"I had Don as a student in the second half of the 1960s. The whole seminary family recognized and appreciated his musical genius. In addition to his exceptional talent. Don distinguished himself by his integrity. Here was an artist that so wanted accurate theological substance for his brilliant artistic style that he studied for four years such foundational disciplines as Hebrew, Greek, and Systematic Theology. In this devotional his virtues come to maturity. Theological accuracy, yes! but beyond that he leads his readers to intimacy, to affection, to communion with God. Saints yearn to walk in an authentic relationship with God—authentic in activity. In short, Don leads us to walk in style with God. What biblical book could be more fitting for such a walk than the Book of Psalms, the epitome of sound theology, brilliant artistry, and intimate affections in active service."
—Dr. Bruce Waltke
Professor of Old Testament and Systematic Theology
Regent College and Reformed Theological Seminary

"My friend, Don Wyrtzen, has been blessed with a rare combination of gifts and experience. He is a brilliant musician, a highly articulate and intelligent spokesman for the faith, and a well-educated theologian. These credentials make him eminently qualified to speak to the church about the Psalms with unique sensitivity and insight. *A Musician Looks at the Psalms* is an important work that I highly recommend."
—William J. Gaither
Songwriter and Christian musician

"In this unique exposure to the message of the Psalms, Don Wyrtzen has combined his clear understanding of Scripture with his heart for music and offered it to us in daily doses of practical help. This book is bound to provide the needed lift along life's way."
—Dr. Joseph M. Stowell
President, The Moody Bible Institute

"Don Wyrtzen is uniquely prepared to minister to God's people today. A trained theologian, he knows what God's Word says about music and worship. As a gifted musician and concert artist, Don is acquainted with every aspect of the contemporary Christian music scene. He is an insightful student of our changing culture who reads widely and thinks perceptively. He communicates with clarity, conviction, and humor; and you go away better understanding the vital part that music plays in the life of the church."
—Dr. Warren W. Wiersbe
Noted author of the "Be" series

"This book could only have been written by Don Wyrtzen. First, it gives echoes of his musical training and remarkable creativity, with references related to both classical and church forms. Second, it demonstrates his theological expertise, with insightful exposition of Scripture that will appeal both to longtime biblical scholars and to newly-converted believers. Finally, it opens a window into the heart of the author, showing him to be a winsome, enthusiastic, and concerned disciple of Jesus Christ."
—Dr. Donald P. Hustad
Senior Professor of Church Music
Southern Baptist Theological Seminary

"Don Wyrtzen has given us a lovely and unique approach to daily devotions. How appropriate for a musician of this caliber to walk us through the devotional journal of the Psalmist. As one who often has quiet times 'at the piano', I found his insights to be educational, inspirational, challenging, and beautiful."
—Twila Paris
artist and contemporary Christian songwriter

"Creative, original, different—just what you would expect from Don Wyrtzen—a combination of helpful inspiration for the lay person and high class biblical instruction for the expert."
—Jill Briscoe
author and speaker

"Who better than an outstanding Christian songwriter and serious student of the Scriptures to give us new and relevant insights into the hymnbook of the Bible. I am excited about Don Wyrtzen's new devotional book . . . superb . . . refreshingly different."
—John W. Peterson
dean of Gospel music songwriters

"Don Wyrtzen has always represented what is the finest in Christian music from both a spiritual and musical perspective. I look forward to using his book as a source of inspiration, comfort, and personal talent.
"Don has a spiritual depth, artistic sense, and understanding of people to marvelously articulate a clear representation of the psalms. This book is from a musician's perspective—but the psalms are for everyone."
—Greg Nelson
songwriter and producer

MUSICIAN LOOKS
at the PSALMS

A

MUSICIAN LOOKS
at the PSALMS

365 DAILY MEDITATIONS

DON WYRTZEN

B&H
PUBLISHING GROUP

NASHVILLE, TENNESSEE

978-0-8054-2774-5

Published by B&H Publishing Group
Nashville, Tennessee

Dewey Classification: 242.5
Subject Heading: DEVOTIONAL LITERATURE \
BIBLE. O.T. PSALMS \ MEDITATIONS

Unless otherwise stated all Scripture citation is from the Holman
Christian Standard Bible® copyright © 1999, 2000, 2001, 2002 by
Holman Bible Publishers. Used by permission. Other versions used
include New International Version, © 1973, 1978, 1984 by International
Bible Society, The Living Bible, copyright © Tyndale House Publishers,
Wheaton, Ill., 1971, used by permission, and the King James Version.

4 5 6 7 8 9   19 18 17 16 15

Dedicated to my parents,
Jack and Marge Wyrtzen,
whose precious gifts to me are reflected in this book.

From my dad comes the gift of his love of the Scriptures.
From my mom came her emotional sensitivity.
Thanks, Dad, and my loving tribute to you, Mom,
for all of life's melodies you have shared with me.

CONTENTS

Notes from the Composer	1
Foreword	3
Quartet of Essays	5
Prelude	29
January	33
Psalms 1–23	
February	64
Psalms 23–30	
March	92
Psalms 31–39	
April	123
Psalms 39–50	
May	153
Psalms 51–64	
June	184
Psalms 64–74	
July	214
Psalms 75–89	
August	245
Psalms 89–105	
September	276
Psalms 105–119	

October   306
    Psalms 119–125

November   337
    Psalms 125–139

December   367
    Psalms 139–150

Postlude   398
Subject Index   402
Musical Terms Index   403
Song Credits   404

Notes from the Composer

❦

On the inception of this work and how it came to be ... Some years ago on my way to a concert at a conference center in western Michigan, I was stressed out. Playing a "praise piano" concert and sharing spiritually with an audience was the last thing I wanted to do. Earlier in the year, I had lost two of the dearest people in the world to me—my mom and my pastor. I was grieving and my spirits were at an all-time low. How could I expect to bring hope, encouragement, and spiritual comfort to others when I couldn't even help myself?

My dad, Jack Wyrtzen, was a great evangelist. He always drummed it into me, "You don't miss a meeting!" "You go on no matter what!" So I did then what I've done many times before and since. I turned it all over to the Lord the best I knew how. Later, sharing intimately and personally about the death of my mom and other losses in my life with the audience, we mutually experienced some profound and exciting thoughts from Psalm 40:1–3:

> I waited patiently for the LORD,
>> and He turned to me and heard my cry for help.
> He brought me up from a desolate pit,
>> out of the muddy clay,
>> and set my feet on a rock,
>> making my steps secure.
> He put a new song in my mouth,
>> a hymn of praise to our God.
>> Many will see and fear,
>> and put their trust in the LORD.

After the concert a dear friend told me that he had been deeply touched and moved by the music and the sharing. A wonderful germ idea was born that night. He suggested that I consider writing a personal devotional journal based on the psalms. He felt that a trained composer, also conversant in theology, could make a unique contribution.

1

The idea grew on me. I had studied the Psalms with the brilliant Hebrew scholar, Dr. Bruce Waltke, had taught them to a large Sunday school class at Calvary Church in Grand Rapids, Michigan, and had read them voraciously for years. Not only that, but much of the praise music I had been writing was also inspired by the Psalms. I decided to accepted the challenge of hand writing a meditation on all 150 psalms for every day of the year.

The process became biblical therapy for me. As I jotted down notes on planes, in motels, or at home on the weekends, I found that I was writing in order to grapple better with reality, to find emotional equilibrium, and to cope with the mysteries, complexities, and relational pain of life. Gradually, I realized that I was experiencing more consistency, stability, and security in my life—that real in-depth change was taking place in me.

My family was very supportive and caring during this project. My wife, Karen, God's special gift to me, helped enormously with the administration of the household, freeing me to write and create. My terrifc kids, D. J. and Kathleen, allowed me to make this large time investment. They grew up, bumping heads underneath the piano while Dad wrote his music. Watching me as I hammered out a book single-handedly was a new challenge for them.

But now that it's all done, my motivation, hope, and prayer is that these artistic musings on the "ancient hymanl of Israel" will be the bread of life and the living water to your soul, that they will nurture, bless, and bring wholeness and peace to you. Most importantly, I want them to be a bridge between you and the Scripture. If they inspire you to read the psalms themselves, then I will be very happy indeed.

Shalom,
Don Wyrtzen
Brentwood, Tennessee

FOREWORD

There is much talk these days about worship but it seems very little real, biblical understanding. How do I know this? Because we American Christians on the whole remain so hungry and shallow. Our "worship" provides for only a narrow spectrum of our emotional and spiritual lives. Rarely does it engage our minds, much less our imaginations. We seek to pour out our praise only to find ourselves empty. If this is at all accurate, how must the true Focus of our impoverished worship feel? Having been blessed by him with so much, how can we go on offering the Lord such pitiful scraps. What are we to do? Where are we to turn?

When we turn to the psalms, we find extreme depth—emotional, theological and spiritual—all seamlessly woven into one fabric of worship. In what can only be seen as a profound mystery as the psalmist pours out all his praise to God, he finds that his heart is, at the same time, filled to overflowing. In worshiping God well he finds his true purpose.

We find in the psalms the entire spectrum of human emotion. We read accusations toward God that make our blood run cold. There are songs of abandonment, desolation and lament which, with one exception, (Ps. 88) turn back nevertheless to praise by the final verse. The psalmist never gives up on God, though again and again he risks breaking his heart with his forsaken songs. He cries out to Someone who he still hopes might be moved by his tears. If we could only learn to sing these psalms once more, imagine what the church might discover, how we might help the world with its pain!

On the other, far end of the scale, the psalms explode with a joyful loving of God that we can scarcely imagine. What we vainly try to emulate with volume, the psalmist genuinely expresses with true passion. It is not that we love God less; it is simply that we lack the lyrical vocabulary, apart from the psalms.

So, if we are ever to return to a biblical understanding of worship, it is with the psalms we must begin and end. The theologians have done much to help us move closer to this point. A few pastors have struggled with the issue, helping us along the way. Sadly, only a few musicians have seriously shouldered this burden. But even still, they have provided a few pieces of the puzzle.

What we've needed all along is someone who represents the rare combination of all these callings, someone with the intuition and imagination of a musician, a pastor's heart and a first rate theological mind. Don Wyrtzen comes closer than anyone else I know to filling this role. He has wrestled with these questions for all of his adult life, addressing many of them musically and now in this book by means of his prose. He does not pretend to have "arrived," but graciously invites us to follow along with him in this journey through the psalms. In the process of looking back through these ancient lyrics, it is our hope that we will discover our own new songs.

Michael Card
Songwriter and Christian musician

Church Music and Worship
in the Twenty-first Century

ॐ

Several years ago I was asked to play a Praise Piano Concert and to lecture on worship and music at a large, traditional church in New Jersey. Their new worship minister had brought in a trap set and placed it on the platform for the Sunday morning services. He did this while very new to the congregation and while the senior pastor was on vacation. Since this is a conservative, well-established church, this precipitated, almost immediately, major worship wars. The older folks polarized against the young people. They were each poised at opposite corners of the ring and were getting ready to duke it out. The stakes were the future of the church.

I was brought in at this juncture to try to be a bridge between the generations. I lectured; I played; I tried to apply Scripture; I had meals with members of the elder board; I had table fellowship with many of the young people; I did a lot of listening; I attempted to apply Scripture to this contemporary situation. I think, in retrospect, that the Lord used me in a small way to be helpful. I know that the Lord used a wise pastor in a big way to keep the church united in community. They avoided a split. Recently, I was invited back. I was pleased to discover a flourishing church, and it is flourishing in the difficult mission field of northern New Jersey.

Many churches have not been so fortunate. Many well-meaning Christians have confused personal taste with spirituality. They mix up "what I like" with "what is right." I often hear comments like, "I don't know much about music, but I know what I like." Usually this means, "I like what I know." Further compounding confusion is the fact that most musicians don't know much about theology and Scripture. This is balanced by the fact that most pastors don't know much about the arts in general and music in particular. Therefore, leaders in both fields tend to misconnect with each other. I believe there are three illiteracies in evangelicalism which tend to fog the issues even further. First, we don't know history. Second, we don't know culture. And third, we don't know Scripture. An attempt to grasp, in general, the broad outlines of each of these can be helpful. Let's begin with the historical perspective.

It is impossible for anyone, except genuine prophets, to predict the future. But one doesn't have any feel for the future unless he understands the present. One cannot understand the present, where we are now, unless he understands the past. The past teaches us about tradition. Tradition is like a large, beautiful tree. That tree must be pruned from time to time in order to grow and flourish. Yet one must be careful, when pruning, that he does not cut the trunk of the tree and cause it to die. It is imperative that we look at the past in order to perceive what is going on now and to have a shot at understanding what may lie ahead.

American church music can be ascertained in five primary movements. First is the New England School. Our old hymnody originated in the British Isles. The great hymn writers such as Isaac Watts, John and Charles Wesley, John Newton, William Cowper, and many others came from England. They had been strongly influenced by the Pietism of the Moravians in Germany. It is a fascinating history to study. These great hymn writers produced such master-pieces as "When I Survey the Wondrous Cross," "And Can It Be that I Should Gain," "Amazing Grace," and "God Moves in a Mysterious Way." These pieces and hundreds more crossed the Atlantic and arrived in Boston in the eighteenth century. Lowell Mason and others arranged these texts, often to new music and new settings. These settings were appropriate to the New World. These classical hymn texts became the foundation of all hymnody in English. They are theologically rich and, for the most part, aesthetically beautiful.

The second movement in American church music would be the African American spirituals. These encompass some of the most exquisitely beautiful songs in all of literature. These were born in profound suffering and injustice. This was also an art form of the slaves. Originally these tunes were not written down and recorded. This was an intense, oral tradition. It produced "There Is a Balm in Gilead," "Swing Low Sweet Chariot," "My Lord, What a Mornin'," and "Wade in the Water." This tradition produced a style that is still deeply ingrained in the American musical culture.

The third movement in American church music would be the Southern Gospel style. In a broad sense these are the white equivalent of the black spirituals. This was also an intense, oral, nonclassical style of music. It produced such folk songs as "Farther Along," "Where Could I Go," and "I'll Fly Away." It also produced singing schools and southern publishing houses such as Vaughn Music Company of Lawrenceberg, Tennessee, and the Stamps-Baxter Music Company of Dallas, Texas. The modern Gaither Homecoming gatherings have strong roots in this tradition.

The fourth movement in American church music would be the Gospel Song style. This style grew out of the nineteenth-century revivals and produced

6

such songwriters as P. P. Bliss, William B. Bradbury, William Howard Doane, Ira Sankey, and of course, the world famous blind songwriter, Fanny Crosby. This was a romantic musical style, designed to reach the unchurched. It is still sung today by Bev Shea, the wonderful baritone with the Billy Graham Crusades. Bev sang at the wedding of my folks, Jack and Marge Wyrtzen. He, himself, has written lovely songs in this style such as "I'd Rather Have Jesus" and "The Wonder of It All." John W. Peterson, who wrote "It Took a Miracle" and "Heaven Came Down and Glory Filled My Soul" is perhaps the last of the great romantic, gospel songwriters.

The fifth and final movement in American church music is the Celebration Era. It started sometime in the 1960s and it has two prongs. First, there is contemporary Christian music. This music is basically soloistic and band oriented. Second, there is praise and worship music, which is generally for congregational singing and participation. Michael W. Smith started in the former and is now a major force in the latter. He has written such songs as "How Majestic Is Your Name in All the Earth," "Great Is the Lord," and "Thy Word." One of the best contemporary hymn writers is Twila Paris. She often has her devotions at the keyboard. She has given us many lovely songs such as "We Will Glorify," "He Is Exalted," and "How Beautiful."

Church music is a lively, ever-changing art form of the people. At present the trend is for blended worship. Blended worship is eclectic—that is, it tries to choose creatively the best of many different styles. This is a biblical approach based on the great apostle Paul's paradigm in Ephesians 5 and Colossians 3 that we are to sing "psalms, hymns, and spiritual songs."

Now we move to the cultural perspective. Understanding culture is of paramount importance. Why? Because it has an immense influence on all of us, particularly in the modern world. Why? Because of the enormous effect of high tech and the media on our lives. Even more telling is the fact that the less people know Scripture, the more they will be dominated by culture. This is why most of us are far more influenced by our cultural context than we are by scriptural principles. Intimate knowledge of Scripture is the only thing that can really offset and cut across secular culture. Many of us have joined this culture in order to reach it with the gospel. When we do this, culture becomes our authority rather than the Word of God. This is not the way Jesus did it. His message and technique were in congruity with the will of his Father.

But even though Christians should not be dominated by culture, they, nevertheless, should understand it. To gain a cultural perspective one must understand the distinguishing marks of the Old World, the New World, and the paradigm shift that took place in the 1960s. First, the Old World was classical, formal, and stressed quality and excellence. The classical world liked European hymns written by the masters of hymnody. Colonial America reveled in these theologically loaded hymns. Early in America, classical literature and music set the standards for all other literature and music worthy of excellence. Even before World War II, the best musical education was found in Europe in places like Fontainebleau, Vienna, and Salzburg. The artistic elites frequented symphony, opera, and ballet.

The Old World emphasized the classics, and it was also a formal world. Formal was preferred to casual. In music formal structure was favored over improvisation. Even in fashion, for example, suits and ties were chosen over T-shirts and jeans. And in popular music Doc Severinson's *Tonight Show* big band was more arranged and formal than Paul Shaeffer's band on the Letterman show.

The Old World also stressed quality and excellence. When I was a kid, the two big guns in world-class piano were Horowitz and Rubenstein. They were two of the best high-wire acts in piano history. In pop music Frank Sinatra and Barbara Streisand held sway with their stylized singing and superbly crafted arrangements.

Then everything shifted in the decade of the 1960s. It was dominated by protests and political unrest. This was the time of Kennedy and Nixon. In the 1970s, the time of Ford and Carter, introspection and psychology held sway. In the 1980s, the time of Reagan and Bush Sr., unrestrained greed and affluence became the prevailing ideology. Tom Wolfe's brilliant novel *The Bonfire of the Vanities* chronicles those days with panache. In the 1990s, the Clinton years, postmodernism commanded the culture. Tolerance and political correctness became the new manners. The only absolute was that there are no absolutes. The only discriminatory judgment possible was not to make any judgments.

These four decades were strongly influenced by what occurred in the 1960s. This is the seminal period. The values of today's leaders were shaped during that decade. Before that time period the two major events that shaped Western culture were the Great Depression and World War II. Then came the avalanche of the baby boomers (those born between 1946 and 1964). Their values were shaped strongly in the 1960s and in the events that dominated that era. This was a period of enormous unrest and upheaval. It was the time of the Vietnam War. During this period Martin Luther King Jr., John F. Kennedy, and Robert Kennedy were assassinated. Also during this time frame Watergate occurred and President Nixon was forced out of office in disgrace. There are many other salient factors, but these are some of the principal ones.

How did this time period affect those people living then? Their impressions created a unique audience. This audience is still with us. What are they like? Here are a few observations. They don't understand theological language. Sin is not their issue. They lack hope. They distrust leaders. They lack direction and discipline. They view truth as relative. They value success and results. Much could be said about each of these, but they show that the old world disappeared and was replaced by a very different new world.

What is the new world like? First, it is an artistically illiterate pop culture. This fits in with United States history. Four of the five movements of American church music cited above were folk forms. The only one of the five that was in any way classical was the old European hymns. The other four movements grew out of grassroots populism. This is born out by sales figures. For approximately the last ten years, prerecorded, classical music has sold 3 to 4 percent worldwide. This obviously means that 96 to 97 percent of prerecorded music sold in the world at this time in history is some form of popular music. In the late 1950s Elvis changed pop music forever. Elvis stood at the crossroads between sexual liberation, racial reconciliation, and mass communication. He took rhythm and blues and hillbilly music from left field to the mainstream. The great novelist and critic, Martin Amis, says of him, "Elvis was a talented hick destroyed by success." However, a trip to Graceland can testify to his enduring attraction and fascination. In February 1964, the Beatles appeared on *The Ed Sullivan Show*. This solidified the titanic cultural tidal wave that was engulfing the world. It was like a tsunami of colossal proportions. All of this coincided with the Japanese development of the personal stereo, which virtually made the youth culture possible. It also took popular music and its pervasive influence all over the world.

Second, the new world is marked by technological change, internationalism and multiculturalism, gender neutrality, a strong emphasis on interpersonal relationships, and postmodernism. Postmodernism is a strong reaction against the Enlightenment. The middle of the seventeenth century ushered in the Enlightenment, an era marked by an absolute faith in human reason. Major advances were made in science and medicine, but reason edged out music and poetry. The Enlightenment laid the groundwork for a loss of truth, goodness, and beauty. Standards were lowered; goodness was modified; standards of beauty were severely moderated. In short, epistemology, ethics, and aesthetics took a big hit. With the Holocaust, human reason, as encompassing all human knowledge, came to an end. Even reflective non-Christians began to see that there is much more to life than human reason alone.

Today there is an insatiable appetite for all kinds of spiritualities. What a grand entree for orthodox, historic Christianity! What an opportunity! Our culture today has many of the same characteristics that marked the ancient world when Christianity turned the world upside down.

But finally and most importantly, we move to the biblical perspective. Colossians 3:16 reads, "Let the word of Christ dwell in you richly as you teach and admonish one another with all wisdom, and as you sing psalms, hymns, and spiritual songs with gratitude in your hearts to God" (NIV). Our worship and music must stress five things. First, there must be a grounding in Scripture. Note the phrase, "let the word of Christ dwell in you richly." The Bible is the foundation and must be stressed. Second, there must be an emphasis on teaching. Note Paul's use of the phrase, "as you teach." This teaching should be stimulating, motivating, and in the power of the Holy Spirit. The emphasis should not be on entertainment. Third, there must be an emphasis on soul-nurturing. Note Paul's use of the word, "counsel." People are hungry for the Bread of Life and thirsty for the Living Water. They desperately need comfort and counsel. Fourth, there must be an emphasis on creativity and variety. The Lord likes a "new song." He likes artistry and creativity. Note Paul's use of the phrase, "psalms, hymns, and spiritual songs." Every church should have a varied diet of these key nutrients for worship. Finally, there should be an emphasis on gratitude. Note Paul's use of the phrase, "with gratitude in your hearts to God." All of our worship should reflect an attitude of praise and thanksgiving.

The apostle Paul also wants us to stress seven virtues in our music and worship. They are found in Philippians 4:8. Here Paul says, "Finally, brothers, whatever is true, whatever is noble, whatever is right, whatever is pure, whatever is lovely, whatever is admirable—if anything is excellent or praiseworthy—think about such things" (NIV). Here are seven virtues that delineate the target for our worship and music practice. Our worship and music must be true, noble (worthy of God's holiness), righteous, pure, lovely, admirable, and excellent. Remember, in a worship service your congregation is not the audience; the Lord is! And he cares a lot about excellence. He wants the best sacrifice of praise.

We confuse worship with evangelism. In a worship service the Lord is the subject, the object, and the audience. In an evangelistic service the congregation is the subject, the object, and the audience. The whole purpose is to connect with the audience, present the gospel to them, and win them to Christ. Non-Christians are incapable of worshipping the Lord until they come to Christ. Does this mean it is bad if someone comes to Christ in a worship service? Of course not. It is glorious. Yet it is imperative that we keep our thinking clear and straight. Worship and evangelism have two different purposes and goals.

We also tend to follow pragmatism (what works) far more than biblical principles. We need to be careful that we don't replace encounters with the living God with human entertainment.

Entertainment can be used judiciously to connect with people. But our worship services must always transcend entertainment. Yielding to the seductive pull of entertainment can be like giving steroids to people, making their souls at risk for infection and disease. The Lord has pleasure and joy to offer us, which we can only begin to imagine. C. S. Lewis said, "We are half-hearted creatures, fooling about with drink and sex and ambition, when infinite joy is offered to us, like an ignorant child who wants to go on making mud pies in a slum because he cannot imagine what is meant by an offer of a holiday at the sea. We are far too easily pleased." Amen!

DEVELOPING A THEOLOGY
OF WORSHIP AND MUSIC

❧

Studying theology is not in vogue at the present time. This is regrettable because in theology and in solid biblical doctrine one comes across pure gold answers that are desperately needed today. I am one of the fortunate ones because I got to study both music and theology. Martin Luther said, "Except for theology, there is no art that can be placed in comparison with music." I learned most of what I know about music from a profoundly gifted teacher named Lillian Hawley Gearhart. My major mentor in theology was Francis Schaeffer. I am so glad I got a solid background in both disciplines when I was young.

Today we are failing to teach theology to just about everybody—especially young people. Author Josh MacDowell claims that 90 percent of evangelical young people do not believe in absolute truth. I've lived in Music City, Nashville, for more than sixteen years. I've often thought that being a theologian in Nashville's music business is a bit like being a seamstress at a nudist colony. Nevertheless, I'm so happy I got pointed in the right direction in these two monumental disciplines many years ago.

The world needs good theology combined with deep compassion and love for people. God's Word is our gold standard for music and worship. Sociology, marketing, research, pragmatism, what others are doing or not doing, and even success are totally inadequate substitutes for God's Word.

Seven key words can help us develop a biblical theology of worship and music. The seven key words are *spirit, truth, balance, theology, community, culture,* and *excellence.* Seven biblical concepts can be built around these words.

First, worship and music must be done in God's way or "in spirit." John 4:23–24 says, "Yet a time is coming and has now come when the true worshipers will worship the Father in spirit and truth, for they are the kind of worshipers the Father seeks. God is spirit, and his worshipers must worship in spirit and in truth." What is God's standard of worship? It is to worship "in spirit" which means to worship "in God's way." A person is a two-part being, having a visible part and an invisible part. He is body and spirit. He is material and immaterial.

Jesus is teaching us that our invisible part—the real, internal person, our spirit—must resonate with the Holy Spirit. Therefore, in a worship service our being must connect with his being. When this happens, we encounter the living Lord in his majesty and glory. This is what happened to the Old Testament prophet Isaiah in Isaiah 6. This was not an encounter with a particular style of worship but was a passionate, frightening meeting with Almighty God. He came into contact with God's transcendent power. So I would say that the test of a worship service should not be, "And a good time was had by all," but rather, "Did you encounter the living Lord today?"

Second, worship and music must be based on God's truth. The apostle John wrote about worshiping "in spirit and in truth." Today many believe that truth is subjective. A person might say, "What's true for you is true for you, but what is true for me is also true for me." But the Word teaches that truth is always exclusive. The Bible does not teach that there are many different ways to God. Jesus himself said in John 14:6, "I am the way and the truth and the life. No one comes to the Father except through me" (NIV). The modern ethos postulates a view that says there are many different hiking trails that lead to the top of the mountain. Even though we may be getting there in a different way from somewhere else, we'll all end up at the same place. This view is modern but totally out of sync with the Scripture.

Pilate, while interviewing Jesus, asked a profound question, "What is truth?" Truth is the living Word, Jesus Christ (see John 1:1, 14). Truth is also the written Word of God (see 2 Tim. 3:16). And God's truth, the Bible, the Scripture, is the gold standard. We evaluate culture, art, aesthetics, liturgy, education, and worship style by Scripture. Wonderful, biblical answers can be found to questions regarding worship and music in a study of Scripture. Should we sing psalms, hymns, or praise choruses? (See Col. 3:16.) Should we disband our choir in favor of a worship team? (See Rev. 5.) What is worship? (See Isa. 6 or John 4.) There is being produced at the present time a burgeoning worship literature. Many of these books are provocative and possess solid insights, yet many of them remain weak in teaching principles and theological concepts that grow right out of the text. They are found wanting when it comes to grappling with the development of a truly biblical theology of worship and music.

Third, worship and music must be balanced. Note the word *balance*. It must involve one's total being. (See Prov. 3:5–6.) It must recognize that we are made in God's image. (See Gen. 1:27.) It must involve the mind. This implicates the objective, the verbal, the cognitive, the left brain, the rational. It accents words and thinking. But worship and music also involve the heart. This implicates the subjective, the nonverbal, the affective, the right brain, the intuitive. It accents symbols, word pictures, and feeling. Music and worship also involve the will. This implicates action, creativity, productivity. It accents the expenditure of energy and doing.

Part of this balance involves basing worship and music on Scripture rather than culture. We all are products of our particular time and place. But for us to praise the Lord in a way that pleases him, we have to ground our adoration and exaltation in his Word. (See Deut. 6:4–6.) If the Word doesn't shape us, culture will. The Bible must have the upper hand. To achieve a just balance one must not just stress the mind, or just the emotions, or just the will. One must cultivate a passionate, intimate relationship with the living Lord that involves one's whole being.

Fourth, worship and music must be grounded in theology. What is theology? The English word is based on the Greek words *theos*, which means "God," and *logos*, which means word. Theology is the study of God. It attempts to discern the whole counsel of God on a given subject from the Scripture. It tries to systematize what the whole Bible says on any given subject. Where does theology come from? It originates from engagement with the text of Scripture. Preaching ought to be grounded in this engagement. But many do not engage with the text of Scripture anymore. How does one engage with the text of Scripture? A good place to begin is to ask three primary questions: (1) What does the text say?(2) What did the text mean when it was written? (3) What am I going to do about it today?

Theology, as a discipline, is at a low point in our time. Consequently, many Christians cannot think through their faith. Much preaching, teaching, and publishing today is fluff. It is kitsch. And yet people today are hungry for substance and content. The next generations, coming along behind the baby boomers, have a strong appetite for meat. They already are demanding content, doctrine, and substance.

Fifth, worship and music must be practiced in community. Americans tend to identify with the Lone Ranger or the Marlboro Man. This strong, virile individualism enabled Americans to be innovative. It enabled early pioneers to conquer the West. It enabled Americans to be creative and entrepreneurial. But it tends to make Christians in America forget that they are part of the body of Christ. They are not meant to go it alone. In fact they are seriously weakened by their own autonomy. Cocooning at home all the time in front of a big-screen TV is not healthy. The couch potato at home tends to become a pew potato at church, and every Christian should be a church member. Why? Because fellowship is important in living well. We are relational beings. Why? Because we are made in God's image, and he is profoundly relational. He exists in three persons, Father, Son, and Holy Spirit. As my mentor, Francis Schaeffer, used to say, "There was love and communication in the Godhead before anything else was created." So we also, being analogous to God, are relational beings at our core. We are also part of God's family—now, in ages past, and in the future. To quote the big Streisand hit "we are people who need people." This is a strong, biblical idea. The psalms were sung in community. The apostle Paul has a vigorous commitment to family in the New Testament. Therefore, worship and music are for the whole family of God—young and old, contemporary and traditional. Ideally we should all worship together at least part of the time. We desperately need the insights that different generations can give to us.

Sixth, worship and music must connect with our culture. Why? It is impossible to fulfill the Great Commission (see Matt. 28) without interacting with culture. The apostle Paul had the three dominant cultures of the ancient world flowing in his veins. He was Jewish; he spoke Greek; and he was a Roman citizen. This made him uniquely suited to communicate to the first century. Human society involves many different families and races. They speak different languages. They have different thought patterns and frames of reference. They prefer different styles. Insight into all of this and acceptance of it renders us capable of using this knowledge in congruity with the Holy Spirit to reach diverse peoples. The gospel can then be presented effectively and powerfully.

Seventh, worship and music must aspire to excellence. The classic passage on this in the New Testament is Philippians 4:8. This is the only time Paul uses the word for excellence (*arete*). It was used in classical Greek to describe the renowned Olympic athletes. Paul is inspiring us to be creative, unique, original. Many of us are too easily satisfied with being derivative, reactive, and committed to cloning other peoples' creative ideas. This passage calls us to learn our craft, and this involves teaching, training, and education. One is born with certain gifts, but one is never born with skill and wisdom. One is not born with impeccable taste. One is not born with a value system. Those things are caught, taught, and learned. They are usually learned from a highly respected mentor or teacher.

Our pluralistic culture has produced an "almost anything goes" approach to art and music. It has embraced a materialistic approach to the arts. If it sells, it's good! It has bought into an efficiency model based on numbers and mass production. Like Kleenex, it's efficient but disposable. This may work well in business, but it does not work well in the church and in making disciples. Secularism is into novelty, fickleness, and waiting for the next big thing. It doesn't produce anything that lasts, that stands the test of time. As the great southern preacher, Vance Havner, used to say, "There is something wrong with the mixture." This shoddy methodology will not produce disciples or saints. Perhaps this is why Christians don't have more influence in the world despite saturation in various forms of media. We often play marbles with diamonds, and we also become eunuchs at the gate.

So in attempting to forge an introduction to a theology of worship and music, we have discussed spirit, truth, balance, theology, community, culture, and excellence. King David, the chief musician of the Old Testament, was perhaps the most artistic, creative person in the Bible. Psalm 78:70–72 offers a beautiful miniature portrait of him: "He chose David His servant and took him from the sheepfolds; He brought him from tending ewes to be shepherd over His people Jacob—over Israel, His inheritance. He shepherded them with a pure heart and guided them with his skillful hands." He was a humble shepherd. He was flawed as a human being and scarred by sin. He conquered his denial; he repented; he was forgiven. He ended up as a "man after God's own heart." Israel lost her heart to him, and he became their greatest king and leader. Why? Because like all profoundly great leaders, he had integrity in his heart and skill in his hands.

Music and God's Glory

༄

There are two primary ways to reach young people today, through athletics and through music. Their heroes, stars, mentors, and models are usually either professional athletes or rock stars. So these two disciplines have immense influence in our society. Young people in America, unlike Europe, go to church. They have brought lots of vitality, energy, and "hot sauce" to what were once conventional worship services. They have experimented a lot and have not been bound, for the most part, by history and tradition.

As Dr. Robert Webber points out, young people today tend to be pursuing either artistry or ecstasy. They are moved by liturgy, pageantry, and personal praise. Their pervasive influence has really shaken up worship style. Consequently, there is more prejudice per square inch when we discuss music than almost any other subject. Leaders have reacted to this state of affairs in different ways. But a common reaction is to equate personal taste with spirituality. A strong leader often imposes his preference on his subjects. Instead of exercising spiritual discernment, he often legislates and censors. There is a crying need for knowledge of biblical principles and the articulation and application of them. After all, the Word is our ultimate authority for faith and practice. This can be a liberating concept to those who are confused about authority and who, therefore, become too dependent on self-styled spokesmen for God.

When one follows biblical principles of praise, God reveals his glory to us. An apt illustration of this was the dedication of King Solomon's temple. Second Chronicles 5:11–14 describes the scene.

> The priests then withdrew from the Holy Place. All the priests who were there had consecrated themselves, regardless of their divisions. All the Levites who were musicians—Asaph, Heman, Jeduthun and their sons and relatives—stood on the east side of the altar, dressed in fine linen and playing cymbals, harps and lyres. They were accompanied by 120 priests sounding trumpets. The trumpeters and singers joined in unison, as with one voice, to give praise and thanks to the LORD. Accompanied by trumpets, cymbals and other instruments, they raised their voices in praise to the LORD and sang:

"He is good;
        his love endures forever."
Then the temple of the LORD was filled with a cloud, and the
priests could not perform, their service because of the cloud, for
the glory of the LORD filled the temple of God (NIV).

One can learn a lot from this passage about the musical leadership in
the temple, the dynamics of the music, the content of the message, and the
display of God's glory.

First, the musicians. We learn that they were skilled. First Chronicles
25:1 says, "David, together with the commanders of the army, set apart some
of the sons of Asaph, Heman and Jeduthun for the ministry of prophesying,
accompanied by harps, lyres and cymbals" (NIV). Verse 7 points out to us that
these musical leaders were all "trained and skilled in music for the LORD"
(NIV). So one had to be a skilled musician in order to serve in ancient Israel.
In Hebrew the word for *skill* encompasses both skill and wisdom. It refers
here to a wedding of knowledge and wisdom in practicing the art of music.
God himself demands skill in worship leadership not musical ineptitude.
Schlock has no place in God's house. Even sincerity is no substitute for skill.

King David, who led a sweeping renaissance of Israelite culture, set the
standards for his leaders. He placed the bar high. As a young man, he was
described by Saul's servant as a young man "who knows how to play the harp."
He was also "a brave man and a warrior." He tells us that "he speaks well and
is a fine-looking man." The most telling phrase he saves for last: "and the
LORD is with him" (1 Sam. 16:18 NIV). The King James Version describes
David as a "cunning" player on the harp. He exuded skill. The Holy Spirit
works with people, most of the time, who have developed craft, who have a
commitment to excellence, and who possess a fusion of knowledge, wisdom,
and experience. On special occasions he uses what he can use, what is available (such as the incident in Numbers 22 with Balaam's donkey).

We learn, second, that the musicians were sanctified. They had "consecrated themselves." The word *sanctify* means "set apart as holy." It refers to a
complete separation from common uses. Even their clothing was different.
They were set apart for life. One could not be a music leader in ancient Israel as
a non-Levite. Music leaders had to have virtually the same qualifications that
were required of the priests. In the new temple Levites will be downgraded
from ministers to servants because of their sinful practices. They will be kept
away from the holy things and offerings. They will only be able to assist the real
worship leaders. They will be replaced by the priests of Zadok, a limited group
of Levites, who were known for one primary thing; they had remained faithful

to God (see Ezek. 44). So King David, the chief musician of the Old Testament, required his musical leaders to be skillful and to be sanctified.

We next learn about the music itself. What was it like stylistically? Was it loud or soft? Was it fast or slow? What was the instrumentation? Was there a choir? What did it sound like? We learn from 1 Chronicles 23:5 that King Solomon had four thousand players in his temple orchestra. So the first thing we learn about this ancient music is that it was exciting.

Second Chronicles 5:12 gives us the instrumentation of the orchestra: cymbals, harps, lyres, and 120 trumpets. These were not modern trumpets. They were ram's horns. Now just try to imagine how that sounded. This would, at first, seem in conflict with David's psalm of thanks recorded in 1 Chronicles 16. Verse 29 enjoins believers to "bring an offering and come before him; worship the LORD in the splendor of his holiness" (NIV). Wouldn't a slow, worshipful, romantic kind of music be well suited for this particular message? But verses 5 and 6 give us the orchestration: lyres, harps, cymbals, and trumpets. Francis Schaeffer used to say that in America we do two things to make music holier. We make it softer and slower. Some of the old German hymns such as "Ein Feste Burg" were evidently sung that way (note the fermatas), and some of the old European hymns would have as many as sixteen verses. I'm sure a lot of roasts were burning during the long services in those days. Some of the English hymns were also sung that way and had an influence on Colonial America. Some of the music in the colonial churches was sung like a dirge, but this is not necessarily biblical.

It is biblical to have meetings that are exciting, stimulating, moving, innovative, and creative. Young people today realize that many styles and forms with varying dynamics can be used in the worship of the Lord. The younger generation is often attentive and involved in their worship experiences. Many of them are passionate. Older congregates must learn to be more open about this. We don't want to be custodians of the cliche and a people straitjacketed in style. We must covet the openness and freedom of the Holy Spirit and his work, particularly in the lives of his young people. We must admire their gifts and their energy. We must encourage them. To do this we must prepare our hearts to worship with them in advance of the worship experience; we must be active and participative during the experience; and we must be responsive after the experience. The Lord likes attentiveness, intimacy, and response.

The second thing we learn about this ancient music is that it was unified. Note 2 Chronicles 5:13, "The trumpeters and singers joined in unison, as with one voice, to give praise and thanks to the LORD" (NIV). This is an apt passage for a conductor. The orchestra and choir were in perfect time and harmony with each other. They were together. There was unity, order, and ensemble. They were synchronized. This was not like the book of Judges where people did "what was right in their own eyes." The Bible has a lot to say about rhythm in nature and in music. There is a rhythm in the seasons—summer, fall, winter, spring. There is a rhythm to our day—morning, afternoon, and evening. There is rhythm in our bodies. We breathe in duple rhythm. Our hearts beat in duple rhythm (unless we are in love). Rhythm is basic to the nature of reality. Just because rhythm is generally more intense today doesn't mean it is evil. On the other hand, not just anything goes rhythmically. Rhythm players, like everybody else in the Lord's orchestra, must learn how to play for the Lord's glory. They need to learn to play with sensitivity, grace, and elegance.

We next learn about the message. It is found in verse 13. "They raised their voices in praise to the LORD and sang: 'He is good; his love endures forever'" (NIV). This was a big message. This was theological praise. They were praising the Lord here for his incomparable attributes of goodness and love. We must learn to scrutinize the texts of hymns and praise songs to make sure they are biblically accurate and theologically precise. Praise music often uses psalm texts and the exact words of Scripture. Calvin, during the Reformation, did not accept texts that were not the exact words of Scripture. Isaac Watts, the great liberator of English hymnody, wrote texts based on Scripture as well. This developed a dynamic, new hymnody that grabbed a huge audience and had staying power. His and the other great English hymn writers set the bar high. All modern music must strive for excellence in its texts. It also must strive for a beautiful wedding or fusion of text and music. There is a wonderful place for both classic hymns and praise and worship music. Hymns are like stars that shine in the firmament. Praise choruses are like fireworks. Praise songs are really miniature hymns.

This was also personal praise. This worship was participative. They used their own voices, their own instruments, their own minds and bodies. This was not a form of entertainment for believers. They did not sit and just watch. They were not just spectators. They were involved and engaged on a personal level. We need whole audiences to get attentive and to be affected on a deep level. We especially need artists, poets, and musicians to get absorbed and enthralled with the Living God.

According to 2 Chronicles 5:13–14, when all of these elements were in place, God visited them in all of his majesty. We read, "Then the temple of the LORD was filled with a cloud, and the priests could not perform their service because of the cloud, for the glory of the LORD filled the temple of God" (NIV). The temple was enveloped in the blazing splendor of God. This congregation was exposed to his flaming holiness. This was scary, frightening, and all encompassing. Christians today need to become aware that their faith is not just an intricate system; it is not just coherent doctrine; it is not just logic. These are all eminently important. But what transcends all of that is a passionate relationship with the living Christ. This might involve tears in the eyes, lumps in the throat, chills going up and down the spine, goose bumps on the surface of the skin. Worship is not just a plaything for children's experimentation. It is an encounter with the King of kings and Lord of lords. So music is not just a part of the preliminaries, not just a prelude to the preaching. Every aspect of the service must involve praise and worship. Every fiber of a person's being must be resonating in harmony with the work of the Holy Spirit in order to exalt the Lord of hosts. St. Augustine wrote in his *Confessions,* "How greatly did I weep in thy hymns and canticles, deeply moved by the voices of thy sweet-speaking church! The voices flowed into mine ears, and the truth was poured forth into my heart, whence the agitation of my piety overflowed, and my tears ran over, and blessed was I therein." Amen!

MUSIC AND GOD'S POWER

❧

Music has a pervasive influence in our culture. It is the world's universal form of communication. According to the Record Industry Association of America, sales worldwide are now at approximately $40 billion annually. The United States has one-third of that worldwide market. The typical consumer is between twenty-five to forty-nine, wants CDs, and listens mostly to rock. For the last ten years classical music has sold only 3 to 4 percent worldwide. That leaves some form of pop music at 96 to 97 percent of worldwide sales.

Music has become democratized and its audience reduced to the lowest common denominator of artistic and aesthetic taste. The biggest stars are those who have perfect pitch for reaching the masses. So we are not talking graduation day at Juilliard here.

All of this has affected the church as well. According to a November 2000 article in Nashville's newspaper the *Tennessean*, gospel music is now a billion-dollar industry. It is now in the top five categories in sales: rhythm and blues, alternative rock, rap, country, and gospel. The article went on to say that it now takes a million dollars just to launch a new, contemporary Christian artist. Nashville's influence has become worldwide. There isn't a city anywhere where its music cannot be heard.

What cultural values dominate this industry? Three things: money, ego, and image. The industry is continually on the lookout for the next big thing. These values have a trickle-down effect on the Christian music industry. Why? Because by and large it has bought into the same value system. It also occurs because this industry is now, for the most part, owned by big, secular conglomerates. How does one relate biblically to all of this? What does the New Testament teach us about music? The Old Testament contains hundreds of references to music. In contrast the New Testament says little about it, yet those passages are of primary significance. This essay will deal with three major New Testament passages that are of major significance in the development of a theology of worship and music. When the art form of music is combined with Scripture, the impact is profound. The Bible gives strong evidence for this in three principles that form the basis of a New Testament theology of music.

The first is the principle of Scripture. In Colossians 3:16 we read, "Let the message about the Messiah dwell richly among you, teaching and admonishing one another in all wisdom, and singing psalms, hymns, and spiritual songs, with gratitude in your hearts to God." This is a classic passage on this subject. Let's unpack it.

First, note the imperative, "Let the message about the Messiah." The Word is commanding all Christians, not just pastors and Christian leaders, to fill themselves with the Word. As one of my favorite seminary professors, Dr. Howard Hendricks, says, "This is not optional; it is essential." My own dad, Jack Wyrtzen, was a great evangelist who was also the founder of Word of Life International. He testified to the fact that the sine qua non of his life and ministry was his commitment to a daily quiet time in the Word.

Second, note that teaching and counseling are related to the music. In the ancient civilization church music was used to teach Christian concepts. After a long, dry period where this was not done in the medieval period, the reformers picked up the torch and started using song to teach again. In fact, Luther did this so well that one Jesuit priest said, "You've damned more souls with your songs than with your teaching." He was unaware that Luther was effectively teaching through his songs.

Unfortunately, sometimes we inculcate bad theology in our lyrics. Some interesting songs have been sent to me. One went, "Onward Christian astronauts zooming into space, With the cross of Jesus leading in the race." Another went this way, "When the saints fly in, other saints will meet them with a grin saying, brethren, where have you been? We will fly up and meet the group and then, zoom in with a loop-de-loop." Songs like "Drop Kick Me Jesus through the Goalposts of Life" and "Did Jesus Ever Kick a Dog?" are not aesthetically pleasing, nor do they teach substantive theology. But the early church engaged with the text and took words seriously. As a result, people learned the content of their faith on a regular basis.

We have a tendency to isolate teaching too much from the music itself. When you sing "Worthy Is the Lamb," you are singing one of the major themes of the Apocalypse. This is not preparation for worship; it is worship in and of itself. When you sing "How Great Thou Art," you already are praising the Lord. When you sing "Fairest Lord Jesus," you already are praying. Music is a potent teaching tool. We must make sure we use it to teach genuinely biblical ideas and concepts rather than nonbiblical ones.

But counseling and comforting also are specified in this text. The King James Version uses the term "admonishing." It really refers to counseling or comforting. This is the Greek word *noutheteo*, which means to instruct, warn, or advise. Larry Richards tells us that "when we examine the passages we sense that 'admonishing' is a ministry calling for much warmth and closeness." He further says, "Paul's admonitions were stimulated by a deep love for young believers. His love was so deep that his admonitions were often accompanied by tears." A primary ministry of music is to comfort people. It often speaks to them beneath the surface of their lives where mere words become inadequate.

As we move through this text, we discover how music was taken seriously in the early body of Christ. Paul mentioned three categories of song: psalms, hymns, and spiritual songs. As eminent church music scholar Dr. Don Hustad says, "Christian song in New Testament times was comprehensive in style, in liturgical purpose, and in theological coverage" (see chapter 6 in his fine work *Jubilate II*).

What were these psalms? They were part of the ancient hymnal of Israel and included the psalms of David, Heman, Jeduthun, Asaph, and many others. What were the hymns? The hymns were theocentric, that is God-centered, songs. Many of them are in the New Testament (see 1 Tim. 3:16; John 1:1–14; Phil. 2:6–11). What were the spiritual songs? They were pneumatic odes—songs that were spontaneous, extemporaneous, and improvisatory. For more detail consult Dr. Gordon Fee's monumental work, *God's Empowering Presence*, which is the gold standard in exegesis of this text and also of Ephesians 5:18, which uses the same phrase.

Our Lord loves variety. He loves when we sing a new song. He loves for us to use the glorious palette of colors and styles that are available to us today. When a church today gets hung up on only one style because the leaders feel only contemporary style is relevant, it is not biblical. Unfortunately, there is precious little real application of these biblical principles today. This is probably because musicians don't study the Bible and theology, and on the other hand, pastors don't study the arts and music. So a lot of misconnection is taking place. Many Christian leaders just follow the old, American philosophy of life—pragmatism. If it works, if the people are coming in, if the numbers are up, what we are doing is good. The major point to keep in mind, however, is that music is a means to express a biblical mind-set. Any other standard and practice are inadequate and deficient.

The second major principle to keep in mind is the principle of Holy Spirit control. In Ephesians 5:18–20 we read, "Don't get drunk with wine, which leads to reckless actions, but be filled with the Spirit: speaking to one another in psalms, hymns, and spiritual songs, singing and making music to the Lord in your heart, giving thanks always for everything to God the Father in the name of our Lord Jesus Christ." This is the parallel passage to Colossians 3:16.

Notice first the analogy Paul uses here—drunkenness. Paul is teaching that just as alcohol can control a person's life, so the Holy Spirit must control the Christian's life. We are to be guided and dominated not by the spirits but by the Holy Spirit. "Be filled with the Spirit" is a present middle imperative. Paul wants us to be continually under the control of the Holy Spirit. This is not a "filling" as in filling up your car's tank with gas but more a question of who is behind the wheel of your life. Except we are not machines or automobiles but people. The verb here, "to fill," means "to control." The Holy Spirit must permeate our lives so that he gains total control of every fiber of our being. It is "in him that we live and move and have our being."

When Christians are filled with the Holy Spirit, four wonderful results follow. We speak to one another through song; we sing and make music to the Lord; we express gratitude and thanksgiving; and we submit to one another. Note, the first two results of the filling of the Spirit have to do with making music. I would have thought Paul would have stressed evangelism, prayer, or Bible study. But he took music much more seriously than we do. It wasn't just part of the preliminaries, or something just preparatory to the sermon, or background to fellowship. It was a direct effect of being filled with the Holy Spirit, and the first two results had to do with the art of making music. This means that those of us who work in this vineyard better take our work a lot more seriously.

We see a logical sequence here. First, we develop a biblical mind-set (see Col. 3). Then we come under the Holy Spirit's control (see Eph. 5:18ff), and then we make music for the Lord's glory. What a mandate! What a joyous calling! King David, the chief musician of the Old Testament, says in Psalm 28:7, "Joy rises in my heart until I burst out in songs of praise to Him" (TLB).

Are you involved with music? Do you ever sing? Or has the modern world squeezed the song out of your life? Or are you a couch potato who spends long hours in front of the TV vegetating with wide eyes and a slack jaw? We must learn to worship not just for an hour of singing praise songs (as wonderful as that is) but in all of life 24–7. And this will lead us to the unleashing of supernatural power in our lives.

The third major principle to keep in mind is the principle of supernatural power. Read and study the story of the missionary trip Paul and Silas took to Philippi (see Acts 16:16–31). Paul and Silas were faithfully preaching the gospel with the anointing of the Spirit and were blessed with miraculous results.

A slave girl with an oracular gift of telling the future was wondrously delivered from demonic possession. Her owners, who were making a lot of money off her, were not amused. They were furious! They trumped up false charges against Paul and Silas, accused them, and had them thrown into prison.

The men were beaten with lictor's rods. The Romans, who were geniuses at torturing people, invented this method of inflicting severe pain. These rods were an ancient cat-o'-nine-tails made of leather and metal or leather and bone. There were many strips of these. One whack on a person's back brought horrible pain and made the back into a bloody pulp. According to 2 Corinthians 11, Paul himself experienced this torture on three separate occasions.

After enduring this ordeal, Paul and Silas were placed in prison and in the inner cell. Renowned Greek scholar Dr. A. T. Robertson said, "The Roman, public prison had a vestibule and outer prison. Behind this was the inner prison which was a veritable dungeon with no light or air except when the door opened." Having been placed in this dungeon, Paul and Silas were placed in stocks. These were not like colonial American stocks. This was another ingenious, Roman torture device. These stocks were made from logs or timber. The Romans would chisel out holes for the legs so they could be forced apart as far as possible to cause cramping pain. How would you have felt in this situation after faithfully preaching the gospel?

Have you ever faced something profoundly difficult? Maybe it was severe rejection. Or perhaps terminal illness. Or loss of a mate, a child, or a job. Have you ever come across some crisis so intensely difficult that it was like a wall you couldn't go around on either side, or climb over, or tunnel underneath? There was no place to go. At such times we either run far away from God, or else we get really close to him.

How did Paul and Silas react after this horrendous ordeal? Acts 16:25 says, "About midnight Paul and Silas were praying and singing hymns to God, and the prisoners were listening to them." Those prisoners were listening because they saw the supernatural power of God in the lives of Paul and Silas. They had chosen obedience to Christ in the miraculous power of the Spirit. The prisoners saw reality, and it was powerful!

Even today your secular neighbors are watching how you handle excessive adversity and the pressures and ups and downs of modern life. Do Christians actually handle major loss differently from non-Christians? How do they die? Is there really any difference?

But note that the Lord was also listening. I heard a marvelous black preacher once preach that when the Lord heard their song he started to tap his foot, and that created a violent earthquake that literally shook the foundation of the prison. It also unlocked the prison doors and unfastened the prisoners' chains. Study Charles Wesley's extraordinary hymn "And Can It Be That I Should Gain," which was inspired by this passage. The end of this story is that even the suicidal jailer came in fear and trembling to Christ. Paul and Silas were still valiantly proclaiming the gospel, "Believe on the Lord Jesus Christ, and you will be saved."

Never underestimate the magnificent power of the combination of Holy Spirit-inspired Scripture with song. Music is perhaps the greatest of all art forms because it speaks to us on so many levels at once. Our whole being is immersed in the artistic experience. Songs can sometimes touch the heart deeply when even words are inadequate.

I once led a choral workshop in New York. At the reception was a woman who waited patiently to see me. When many of the people had left, she finally came to talk with me. She was very shy. She quietly said to me, "Thank you for your song, 'God Said Farewell.'" She told me that the Lord had used that song to hold her marriage together.

She immediately got my attention for two reasons. First, hardly anyone knows that particular song of mine. Second, it is a Christmas lullaby and has virtually nothing to do with marriage. So with a little coaxing from me, she told me her moving story.

She had fallen in love with a fine Christian man, and they eventually married. The Lord blessed their marriage with the birth of a beautiful baby boy who became the center of their lives. Things couldn't have been better. Life was really good, happy and fulfilling.

One day when this boy was six years old, he was playing ball. He went into the street to retrieve his ball and was accidentally hit by a car and instantly killed. His father was coming home from work, late in the afternoon, and when he turned the corner, he saw his own son crushed by an automobile. Their lives also were crushed. The mother said it was like taking a sledgehammer to a Tiffany stained-glass window: Their lives broke into a million fragments. She said that people would come to her and her husband and try to be comforting. They would promise to pray for them. They also would confess to a deep fear of losing their own children.

One day, she said, her worship minister came to her and invited her to bring her husband to a choir rehearsal. This worship minister confessed that he didn't know what to say to her, that he couldn't even begin to imagine what she was going through. He said that if she would come with her husband, she would not have to do anything—to sing, pray, or participate in any way. He told her that the choir just wanted them to sit in the middle of the choir and let them sing to them. They just wanted to surround this couple with their love.

Finally, to get this music minister off her back, she and her husband came. That night the choir was rehearsing one of my songs, "God Said Farewell." It pictures God, the Heavenly Father, standing on the battlements of glory and saying good-bye to his only Son when he came to this earth. The first line of the song goes, "God said farewell to his only Son as he stood on the threshold of glory." This lady, then, with tears streaming down her face, told me that she and her husband had changed my lyric to "we said farewell to our only son as he stood on the threshold of glory." I was profoundly touched and moved to tears.

Looking back, I believe that the Lord sent that woman to share that with me. I desperately needed to hear her story. At that time I was flying high. I was making records with the London Symphony and with some of the finest singers in Hollywood. I was doing well. I was fulfilled in my career and family. But I had forgotten the immense power of a gospel song to touch a person's life and to initiate the healing of a broken heart.

My mom once told me that one day I would learn how to use my musical gift not to impress but to comfort people. The Lord used this broken couple to minister to me profoundly and to touch my life. My mandate now is not to build an empire, not to make a lot of money, not to become famous, but to use the beautiful, musical gift God gave me for his glory and for his kingdom. I want to spend the rest of my life doing that. I want to be like King David, who said, "I will praise You with all my heart, Lord my God, and will honor Your name forever" (Ps. 86:12).

PRELUDE

Don Wyrtzen

∽

The Psalter, the ancient hymnal of Israel, gives a magnificent picture of reality. The Psalter's lyricists and composers wrestled with the nitty-gritty of life in the ancient world. They wrote honest and beautiful songs about their struggles and triumphs. Some of what they wrote seems messy to a purely rationalistic mind, but it all rings true to a full view of reality.

I believe the Lord wants us to relate to him with our whole beings with the totality of our personalities. But many of us intellectualize Christianity. We approach it much as we would a crossword puzzle in the *New York Times*. We are satisfied if all the little squares are filled in properly, both horizontally and vertically. If everything fits, matches, goes together, we feel content. However, a vital relationship with the Lord is based on more than head knowledge! He wants to get inside our hearts too—our psyches, our *personas*.

I also believe that intellectualized Christianity is too brittle and rigid for life. Brittle things tend to snap! Modern life is unpredictable, constantly changing, and complex. Both our external and internal worlds keep shifting and moving. Life seems to have a rhythm—work to rest, tension to resolution, and dissonance to consonance. We even tend to think in terms of black versus white and of relative versus absolute.

What do we need? What will give us comfort and direction in our complex modern society? We need an adequate view of reality! Intellectual precision, sound doctrine, and impeccable theology are essential, but they are not enough. They are basic blocks in the structure of reality, but they are not the whole building. Those of us who have bought into that system, to the neglect of other crucial areas of our personality, have sooner or later found our lives bankrupt.

The Lord isn't interested in a halfhearted, casual relationship. Hear his compelling command: "Love the LORD your God with all your heart and with all your soul and with all your strength" (Deut. 6:5 NIV). He demands that we love him with our hearts, the seat of our love and emotions; with our souls (*nephesh*), the center of our personalities and self-consciousness; and with our strength, our physical bodies.

29

This is at the fountainhead of living on the basis of the Law. In love the Israelites were to obey the Law because of an awesome respect (fear) and reverence for Yahweh. In the New Testament the Messiah taught us that the whole Law and the Prophets hang on two great commandments—loving God with our whole beings and loving our neighbors as ourselves (see Matt. 22:37–40).

The love of God was displayed not only in the Law but also on a grand and glorious scale through his "one and only Son" (John 3:16 NIV). The thrill of the gospel is that is enables us, as never before, to live on the basis of these two great commandments. As we do, we come to know the Lord with our whole beings.

As I've written this journal, I have identified with these ancient songwriters. Their sharing with me, under the power and inspiration of the Holy Spirit, has taken me to new heights and depths of reality. They have pulled, stretched, challenged, and comforted me.

The motifs and musings that follow are personal. These are not an exegetical and theological treatises. They are written from an artistic, musical, and emotional perspective. All 150 psalms are included, with a few key thoughts for each day of the year.

Art must be perceived in terms of both form and content. *Form* refers to how something is said; *content* refers to what is said. Form relates to style; content relates to substance. There should be congruity between the form and the content (i.e., you don't depict a thunderstorm with a piccolo solo!). Form is important, though often neglected. I don't think it was an accident that Psalm 51, David's magnificent poem of confession, was written in poetic form. Poetry is much more passionate and multi-layered than prose. So both form and content are highly significant in this journal.

A sonata or symphony (a sonata for orchestra) generally has three parts: exposition of the theme, development of the theme, and recapitulation of the theme. I have loosely followed that format in my journal.

The book itself is a three-part form—prelude, body, postlude. For each day there are three sections:

Theme—usually several key verses from each psalm
Development—some personal thoughts on those verses
Personal prayer—an attempt to apply by faith a biblical concept for each day

I've also included some traditional hymns and contemporary lyrics along the way.

Where possible, I have tried to tie in a musical perspective because I believe that music can be seen as a metaphor for life. What's wrong with many of us is that the song has gone out of our lives!

I have given each psalm its own title, using modern musical forms—sonatas, fugues, variations, rhapsodies, dirges, marches, hymns—to enhance the meaning of the text. I also have tied in some of the literary forms of the psalms—descriptive praise, individual and national lament, imprecatory, enthronement—which have only recently been discovered.

King David, the chief musician, says:
The instruction of the LORD is perfect, reviving the soul;
the testimony of the LORD is trustworthy, making the inexperienced
     wise.
The precepts of the LORD are right, making the heart glad;
the commandment of the LORD is radiant, making the eyes light up.
The fear of the LORD is pure, enduring forever;
the ordinances of the LORD are reliable and altogether righteous.
They are more desirable than gold—than an abundance of pure gold;
and sweeter than honey—than honey dripping from the comb.
In addition, Your servant is warned by them;
there is great reward in keeping them.
Amen! (Ps. 19:7–11)

A Contemporary Lyric

Adoration

May I love You, Lord, with all my heart,
  With my whole life, not just in part;
May I love You, Lord with all my soul,
  Make loving You my highest goal.

May I love You, Lord, with all my might,
  Fill my being with radiant light;
May I worship You more than anything,
  Filled with glorious praise I'll sing.

May I bow before You, Lord, on high,
  As Your holy name I glorify;
May I worship You on bended knee,
  King of Kings who reigns in majesty.

May I learn to know You more each day,
  With my family walking by the way;
May I worship You more than anything,
  Filled with glorious praise I'll sing.

Words and music by Don Wyrtzen   © 1984 Singspiration. (Based on Deut. 6:5–7.)

31

ODE TO JOY

FIRST MOVEMENT—IN MINOR

❧ Psalm 1 ❧

How happy is the man who does not follow the advice of the wicked, or take the path of sinners, or join a group of mockers! (v. 1).

Deep inside I long to be happy. At the core of my being, I crave fulfillment, meaning, and significance. The mind-set I choose and the lifestyle I live can only partly satisfy these longings.

To get a clear picture of happiness, I need to come to grips with what sort of behavior brings unhappiness. Taking advice from the ungodly, hanging around with sinners, and socializing with scoffers will sap my life of meaning and joy.

The people close to me—arrangers, composers, vocalists, and instrumentalists—strongly influence me. They have a subtle yet pervasive effect on my life. How easy it would be for me to impress them with my gifts and abilities in an attempt to make it big in records, films, or television. I don't want to compromise my commitment to Christian music; but if I'm not careful, I will walk, then stand, and ultimately sit with people who couldn't care less about God.

If I choose friends from a secular environment, my personal values will gradually change, the song of my life will shift to a minor key, and I'll lose a deep sense of personal joy. I need to keep my motives pure in my professional dealings; I don't want to become a clone of someone I admire.

Personal Prayer

Lord, help me not to be brainwashed by materialistic society, but give me a deep sense of personal joy in knowing You.

A Contemporary Psalm

Appreciation for Music
by Joseph T. Bayly

Thank You for music Lord
Handel and Haydn Society
and Boston Symphony
present Handel's Messiah
He shall feed His flock
like a shepherd
shall gather the lambs with His arm
and carry them in His bosom.
Students on Fairview Island singing
Who is on the Lord's side
who will serve the King?
Mother holding little boy rocking
humming
All through the night
my Savior will be watching
and Like a river glorious
is God's perfect peace.
Little group of people
before an open grave singing
My Jesus I love Thee
and up from the grave He arose.

From Psalms of My Life © 1987. Used by permission of David C. Cook Publishing Company.

ODE TO JOY
SECOND MOVEMENT—IN MAJOR

ᗡᗡ Psalm 1 ᗡᗡ

Instead, his delight is in the LORD's instruction,
and he meditates on it day and night (v. 2).

My mind is the key to my happiness, joy, and personal meaning. I am "transformed by the renewing of your mind" (Rom. 12:2). I must delight in the magnificence of the law. I must revel in the glory of biblical truth so that it shapes my thinking and changes my life.

I must meditate on it, fantasize about it, and be imaginative with it. I often struggle with low self-esteem and feel inadequate. But I know that when I'm weak, the Lord gives me strength. My source of strength and adequacy is the Lord, not myself. As I learn to pray more honestly, I will apply the Word more personally. Inspired by the Word, my life will burst forth with song.

What made the ancient Jews distinctive from the surrounding nations? The magnificence and glory of the Mosaic Law. What will make my life ring true today in the modern world? God's truth, the Holy Scripture! I must move beyond a cognitive perception of it and relate it to my total personality. I must delight in it!

Personal Prayer
Heavenly Father, I'm moved by the lyric poetry of your Word.
May my life become a motif of praise as I learn to love your truth.

A Contemporary Lyric

Psalm of My Life

Like worthless chaff the wind blows away,
Scorched by the bright desert sun through the day,
No root below, no fruit borne above,
My life was thirsting for rains of His love.
While roaming far away on my own,
I stood with sinners with hearts cold like stone,
I sat with scoffing cynics at play,
Until my life changed direction one day.

While meditating day and night,
His Word brought pleasure and highest delight,
It quenched my thirst and nurtured my soul,
It satisfied me and made my life whole.
Then, like a lovely well-watered tree,
Nourished by rivers that flow endlessly,
Weighed down with luscious fruit from His hand,
My full life prospered for Him in the land.

Words and music by Don Wyrtzen © 1975 Singspiration.

ODE TO JOY

THIRD MOVEMENT
Righteousness in Three Parts:
Planted, Productive, Prosperous

∽ Psalm 1 ∽

He is like a tree planted beside streams of water that bears its fruit
in season and whose leaf does not wither. Whatever he does prospers (v. 3).

When water flows through a pipe, the pipe remains unchanged; but when it flows through a tree, the tree receives nourishment and is changed, for a tree is a living organism.

In this passage we learn three things about this tree: it is planted; it is productive; and it is prosperous. This beautiful, flourishing tree is a stunning simile for the righteous person. The chaff of verse 4 is an apt word picture for the person who throws his life away.

When I read this passage, I think of my friend D. J. DePree, founder of the Herman Miller furniture firm. He was the only man I knew who was equally competent in biblical studies, in business, and in the arts. He walked with the Lord for over seventy years. Perhaps his greatest contribution was his Sunday school teaching, which he faithfully performed into his nineties.

I want to be like D. J. DePree:

+ Planted—firmly rooted and stable
+ Productive—marked by effectiveness
+ Prosperous—showcasing God's blessing

Personal Prayer
Lord, make my life a well-watered tree
rather than chaff that the wind blows away.

Ode

A poem of variable metric and verse structure that is usually festive in nature and addressed to a deity.

The last movement of Beethoven's Ninth Symphony (the Choral Symphony) is called "Ode to Joy." The magnificent hymn, "Joyful, Joyful, We Adore Thee" is based on this glorious theme.

ODE TO JOY
RECAPITULATION

❧ Psalm 1 ❧
For the LORD watches over the way of the righteous,
but the way of the wicked leads to ruin (v. 6).

This psalm presupposes two destinies: the destiny of the righteous and the destiny of the unrighteous. The godly person, living on the basis of the law of the Lord, ends up holy and happy. The ungodly person, living on the basis of a secular environment, ends up condemned and doomed. The Lord deeply cares about both. We will hear a lot more from this righteous person. He is the man of prayer who speaks most often in the Psalms.

Personal Prayer
Lord, remind me of life's destinies.
Help me choose righteousness over unrighteousness.

A Contemporary Lyric

My Everything

Lord, You are my everything,
  My highest joy and prize;
You meet my needs in every way with
  grace that satisfies.
Lord, You are my everything,
  My food and drink today;
You lead to brooks and meadows green
  and guide in a special way.
Since I am your own precious sheep,
  You watch me even when I sleep;
You have become my All-in-all,
  You always lift me when I fall.
Lord, You are my everything,
  My highest joy and prize;
You meet my needs in every way with
  grace that satisfies.

Lord, You are my everything,
  My highest joy and prize;
You meet my needs in every way with
  grace that satisfies.
Lord, You are my everything,
  My Shelter, Refuge, Friend;
You are my great Inheritance,
  Whose blessings never end.
You give me wisdom in the night,
  You fill me with complete delight;
Your presence fills my heart with joy,
  Which nothing ever can destroy.
Lord, You are my everything,
  My highest joy and prize;
You meet my needs in every way with
  grace with satisfies.

Words and music by Don Wyrtzen © 1981.

KING OF KINGS
AND LORD OF LORDS

✑ Psalm 2 ✑

"I have consecrated My King on Zion, My holy mountain."
I will declare the LORD's decree: He said to Me, "You are My Son;
today I have become Your Father (vv. 6–7).

King of kings and Lord of lords . . . and he shall reign forever and ever." My ear keeps playing Handel's *Messiah* as I approach Psalm 2, and I am overwhelmed by its majesty and glory. My friend Larry McGuill had a similar experience when he sang Handel's *Messiah* with four thousand others. During the "Hallelujah Chorus," he was so overcome with the beauty and intricacy of the music as well as the message that tears flowed down his cheeks and he was unable to sing.

God chose King David, the chief musician, to be the greatest king in Israel's history. But God also chose David's great Son to be King of kings. His kingdom will be established, and his reign will be forever. Verses 6–7, the centerpiece of this psalm, speak of the coronation of the King and the pledge of adoption given to David's heir. As Christ, the Messiah, fulfills this, he becomes the basis for missionary ventures throughout the world.

As I enter the throne room of God through this psalm, the nations of the world come into focus and perspective. But in a more compelling manner, I am overwhelmed by the dignity, solemnity, and majesty of this King of all the universe. May I learn to give him my full allegiance and loyalty today. May I learn to worship him, adore him, glorify him, and enjoy him! But may the awesomeness of his majesty not rob me of personal intimacy with him.

Personal Prayer

Thank You, Lord, that I can approach your throne of grace with confidence
and can receive your grace and help as I need them.

ELEGY IN THE NIGHT
FIRST MOVEMENT

∽ Psalm 3 ∽

I lie down and sleep; I wake again because the LORD sustains me.
I am not afraid of the thousands of people who have taken
their stand against me on every side (vv. 5–6).

Anxiety is deep and profound. Fear controls and dominates. Long nights become threatening. Children cause distress and personal grief. Big questions start to press upon me, and I start to feel that God has withdrawn from me. Sometimes in the middle of the night, I awake disturbed over the changes and uncertainties in the music business; other times I feel uncertain if I don't have my wife's approval on a major issue. How vulnerable and needy I am.

At times like this I'm learning to pour out my soul to my Heavenly Father. I'm learning that spirituality begins with honesty. I'm learning to express myself emotionally to God. I don't want to have just a cognitive relationship to him. I want to learn to share my total personality with him: the mood swings, the ups and downs, the consonance as well as the dissonance of my life, the harmony as well as the disharmony. There is no resolution without tension. And this it true whether in symphonic form or in the structure of my own life.

King David experienced all of these textures in his full but turbulent life. He even had to cope with a son, who though so full of promise and potential, out of rebellion was trying to kill him. Yet somehow David was able to roll all this trauma over on the Lord. He entrusted his troubles to the Lord, overwhelming as they were, and turned over and got a good night's sleep. He learned that faith could flourish in the soil of fear and that anxiety could be transformed into tranquility.

Personal Prayer

Teach me, Lord, to lament honestly.
Then when you miraculously deliver me,
I can really praise you.

The Language of Music

Elegy

A mournful, plaintive, sorrowful poem or song.

The Scripture is full of lamentation (The Psalms, Jeremiah, Lamentations). In Romans 8:26 we learn that the Holy Spirit "intercedes for us with groans that words cannot express."

ELEGY IN THE NIGHT

SECOND MOVEMENT

◦◦ Psalm 4 ◦◦

*Answer me when I call, O God who vindicates me. You freed me from affliction;
be gracious to me and hear my prayer. Many are saying, "Who can show us
anything good?" Look on us with favor, LORD. You have put more joy in my
heart than they have when their grain and new wine abound. I will both lie down
and sleep in peace, for You alone, LORD, make me live in safety (vv. 1, 6–8).*

K ing David had a melancholic cast to his psyche. Artistic, sensitive, and
creative by nature, he also tended to be a perfectionist. But unlike many
creative people, who often feel inadequate because they can't do everything perfectly, he didn't allow his perfectionism to add to his guilt. Instead he allowed
the nightmares of his life to motivate him to express himself intuitively as well
as intellectually. Recently I wrote a theme that I called "Elegy in the Night."
I was hurting so much when I wrote it, I expressed my emotions musically but
not lyrically. I don't know if I'll ever be able to find the words for that melody.

When humiliated, exasperated, surrounded by lies, and filled with
doom and gloom, David took all of this to God in prayer. He also wrote
songs about all of it—songs that reveal the innermost working of his soul
and lead other believers into profound, personal worship.

In distress David learned to pray more meaningfully, to trust God more
implicitly, and as a result, to compose more freely and imaginatively. As
David learned to bring his experiences into harmony with his artistic tem-
perament, God led him to a deep wellspring of peace and contentment. The
New Testament insight on this is 1 Peter 5:7: "Casting all your care upon
Him, because He cares about you."

Personal Prayer

*Just as the dominant seventh pulls toward a deeply satisfying
resolution in the tonic chord, may the tensions of my personal life be
resolved in you, O Lord, my Deliverer.*

Morning Song

∽ Psalm 5 ∽

*At daybreak, LORD, You hear my voice; at daybreak I plead my case
to You and watch expectantly. But let all who take refuge in You rejoice;
let them shout for joy forever. May You shelter them, and may those
who love Your name boast about You (vv. 3, 11).*

*L*iving in the complexity of the modern world puts me under a lot of
stress. My mind continually mulls over unresolved personal conflicts,
domestic hassles, competitiveness at work, and the pressure to perform. All
of this rises to the surface early in the morning. At my first moments of consciousness, I often feel despair. For me many days are blue Mondays.

Often beneath creativity lies a fragile psyche. When I immaturely
demand the respect and admiration of my colleagues, an honest, too objective criticism deeply hurts me. I have experienced undue depression because
I have placed too much value in myself instead of in the Lord.

Sensitive, artistic, and high-strung, King David also experienced severe
depression early in the morning. Yet he didn't wallow in despair or nurture his
black moods. Instead, he started his day with God by offering daily sacrifice to
God's threshold. He met God there, spoke with him, and committed all of his
troubles to the Lord.

David approached God with great expectation. He didn't deny him
many problems, but he broke free of his loneliness. He realized he was not
alone in the world but part of a company of believers who could join him in
praise. God responded by covering him, encircling him, and caring for him.
And the sun came up, and the black clouds were blown away.

Personal Prayer

*Dear Lord, I praise you and thank you that I am not alone
in the universe. Because of the presence of Christ in my life,
I can live today with deep peace and joy.*

KYRIE—
"LORD, HAVE MERCY!"

◌ Psalm 6 ◌

LORD, *do not rebuke me in Your anger; do not discipline me in Your wrath.*
Be gracious to me, LORD, for I am weak; heal me, LORD, for my bones are shaking;
my whole being is shaken with terror. And You, LORD—how long?
The LORD has heard my plea for help; the LORD accepts my prayer (vv. 1–3, 9).

The painful, heart-wrenching discipline of the Lord caused David to cry out for mercy. But the Heavenly Father, an example to all fathers, had to discipline his son. Hebrews 12:5–6, the classic New Testament commentary on discipline, says, "My son, do not make light of the Lord's discipline, and do not lose heart when he rebukes you, because the Lord disciplines those he loves, and punishes everyone he accepts as a son" (NIV).

Deeply troubled and alarmed, David almost lost heart. His conscience was uneasy, and he was exhausted and depressed. Even his prayer had died away. He could only weep.

Unlike David, I sometimes deny such feelings or at least compound my problems with rationalization. I find it hard to be vulnerable enough to face my predicament, to come to grips with my life, and to share my hurt and pain with brothers or sisters in Christ who are close to me.

David faced squarely the reality of his messed-up life. He cried out to his Heavenly Father for mercy and discovered that his walk with the Lord must begin with reality. He moved from petition to praise and found answered prayer. Then he wrote this moving psalm for those of us who have a hard time admitting, much less expressing, the deep hurt and pain of our lives. When we do as David did, God goes to work for our lives, giving us authentic reasons to praise him.

The Language of Music

Kyrie

A Greek term for "O Lord."

The complete phrase is <u>Kyrie eleison,</u> "Lord, have mercy." David said, "I am in deep distress. Let me fall into the hands of the Lord, for his mercy is very great" (1 Chron. 21:13 NIV).

Personal Prayer

Lord, make the tough things in my life a black velvet backdrop against which you showcase the diamond of your grace.

SONG OF
THE SLANDERED SAINT
SUGGESTED BY SPURGEON

∽ Psalm 7 ∽

LORD my God, I seek refuge in You; save me from all my pursuers and rescue me, or they will tear me like a lion, ripping me apart, with no one to rescue me. Let the evil of the wicked come to an end, but establish the righteous. The One who examines the thoughts and emotions is a righteous God. I will thank the LORD for His righteousness; I will sing about the name of the LORD, the Most High (vv. 1–2, 9, 17).

Betrayed, hounded, and unjustly accused as a result of Saul's jealousy and rivalry, David broke forth with a plea, "Lord, it isn't fair!" I remember a producer who accused me of too much self-confidence and arrogance when actually I had many self-doubts. I felt I had been judged unfairly.

David didn't just complain. He moved on to honest prayer and finally to praise. He came down on the side of God instead of on the side of despair. Deep in his soul David knew that the "Judge of all the earth will do right" (see Gen. 18:25). He found security in God's righteousness (v. 9). He practiced in the ancient world what the apostle Paul later taught: "Don't worry about anything, but in everything, through prayer and petition with thanksgiving, let your requests be made known to God. And the peace of God, which surpasses every thought, will guard your hearts and your minds in Christ Jesus" (Phil. 4:6–7).

Personal Prayer

O Lord Most High, may I not wallow in despair today, but may I completely trust your righteousness and fairness.

How Majestic Is Your Name in All the Earth

∾ Psalm 8 ∾

O Lord, our Lord, how magnificent is Your name throughout the earth!
You have covered the heavens with Your majesty. Because of Your adversaries,
You have established a stronghold from the mouths of children and nursing
infants, to silence the enemy and the avenger (vv. 1–2).

Psalm 8, a consummate example of what a hymn should be, celebrates the glory and the grace of God. Its major thesis is "How excellent is your name." in *Reflections on the Psalms*. C. S. Lewis reminds us that "to glorify God is to enjoy Him."

Majesty combined with intimacy characterizes our relationship with God. On one hand, we can relate to Isaiah, who witnessed the holiness of God: "Woe to me!" he cried. "I am ruined! For I am a man of unclean lips, and I live among a people of unclean lips, and my eyes have seen the King, the Lord Almighty" (Isa. 6:5 NIV). On the other hand, God wants us to approach his throne with confidence so that we may receive mercy and find grace (see Heb. 4:16).

That the Sovereign of the universe desires a close, personal relationship with me is almost beyond comprehension. He is my Heavenly Father, and I am his child.

Personal Prayer

Lord, may I move from sterile, inattentive worship
to an intimate relationship with you.
May I learn to enjoy your presence!

THE MAJESTY OF MAN

∽ Psalm 8 ∽
You made him little less than God
and crowned him with glory and honor (v. 5).

When compared to the vastness of the universe, I am infinitesimal. Yet even though I am dwarfed by the magnitude of God's creation, I have profound meaning and significance because I am made in God's image (Gen. 1:26–27). Because his glory is revealed not only in nature but also in me, I possess majesty. Even though I may not like certain things about myself (my height, my weight, my age), I need to remember that I am a reflection of the image of God.

Humanism has deified man and attempted to make him the "measure of all things." I sometimes overreact to this and think that I am nothing. But I am only a little lower than the angels in God's hierarchy. I am crowned with glory and honor. I reflect God's glory just as much as the starry heavens do.

Unlike the animals, which also reflect God's incredible imagination, I have a sense of my own existence and I can experience community. But even more significant, I can pray directly to the Lord of hosts. Because I'm part of God's family, the universe isn't meaningless and empty; it is my home.

In size I may be infinitesimal, but in worth I am infinitely valuable because I reflect God's glory.

Personal Prayer
Lord, help me to think soberly and objectively about myself.
May I not get so wrapped up in my weaknesses that I forget
that your glory and majesty are revealed in me.

Triumphal March

∽ Psalm 9 ∽

*I will thank the LORD with all my heart; I will declare all Your wonderful
works. I will rejoice and boast about You; I will sing about Your name,
Most High. When my enemies retreat, they stumble and perish before
You. For You have upheld my just cause; You are seated on Your throne
as a righteous judge (vv. 1–4).*

This psalm, a stirring lyric to a triumphal march, celebrates a glorious
victory in battle. Although flushed with the new wine of success, David
didn't use the occasion to boast; instead he broke forth in praise, celebrating
God's actions and his person.

David was happy about his victory, but he also saw the bigger picture.
As God worked in David's personal life and daily experiences, he also works
in history through great redemptive acts. David knew that the Lord would
ultimately triumph and usher in a worldwide reign of justice.

This psalm assures me that I can live in confidence, knowing that God
has a firm hold on history. Things are not careening out of control! He holds
the momentous events of the future as well as the ordinary events of my daily
life in his hands. I recall when I really tasted success for the first time. A top-
notch London symphony played my scores for a recording session. I had to
fight to retain my composure as I conducted the orchestra. That experience
really affirmed me and boosted my sagging self-image.

As I taste the sweet elixir of success from time to time, may I not become
drunk with personal pride. May I be reminded that God is the One who has
composed the score and has personally orchestrated my life.

Personal Prayer
*O Lord Most High, I praise you for being in control of history,
including the details of my life today.*

A Mournful Lament

◌⟋ Psalm 10 ⟍◌

Lord, why do You stand so far away? Why do You hide in times of trouble?
In all his scheming, the wicked arrogantly thinks: "There is no accountability,
[since] God does not exist." He crouches and bends down; the helpless fall
because of his strength. Lord, You have heard the desire of the humble;
You will strengthen their hearts. You will listen carefully, doing justice
for the fatherless and the oppressed, so that men of the earth may
terrify [them] no more (vv. 1, 4, 10, 17–18).

When I desperately need God, where is he? I feel the terror of being abandoned. God seems far away, as if he is in hiding. How must I react when I'm in this kind of corner?

First, *I can lament.* As David did, I can pour out my soul to God and let my raw emotions flow out to my Creator.

Second, *I can face reality.* In verses 2–11, the psalmist described a wicked tyrant who is boastful, greedy, blasphemous, and atheistic. Yet he appeared to be prosperous, stable, and happy. This harmony between evil and success seems grossly unfair! But the psalmist faced squarely the tyranny of this wicked ruler and confronted God with his responsibility.

Third, *I can pray.* The psalmist prayed for God to remember the helpless, to see their trouble and grief, and to break the power of this evil man. This response is an excellent model for me to follow when I face problems. God is much greater than any problem, so I need not fear that I'm asking too much.

Fourth, *I can praise.* David expressed faith that the Lord hears, listens, encourages, and defends. As he worshiped the Lord of eternity, his terror diminished.

I too must learn to lament, to face reality, to pray, and to praise. I must free myself of empty clichés and repetitive, timeworn phrases. When I'm honest with my Heavenly Father, I will begin to praise him with my whole being.

Personal Prayer
Instead of internalizing anxiety and anger,
May I learn to lament to you, O Lord, my King forever.

FINDING REFUGE

∾ Psalm 11 ∾

I have taken refuge in the LORD. How can you say to me,
"Escape to the mountain like a bird! The LORD is in His holy temple;
the LORD's throne is in heaven. His eyes watch; He examines everyone.
For the LORD is righteous; He loves righteous deeds.
The upright will see His face (vv. 1, 4, 7).

David's friends advised him to flee to a mountain cave for safety. He was being pursued—perhaps by Saul or by Absalom. But instead of giving in to panic, he placed his faith in the Lord as his refuge.

I'm a peacemaker. I'll go to any lengths to avoid conflict and as a result experience much distress in interpersonal relationships. I'm not alone—people today flee pain and stress through the misuse of work (even the Lord's work), sex, drugs, and alcohol.

The Lord is in residence, not in flight. He is always there as a refuge and shelter for his people. His city has foundations; his temple is secure. Instead of wallowing in fear, David exercised faith and found a complete and satisfying security in the righteousness and justice of God.

When I feel trapped, I must trust God and believe in the freedom that comes from his truth (John 8:31–32). Because of his just rule, the wicked will go down in judgment and ruin, but I will behold him face-to-face. The child of God always has a happy ending to look forward to.

Personal Prayer

O Lord, as I live in the middle of a rootlessness and complexity
of modern life, may I find my refuge and shelter in you.

A Gospel Song Lyric

A Shelter in the Time of Storm

The Lord's our Rock, in Him we hide,
A Shelter in the time of storm;
Secure whatever ill betide,
A Shelter in the time of storm.
O Jesus is a Rock in a weary land,

A weary land, a weary land;
O Jesus is a Rock in a weary land,
A Shelter in the time of storm.
O Rock divine, O Refuge dear,
A Shelter in the time of storm;
Be Thou our helper ever near,
A Shelter in the time of storm.

Words by Vernon J. Charlesworth. Music by Ira D. Sankey.

DOUBLE-TONGUING

∽ Psalm 12 ∽

Help, LORD, for no faithful one remains; the loyal have disappeared
from the human race. They lie to one another; they speak with flattering
lips and deceptive hearts. The words of the LORD are pure words,
like silver refined in an earthen furnace, purified seven times (vv. 1–2, 6).

*I*n music the effect of double-tonguing is delightful. In life, it is devastating and cruel. James tells us that "no man can tame the tongue. It is a restless evil, full of deadly poison" (3:8). The music industry is notorious for its hype and its manipulation of people. Since the art form of music is so subjective and since aesthetic taste is so personal, relationships between people are very important. Unfortunately, positive, healthy relationships can easily degenerate into negative, unhealthy "politics."

A Contemporary Lyric
The Refiner's Fire
The words of the Lord are flawless
Like silver refined I the furnace of clay,
Purified in the refiner's fire,
They will stand sure on the Judgment Day!
Words by Don Wyrtzen © 1988.

The untamed tongue of Psalm 12 lies, flatters, deceives, and boasts. Empty talk, smooth talk, and double-talk take the place of satisfying communication; and deceit and manipulation rule. I'm amazed at how deceitful my own heart is. As I read Crabb's *The Marriage Builder,* I see how often I use manipulation for my own ends in our marriage. Often I don't even realize it! By nature I am unaware of my own deceitfulness.

In stark contrast stand the flawless and pure words of the Lord, a wealth of silver refined in God's crucible.

I want my life to be permeated with God's words, not marked by an uncontrollable tongue. If I'm controlled by the Spirit, I won't manipulate people. I will minister to them. And I will experience fullness in place of emptiness, wholeness in place of fragmentation, and fellowship in place of loneliness.

Personal Prayer
Help me, Lord, to minister
to people rather than
manipulate them.

The Language of Music
Dirge
A song or hymn of grief or lamentation.
Dirges are especially intended to accompany funeral or memorial rites. They are slow, solemn, and mournful. The "teacher" tells us in Ecclesiastes 3:4 that there is "a time to weep and a time to laugh, a time to mourn and a time to dance."

Dirge of Depression to Descant of Delight

∽ Psalm 13 ∽

*Lord, how long will You continually forget me? How long will
You hide Your face from me? How long will I store up anxious concerns
within me, agony in my mind every day? How long will my enemy dominate
me? But I have trusted in Your faithful love; my heart will rejoice in Your
deliverance. I will sing to the Lord because He has treated me
generously (vv. 1–2, 5–6).*

How long? Repeated four times, this question indicates that David was distressed with God, with himself, and with his enemy. Much good can come from tension. For example, the music from stringed instruments is a result of tension. For me there is nothing like a glorious resolution of the rising tension produced in a Beethoven symphony.

David was restless. His mind was in turmoil, and he felt dejected. His enemy seemed to be ascending, threatening his kingship, and causing personal humiliation. God seemed distant. The friendship between David and his Lord has clouded over.

Things are not always as they seem. Part of David's genius was his ability to transcend such difficulties. Without tension there can be no resolution. The tension in David's life came from his difficulties with the enemy and his devotion to God. This conflict led to personal maturity, which he attained because he maintained intimacy with God.

His dirge of depression became a descant of delight. Like an eagle, David soared to new heights. His life took flight when he pledged himself to God's unfailing love, when he chose to praise and thank God, when he realized that God had a higher purpose. "His ways are not our ways, and his thoughts are not our thoughts" (Isa. 55:8 NIV). A spiritual metamorphosis took place when David wrapped himself in God's love instead of in his besetting circumstances. He reached the loftiest height of all when he started to sing of God's goodness.

The Language of Music

Descant

A soaring counter melody, usually sung by several sopranos.

Used as a decorative addition to a hymn, the descant is a very effective musical device which can leave listeners feeling exhilarated.

Personal Prayer

*Lord, I want to trust in your unfailing
love, rejoice in your salvation, and sing
of your goodness today.*

DISCORD OF DEPRAVITY

✑ Psalm 14 ✑

The fool says in his heart, "God does not exist." They are corrupt; their actions are revolting. There is no one who does good. All have turned away; they have all become corrupt. There is no one who does good, not even one (vv. 1, 3; also see Rom. 1).

The mood of this piece is arrogant. The theme is total depravity—leaving God out of life. The motifs are materialism, secularism, exploitation, and corruption. The essence of living in the flesh is to live as if God doesn't exist. I know of a former prominent evangelist who arrogantly decided to no longer call God his Father.

What happens when we leave God out of our lives? Psalm 14 graphically and poetically answers the question.

Denying God begins a downward progression. Suppressing the truth leads to idolatry, self-destructiveness, and gross immorality. Error replaces truth, behavior becomes totally depraved, and people are oppressed.

Apostates think they are wise, but they are fools. When we choose the foolish route of denying God, we end up in rebellion against God, in alienation from others, and in personal corruption because we have killed off the source of all love and meaning for our lives.

This psalm is discordant and dissonant until the last verse, when David returns to the theme of salvation. The Lord will restore the fortunes of his people and make them glad. We don't need to be mannequins—lifeless and stripped of all love and meaning.

Personal Prayer

Heavenly Father, make me fully aware that it is your existence alone that fills my life with love and gives it meaning.

The Language of Music

Discord

A musical dynamic characterized by dissonance and unpleasantness.

The opposite of discord is "concord" which emphasizes consonance and pleasantness. Our Lord encourages harmony and unity (John 17:23). Like darkness and light, however, discord and concord would lack definition without their opposites.

RHAPSODY
OF RIGHTEOUSNESS

∽ Psalm 15 ∽

LORD, who can dwell in Your tent? Who can live on Your holy
mountain? The one who lives honestly, practices righteousness,
and acknowledges the truth in his heart—(vv. 1–2).

Psalm 15 portrays a man of integrity who stands in bold contrast to the depraved man of Psalm 14.

Because he is a man of worship and sacrifice, his sins are covered by the blood. Therefore he has nothing to hide and he deceives no one. He is marked by five sterling characteristics:

1. *Integrity* (v. 2)
2. *Truth* (v. 3)
3. *Allegiance* (v. 4)
4. *Honor* (vv. 4–5)
5. *Stability* (v. 5)

One of the most authentic people I know is my friend Bill Rigg. He is filled with quiet, steadfast conviction. When he spoke at the funeral service for his fifteen-year-old son, Jim, I saw unbelievable pain, but I also saw the reality of Jesus Christ.

I want God to create these personality strengths in me. They will be God's gift to me when I place complete trust in him.

Personal Prayer
Lord, I pray that you will produce transparency,
authenticity, and integrity in my life.

A Contemporary Lyric

Make Me Real, Lord

Make me real, Lord,
Marked by integrity;
May what I say be one with what I am!
Make me true, Lord,
Living reality;
And make my life ring true—not a
   sham.

May my instrument give forth a pure,
Wholehearted sound,
May the choices of my life in truth
abound.
Make me real, Lord,
Create transparency;
And may I glorify the Great I Am,
And may I magnify the Spotless Lamb!
Words by Don Wyrtzen © 1998.

SONG OF SECURITY

IN LIFE AND IN DEATH

∽ Psalm 16 ∽

*Protect me, God, for I take refuge in You. I said to the LORD, "You are my Lord;
I have no good besides You." Therefore my heart is glad, and my spirit rejoices;
my body also rests securely. For You will not abandon me to Sheol;
You will not allow Your Faithful One to see the Pit. You reveal the path of
life to me; in Your presence is abundant joy; in Your right hand
are eternal pleasures (vv. 1–2, 9–11).*

How can I be secure in life when I know I will someday die and when I feel at times that I am only an animal, a machine, or a combination of molecules? Death fascinates me, yet I was shocked by my mother's sudden death. Death seems to be an assault on humanity, impossible to grasp and comprehend.

Though aware of my mortality and fallenness, I know that I bear God's image. As St. Augustine reminds me, my heart has a God-shaped vacuum that will never be satisfied apart from the Lord. In short, my security must be in him. My profound need to be loved and accepted must be met by God.

How will he meet my deep longing for security?

1. He assigns me my portion and holds my future (v. 5).
2. He gives me a beautiful inheritance (v. 6).
3. He helps my conscience instruct me (v. 7).
4. His presence is at my right hand (v. 8).
5. He gives me a glad heart, and my spirit rejoices (v. 9).
6. He watches over my body—even after death (v. 9, also Acts 2:22–37).
7. He reveals the path of life to me; His presence is abundant joy; at His right hand are eternal pleasures (v. 11).

Therefore, I will place my faith in these promises and let the Lord be my reference point. I will let him integrate, authenticate, and inform my life. As he brings wholeness, my insecurities will be transformed into peace and rest. My fears will begin to disappear, and I will be able to face life and even death with confidence.

Personal Prayer

*Lord, I praise you because I am one of your loved ones.
Help me to count on the fact that because I am in you,
no one could be more secure.*

PRAYER FOR JUSTICE

✑ Psalm 17 ✑

LORD, hear a just cause; pay attention to my cry; listen to my prayer—
from lips free of deceit. Let my vindication come from You, [for] You see
what is right. I call on You, God, because You will answer me; listen closely
to me; hear what I say. Display the wonders of Your faithful love, Savior of
all who seek refuge from those who rebel against Your right hand. Guard me as
the apple of Your eye; hide me in the shadow of Your wings (vv. 1–2, 6–8).

I want to pray with the same warmth, intimacy, and immediacy with which
King David prayed. He unveiled his inner self, crying out to God and
pleading for refuge. The old gospel song says it so well:

Under His wings I am safely abiding,
Tho' the night deepens and tempests are wile;
Still I can trust Him, I know he will keep me,
He has redeemed me and I am His child.
Under His wings, under His wings,
Who from His love can sever?
Under His wings my soul shall abide,
Safely abide forever.
Under His wings, O what precious enjoyment!
There will I hide till life's trials are o'er;
Sheltered, protected, no evil can harm me,
Resting in Jesus I'm safe evermore.
Words by William O. Cushing. Music by Ira D. Sankey.

Once again David confronted his problem head-on and talked honestly to
God about his callous, arrogant, and murderous enemies who were frustrating
him on every side.

He ends with an exquisitely beautiful verse: "But I will see Your face in
righteousness; when I awake, I will be satisfied with Your presence" (v. 15).

Personal Prayer

Help me, Lord, to give up my quest to find satisfaction in anyone but you.
Make me intensely aware that only you can totally satisfy.

Doxology

ᥴᕽᕽ Psalm 18 ᕽᕽᥴ

I love You, Lord, my strength. The Lord is my rock, my fortress,
and my deliverer, my God, my mountain where I seek refuge,
my shield and the horn of my salvation, my stronghold. I called to the Lord,
who is worthy of praise, and I was saved from my enemies (vv. 1–3).

The psalms contain more lament than praise. Uninhibited praise is usually preceded by authentic lament. Perhaps today our praise and worship are sometimes shallow and superficial because we have not learned to lament. Unlike David we have little or no concept of how profound our personal need is.

Miraculously delivered from his enemies and from Saul (see 2 Sam. 8, 22), David broke forth in this moving song with intense feeling. Because of his artistic discipline, he was able to hone this experience into a carefully crafted psalm of beautiful structure and symmetry:

Doxology (vv. 1–3)
Metaphors of deliverance (vv. 4–6)
Theophany (vv. 7–15)
Personal application (vv. 16–45)
Doxology (vv. 46–50)

This song deals with David's dramatic deliverance from Saul and from his enemies, but it also deals with the quintessential Deliverer to come, the Messiah. In Romans 15:9, Paul applies Psalm 18:49 directly to Christ, our Messiah.

Psalm 18 comforts and encourages me. Like David, I can be set free—physically and emotionally. The liberation of my personality will occur as I place more and more trust in Christ, my Deliverer, rather than in human effort unempowered by God.

Personal Prayer

I praise you, Yahweh, for being my Rock,
my Savior, and my Deliverer. May you
be exalted in my life today, and may
I sing praises to your name.

The Language of Music

Doxology

An expression of praise to God, this term is based on the Greek word <u>Doxa,</u> which means "glory."

Louis Bourgeois's "Doxology" from the Genevan Psalter is an excellent example:

Praise God, from whom all
blessings flow;
Praise Him, all creatures
here below;
Praise Him above, ye heavenly
host;
Praise Father, Son, and Holy
Ghost. Amen!

Glorious Proclamation

∽ Psalm 19 ∽

The heavens declare the glory of God, and the sky proclaims the work of His hands. The instruction of the LORD is perfect, reviving the soul; the testimony of the LORD is trustworthy, making the inexperienced wise. May the words of my mouth and the meditation of my heart be acceptable to You, O LORD, my rock and my Redeemer (vv. 1, 7, 14).

No nobler, more majestic psalm has ever been written about God's revelation than Psalm 19. It tells us how God took the initiative to reveal himself to us—a concept beyond my comprehension. He did not leave us in darkness; he communicated through the sky and the Scripture.

Creation reveals God's invisible qualities. His power and divine nature can be seen clearly in what he has made (Rom. 1). He holds each of us accountable for our response to this revelation. If we respond favorably, he sends more revelation (Acts 10). If we suppress this truth, we have no excuse!

Our Heavenly Father, a creative virtuoso, dazzles us with his power and might. Yet because he wants to be close to us, he bridged the distance between us with his Word, making possible an intimate relationship. His Word is perfect, restorative, and trustworthy (v. 7). It brings wisdom, joy, radiance, and light (vv. 7–8). His ordinances are pure, eternal, sure, and righteous (v. 9). They are more precious than gold and sweeter than honey (v. 10). Living on the basis of the law has its own great reward (v. 11).

The compelling message of the lyric, "But Greater Still," convinces me that the value of God's Word defies description. Its worth to me is intensely personal. It nourishes my soul, and its truth sets me free.

Personal Prayer
O Lord, my Rock and my Redeemer,
may the words of my mouth
and the meditation of my heart
be pleasing in your sight.

INVOCATION

PRAYER BEFORE BATTLE

∞ Psalm 20 ∞

May the LORD answer you in a day of trouble; may the name of
Jacob's God protect you. May He give you what your heart desires and
fulfill your whole purpose. Let us shout for joy at your victory and lift the
banner in the name of our God. May the LORD fulfill all your requests.
Some take pride in a chariot, and others in horses, but we take
pride in the name of the LORD our God (vv. 1, 4–5, 7).

Knowing he faced a life-or-death struggle, David prepared for battle by offering prayers and sacrifices. The congregation prayed for him, and David voiced his certainty of God's answer (vv. 6–8).

The focus of David's cry for help was the name of the Lord, which he knew had power. Any hope for conquest, and all protection, support, and help, come only from that name. The most formidable weapons of the ancient world were impotent against the name of the Lord.

I too face confrontation—in the big hassles of life and the small hassles of daily living. I don't want to rely on modern insights or popular solutions. They are sterile and useless. Only the name of the Lord can give me relief and support. I don't want it to be the last place I go for help. I don't have the resources to make it on my own. I'm a dependent person. When I am weak, then I am strong. As Sandi Patti sings so gloriously, "There is power in the name of the Lord."

Personal Prayer

Lord, keep me from placing
my trust in the might of men;
remind me that your name is
the only reliable source of strength.

The Language of Music

Invocation

The act or process of petitioning for help or support.

An invocation can be a prayer or a musical composition at the beginning of a worship service. A beautiful example is "God Is Here" by Norman Johnson:

> God is here and waits to
> speak with us;
> God is here to start this
> week with us.
> With open hearts and minds
> let us respond to Him—
> And keep our appointment
> with God!

© 1970 Singspiration.

Victory March

∽ Psalm 21 ∽

Lord, the king finds joy in Your strength. How greatly
he rejoices in Your victory! You have given him his heart's
desire and have not denied the request of his lips. Selah
For the king relies on the Lord; through the faithful love of the
Most High he is not shaken. Be exalted, Lord, in Your strength;
we will sing and praise Your might (vv. 1–2, 7, 13).

After pouring out my soul in lament and prayer, I need to wait patiently for the Lord to answer. As he answered David, he also will answer me. In Psalm 21, a glorious royal hymn, David celebrated the Lord's answer to his petition. The Lord brought victory rather than defeat, gave life instead of death, and blessed David by granting him his heart's desire.

Even under pressure David modeled stability and security. I too need to grasp that my safety, steadiness, and confidence are based on God's loyal love (see Rom. 8:35–39). David's faith, centered squarely on the rock-solid, permanent, eternal love of the Lord, stabilized and strengthened him.

David didn't win the battle with his own strength, expertise, or military genius. But that didn't diminish his exhilaration. To celebrate God's victory, David wrote glorious music. Like David, I too will sing praise when I lift up my life to the Lord, and he will bring music back into my life.

The Language of Music

March

Music for soldiers, usually involving strongly accented beats in groups of four.

Marches are usually dignified, ceremonial, and military. A good example is Arthur Sullivan's stirring hymn, "Onward Christian Soldiers."

Personal Prayer
Lord, may I learn to throw
a party to celebrate your
glory, majesty, and unfailing love.

SONG OF THE SUFFERING SERVANT

FIRST MOVEMENT
The Eloquence of Darkness—Part 1

∽ Psalm 22 ∽

My God, my God, why have You forsaken me? [Why are You] so far
from my deliverance and from my words of groaning? (v. 1).

When I face an obstacle that I can't go over, under, or around, I need to acknowledge my pain and helplessness. Denial and fantasy only compound my problem with dishonesty. I need to look squarely at my situation and admit my inability to resolve it.

The parallels between this psalm and Christ's crucifixion are astounding. This exquisite lyric poetry portrays deep personal shame and intense suffering. Reading it makes me feel vicariously what Christ went through to win my redemption on the darkest day in history. Since Christ lived the experiences described here and quotes it in the New Testament, I believe this lament applies to him.

Throbbing with urgency and immediacy, the first movement of this psalm (vv. 1–21) eloquently portrays darkness in several related themes:

First, *David cried out to God* (vv. 1–2). "My God, my God, why have You forsaken me?" According to Gospel accounts, Christ said these exact words at the height of his agony on the cross (Matt. 27:46; Mark 15:34). As death closed in, Christ felt that his Father had turned his back on him and had withdrawn protection. He felt helpless, disoriented, and betrayed.

Second, *David remembered history* (vv. 3–5). He praised the Lord and affirmed his holiness by citing the experiences of his fathers who trusted God through adversity and were delivered.

Third, *David described the suffering servant's experience of shame* (vv. 6–8). Scorned and despised, he was mocked by a blood-thirsty crowd that was cynical and cruel.

Fourth, *David reflected on God's care* (vv. 9–11). The Hebrew word for trust means "to lie prone—completely helpless." David trusted God from the beginning—even from birth. He pleaded for God to be close because there was no one else to help.

Personal Prayer
Help me, Father, to identify my suffering and need with the Savior. Help me, by faith,
to become aware that when I participate in his sufferings, I also share in his glory.

SONG OF THE SUFFERING SERVANT

FIRST MOVEMENT
The Eloquence of Darkness—Part 2

✑ Psalm 22 ✑

Many bulls surround me; strong ones of Bashan encircle me. They open
their mouths against me—lions, mauling and roaring (vv. 12–13).

Continuing the theme of suffering, David portrayed a fifth scene of darkness: Christ's intense suffering on the cross. He pictured the mocking crowd as a menagerie of wild animals. They were like ravenous wolves closing in on their prey. Murder, sin, and hate filled their wild eyes.

Verses 16–18 describe in uncanny detail the Roman execution—piercing the hands and feet, counting the bones, people staring and gloating, soldiers dividing the garments and casting lots for them.

David pleads for immediate help (vv. 19–21). He prays intensely for God to come close and deliver him from these wild, murderous, unclean predators.

What a model for me to follow when I am called to suffer. Romans 8:17–18 says it all: "And if children, also heirs—heirs of God and co-heirs with Christ—seeing that we suffer with Him so that we may also be glorified with Him. For I consider that the sufferings of this present time are not worth comparing with the glory that is going to be revealed to us."

It is easy to live under the mistaken notion that if I do the will of God, my life will be a paragon of perfection, free from anxiety and trauma. But I need to recognize that I may suffer because I am doing the will of God. This happened to David, and it happened to Christ in Gethsemane and on the cross.

My goal in life should be holiness, not happiness. But grabbing hold of this concept in our affluent society is difficult at best. The fullest, most richly textured life is the holy life. Only the refiner's fire produces pure gold. The holy life yields the richest, most enduring rewards.

A Gospel Chorus Lyric

Eternity's Values in View
With eternity's values in view, Lord,
With eternity's values in view;
May I do each day's work for Jesus,
With eternity's values in view.
Words and music by Alfred B. Smith © 1941. Renewed 1969.

Personal Prayer
Lord, though I live in a pagan, materialistic culture, may I commit my life to the higher value of holiness over happiness. Let me experience a deep wellspring of joy, no matter what happens.

SONG OF THE SUFFERING SERVANT
SECOND MOVEMENT—
The Joyful Feast

∾ Psalm 22 ∾
I will proclaim Your name to my brothers;
I will praise You in the congregation (v. 22).

After the powerful lament of verses 1–21, the Lord miraculously hears and delivers. Heart-wrenching, soul-searching lament is the basis for the true praise of God.

In the Old Testament economy, this praise and worship was accomplished through prayer, sacrifice, a commemorative feast, and vows of service to God (Lev. 7:16). Joy and happiness were to be kept private. Servants, poor people, and especially Levites were to be invited to the feast (Deut. 12:17–19). The whole congregation was to celebrate what God had done for them.

David threw a party in the Lord's honor. He got carried away with expressions of thanksgiving and praise (vv. 27–31). He sang a stirring canticle of blessing, and his worship found its ultimate focus on God's eternal kingdom—where the poor will be fed, where nations will bow down before the Lord, and where his righteousness will be proclaimed to people yet to be born.

> **The Language of Music**
>
> ### Song
> The act or art of singing.
>
> The word <u>song</u> can also designate a poetical composition or a short, musical composition of words and music. It also refers to a melody for a lyric, ballad, or poem. The psalmist says, "Your statutes are the theme of my song during my earthly life" (Ps. 119:54).

The secular mind looks at life and says, "Is this all there is?" The believer looks at life and sees a party to look forward to.

Personal Prayer
Lord, may I move today from lament
to praise, from darkness to light,
and from ordinary business to celestial celebration.

SATISFACTION

∽ Psalm 23 ∽
The LORD is my shepherd;
there is nothing I lack (v. 1).

Perhaps the most creative and artistic person in the Bible, David was a virtuoso harpist, a military genius, a capable administrator, and a cultural innovator. He led a sweeping renaissance of Jewish culture. Perhaps his most enduring literary achievement was to write and/or compile this psalm, the most-loved and well-known of all. It comforts, satisfies, and meets the deepest longings of the human heart.

It starts straightforwardly with the simple words, "The LORD is my shepherd." "LORD" is emphatic here. It is the Lord who makes our faith distinctive. No other person fits: not Mohammed, not Buddha, not Gandi. "My" personalizes the relationship, revealing intimacy and closeness.

"Shepherd" is the most comprehensive and intimate metaphor in the Psalms. The shepherd lives with his flock and is everything to it—guide, physician, and protector.

The last phrase, "there is nothing I lack," means that God will fulfill my deepest personal needs and that I will find meaning and true identity in him. In short, I don't need God plus anything or anyone. All my emotional and psychological longings for significance and security will find fulfillment in the Lord.

Personal Prayer
Thank you, Lord, that you meet all my needs and that
you are the key to my wholeness and fulfillment.

REST

∽ Psalm 23 ∽

He lets me lie down in green pastures;
He leads me beside quiet waters (v. 2).

Just as the ark of the covenant went ahead of Israel to find places of rest, so the Lord guides us to refreshment and relaxation. He provides green pastures and quiet waters. He doesn't want us to work nonstop.

Sometimes, I need to be intellectually "driven" in my work. I used to work on a fairly regular basis with the London Symphony musicians doing recording projects. On many occasions I would fly all night to London, write music the first day, record the following day, write all that night, and record the next day. By that time I was more like a zombie than an arranger-composer badly in need of rest.

A shepherd thinks in terms of the needs of his flock just as a father thinks in terms of the needs of his family. God has taken on a flock, a family. He is involved with us, bound up with us, and deeply concerned about meeting our innermost personal needs. Modern psychology has pointed out how essential it is for normal, emotional development that we have an adequate father. Ultimately, only our Heavenly Father is adequate.

I want the Lord to balance my life today, to define my lifestyle and my priorities, to deliver me from neurotic activity and workaholism, and to keep me from trying to meet my own needs through work and achievement instead of through him.

Personal Prayer

Lord, help me to turn over to you the pressure and stress that I feel. Teach me to relax in your Spirit.

A Shepherd's Perspective

My Creator—Shepherd
by Phillip Keller

"It is a staggering fact that Christ, the Creator of an enormous universe of overwhelming magnitude deigns to call Himself my Shepherd and invites me to consider myself His sheep—His special object of affection and attention. Who better could care for me?"

A Shepherd Looks at Psalm 23 © 1970. Zondervan Publishing House.

GUIDANCE

℘ Psalm 23 ℘

He renews my life;
He leads me along the right paths
for His name's sake (v. 3).

The Lord not only renews my life physically and emotionally, but he also guides me in paths of righteousness. I need to trust the authority of Scripture as my rule of faith and behavior. I need to commit myself to doing God's will, whatever it is. And I need to walk closely with God so I know him intimately. If I trust him and nurture and cultivate intimacy with him, he makes my paths smooth and straight (Prov. 3:5–6). Living righteously and blamelessly has its own reward. If we place God's authority and our commitment to and intimacy with him in proper perspective, he leads us by the hand through life and manages our affairs. What a comfort to know that the Lord is right in front of me, removing obstacles!

Why does the Lord do this for me? "For his name's sake." The Lord takes his name seriously. We are to uphold his holy name. When we do, God makes us new. In Ezekiel 36:22, 26 the Lord says, "It is not for your sake, O house of Israel, that I am going to do these things, but for the sake of my holy name. . . . I will give you a new heart and put a new spirit in you; I will remove from you your heart of stone and give you a heart of flesh" (NIV).

Personal Prayer
Sovereign Lord, I lift up your holy name today.
Renew my spirit and give me a new heart.

COMFORT

∽ Psalm 23 ∽

Even when I walk through the darkest valley, I fear no danger, for You are with me;
Your rod and Your staff—they comfort me (v. 4).

The greatest insult to humanity is the specter of death. At certain moments the fear of it grips and mystifies us. When it does, we need to come to the soothing, timeless truth of Psalm 23:4.

I will never forget the night my mom died. We had just experienced a joyous reunion with my parents over the Christmas holidays. Because of a business trip, I had left my family in northern Michigan for a skiing vacation and returned home. When I arrived, I heard the phone ringing. My friend Bob Steed told me my mom had gone to be with the Lord. I was shocked! That long night became a mélange of crying, reminiscing, praying, and fitful sleeping. But I didn't feel alone; I felt the Lord walking with me through my grief.

The valley of the shadow is a dark ravine. Yet, like the green pastures (v. 3), it too is a right path. People today fear death, so they don't talk about it often. But the Bible discusses it in comforting terms as part of the nature of reality.

In verse 4, the lyric switches from "he" (vv. 2–3) to "you," a much more personal pronoun. I am to fear no evil for "you are with me." Instead of walking ahead of me, the Lord now walks alongside me as an escort. He is not distant and impersonal. He is my companion—even in death. His presence overcomes the worst thing that remains: fear.

Armed as he walks beside us, our Shepherd and Companion protects us with his rod and staff. The rod—a cudgel or short, heavy club—symbolized defense. The staff, which the shepherd used to help him walk or to round up the flock, symbolized control. The Lord defends us even in death and gives us his security.

Personal Prayer
Lord, I thank you that you walk beside me
as my Friend and Companion.
I thank you that you are at my side
even at the moment of death.

INTERLUDE

∽ 1 Corinthians 15 ∽

O Death, where is your victory? O Death, where is your sting? Now the sting of death is sin, and the power of sin is the law. But thanks be to God, who gives us the victory through our Lord Jesus Christ! (vv. 55–57).

The apostle Paul gave us the New Testament picture of death in 1 Corinthians 15:55–57 and in 2 Corinthians 5:7–9. The more we see death from the biblical perspective, the more our fear will melt away. The events described in Psalm 23:4 happen instantaneously. In the light of eternity, death is just a walk through the gates of glory to a forever of eternal joy.

Originally written for Dr. W. A. Criswell, pastor of First Baptist Church in Dallas, Texas, the song "Finally Home" has brought peace and comfort to hundreds of people. Dr. Criswell's daughter Anne first sang the chorus coupled with a chorus of "The Glory Song" because we didn't have any verses yet. John W. Peterson, one of my mentors and a noted songwriter, encouraged me to write verses that would describe a human's fear of death and provide the background for this glorious chorus. I wrote the lyrics and music; the Lord gave the song his special touch.

Personal Prayer
Lord, I thank you and praise you that someday I will wake up in glory and discover that I've finally arrived home.

A Contemporary Lyric

Finally Home
When alarmed by the fury of the restless sea,
Towering waves before you roll;
At the end of doubt and peril is eternity,
Though fear and conflict seize your soul:
When surrounded by the blackness of the darkest night,
O how lonely death can be;
At the end of this long tunnel is a shining light,
For death is swallowed up in victory!
But just think of stepping on shore and finding it heaven!
Of touching a hand and finding it God's!
Of breathing new air and finding it celestial!
Of waking up in glory and finding it home!

Words © by L. E. Singer and Don Wyrtzen. Music © by Don Wyrtzen.

CELEBRATION

✏ Psalm 23 ✏

You prepare a table before me in the presence of my enemies;
You anoint my head with oil; my cup overflows (v. 5).

As great art so frequently does, verse 5 throws us a curve. What do a table, oil, and a cup have to do with sheep? The answer is—nothing. The songwriter simply changed his imagery from that of the shepherd to one of even greater intimacy and closeness: the friend.

The threat of verse 4 becomes the triumph of verse 5. We transcend the depths of the valley to the heights of a victory celebration. The Lord not only leads through the dark valley, but he provides a feast for us as well. Our enemies are present, but they are captives.

I felt a genuine sense of injustice when another musician was chosen to do a project that had been promised to me. When I realized my vulnerability to jealousy, I committed the entire matter to the Lord in prayer. Later I became involved in two other projects that were so well received that my musical ministry was given an enormous boost.

The Lord, our Host, provides abundantly. He sets a beautiful table, anoints us with costly perfume, and fills our cups to the brim. In other words, he more than meets our needs.

How limited is our faith! The Lord, our Friend and Host, wants to supply us abundantly. Believers, of all people, should not be running scared. As the old Sunday school song says, "My cup is full and running over."

Personal Prayer
Lord, thank you for bringing truth and beauty into my life.
Thank you that I don't have to live in poverty but can be
satiated by your glorious riches.

PROSPERITY

✑ Psalm 23 ✑
Only goodness and faithful love will pursue me all the
days of my life, and I will dwell in the house
of the LORD as long as I live (v. 6).

The modern perspective on success and prosperity is often narrow, defined only in materialistic terms. But David defined true prosperity in Psalm 23:6. Rather than being pursued by enemies, the believer is pursued by the Lord's prosperity. The Lord's goodness and love define that prosperity.

The most richly textured Hebrew word for love, *hesed*, is used here. It's also used to describe Hosea's miraculous love for his prostitute wife and to describe God's love for Israel even when the people worshipped idols. Similar to *agape*, the Greek word for *love* used in the New Testament, *hesed* describes God's loyal, unfailing, unconditional love. This love is hard for us to comprehend because human love so frequently has mixed motives.

Even though he knows everything there is to know about us (Ps. 139), God loves us. Even though we stand naked before him, he fully accepts us. The Lord's love for us is also the core of the gospel message. That I can be fully exposed and yet totally accepted is the thrill of the gospel.

When we learn to accept this love, we will be able to think soberly about ourselves, which is the foundation for true self-worth. Then we'll also be free to love other people, which is the basis for friendships, marriage, and a fulfilled family life. In the arms of our Heavenly Father, we are vulnerable yet fully safe.

I am beginning to be aware of God's love for me. I see wonder in ordinary things, and I accept them as gifts of God's grace. God's love is so vast, it is impossible for me to comprehend fully.

What a promise the last phrase is! "I will dwell in the house of the LORD forever!" Death is not a threat to me. I don't go into oblivion, buried beneath the sod. I have no cause for despair. "I will dwell in the house of the Lord, forever!" I wonder what resplendent music the chief musician wrote for that!

Personal Prayer
I praise you, Lord, that I don't have to live in fear—
even of death—because you have
promised I can dwell in your house forever.

THE KING OF GLORY PROCESSIONAL

FIRST MOVEMENT—THE LORD'S CREATIVITY

∞ Psalm 24 ∞

The earth and everything in it, the world and its inhabitants, belong to the LORD;
for He laid its foundation on the seas and established it on the rivers (vv. 1–2).

The creative power of God inspires awe. I'm filled with reverent wonder as I contemplate it. To think that he spoke and worlds came into being! In contrast to God, I work with raw materials that he created. My creativity is derived from his. I put the wrapping paper and ribbon on his packages.

Several years ago Karen and I traveled to Brazil. Along with lecturing and ministering to missionaries, we scheduled some sightseeing. I will never forget the awesome Iguacú Falls. There in the majestic grandeur of cascading water, I saw the omnipotence of Almighty God. I shouted spontaneously, "How great thou art!"

Because the Lord made the earth and everything on it, he owns it. He founded the earth (Gen. 1) and established it upon the waters. The heathen nations feared the restless, perilous, foaming seas. But even the violent waters belong to God and reflect the variety and depth of his creative imagination.

The Lord didn't create the earth and then abandon it. He is intimately involved with sustaining it. He watches over what belongs to him. My Lord doesn't like loose ends! He not only sustains his creation; he watches over me too and allows me to reflect his creativity!

> **The Language of Music**
>
> ### Processional
>
> A musical composition, such as a hymn, designed for a procession—a group of individuals moving along in an orderly, often ceremonial, fashion.
>
> The psalmist declares, "The LORD is God and has given us light. Bind the festival sacrifice with cords to the horns of the alter" (Ps. 118:27).

Personal Prayer

I praise you, Lord, for your incredible imagination and creativity.
I thank you that I can, in a small way, imitate it.

THE KING OF
GLORY PROCESSIONAL

SECOND MOVEMENT—THE LORD'S HOLINESS

∽ Psalm 24 ∽

Who may ascend the mountain of the LORD? Who may stand in his holy place?
The one who has clean hands and a pure heart, who has not set his mind on
what is false, and who has not sworn deceitfully. He will receive blessing from
the LORD, and righteousness from the God of his salvation (vv. 3–5).

David speaks eloquently about God's holiness and our need for purity, which, in today's language, we would call integrity. He concludes that only a person marked by integrity can stand before God's absolute holiness.

Isaiah understood that purity is the prerequisite for knowing God. When exposed to the stunning radiance of God, he said, "I am a man of unclean lips, and I live among a people of unclean lips, and my eyes have seen the King, the LORD Almighty" (Isa. 6:5 NIV). Jesus himself taught that only the pure in heart would see God (Matt. 5:8). And the apostle Paul drove home the same point when he said, "I want you to be wise about what is good, and innocent about what is evil" (Rom. 16:19). We cannot begin to know the holiness of God until we cultivate purity in our personal lives.

The quest for purity and integrity challenges believers today. Modern technology provides easy and private access to seductive entertainment. Nuances of temptation common today were unknown in the ancient world. Yet even so, David's words remain true today. Integrity is the prerequisite for knowing God and being able to stand before his holiness.

Personal Prayer
Heavenly Father, my desire is to have clean hands
and a pure heart today. By your Spirit,
change me into a person of integrity and purity.

THE KING OF GLORY PROCESSIONAL
THIRD MOVEMENT—THE LORD'S MIGHT

∽ Psalm 24 ∽

Lift up your heads, O gates! Rise up, O ancient doors!
Then the King of glory will come in.
Who is He, this King of glory? The LORD of Hosts,
He is the King of glory. Selah (vv. 9–10).

The dramatic scene at the end of Psalm 24 may have been enacted as the processional arrived at the city gates. Begun in Egypt, this stately march ascended to Zion and broke forth into a dazzling festival of praise.

There have been a number of times in my life when a musical experience has also become a spiritual experience. During the World's Fair in New York, I directed a mass choir of a thousand Christian women. As I fought to keep my composure, my heart overflowed with praises for God.

As the ancient doors swung open, the spotlight focused on the King of glory riding through the gates. He was a King of towering stature, strong and mighty in battle, the Warrior of warriors! No doubt the marching band started to sing and play the song of Miriam and Moses: "The Lord is a warrior; the LORD is his name" (Exod. 15:3 NIV).

What pageantry and excitement they had in their worship! Not lifeless, boring, predictable rituals. They exulted in praise to the King of glory. They celebrated his creativity (24:1–2), his holiness (24:3–6), and his might (24:7–10). What a battle cry for us today as we look forward to seeing the King of glory face-to-face!

Personal Prayer
Lord, teach me to worship you
with genuine fervor and vitality.
May I be excited by your presence
rather than embalmed by lifeless liturgy.

A Personal Hymn
for the Congregation
FIRST MOTIF—PROTECTION

∽ Psalm 25 ∽

LORD, I turn my hope to You. My God, I trust in You. Do not let me be disgraced; do not let my enemies gloat over me. . . . Guard me and deliver me; do not let me be put to shame, for I take refuge in You. May integrity and uprightness keep me, for I wait for You (vv. 1–2, 20–21).

Although written as a hymn for the whole congregation, Psalm 25 is very personal. And, like many of David's artistic creations, it is highly structured. Crafted around the Hebrew alphabet, it is difficult to outline. But David seems to have focused on four basic motifs: protection from his enemies, guidance for his life, forgiveness from sin, and hope for deliverance.

Knowing that only integrity and uprightness could protect him from his enemies, David asked for forgiveness from past sins. And knowing that only those whose hope is in the Lord could walk in integrity, he asked for guidance and placed his hope in God.

Like David and my dad, I want the kind of personal integrity and uprightness that I can depend on for protection. *Integrity* is a word that beautifully encompasses honor, sincerity, and wholeness. My dad, who lives consistently on the basis of his convictions, personifies integrity. He advances his evangelism on the basis of biblical principles and is not easily distracted from reaching his goals. By daily example, he teaches me that if my hope is truly in the Lord, not in secular thinking and methods, I will be able to cultivate personal integrity and be protected.

Personal Prayer
*Lord, may I be preoccupied with you
rather than with the enemies who surround me.
Mark my life with integrity and uprightness.*

A Personal Hymn
for the Congregation
SECOND MOTIF—GUIDANCE

∽ Psalm 25 ∽

Make Your ways known to me, Lord; teach me Your paths.
Guide me in Your truth and teach me, for You are the God of my salvation; I wait for
You all day long.... The Lord is good and upright; therefore He shows sinners the
way. He leads the humble in what is right and teaches them His way (vv. 4–5, 8–9).

Pagans had an irrational approach to guidance. They trusted magical pointers and omens. David, in stark contrast, had an intimate walk with his Lord. Walking with the Lord may seem irrational to modern minds; however, when in severe trauma or stress, I believe we naturally cry out to our Heavenly Father for help, as Christ cried out to him on the cross.

In this psalm David listed four characteristics necessary for knowing God's will: discernment, persistence, obedience, and reverence.

Discernment is the ability to distinguish good from evil (Heb. 5:14). Because God's will is always true and good, those who have poor discernment—who cannot distinguish between truth and falsehood, good and evil, right and wrong—cannot know God's will.

David demonstrated persistence by keeping his eyes "always on the Lord" (v. 15). His hope was not a fly-by-night thing; it was in the Lord "all day long" (v. 5).

Doing what is right doesn't come naturally, either. We need lots of practice. Obedience, therefore, is another prerequisite for knowing God's will. David modeled obedience by being good, upright, humble, and teachable (vv. 8–9).

Obeying God's will is to obey his Word. As the prophet told King Saul, "Does the Lord delight in burnt offerings and sacrifices as much as in obeying the voice of the Lord? To obey is better than sacrifice, and to heed is better than the fat of rams" (1 Sam. 15:22).

Because "the Lord is for those who fear him" (v. 14), those who want to know God's will need to learn reverence. David viewed the Lord with awe and respect, and the Lord became his friend.

Personal Prayer
Lord, may I walk closely and intimately with you
so that I will experience your guidance
and direction in my life.

A Personal Hymn
for the Congregation
THIRD MOTIF—FORGIVENESS

∽ Psalm 25 ∽

Do not remember the sins of my youth or my acts of rebellion; in keeping with Your faithful love, remember me because of Your goodness, LORD. The LORD is good and upright; therefore He shows sinners the way.... Turn to me and be gracious to me, for I am alone and afflicted. The distresses of my heart increase; bring me out of my sufferings. Consider my affliction and trouble, and take away all my sins (vv. 7–8, 16–18).

David readily admitted his sins; he didn't hide behind rationalization. His honesty reflected a clear-cut, ethical value system that today's world seriously lacks. It is rare to hear someone say, "I lied!" We often hide behind highfalutin phrases and euphemisms; Charles Van Doren vividly illustrates this. Instead of saying, "I lied," he said, "I've been involved in an incredible delusion." This was his statement after he was found to be cheating in television quiz scandals.

Guilt had been eating away at David, and his troubles had multiplied. He knew that only the Lord could relieve him of his affliction, and so he cried out for the Lord to "take away all my sins" (v. 18). Confession is still the only way out of anxiety caused by sin and guilt. A clear conscience leads to good health. A solid theology is the route to a balanced, fulfilled life.

As New Testament Christians, we need never surrender to the erosion of unresolved guilt. We can claim the apostle John's promise: "If we confess our sins, He is faithful and righteous to forgive us our sins and to cleanse us from all unrighteousness" (1 John 1:9).

Personal Prayer
To you, O Lord, I lift up my soul. Deliver me from trouble today and take away all my sins.

The Language of Music

Hymn
A song of praise to God that involves adoration, worship, and reverence.

Paul admonishes us, "Let the message about the Messiah dwell richly among you, teaching and admonishing one another in all wisdom, and singing psalms, hymns, and spiritual songs, with gratitude in your hearts to God" (Col. 3:16).

A PERSONAL HYMN
FOR THE CONGREGATION
FOURTH MOTIF—HOPE

◌∾ Psalm 25 ∾◌
*LORD, I turn my hope to You. My God, I trust
in You. Do not let me be disgraced;
do not let my enemies gloat over me (vv. 1–2).*

Instead of feeling anxious because of the stress in his life, David had a sense of well-being and security. Because his confidence was in the Lord, he had no fear. He did not base his hope on his own righteousness; he based it on the loyal love (*hesed*) of the Lord. He didn't trust sacred formulas and structures; he trusted the faithfulness of God. David was fully aware of the graciousness and dependability of his Lord. For him to place his confidence in anything or anyone else would be groundless.

Only the Lord can provide the deep inner sense of security, which, I believe, we all long to feel. God doesn't promise insulation from all harm. Nor does he guarantee that ungodly people will not prosper or succeed. But he does promise to take us through the storms of life if we place our trust in him, not ourselves. We must risk the life of faith to become truly secure.

David was high-strung, sensitive, and fragile, yet he exhibited unusual strength and authority. What really informed his leadership was bedrock security that came from his trust in the Lord.

Personal Prayer
*Lord, I thank you that you are fully aware of all
my insecurities. I turn them all over to you today because
I choose to place my complete trust in you.*

DEVOTIONAL LEITMOTIFS
FIRST LEITMOTIF—PERSONAL INTEGRITY

⁒ Psalm 26 ⁒
Vindicate me, LORD, because I have lived with integrity
and have trusted in the LORD without wavering.
Test me, LORD, and try me; examine my heart and mind (vv. 1–2).

Psalm 26 is all about personal integrity. Integrity signifies soundness, completeness, and honesty. People with these characteristics identity with Yahweh and keep themselves separate from sinners.

The psalmist petitioned the Lord for two things: vindication and examination. On the basis of his integrity, he asked to be delivered and avenged. He also asked to be critically examined. He wanted his heart and his mind tested because he was confident of his integrity. His life had not been dominated by ulterior motives, nor had he played political games. He had been singular in his purpose to trust the Lord.

How I need to cultivate total openness before the Lord! Transparency is the prelude to genuine spiritual intimacy. Because David experienced this, he was a man after God's own heart (Acts 13:22). No higher compliment could ever be paid!

Personal Prayer
Lord, may my life be an open book before you!

The Language of Music

Leitmotif
A German term meaning "leading motif."

Refers to a short theme or musical idea linked with a character, object, place, situation, or recurring idea. It is like a mini-theme, consistently repeated, to give a musical piece unity and cohesion.

DEVOTIONAL LEITMOTIFS
SECOND LEITMOTIF—SEPARATION FROM SINNERS

✑ Psalm 26 ✑

For Your faithful love is before my eyes, and I live by Your truth.
I do not sit with the worthless or associate with hypocrites. I hate a
crowd of evildoers, and I do not sit with the wicked (vv. 3–5).

David demonstrated his integrity in two specific ways: his separation from sinners and his identification with Yahweh. The structure of David's life rested on two pillars: God's love and God's truth.

David kept God's unconditional love before him. Knowing that God would love him no matter what he thought of himself or what behavior he engaged in, David walked confidently through life.

He also walked continually in God's truth. Because he knew that friends and associates would play a major role in shaping his attitudes and values, he chose them carefully. Deceivers, hypocrites, evildoers, and other wicked people were not part of his group. It wasn't that he disapproved of them socially but rather that he would not align himself with them spiritually. For as Solomon warned his young son, "Don't travel that road with them or set foot on their path" (Prov. 1:15). Their way of life leads to spiritual death.

I need to model David in his careful choice of personal friends and confidants because they do influence my value system. In this David showed great wisdom because his friends affirmed him and kept him on track.

Personal Prayer
O Lord, lead me to friends who will
encourage me and lead me closer to you.

DEVOTIONAL LEITMOTIFS

THIRD LEITMOTIF—IDENTIFICATION WITH YAHWEH

∾ Psalm 26 ∾

I wash my hands in innocence and go around Your altar, LORD, raising my voice in thanksgiving and telling about Your wonderful works. LORD, I love the house where You dwell, the place where Your glory resides (vv. 6–8).

Picture in your mind an open court with singers marching around the altar. Before the priests approached this altar, they stopped at the laver for cleansing. David put himself in this picture and used it to personalize his praise.

David loved to "let go" in praise of the Lord. He told of God's wonderful deeds, and he did it loudly in songs of thanksgiving. He loved the Lord's house because the glory of the Lord dwelt there.

One time I attended The Praise Gathering, where Ronn Huff led ten thousand of us in singing Michael W. Smith's "Great Is the Lord." The voices of the mass choir—accompanied by brass, percussion, and organ—lifted us right out of our seats. Then, without accompaniment, we sang "Great Is Thy Faithfulness." What a sense of the Lord's presence!

In praising the Lord and expressing love for his house, David clearly identified himself with Yahweh. He proved this by his actions: he offered acknowledgment to his Lord.

Like David, I want to praise the Lord continually with my imagination, animation, and with everything I've got. Above all I want to avoid boredom in God's house. With words and music I want to bring excitement about the Lord to his dwelling place.

Personal Prayer

Lord, as I identify with you and with your house,
help me find my own personal identity.

DEVOTIONAL LEITMOTIFS

FOURTH LEITMOTIF—PETITION FOR REDEMPTION

∾ Psalm 26 ∾

Do not destroy me along with sinners, or my life along with men of bloodshed in whose hands are evil schemes, and whose right hands are filled with bribes. But I live with integrity; redeem me and be gracious to me. My foot stands on level ground; I will praise the LORD in the assemblies (vv. 9–12).

David prayed for deliverance from the fate of sinners and petitioned the Lord to redeem him. He trusted Yahweh to spare him from the fate inevitably coming to the wicked.

David's beautiful prayer unveiled his true character. In it we see his authenticity, integrity, and deep humility. Wholehearted in his commitment, David would continue to walk along the path he had chosen. His life was characterized by loyalty and righteousness.

Assured of God's deliverance, he ended the psalm by praising and blessing the Lord. He added his voice to a choir of believers whose lives rang true to reality because they trusted the Lord.

Making music is part of the fellowship that binds believers together. The enjoyment of music is enhanced when we listen with another person. If we participate in a vocal or instrumental ensemble, our pleasure is even greater. Ultimately, personal involvement is the key to the joy of music. Just as David got involved musically with the congregation, we too must get involved personally in making music for the glory of God.

Personal Prayer

Lord, I thank you for your loyal love. Continue to build integrity and humility into my life as I place my trust in you.

FREEDOM

FIRST VARIATION—FREEDOM FROM FEAR

∾ Psalm 27 ∾

The LORD is my light and my salvation— whom should I fear? The LORD
is the stronghold of my life—of whom should I be afraid? When evildoers came
against me to devour my flesh, my foes and my enemies stumbled and fell.
Though an army deploy against me, my heart is not afraid; though war
break out against me, still I am confident (vv. 1–3).

My wife, Karen, and I were with our beloved pastor, George Gardiner, when he lost his two-year bout with cancer and went to be with the Lord. Shortly before his home-going, he shared with me his paraphrase of Psalm 27:1–2: "The Lord is my light and my radiation—whom shall I fear? The Lord is the stronghold of my life—of whom shall I be afraid? When cancer advances against me to devour my flesh, even then will I be confident." Fear can cripple us and keep us in bondage. Some of us allow anxiety, a type of fear common in modern culture, to dominate us and keep us from developing our full potential.

In two fitting and beautiful metaphors that describe the Lord, David gave the antidote to fear: light and salvation.

Light is an appropriate symbol for truth, goodness, and joy. When the Lord is our centerpiece, his light will dispel the darkness of our fear. Amen!

The Lord also *saves us* from our enemies. When they advance and attack, the Lord will make them stumble and fall. David built a crescendo in verse 3. He asserted his freedom from fear and his overwhelming confidence.

Like Pastor Gardiner, we can face courageously whatever confronts us if we remember that the Lord has already conquered fear. Worry will disintegrate if we remember that he is our light and salvation.

Personal Prayer

Lord, instead of continuing to be overcome by fear, help me to find rest
in perceiving you as my Light and my Salvation.

FREEDOM

SECOND VARIATION—FREEDOM TO PRAISE

∽ Psalm 27 ∽

I have asked one thing from the LORD; it is what I desire: to dwell in the house of the LORD all the days of my life, gazing on the beauty of the LORD and seeking [Him] in His temple. For He will conceal me in His shelter in the day of adversity; He will hide me under the cover of His tent; He will set me high on a rock. Then my head will be high above my enemies around me; I will offer sacrifices in His tent with shouts of joy. I will sing and make music to the LORD (vv. 4–6).

Worship is another antidote for worry. David understood that praising the Lord was the one thing that could dispel fear (v. 4). There is safety and security in the Lord's sanctuary.

Filled with love for God's house, David used five different words to describe it: house, temple, dwelling, shelter, and tabernacle. David did not isolate himself. He did not face his troubles alone. He faced trial within the context of a community of believers. God's house was his place of safety and security.

David did not visit God's house merely to observe. He got personally involved in singing and making music to the Lord. His answer to deep, personal fear and insecurity was to make music for God's glory.

We must not let the pressure of modern life squeeze the song out of our lives. We must learn to sing in the night, when we're hurting and when we're afraid. Renewal and recovery come when we praise God for his sovereign control.

Then the joy of the Lord will come flooding in, bringing with it his serenity and safety. Isaiah says it so beautifully, "You will keep in perfect peace him whose mind is steadfast, because he trusts in you" (Isa. 26:3 NIV).

Personal Prayer

Lord, no matter what my circumstances turn out to be today, help me to sing and make music to your holy name!

The Language of Music

Variations

Modifications of a theme.

The form—theme and variations—is an apt musical picture of unity and diversity. The Trinity is the divine metaphor.

FREEDOM

THIRD VARIATION—FREEDOM FROM REJECTION

∾ Psalm 27 ∾

LORD, hear my voice when I call; be gracious to me and answer me. In Your behalf my heart says, "Seek My face." LORD, I will seek Your face. Do not hide Your face from me; do not turn Your servant away in anger. You have been my help; do not leave me or abandon me, O God of my salvation. Even if my father and mother abandon me, the LORD cares for me. Because of my adversaries, show me Your way, LORD, and lead me on a level path. Do not give me over to the will of my foes, for false witnesses rise up against me, breathing violence (vv. 7–12).

To David, ultimate rejection would be to have the Lord turn his face from him. Acutely aware of the gulf between his own impurity and God's absolute holiness, David appealed to God's mercy and pleaded to be spared from rejection.

Rejection is incredibly difficult to deal with, especially when it comes from those ordinarily close to us, such as family members or friends. This happens to many people, and it causes all kinds of emotional and personal pain. But even when rejected by loved ones, we can attain intimacy because the Lord never turns his face from those who seek him.

One of the keys to successful songwriting is to be able to handle rejection. Songs are subjective; unlike numbers, lyrics and music have nuances, so there can be a wide range of opinions about the value of a particular song. Perhaps it takes more courage than talent to be a songwriter. Rejection is painful, though, especially the personal rejection in a wife-husband, parent-child relationship.

David's point here is that even when we are rejected by those who are supposed to love us, the Lord will not reject us. Someone I love may push me off a cliff, but God has suspended himself like a net to catch me. For believers, the Lord is always our safety net.

Personal Prayer

Thank you, Lord, that you have suspended a safety net beneath me. Continue to deliver me from the fear of falling.

FREEDOM

FOURTH VARIATION—FREEDOM TO BE PATIENT

∽ Psalm 27 ∽

I am certain that I will see the LORD's goodness in the land of the living. Wait for the LORD; be courageous and let your heart be strong. Wait for the LORD (vv. 13–14).

The final thought of this magnificent psalm is a statement of faith. David had the assurance that God was worth waiting for, and he had freely placed his confidence in the goodness and fairness of the Lord. He knew that the Lord would have the last word.

Relocation can be a traumatic experience for a family. Our move from Grand Rapids, Michigan, to Nashville, Tennessee, caused us to experience many conflicting emotions—sometimes feeling uprooted, confused, or churned-up! I believe it is possible to do the right thing yet feel strange doing it. The only way to gain perspective is to wait on the Lord.

Fear can render us ineffective and lifeless. But God gives us the answer to this phantom of the night: himself. He is our Light and our Salvation. Therefore, we need not be dominated by fear or rejection. We are free to praise and to be patient. Praise brings the shining light of his presence into our lives to replace darkness. And confidence in the Lord builds patience.

Faith stands in bold contrast to fear. When we seek the Lord, he delivers us from all our fears (Ps. 34:4).

Personal Prayer

Lord, help me to place my complete confidence in you and to wait for you.
Give me the ability to trust in your overwhelming goodness.

BURSTING OUT IN SONG
A MOURNFUL MELODY

∽ Psalm 28 ∽

LORD, I call to You; my rock, do not be deaf to me. If You remain silent to me, I will be like those going down to the Pit. Listen to the sound of my pleading when I cry to You for help, when I lift up my hands toward Your holy sanctuary. Do not drag me away with the wicked, with the evildoers, who speak in friendly ways with their neighbors, while malice is in their hearts. Repay them according to what they have done—according to the evil of their deeds. Repay them according to the work of their hands; give them back what they deserve (vv. 1–4).

Forced to look into the eye of death, David pleaded for salvation. He asked the Lord to distinguish between himself and the wicked and requested that he not face a common death with them. He prayed specifically for three things: (1) that the Lord would hear him and help him; (2) that the Lord would not identify him with hypocritical sinners; (3) that the Lord would be fair in rendering judgment.

What strength there is in placing our trust in the goodness and justice of God! When Abraham prayed for Sodom, he spoke profoundly when he said, "Will not the Judge of all the earth do right?" Focusing our faith in Yahweh and his righteousness answers a myriad of unsettling philosophical questions. One of the most profound is the question of our final destiny.

Personal Prayer
*Lord, I praise you that I can leave my eternal destiny in your hands.
I believe in your righteousness and justice.*

The Language of Music

Melody
A succession of tones, as opposed to harmony (tones sounded simultaneously).

Musical texture is comprised of both horizontal (melodic) and vertical (harmonic) elements. A melody can soar and deeply touch the soul.

BURSTING OUT IN SONG
A JOYFUL MELODY

✑ Psalm 28 ✑

Because they do not consider what the LORD has done or the work of His hands,
He will tear them down and not rebuild them. May the LORD be praised, for
He has heard the sound of my pleading. The LORD is my strength and my shield;
my heart trusts in Him, and I am helped. Therefore my heart rejoices, and I praise
Him with my song. The LORD is the strength of His people; He is a stronghold
of salvation for His anointed (vv. 5–8).

In these verses David expressed supreme confidence that the Lord would answer his prayer and would eventually overthrow the wicked.

This confidence put David in a mood to praise the Lord. He praised the Lord for three things: (1) for hearing his prayer, (2) for being his strength and shield, (3) for being the salvation of Israel.

David made these points with increasing intensity. Like a mighty musical crescendo climaxing with cymbals crashing, he burst out in song and praise. His heart leaped and he was filled with thanksgiving. Convinced that the Lord was his strength, his salvation, and his song, David worshipped the Lord in the beauty of holiness.

There is no better way to express such ardent emotion than through the art form of music. Music allowed David to express the inexpressible.

I find that when I'm overburdened with my own melancholia (feeling "down"), thinking about God's goodness helps me. I like to substitute praise songs for negative thoughts, so I wrote a little chorus, "He Satisfies My Life," to concentrate on the theme "God is good."

A Contemporary Lyric

He Satisfies My Life
As I lift my voice in praise my heart sings,
For He satisfies my life with good things.
I can't describe the joy that He brings,
For He satisfies my life with good things.
Words and music by Don Wyrtzen © 1985.

Personal Prayer

May joy rise in my heart so that I may burst out in songs of praise to him!
(Ps. 28:7 TLB).

BURSTING OUT IN SONG

AN ENTREATING MELODY

✑ Psalm 28 ✑

Save Your people, bless Your possession, shepherd them, and carry them forever (v. 9).

David was much more than an average citizen. He was the prototype of the Messiah. Because of this special position, David bestowed God's grace on the people. This concept reached full maturation in Christ of the New Testament "who has blessed us with every spiritual blessing in the heavens" (Eph. 1:3).

The final verse of this psalm is a prayer that has become part of the "Te Deum," a celebrated song of praise, rejoicing, and thanksgiving. In it David importunes God for the salvation, blessing, and sustenance of his people. Using the shepherd motif again, David asked the Lord to lift up his people and carry them forever.

David started in minor but ended in major. He began in the dark but ended in the light. He went from being low in spirit to being high with joy. He moved from lamentation to praise. What an appropriate model for worship and prayer!

Like David, I want to be able to honestly pour out my soul to my Heavenly Father, trusting that he will carry me. What comfort this will bring when I feel stress from the complexity of modern life!

Personal Prayer

Lord, I thank and praise you for your grace,
for your salvation,
for the blessing of your inheritance,
and for shepherding me forever.

A Contemporary Lyric

Unbounded Grace

Unbounded Grace—it reached to me
When hope was gone from view;
In my despair, Christ came to me
As He alone could do.
Grace was for me the only way
My guilt could find relief;
My destiny was changed that day
I reached out in belief.

God's grace does not on me depend—
It's God who is my Stay;
His love is offered without end,
He walks with me each day.
The universe with joy will ring
When grace has won the day;
As all creation joins to sing,
"Praise God, who paid the way!"

Words by John E. Walvoord. Music by Don Wyrtzen © 1971 Singspiration.

MAJESTY

HIS SPLENDOR

‿ Psalm 29 ‿

Give the LORD—you heavenly beings—give the LORD glory and strength. Give the LORD the glory due His name; worship the LORD in holy splendor (vv. 1–2).

Our Lord's absolute holiness, transcendence, and majesty are incomprehensible and unfathomable to mere mortals. For this reason David threw logic and analysis to the wind and allowed the flow of Hebrew poetry to take over in Psalm 29. Reminiscent of the Song of the Sea (Exod. 15), the oracles of Balaam (Num. 23–24), and the Song of Deborah (Judg. 5), this psalm lets us feel through poetry the towering majesty of the Lord.

The scene opened with angels singing themes of true worship and adoration. In them we see that declaring the greatness of God involves the total personality.

It may be true that we have a more intimate relationship with God than the angels do. Angels are awestruck by the greatness of God, but they do not experience the thrill of the gospel as we do. God took the initiative to relate to us personally through Jesus Christ. Though we are "a little lower than the angels" in God's hierarchy, we have a unique entrée to him.

Like the angels I am to be filled with love and wonder at the mention of his name. I am to worship him for the splendor of his holiness. Through meditation, prayer, music, and poetry, I can do this. And because of who God is and what he does, I will do it. A. W. Tozer called worship "the missing jewel of evangelicalism." Instead of learning about worship from religious leaders, I need to learn about it from the angels who are uninhibited and unrestrained in their praise of God.

Personal Prayer
Lord, make me aware of your holiness and transcendence and teach me how to reflect them back to you.

A Gospel Song Lyric

Holy, Holy Is What the Angels Sing
Holy, holy is what the angels sing,
And I expect to help them make the courts of heaven ring;
And when they sing redemption's story,
They will fold their wings
For angels never felt the joy that our salvation brings.
Words by Johnson Oatman Jr. Music by John R. Sweeney.

MAJESTY
HIS STORM

∽ Psalm 29 ∽

The voice of the LORD is above the waters. The God of glory thunders—the voice of the LORD in power, the LORD, above vast waters, the voice of the LORD in splendor. The voice of the LORD breaks the cedars; the LORD shatters the cedars of Lebanon. He makes Lebanon skip like a calf, and Sirion, like a young wild ox. The voice of the LORD flashes flames of fire. The voice of the LORD shakes the wilderness; the LORD shakes the wilderness of Kadesh. The voice of the LORD makes the deer give birth and strips the woodlands bare. In His temple all cry, "Glory!" (vv. 3–9).

The magnificence of nature reflects the power and might of God (Rom. 1:20). All of nature trembles at the sound of his voice. It calmed the raging sea of Galilee and caused Jesus' disciples to exclaim, "Who is this? He commands even the winds and the water, and they obey him" (Luke 8:25). And it made everyone in the temple shout, "Glory!"

In our day we think of man as being bigger than he is and of God as being smaller than he is. This distortion makes us lose perspective on what is important and causes us to major on minor issues. We major on minor issues when we reduce the mystery of the Godhead to a rationalistic system, when we get wrapped up in external behaviors rather than in internal reality, and when we explain Christianity in numbers rather than by an intimate relationship with the Lord. We need to hear again the voice of Almighty God as it resounds like timpani rolling, cymbals crashing, and brass bands playing fanfares—all climaxing in one eruption of praise and a mighty crescendo of glory.

Personal Prayer
*Lord, give me an acute awareness of your power and might.
And give me a foretaste of heaven by letting me
experience some of your glorious presence now.*

MAJESTY
HIS SALVATION

☙ Psalm 29 ☙

The LORD sat enthroned at the flood; the LORD sits enthroned, King forever. The LORD gives His people strength; the LORD blesses His people with peace (vv. 10–11).

The Hebrew word for *flood* (v. 10) appears just one other time in the Old Testament—in Genesis 6. Psalm 29:10 means, therefore, that our Lord has the power to unleash the violent forces of nature just as he did during Noah's flood (Gen. 6–11).

The Lord Jesus, God incarnate, used his voice to display supernatural power. He said to the churning sea, "Quiet! Be still!" Then the wind died down, and it was completely calm (Mark 4:39). He also used his voice to raise Lazarus from the dead, "Lazarus, come out!" and the dead man obeyed (John 11:43–44). God speaks with awesome authority and might.

Verse 11 gives us a glimpse into the future. The Lord will give, and the Lord will bless. The Lord uses his voice not for a gratuitous show of force but as an instrument of judgment and salvation.

Franz Delitzch, a brilliant nineteenth-century Old Testament scholar, viewed the closing words "with peace" as a rainbow arching over the psalm. We can either experience the *force* of God's wrath or the *peace* of his salvation. We can choose between the awesome power he uses against his enemies or the compassionate intimacy he offers to his children.

Personal Prayer
Lord, I am fully aware that you are enthroned as King forever.
I praise you for giving me strength, blessing, and peace.

Joy Comes
in the Morning
OUTBURST OF PRAISE

∽ Psalm 30 ∽

I will exalt You, Lord, because You have lifted me up and have not allowed my enemies
to triumph over me. O Lord my God, I cried to You for help, and You healed me.
O Lord, You brought me up from Sheol; You spared me from among those going down
to the Pit. Sing to the Lord, you His faithful ones, and praise His holy name.
For His anger lasts only a moment, but His favor, a lifetime. Weeping may
spend the night, but there is joy in the morning (vv. 1–5).

Restoration follows confession. David wrote Psalm 30 after experiencing this glorious truth.

Perhaps the most innovative, imaginative, and creative person in Scripture, David was vulnerable to the sin of pride. To chasten David for arrogantly numbering the fighting men of Israel (1 Chron. 21), God allowed him to be placed near death.

David was aware of the contrasts between sorrow and joy, the momentary and the eternal, the troubles that weigh little and the glory that outweighs everything (2 Cor. 4:16–18). He praised God that his anger lasts only for a moment but that his favor lasts for a lifetime (v. 5).

David experienced momentary personal pleasure with Bathsheba (2 Sam. 11). This affair produced unalterable consequences for David, Bathsheba, and their families. Yet because David had an intimate relationship with God, he confessed his sin (Ps. 51). God responded by restoring and renewing him (Gal. 6:1).

What an encouragement to those who have given in to temptation and are living with the inevitable stress! The answer is confession, which leads to restoration and praise.

Personal Prayer
Lord, teach me how to keep short accounts with you.
Teach me also to regularly praise your precious name.

Joy Comes
in the Morning
OUTBURST OF CONFESSION

∽ Psalm 30 ∽

When I was secure, I said, "I will never be shaken." LORD, when You showed Your favor, You made me stand like a strong mountain; when You hid Your face, I was terrified. LORD, I called to You; I sought favor from my Lord: "What gain is there in my death, in my descending to the Pit? Will the dust praise You? Will it proclaim Your truth? LORD, listen and be gracious to me; LORD, be my helper" (vv. 6–10).

David had turned from God and was leaving him out of his life. But when God turned his face from him, David felt cold, raw fear. He saw his unfaithfulness as frailty and his carefree lifestyle as carelessness.

Reciting his emotional disintegration, his personal destruction, and his feelings of deep insecurity, David cried out for mercy. At the end of himself, David abandoned his independence, his cleverness, and all his human resources, realizing that the solidarity of his kingdom depended on God's favor, not on his own ingenuity (vv. 6–7). Knowing that he had been out of tune with God, David tightened the strings of his life through a mighty outburst of confession.

In numerous ways my inadequacy comes to the surface every day. I reveal it when I'm threatened by competition, when I'm defensive with Karen, or when I desire to simplify the mysteries of life. I'm just learning to admit my incompetence by not denying it. I'm even learning to rejoice in it, though a bit guardedly I admit, because Paul teaches us, "When I am weak, then I am strong" (2 Cor. 12:10). Dependency on the Lord is the key to security.

Without the Lord we are dust (v. 9). David's artistic and administrative genius, apart from God's special touch, were no match for the pressures and complexities already apparent in the ancient world.

Personal Prayer
*Lord, forgive me for leaving you out of my life,
for trying to "go it alone."
I confess my tendency toward self-sufficiency and
now thrust myself upon you for mercy and help.*

Joy Comes in the Morning

Outburst of Joy

∽ Psalm 30 ∽

You turned my lament into dancing; You removed my sackcloth and clothed me with gladness, so that I can sing to You and not be silent. Lord my God, I will praise You forever (vv. 11–12).

David's richly textured personality and artistic temperament were expressed on many emotional levels. In this psalm he was as uninhibited in his praise as when he "danced before the Lord with all his might" (2 Sam. 6:14 NIV). David wasn't shy about expressing the intensity of his joy.

In the first movement of this psalm, David felt the exuberance of praise (vv. 1–5). In the second movement, he felt the depression of guilt over his sin (vv. 6–10). In this movement, after a moving confession, David felt the exhilaration and freedom of forgiveness, and it culminated in an outburst of joy (vv. 11–12).

What colorful contrasts David experienced: from wailing to dancing, sackcloths of despair to garments of joy, sounds of silence to songs of joy, independence to dependence, disintegration to integration, cynicism to caring, and from needing no one to trusting God. He exchanged a growing insecurity for unshakeable confidence. No wonder he vowed to praise the Lord and to give thanks to him forever!

I also feel stark contrasts, fluctuating mood swings, and mixed motives in my life. I've conducted some of the finest musicians in the world, but I'm often plagued by self-doubts. I deeply desire to glorify God in writing this book. But I'm also conscious of my concern about how I'm coming across to you. Even though many would consider my life to be *successful*, I sometimes wonder how *significant* it has been. But I'm learning to praise God persistently in the midst of it all; and every once in a while, like C. S. Lewis, I'm surprised by joy.

Personal Prayer

Dear Father, may I not continue to be content
with my self-centered and self-contained life.
May I not eat husks when I can feast at your banquet table.

DAVID FACES CRISIS

REJECTION!

∽ Psalm 31 ∽

*Be gracious to me, LORD, because I am in distress; my eyes are worn out from
angry sorrow—my whole being as well. . . . I am ridiculed by all my adversaries
and even by my neighbors. I am an object of dread to my acquaintances; those who
see me in the street run from me. I am forgotten: gone from memory like a dead
person—like broken pottery. . . . But I trust in You, LORD; I say, "You are my God."
The course of my life is in Your power; deliver me from the power of my enemies
and from my persecutors. . . . Love the LORD, all His faithful ones. The LORD
protects the loyal, but fully repays the arrogant. Be strong and courageous,
all you who hope in the LORD (vv. 9, 11–12, 14–15, 23–24).*

David knew what it was like to experience discouragement, despair,
grief, and gloom. When he was depressed, he felt isolated and rejected.
The picture he painted in Psalm 31:9–13 is black; and his use of graphic
and descriptive nouns—distress, sorrow, grief, anguish, groaning, affliction,
contempt, dread, and terror—helps us feel what he felt.

I'm certain that we all struggle with the pain of rejection. I feel rejected
spiritually when I don't sense God's presence in my life. I feel rejected
domestically when Karen and I disagree. And I feel rejected professionally
when someone doesn't like a new song I've written.

David's response to his rejection is a model for me today. Once again he
prayed and praised. After affirming his faith in the Lord and praying for
deliverance from his enemies, for the shame and death of the wicked, and
for his own purity, he moved again to a crescendo of praise (vv. 19–24). The
first pair of verses speak eloquently of God's care for his own (vv. 19–20).
The next pair personalize the message. David praised the Lord for his wonderful love and indescribable mercy (vv. 21–22).

Four brief but powerful concepts end this psalm of crisis: Love the
Lord! Be faithful! Be humble! Be strong and take heart!

Personal Prayer
*Lord, help me to wait for you! Help me to put my faith in what
I know rather than in what I feel!*

WHITER THAN SNOW

FORGIVENESS

∽ Psalm 32 ∽

How happy is the one whose transgression is forgiven, whose sin is covered!
How happy is the man whom the LORD does not charge with sin, and in
whose spirit is no deceit! . . . Then I acknowledged my sin to You and
did not conceal my iniquity. I said, "I will confess my transgressions to
the LORD," and You took away the guilt of my sin. (vv. 1–2, 5).

In the Psalter, David composed many variations on the theme of forgiveness. Psalm 32 zeroes in on the exhilarating emotional release that comes from forgiveness after confession.

David gave two reasons for personal contentment and happiness: First, we are happy (blessed) when our sins are forgiven; second, we are happy when we are counted righteous. The New Testament teaches that forgiveness and imputation of personal righteousness hinge on Christ's atonement for our sin. (David's faith prefigured Christ's sacrifice. See Rom. 4:6–8.)

Like many of us, I too often choose short-term gratification over long-term benefits. My eating habits are an example. I'd rather have an ice cream cone now than be in great physical shape later. There is a pleasure now but misery later when I feel guilty.

As David continued to sin, his bones wasted away, but his conscience remained very much alive. He groaned all day long from the weight of God's heavy hand on him. He had all of the symptoms of guilt. But he confessed his sins, acknowledged his transgressions, and experienced complete forgiveness.

Why do I sometimes continue in my sin? Why don't I listen to my conscience and follow David's example? When I face reality and acknowledge and confess my sin, I, like David, experience the exhilaration of forgiveness. I feel healthier too.

Personal Prayer
Lord, wash me and I shall be whiter than snow.

WHITER THAN SNOW

DELIVERANCE

◌ Psalm 32 ◌

Therefore let everyone who is faithful pray to You at a time that You may be found. When great floodwaters come, they will not reach him. You are my hiding place; You protect me from trouble. You surround me with joyful shouts of deliverance. (vv. 6–7).

When the mighty waters of trouble rise and I am about to go under, I can cry out, "Lord save me!" And he will. Peter also experienced deliverance in Matthew 14:28–33.

David was going through deep waters when he wrote Psalm 32. In danger of going under, he sought the Lord, and the Lord miraculously delivered him. Through this, David learned that trusting the Lord was the only safe place to be and his only real security. The Lord protected David from trouble and surrounded him "with songs of deliverance."

Music can be the perfect vehicle of comfort and protection. One day when I was flying in a small plane through vicious, clear-air turbulence, I had an anxiety attack and began hyperventilating. I started to sing to myself Joe Park's "He Holdeth Me." Then I remembered Moses' magnificent blessing, "The eternal God is your refuge, and underneath are the everlasting arms" (Deut. 33:27 NIV). As the Lord lovingly replaced my anxiety with the security of his arms, I became calm.

Saved from adversity, David composed his own songs of deliverance so that others could worship with him. How marvelous that he shared his discovery! What a motivation for me to make music that celebrates my deliverance.

Personal Prayer

Lord, thank you that I am safe in you, and that you deliver me from the complex problems of life today!

WHITER THAN SNOW

JOY

∾ Psalm 32 ∾

I will instruct you and show you the way to go; with My eye on you, I will give counsel. Do not be like a horse or mule, without understanding, that must be controlled with bit and bridle, or else it will not come near you. Many pains come to the wicked, but the one who trusts in the LORD will have faithful love surrounding him. Be glad in the LORD and rejoice, you righteous ones; shout for joy, all you upright in heart (vv. 8–11).

David progressed from sin to joy. Not only did he find exhilaration in forgiveness; he also found great joy in fellowship with the Lord. David felt God's chastening, then he experienced God's care.

Wicked people, because they don't understand or obey the truth, are like horses and mules; they can be controlled only by uncomfortable bits and bridles. Consequently, they experience many woes. In contrast, the righteous are surrounded by the Lord's unfailing truth and love. The Lord promises to instruct, counsel, and watch over us, which will keep us out of trouble.

What a promise for us as we face life's day-to-day stresses! What a reason for celebration, singing, and joy! The Lord's truth leads to personal freedom. And that freedom results in a deep sense of joy.

Personal Prayer

Heavenly Father, I praise you for counseling me and watching over me. When I contemplate your unfailing love, my heart is filled with joy, and I want to make music.

A Wonderful Old Hymn

Whiter Than Snow

Lord Jesus, I long to be perfectly whole,
I want You forever to live in my soul;
Break down every idol, cast out every foe—
Now wash me and I shall be whiter than snow.
Lord Jesus, for this I most humbly entreat,
I wait, blessed Lord, at Your crucified feet;

By faith, for my cleansing I see Your blood flow—
Now wash me and I shall be whiter than snow.
Lord Jesus, before You I patiently wait,
Come now and within me a new heart create;
To those who have sought You, You never said "No"—
Now wash me and I shall be whiter than snow.

Words by James Nicholson. Music by William G. Fisher.

HYMN OF PRAISE
BEAUTY

ᢒᢒ Psalm 33 ᢒᢒ

Rejoice in the LORD, O you righteous ones; praise from the upright is beautiful. Praise the LORD with the lyre; make music to Him with a ten-stringed harp. Sing a new song to Him; play skillfully on the strings, with a joyful shout (vv. 1–3).

The psalmist starts this magnificent hymn of praise with a plea for music-making executed with excellence. The Lord wants to hear a new song, and he wants to hear it played skillfully. He despises frozen forms and sacred clichés because sometimes rituals lose their meaning and traditions turn stale.

Having reviewed hundreds of unsolicited music manuscripts, I can honestly say that most of them are imitative and derivative rather than truly creative and innovative. The Lord is unimpressed with echoes; he rewards uniqueness.

The nature of music is to change—and true artists, by definition, grow steadily, change constantly, and create regularly. By doing so, they remain contemporary and relevant. Genuine art reflects the Lord's beauty and skill, so sincerity alone is never enough. The Lord wants freshness and good technique as well as fervor.

When I sing a new song, play my instrument with skill, and shout for joy, the Lord will lift me out of my own small, circumscribed world, and I will join all true believers and heaven's angels in sacred song!

Praising God through artistic expression enhances my inner beauty the way a diamond tiara enhances the outward beauty of a lovely woman.

Personal Prayer
*Dear Lord, may I use my voice and my instrument
to bring glory to your name today.*

HYMN OF PRAISE

TRUTH

✍ Psalm 33 ✍

Let the whole earth tremble before the LORD; let all the inhabitants of the world stand in awe of Him. For He spoke, and it came into being; He commanded, and it came into existence (vv. 8–9).

I find profound personal comfort in order and design. I observe it in nature when I drive up the Maine coast and when I scan a symphonic score by Mozart. Even though I admire the sensitivity of modern existentialists and can empathize with their despair, like the sweet psalmist of Israel, I find security in knowing that God has a specific plan for the universe—and one for my life too.

I cannot begin to understand the truth of God's power, but I see it in the wonder of creation and in the creative acts of history. Only the plans of the Lord are sure. They stand firm through all generations. The geopolitical manipulations of earth's rulers succeed or fail according to God's overarching plan. Nebuchadnezzar, Darius, Alexander the Great, Caesar, Napoleon—all were mere instrumentalists contributing to God's score for the universe. The Lord is the Master Orchestrator of history.

The awesome truth of God's creative power stretches far beyond my imagination. God spoke and worlds came into being. And if he chose to do so, he could gather the majestic sea into a jar. The Lord's hallmark is faithfulness, and his Word is truth. The only rational response is respectful fear and reverence.

Personal Prayer

I praise you, Lord, for your powerful Word. Thank you for using it to create the universe and to act in history.

Hymn of Praise

LOVE

∽ Psalm 33 ∽

He loves righteousness and justice; the earth is full of the Lord's unfailing love. . . .
Now the eye of the Lord is on those who fear Him—those who depend on
His faithful love (vv. 5, 18).

God not only sees all people and everything they do from his exalted position in the heavens, he also sees their inward thoughts and motives. No one can hide from him! When God sees reliance upon self, rather than on him, he withholds his reward. The use of huge armies, great personal strength, and the latest technology will lead to death, not victory.

The only hope for the arrogant and autonomous is for them to place their trust in the Lord, who watches over those who fear him, and to place their hope in his love.

The Lord doesn't really need articulate people, as Joseph proved before Pharaoh. The Lord doesn't really need strong people, as the young shepherd boy David proved before Goliath. And the Lord doesn't really need brilliant people. Paul tells us that God chooses "the world's weak things to shame the strong" (1 Cor. 1:27).

If I place my confidence in my own cleverness, energy, charm, or other human resources, I will fail. Real inner strength to meet the challenges of my life will come only when I give the Lord reverence and when I trust totally in his unfailing love of righteousness.

Personal Prayer

I praise you, Lord, that your love for justice and righteousness
will finally win and that I don't have to harbor bitterness
and resentment over today's injustices.

HYMN OF PRAISE

HOLINESS

✂ Psalm 33 ✂

We wait for the LORD; He is our help and shield. For our hearts rejoice in Him, because we trust in His holy name. May Your faithful love rest on us, LORD, for we hope in You (vv. 20–22).

The psalmist concluded this majestic hymn of praise by leading his congregation in asserting their faith in the holiness of the Lord!

They asserted their faith by waiting in hope for the Lord (v. 20), by rejoicing in him (v. 21), and by praying for the Lord's faithful love (v. 22). Their finale is a promise that they have placed all of their hope in the Lord.

Wait, rejoice, petition—what a paradigm for personal praise! Praise must be the top priority in our lives.

When Isaiah saw the Lord face-to-face, he trembled in fear because of his sins. In Isaiah 6, we can only imagine the utter majesty and glory of the Lord, which Isaiah saw. But even *this* tiny glimpse of God's holiness (Ps. 33) can result in our own trembling and sometimes terror; sometimes, in uninhibited praise and worship. "Therefore, through Him, let us continually offer up to God a sacrifice of praise, that is, the fruit of our lips that confess His name" (Heb. 13:15).

Personal Prayer
*Lord, I praise you for filling my heart with joy
because I have trusted in your holy name.*

SONG OF EXALTATION
EXTOLLING THE LORD

∽ Psalm 34 ∽

*I will praise the LORD at all times; His praise will always be on my lips.
I will boast in the LORD; the humble will hear and be glad. Proclaim with
me the LORD's greatness; let us exalt His name together (vv. 1–3).*

*D*avid knew how to praise the Lord. The rich texture of his highly sensitive personality made exaltation the focus of his life. As my mentor, he teaches me three facets of worship.

First, I am to extol the Lord. Praising him must become second nature to me, part of the daily rhythm of my life. Praise must be an inner voice of worship, not a lifeless liturgy.

How do I do this? Sometimes I paraphrase Scripture when I write poetry about the Lord and compose songs for his glory. I call upon his name in prayer and sing songs of praise to him. No matter where I am, I try to glorify his name in simple, practical ways.

Second, I am to boast in the Lord. At dinner parties and other social occasions, my conversation must be dominated by stories of the great things God has done for me, not by what I have done for myself. Discussions about who I know, where I have been, and what I have done reveal my insecurity. Only by putting the spotlight on the Lord and focusing on him will I find true security.

Third, I am to glorify the Lord. As C. S. Lewis observed, "To glorify is to enjoy." Ironically, the overstimulation of modern life leads to boredom. I need to move away from the emptiness the world offers to find the fulfillment of the Lord. Enjoying the Lord in the company of my brothers and sisters in Christ enhances this joy.

Personal Prayer
Dear Lord, I extol you, I boast in you, and I glorify you. In your precious name, Amen!

A Contemporary Lyric

We Will Glorify
We will glorify the King of Kings,
We will glorify the Lamb,
We will glorify the Lord of Lords,
Who is the great I Am.
Who is the great I Am!

Words and music by Twila Paris © 1982 Singspiration.

SONG OF EXALTATION
SEEKING THE LORD

∽ Psalm 34 ∽

I sought the LORD, and He answered me and delivered me from all my fears. Those who look to Him are radiant with joy; their faces will never be ashamed. This poor man cried, and the LORD heard [him] and saved him from all his troubles. The angel of the LORD encamps around those who fear Him, and rescues them (vv. 4–7).

The elusive monster of fear lurks in the shadows waiting to claw my soul to shreds. As one prone to melancholia, I see its ugly face often: when I'm struggling with the emotional stress of a difficult relationship, when I'm afraid failure is just around the corner, when success seems too hard to handle, and on days when free-floating anxiety is getting the best of me.

Ironically, the Lord delivers from fear all those who fear him. So when I am afraid, I need to seek the Lord, who will hear me and save me from all my troubles.

Furthermore, the Lord promises me radiance. I can hold my head high and look straight ahead because he has covered my shame. Forgiveness leads to transparency and transparency to intimacy. And, as if that were not enough, he gives me inner beauty that is reflected in outer radiance. Praise his holy name!

Personal Prayer
I praise you, Lord, for replacing fear and
trouble with peace and radiance.

SONG OF EXALTATION
TASTING THE LORD'S GOODNESS

∽ Psalm 34 ∽

Taste and see that the LORD is good. How happy is the man who takes refuge in Him! Fear the LORD, you His saints, for those who fear Him lack nothing. Young lions lack food and go hungry, but those who seek the LORD will not lack any good thing (vv. 8–10).

Many who believe they have "tasted the Lord" have only a superficial knowledge of him. They say they have tried him, think they know all about him, and claim they have been disappointed in him. But "tasting the Lord" involves more than a casual glance, a brief encounter, or a simple, memorized formula. To taste the Lord, I need to embrace him, to relate to him with my whole being!

I need also to fear the Lord. To do this I must concentrate on him, not on myself. Narcissism subtly kills spiritual intimacy. Because I am very sensitive, I tend to be neurotic. Instead of looking outside myself and to the Lord, I tend to turn inward, which leads to despair. I would do better to focus less on self, serve others, and trust the Lord more. When I respect him as I should, I will lack nothing.

Even the king of the jungle grows weak from hunger. But the one who seeks the Lord lacks no good thing. Those who have the Lord have no need for anything else, for he alone is complete. As a result, the anxiety I feel about competitiveness will dissolve. And my struggles for power and prestige will be replaced by knowing intimately the One who holds all power and deserves all prestige.

Personal Prayer
Help me to taste and see your goodness, Lord. Help me to find all the power and prestige I need in my relationship with you.

Song of Exaltation

FEARING THE LORD

∽ Psalm 34 ∽

Come, children, listen to me; I will teach you the fear of the LORD. Who is the man who delights in life, loving a long life to enjoy what is good? Keep your tongue from evil and your lips from deceitful speech. Turn away from evil and do good; seek peace and pursue it (vv. 11–14).

I am to reject the lie that there is fulfillment outside the will of God. Reverence for the Lord is the only way to personal enrichment. From David, I learn that two big changes will occur in my life when I reverence God.

First, I will speak the truth. Deception comes easily and naturally for me. I never had to learn to lie. When I was a kid, I remember calling the operator just to say something rude and brash to her. When she called back, my dad answered the phone. He asked me if I had made the call. I lied. Even though it was easy to lie, deceiving my dad wasn't wise. As David says, if I commit myself to speaking the truth, I will have many good days and a long life.

Second, I will do good and pursue peace. The fringe benefits will be personal fulfillment and spiritual enrichment because my goals and behavior will be in harmony with the will of God.

Personal Prayer

*Lord, teach me to speak the truth and to turn from evil.
I can't do it on my own, so empower me,
that I may experience the fulfillment
that comes from doing your will.*

SONG OF EXALTATION
CRYING OUT TO THE LORD

❧ Psalm 34 ❧

The eyes of the LORD are on the righteous, and His ears are open to their cry for help. The face of the LORD is set against those who do evil, to erase all memory of them from the earth. The righteous cry out, and the LORD hears, and delivers them from all their troubles. The LORD is near the brokenhearted; He saves those crushed in spirit (vv. 15–18).

A certain comfort comes from crying, and there is virtue in ventilation. Before I can really praise the Lord, I must lament honestly and deeply. I must be vulnerable enough to let my wife and children see me cry because genuine spirituality begins with honesty about my own feelings. Not long ago as Karen, Kathy, D. J., and I prayed for a bereaved family, I cried. I was so overcome with sadness for this good friend, I lost control in the middle of the prayer. I felt embarrassed and uncomfortable because I like to be in control. But crying was the best and most natural thing for me to do in order to give God complete control. I must remember that I do not live in exile, estranged from God, where there is darkness and no hope.

Though not denying the reality of sin, pain, suffering, and death, I need to embrace the greater reality—that the Lord is Victor over these. He has conquered the negatives of my life. He is my Savior and Deliverer. When I begin to see that, laborious lament is transformed into uproarious praise.

Personal Prayer
Thank you, Lord, that you are close to the brokenhearted and that you save those who are crushed in spirit.

SONG OF EXALTATION

FINDING SAFETY IN THE LORD

ᴖ Psalm 34 ᴖ

Many adversities come to the one who is righteous, but the LORD *delivers him from them all. He protects all his bones; not one of them is broken. Evil brings death to the sinner, and those who hate the righteous will be punished. The* LORD *redeems the life of His servants, and all who take refuge in Him will not be punished (vv. 19–22).*

This promise was fulfilled beautifully after Jesus' death. Following Roman custom, the two condemned malefactors were removed from their crosses after having had their legs broken. But when they came to Jesus, "they did not break his legs" (John 19:33).

The Lord not only cares about me psychologically but physically as well. My psyche and my body reflect his image.

The Lord kept me safe on a particularly dangerous, icy road when I was in college. As I crested the hill, I saw two other cars had already collided at the bottom. Naturally, I braked hard, which was enough to propel me down the hill faster into the other two cars. Although I was badly shaken, no one was hurt. The Lord protected and delivered me that day.

David here vividly contrasts the wicked and the righteous. The wicked are slain by evil, but foes of the righteous are condemned. The Lord redeems his own. No one who finds refuge in the Lord is condemned. As a righteous person, I may have many troubles, but the Lord will deliver me from all of them.

This great worship anthem, "Song of Exaltation," gives six specific steps toward personal fulfillment. I am to *extol* the Lord, *seek* the Lord, *taste* the goodness of the Lord, *fear* the Lord, *cry out* to the Lord, and *find safety* in the Lord. The key is in the object—the Lord! Faith in any person other than the Lord is foolishness.

Personal Prayer
*Lord, I praise you that no matter what
my external circumstances will ever be,
I am safe in your care!*

LIMITED
PERSPECTIVE

IMPATIENCE WITH GOD—FIRST MOVEMENT

ᴄᴐ Psalm 35 ᴄᴐ

Let those who seek to kill me be disgraced and humiliated; let those who plan to harm me be turned back and ashamed. . . . Then I will rejoice in the LORD; I will delight in His deliverance. My very bones will say, "LORD, who is like You, rescuing the poor from one too strong for him, the poor or the needy from one who robs him?" (vv. 4, 9–10).

David was impatient. The Lord, it seemed, was not listening to his prayers. While his enemies plotted against him, David tried to come to grips with God's seeming silence. The striking contrasts of his poetry reflect the ups and downs of his life.

David was being hassled and harassed, but his real problem was his limited perspective. One of the key issues in life is time. When we get preoccupied with "now," we lose perspective. When we get hung up on the present, we lose sight of the future.

At times I become overly concerned about time. How much do I have left? Is what I'm doing important? Have I accomplished anything significant in my life? Since only God sees the big picture, we need to place complete trust in his will. His plan encompasses the whole universe, but it also includes me in detail as an individual.

Personal Prayer

Dear Father, forgive me for being angry and impatient with you. Help me to place my complete faith in you and your plan.

LIMITED PERSPECTIVE

IMPATIENCE WITH GOD—SECOND MOVEMENT

⟡ Psalm 35 ⟡

Yet when they were sick, my clothing was sackcloth; I humbled myself with fasting, and my prayer was genuine. I went about [grieving] as if for my friend or brother; I was bowed down with grief, like one mourning a mother. . . . I will praise You in the great congregation; I will exalt You among many people (vv. 13–14, 18).

The Lord had not yet answered David's prayer. Ruthless witnesses accused him. When he stumbled, they attacked maliciously. When he faltered, they gathered in glee. David had every human reason to get angry at God, but he responded by praising and thanking him.

David went public with his confession. He worshipped in the company of believers, shared the reality of his plight, and told of his decision to trust God no matter what. His brothers and sisters participated in both his pain and his praise.

How often we hide when we are hurting! How often we pretend all is well when everything is falling apart! How often we try to maintain an image of stability when the foundation of our lives is crumbling! What emotional energy we waste building facades!

I come from a background that rewards performance. Consequently, even when my world seems to be falling apart round me, the show goes on. Even when I'm despondent and on the emotional brink, I still try to play or speak. But I'm learning to open up to a few trusted friends. I'm gradually learning that being vulnerable is how we share our lives and our love.

David shared honestly and candidly. He wasn't afraid to cry in front of his family, and that was one of the secrets behind his powerful praise.

Personal Prayer
*Dear Father, I praise and thank you. I know you will answer
my prayers in your perfect time.*

LIMITED
PERSPECTIVE

IMPATIENCE WITH GOD—THIRD MOVEMENT

❧ Psalm 35 ❧

Vindicate me, LORD, my God, in keeping with Your righteousness, and do not let them rejoice over me. . . . Let those who want my vindication shout for joy and be glad; let them continually say, "The LORD be exalted, who wants His servant's well-being." And my tongue will proclaim Your righteousness, Your praise all day long (vv. 24, 27–28).

Still grappling with the silence and distance of the Lord, David longed for vindication. He wanted to see his enemies defeated, disgraced, and put to confusion.

But instead of letting his sorrow get him down, David lifted up praise to the Lord. Though still concerned for his own acquittal, he concentrated on worship! And when he praised, his ambivalence melted away. I am just beginning to pray when I'm sad, to give thanks when I'm sorrowful or suffering, and to praise God when I'm experiencing pain. After praise and worship, David had a small problem and a big concept of God instead of a big problem and a small concept of God.

Personal Prayer
*Lord, may my tongue speak of your righteousness
and your praises all day long.*

A Musical Play
ACT ONE: PORTRAIT OF WICKEDNESS

∽ Psalm 36 ∽

An oracle within my heart concerning the transgression of the wicked:
There is no dread of God before his eyes (v. 1).

In this surprising oracle, David defined the wicked as those who lack the fear of God. In contrast to the righteous, who recognize their sin and fear God, the wicked flatter themselves too much to detect or hate their sin.

Their self-delusion and recklessness affect their communication, and they are deceitful. Even at night they plot evil schemes and sinful courses of action. They completely lack spiritual values. Their thoughts, wills, and feeling are all corrupt, and this interior rottenness leads to corrupt behavior.

I think of pornographers that exploit women and children for money and power. Of drug runners who pander to the needs of addicts. And of abusers of all types who use their strength to dominate innocent victims.

Apart from God, man is powerless to help himself. He doesn't even know he needs help. Wallowing in his own corruption, he desperately needs God's love and righteousness, but he doesn't know it.

Personal Prayer
O God, I thank you that because of your grace,
I don't need to wallow in wickedness.

A Contemporary Lyric

Love Was When

Love was when God became a man
Locked in time and space without rank or place;
Love was God born of Jewish kin,
Just a carpenter with some fishermen.
Love was when Jesus walked in history—
Lovingly He brought a new life that's free;
Love was God nailed to bleed and die
To reach and love one such as I.

Words by John E. Walvoord. Music by Don Wyrtzen © 1970 by Singspiration.

A Musical Play
ACT TWO: PARADIGM OF RIGHTEOUSNESS

✑ Psalm 36 ✑

Lord, Your faithful love [reaches] to heaven, Your faithfulness to the skies.
Your righteousness is like the highest mountain; Your judgments, like the
deepest sea. Lord, You preserve man and beast (vv. 5–6).

When words are inadequate to define the love of God, the music of poetry helps me express it. So do analogies. David used word pictures of finite things—the heavens, skies, mountains, and seas—to explain infinite things—love, faithfulness, righteousness, and justice. This description of the indescribable is more accurate than simple words could ever be.

Poets and lyricists revel in the use of vivid word pictures. An excellent example of Frederick Lehman's exquisite lyric, "The Love of God."

After describing God's unsearchable, inexhaustible, and unfathomable love, David becomes more intimate. He tells of the pricelessness of God's unfailing love and affirms that all men, whatever their station in life, can find security ("refuge in the shadow of your wings"), sustenance ("feast on the abundance of your house"), and satisfaction ("drink from your river of delights"). He is the Fountain of life, the Source of all light and joy.

What cause for rejoicing and singing today! What themes to inspire magnificent music-making!

Personal Prayer
O Lord, help me to feast at your table and drink from your fountain
that I may be filled with eternal joy.

A Lovely Gospel Hymn

The Love of God
Could we with ink the ocean fill
And were the skies of parchment made.
Were every stalk on earth a quill
And every man a scribe by trade.
To write the love of God above
Would drain the ocean dry,
Nor could the scroll contain the whole
Tho stretched from sky to sky.
© 1917. Renewal 1945 by Nazarene Publishing House.

A Musical Play

ACT THREE: PRAYER OF CONFIDENCE

∽ Psalm 36 ∽

Spread Your faithful love over those who know You, and Your
righteousness over the upright in heart (v. 10).

Overwhelmed by the stark contrast between human depravity and divine grace, David was driven to prayer. He pleaded for God's continued love and righteousness and for protection from arrogant and wicked men. Then he painted a word picture of the final doom of evildoers who lay fallen, thrown down, and unable to rise.

Ready to fight wickedness (act 1) and to embrace God's grace (act 2), David gets caught up in urgent prayer (act 3).

What are the lessons for me today? My life should be totally different from the person who has "no dread of God before his eyes" (v. 1). I don't want to be flippant about the holiness of God, casual about the grace of God, or unduly wise about evil. As Vance Havner so aptly said, "I don't want to be guilty of playing marbles with diamonds."

My life should be a paradigm of God's righteousness because my personality is being radically transformed by God's grace. Therefore, I can join David in this timeless prayer of confidence.

Personal Prayer

O Lord, make me a paradigm of your righteousness.
May your grace transform my life today.

HARMONIC PROGRESSIONS
HARMONY IN WISDOM

∞ Psalm 37 ∞

Trust in the LORD and do good; dwell in the land and live securely. Take delight in the LORD, and He will give you your heart's desires. Commit your way to the LORD; trust in Him, and He will act, making your righteousness shine like the dawn, your justice like the noonday. Be silent before the LORD and wait expectantly for Him; do not be agitated by one who prospers in his way, by the man who carries out evil plans. Refrain from anger and give up [your] rage; do not be agitated—it can only bring harm (vv. 3–8).

Jesus said, "Blessed are the meek, for they will inherit the earth" (Matt. 5:5). David taught the same truth in this psalm: "But the humble will inherit the land and enjoy abundant prosperity" (v. 11). The person who follows David's instruction will be wise.

Like the flowers of the field, the wicked are only temporary; they eventually wither and die. Therefore, we are not to get upset over them. Instead, we are to concentrate on doing good, and David gives five steps to personal peace, wisdom, and tranquility:

First, we are "to trust in the Lord and do good." When we do this, we will experience deep inner security.

Second, we are "to delight in the Lord." When we do, a spiritual metamorphosis takes place, and his desires become ours.

Third, we are "to commit our way to the Lord." The Hebrew word for *commit* is *roll*—as though getting rid of a burden. We are to entrust our lives to our Lord's care.

Fourth, we are "to be silent before the Lord." We are to wait patiently for the Lord to work out his plans and not be impressed with the success of others.

Fifth, we are "to refrain from anger." We are to resist anger by turning away from it.

Those of us who follow these five imperatives will experience deep peace and inner serenity but not a total absence of upheaval in our personal lives. David teaches us that the storms of life are only on the surface; underneath is the calm of his security and strength. Those who obey the Lord will resist self-assertion and be following the path of patient faith. How do I know for sure? The Lord promises that they will inherit the earth and enjoy great peace.

Personal Prayer

Dear Lord, I praise you for your promise of deep personal security. Help me not to continue to search for it elsewhere.

HARMONIC PROGRESSIONS

DISSONANCE IN WICKEDNESS

∾ Psalm 37 ∾

Better the little that the righteous man has than the abundance of many wicked people. For the arms of the wicked will be broken, but the LORD supports the righteous (vv. 16–17).

Wise people are righteous; foolish people are wicked. They stand in bold contrast to each other in this psalm. David described the wicked vividly. They plot against the righteous. They attack by drawing the sword and bending the bow. They slay poor, needy, and righteous people. They are violent and hostile.

The Lord, however, will have the last word. He will laugh at the wicked. He knows their day is coming. He turns their own weapons against them. He breaks their power and renders their wealth useless. He predicts their final denouement. Like the flowers of the field, they will vanish and disappear. The righteous, on the other hand, will be upheld. Their inheritance will endure forever. Even in days of famine, they will enjoy plenty.

Though the wicked often prosper while the righteous suffer, in the end God will uphold his justice. He will destroy the wicked and bless the righteous. In the long run it pays to serve the Lord and to live righteously. Personal fulfillment is a fringe benefit.

Personal Prayer

I praise you, Lord, for your power and justice.
I thank you that you will eternally reward personal righteousness.

The Language of Music
_____

Harmony

Tones sounded simultaneously as opposed to melody which is a succession of tones.

Harmony can be either consonant (pleasant sounding) or dissonant (unpleasant sounding). "How good and pleasant it is when brothers can live together" (Ps. 133:1).

HARMONIC PROGRESSIONS
CONSONANCE IN RIGHTEOUSNESS

∽ Psalm 37 ∽

I have been young and now I am old, yet I have not seen the righteous abandoned or his children begging bread. He is always generous, always lending, and his children are a blessing. . . . The mouth of the righteous utters wisdom; his tongue speaks what is just. The instruction of his God is in his heart; his steps do not falter (vv. 25–26, 30–31).

Would I like to give generously, experience the Lord's blessing, and look forward to an eternal inheritance? Would I like stability and steadiness in my personal life?

What would it be like to be blessed physically, materially, and to have inner security? Is it possible that I could speak wisdom, proclaim justice, and generally integrate God's truth into my personality? Could I ever be the focus of the Lord's delight? Because God's Word is my reference point for the nature of reality, the more I absorb and obey it, the more I fulfill my destiny. Then I can become an accomplished, complete person.

These are the blessings and benefits the Lord gives to the righteous, to those who fill their hearts with the law of God. Their "feet do not slip."

What promises! My security and wealth don't lie in uncertain riches but in the Lord himself. Therefore, I'm able to give and lend constantly, and I can be a lasting blessing to society through the family that I lead. What a comfort to know that even though I experience ups and downs, the Lord's hand holds me steady! The Lord himself establishes my steps and delights in my way. He makes harmony out of my life.

Personal Prayer
Lord, fill my heart with your law
so that my feet will not slip.

Harmonic Progressions

FINALE: INTERPLAY BETWEEN HARMONY AND DISHARMONY

∽ Psalm 37 ∽

*I have seen a wicked, violent man well-rooted like a flourishing native tree. Then
I passed by and noticed he was gone; I searched for him, but he could not be found. . . .
The salvation of the righteous is from the LORD, their refuge in a time of distress. The
LORD helps and delivers them; He will deliver them from the wicked and will save
them because they take refuge in Him (vv. 35–36, 39–40).*

In tying up the loose ends of this moving psalm, David lets us see the final
end of the wicked and righteous person. The last verses are a moving
finale, an exciting interplay between harmony and disharmony.

The wicked lie in wait for the righteous, but the Lord renders them impotent. The metaphor used to picture the wicked, ruthless man is a flourishing
green tree. But that tree soon withers, dies, falls down, and rots. It vanishes
without a trace.

Hitler, architect and fuhrer of Germany's Third Reich, became a broken
man. On April 30, 1945, in a bomb shelter of the chancellery, Hitler and his
wife, Eva Braun, swallowed poison. Aides burned their bodies with gasoline.

In bold contrast the righteous are exalted. They possess the land. They
have a glorious future because their salvation comes from the Lord. The Lord
helps them, protects them, and delivers them in times of trouble. He is their
shelter and their refuge.

This uplifting psalm ends with peace, serenity, and calm objectivity—a
totally different mood from the fretful impatience and anxiety David
expresses at the beginning of this psalm.

Personal Prayer
*Lord, I live in a frantic society and experience stress and pressure.
Be my refuge and shelter.*

Dirge of Discouragement

GUILT

∽ Psalm 38 ∽

O LORD, do not punish me in Your anger or discipline me in Your wrath. For Your arrows have sunk into me, and Your hand has pressed down on me. There is no soundness in my body because of Your indignation; there is no health in my bones because of my sin. For my sins have flooded over my head; they are a burden too heavy for me to bear (vv. 1–4).

Our Heavenly Father is attentive. He disciplines the children he loves (Prov. 3:11–12). David was experiencing the profound, searing devastation of internal guilt. It gnawed away at him.

Since he feared God's anger and wrath, David cried out for mercy. Emotional tension erupted into physical illness because his guilt was so overwhelming.

We must never assume that all sickness is a punishment, although I believe that sometimes physical illness is directly related to guilt over irresponsible behavior. Here we have a clear-cut case of illness resulting from sin. David said, "My wounds fester and are loathsome because of my sinful folly." He was paying the wages of sin with mental anguish and physical agony.

What is the bottom line of sinful behavior? David said, "I am feeble and utterly crushed. I groan in anguish of heart." Authentic lament almost always precedes genuine praise. I admire David's honesty. His life throbbed with reality and authenticity.

Personal Prayer

I thank you, Lord, for giving me a sensitive conscience that serves as a spiritual gyroscope for my life.

DIRGE OF DISCOURAGEMENT

ISOLATION

∽ Psalm 38 ∽

Lord, my every desire is known to You; my sighing is not hidden from You. My heart races, my strength leaves me, and even the light of my eyes has faded. My loved ones and friends stand back from my affliction, and my relatives stand at a distance (vv. 9–11).

The more David needed the support of friends, the less attention he received from them because of his abnormality. He was caught in the same vicious cycle many of us find ourselves in. Sin has led to guilt; guilt has led to emotional and physical illness; illness has led to suffering and pain; and pain has led to isolation and loneliness. David was like a modern-day AIDS victim. He said, "My loved ones and friends stand back from my affliction, and my relatives stand at a distance" (38:11).

David felt the effects of alienation. Estranged from his Heavenly Father as well as his community of friends, David—like many of us—was lonely and despondent. He was at a point where only the Lord could meet this incredible need. He was ready and open for a deep work of God in his life.

Personal Prayer
I cry to you, Lord, out of my deep loneliness and despair.
Please come to me, minister to me, and fully meet my need!

DIRGE OF DISCOURAGEMENT

PATICE
PATIENCE

∽ Psalm 38 ∽

I hope in You, LORD; You will answer, Lord my God. For I said, "Don't let them rejoice over me—those who are arrogant toward me when I stumble" (vv. 15–16).

Despite David's instability and anxiety, he was able to wait on God. Though mired in a morass of sin, guilt, and suffering, he still exercised faith.

David faced his sin squarely and confessed his iniquity. His sensitivity to the inner voice of God's Spirit had not been seared, and he did not have a jaded conscience. Once Karen and I attended a bullfight in Mexico City. We were in a large stadium surrounded by thousands of excited Latin people. We watched as the first bull was manipulated by the matador with his banderillas. In time the bull was outmaneuvered and killed. Seeing blood flow for the first time made us queasy. But after seeing ten bulls killed in a similar way, we weren't as queasy. I believe we can become anesthetized to sin in much the same way. David wasn't like this. He was still deeply troubled by his sin and was beyond making excuses or rationalizations for it.

All of this is testimony to the fact that David was God's child. Heathen people are not profoundly troubled by their sin. The fact that David felt God's chastening hand was one more proof that he was a son. Guilt is also tacit evidence for the holiness of God, the absolute standard by which all ethics and values are measured.

Personal Prayer

Heavenly Father, I confess my sin before you today. Bind my wandering heart to you. Amen.

An Apt Hymn

Come Thou Fount
O to grace how great a debtor
Daily, I'm constrained to be!
Let Thy goodness like a fetter
Bind my wandering heart to Thee.
Prone to wander—Lord, I feel it—
Prone to leave the God I love.
Here's my heart—O take and seal it,
Seal it for Thy courts above.
Words by Robert Robinson. Music by John Wyeth.

Dirge of Discouragement

CALLING ON GOD

ᢓᢙ Psalm 38 ᢙᢖ

Lord, do not abandon me; my God, do not be far from me.
Hurry to help me, O Lord, my Savior (vv. 21–22).

*A*t the end of this penitential psalm, David cried out to God. He could no longer endure being alone.

David had an intimate knowledge of his Lord. He knew him by his deepest, most personal name—*Yahweh*. He also was related to God by covenant. He knew the Lord as his Master and Savior and addressed the Lord from these perspectives in verses 21–22.

David had three final requests: that the Lord would not forsake him, that the Lord would be close, and that the Lord would come quickly to help.

Being right all the time is really important to me. Therefore, saying "I'm sorry" isn't easy for me. But I'm learning that I don't have to be so perfectionistic and that being vulnerable can be liberating. I'm just beginning to learn how to be released through repentance. Apologizing brings real freedom to my life; repentance provides the only true resolution for my guilty conscience.

Personal Prayer
Lord, I identify with David, the ancient King of Israel.
Please don't forsake me; be close, and come quickly to help.
To get right to the point: forgive my sin.

ARIA ON ANXIETY
VERBALIZING FEELINGS

∽ Psalm 39 ∽

I said, "I will guard my ways so that I may not sin with my tongue; I will guard my mouth with a muzzle as long as the wicked are in my presence." I was speechless and quiet; I kept silent, even from [speaking] good, and my pain intensified. My heart grew hot within me; as I mused, a fire burned. I spoke with my tongue: (vv. 1–3).

David learned to verbalize his feelings, to communicate his anxiety, and to articulate his inner thoughts.

Silence and stillness had made David sick. Not facing reality had increased his anxiety. He had become a pressure cooker, and the lid was ready to blow off!

I'm a goal-oriented person. When my goal is blocked, I become angry. When my goal is uncertain, I become anxious. Often I deny or block out how I'm really feeling, which forces my feelings to escalate out of control. I have found that feelings, good or bad, must be acknowledged or they will destroy me.

David didn't acknowledge his feelings in front of the wicked. He restrained himself from venting them in the wrong company. Unrestrained ventilation could be misconstrued by unbelievers as disloyalty or even blasphemy.

He took his pent-up protest to the Lord. Lament as well as praise were an integral part of his prayer. His relationship with the Lord was honest and down-to-earth—the way I want mine to be today.

Personal Prayer
Help me, Lord, to watch my ways and to keep my tongue from sin. Help me to bring my gravest concerns to you.

The Language of Music

Aria
In contrast to songs, arias are complex, virtuoso solos.
   Accompanied by instruments, they figure prominently in operas, oratorios, and cantatas.

Aria on Anxiety

ASSESSING LIFE'S BREVITY

∞ Psalm 39 ∞

*"Lord, reveal to me the end of my life and the number of my days. Let me know
how transitory I am. You, indeed, have made my days short in length, and my life
span as nothing in Your sight. Yes, every mortal man is only a vapor.
Certainly, man walks about like a mere shadow. Indeed, they frantically rush around
in vain, gathering possessions without knowing who will get them"* (vv. 4–6).

Life is brief. Like a vapor, a mist, a breath, it is soon over. James says, "You
don't even know what tomorrow will bring—what your life will be! For you
are a bit of smoke that appears for a little while, then vanishes" (James 4:14).

Our busyness makes us think we are more important than we really are.
Yet in all of our bustle and activity, we are still mere phantoms. We have little
control over the destiny of our heaped-up wealth. Our life span is nothing
before God. And life itself is empty without him.

Midlife is a time of critical evaluation for most of us. We are preoccupied
with time. Accomplishments and achievements are carefully scrutinized as we
look to the future. How much time do I have left? becomes a nagging question
for us to answer. The dangerous temptation to live for false gods results in the
emptiness we are so frantically fleeing. David, too, was aware of time's passing.

What caused David to number his days? What made him suddenly look
at things from God's point of view? The answer: intense suffering. Extreme
pain opened David to a deep work of God in his life. Suffering is God's mega-
phone to reach those of us with deaf ears.

Personal Prayer

*Lord, help me to become aware of just how fleeting my life really is.
Help me to make today really count for you.*

ARIA ON ANXIETY
EXPERIENCING DISCIPLINE

✑ Psalm 39 ✑

"Now, Lord, what do I wait for? My hope is in You. Deliver me from all my transgressions; do not make me the taunt of fools. I am speechless; I do not open my mouth because of what You have done. Remove Your torment from me; I fade away because of the force of Your hand. You discipline a man with punishment for sin, consuming like a moth what is precious to him; every man is a mere vapor" (vv. 7–11).

After experiencing the shattering cruelty of friends (Ps. 38), David felt the crushing severity of the Lord.

Overcome by God's heavy-handed treatment, David prayed to be released from the pressure. Despondent, he cried out to God, pouring out his soul about how brief and fragile life is.

Though nearly overwhelmed by his own mortality, David knew that salvation came from the Lord. He affirmed that faith by crying out, "My hope is in you!"

The year 1984 was one of profound loss for me. Norman Johnson, our senior editor at Singspiration Music, went to be with the Lord. Then shortly after his death, my mom died. A few months later, my pastor, Reverend George Gardiner, passed away. These losses caused me to realize how fleeting life is and how near eternity is. Just the time span of the twinkling of an eye separates us from God. "Only one life, 'twill soon be past, only what's done for Christ will last!"

God isn't a sadomasochist, but he has built suffering and adversity into the mysterious nature of reality. God used pain and hardship to give David perspective—on his transient life on earth and on his hope for eternity. In other words, dissonance is an essential element of harmony. For it is the tension between consonance and dissonance that creates music.

Personal Prayer
*Lord, no matter how dark and grave my circumstances become,
help me to affirm my faith and trust in you. And I trust you to make music
even out of the disharmony of my life.*

ARIA ON ANXIETY

PETITIONING GOD'S HELP

✑ Psalm 39 ✑

"Hear my prayer, LORD, and listen to my cry for help; do not be silent at my tears. For I am a foreigner residing with You, a sojourner like all my fathers. Turn Your angry gaze from me so that I may be cheered up before I die and am gone" (vv. 12–13).

David, feeling alienated and estranged from God, cries out for help. He even wonders if the Lord hears his weeping, for he feels like an outcast—a foreigner in Israel, a mere passing guest or sojourner. For the moment all he can see is his own death looming before him.

As a Christian music executive in a secular world, I have felt this kind of alienation. Then I remind myself that I'm just a pilgrim here, and I think of the words of that old southern gospel song, "This World Is Not My Home."

Despite David's desperation, alienation, and estrangement, he prays, and this prayer is a testimony of his bedrock faith and trust in God. Though he can't put his circumstances together rationally, he still clings to an existential relationship with God.

The most natural thing for a believer to do, in times of despair and despondency, is to turn to the Heavenly Father. All true spirituality begins with this basic kind of honest lament.

Personal Prayer

Heavenly Father, I may be a stranger in this world, but I don't want to be a stranger to you. Don't let me blend with the voices of the world, but help me to sound a clear note of faith in the midst of doubt and disillusionment.

A Southern Gospel Song
_____

This World Is Not My Home

This world is not my home, I'm just a-passin' thru,
My treasures are laid up somewhere beyond the blue;
The angels beckon me from heaven's open door,
And I can't feel at home in this world anymore.
O Lord, You know I have no friend like You,
If Heaven's not my home, then, Lord, what will I do?
The angels beckon me from Heaven's open door,
And I can't feel at home in this world anymore.
© 1946 Albert E. Brumley & Sons © 1974 Renewal.

SONATINA OF SACRIFICE

JOY

∾ Psalm 40 ∾

"I waited patiently for the LORD, and He turned to me and heard my cry for help. He brought me up from a desolate pit, out of the muddy clay, and set my feet on a rock, making my steps secure. He put a new song in my mouth, a hymn of praise to our God. Many will see and fear, and put their trust in the LORD (vv. 1–3).

In three magnificent movements treating the subjects of joy (vv. 1–4), thanksgiving (vv. 5–10), and prayer (vv. 11–17), David has flawlessly crafted a sonatina on the sacrifice of praise.

Most likely the psalmist has recently been near death, for he uses the metaphor of a deep pit, lined with slime, to describe his precarious position. But the Lord hears his cry and delivers him—and what a deliverance! Now David's feet are firmly planted on a rock.

Released from distress, he moves quickly from anxiety to a joyous celebration of God's power. This fresh vision of God gives David exciting material for a "new song." He may have arranged an old hymn—and discovering its genius—added fresh color and new insights. Or perhaps, in the rush of creativity and exhilaration, he composed an entirely new song. Inner joy results in music!

This event, and other miraculous deliverances in David's life, were the inspiration for many of his great hymns of praise, shared with his congregation and recorded for generations to come. As a result, thousands "fear and put their trust in the Lord." Worship becomes witness!

I also will be used of the Lord today in the extent that I place my faith and trust in him and lead others to do so. This is the source of both my joy and my music.

Personal Prayer

*Lord, help me not to seek joy and happiness apart from you.
And may the songs that come from the deep springs of my heart
point others to the Source of all satisfaction.*

The Language of Music

Sonatina
**A brief sonata marked by simplicity and designed for instruction.
It is analogous to a good, brief three-point sermon.**

SONATINA OF SACRIFICE

THANKSGIVING

∾ Psalm 40 ∾

LORD my God, You have done many things—Your wonderful works and Your plans for us; none can compare with You. If I were to report and speak [of them], they are more than can be told. You do not delight in sacrifice and offering; You open my ears to listen. You do not ask for a whole burnt offering or a sin offering. Then I said, "See, I have come; it is written about me in the volume of the scroll. I delight to do Your will, my God; Your instruction resides within me" (vv. 5–8).

Caught up in the vortex of an exhilarating experience with the Lord, David breaks forth with thanksgiving. As his imagination soars, he is reminded of many other miraculous works God has wrought on behalf of his people. David's whole being, permeated with God's truth, is turned to his will, and the psalmist discovers that God desires the sacrifice of a pure heart and attitude rather than external, and sometimes empty, worship practices.

In music ministry it is easy to depend upon natural gifts, experience, and craftsmanship as a substitute for real inspiration. But David's time with the Lord becomes the deep reservoir out of which flow his hymns of praise.

Elated with this discovery, David can't keep still in "the great assembly" (v. 9). His lips, unsealed, proclaim the righteousness of God reigning in his heart, and he shares four major themes with the congregation: God's faithfulness, salvation, love, and truth. Suddenly David finds himself in the middle of a revival resulting from his own praise and thanksgiving!

Personal Prayer

Lord, fill me with your steadfast love and perfect truth so that the music
I write will reflect my gratitude.

SONATINA OF SACRIFICE
PRAYER

∽ Psalm 40 ∽

LORD, do not withhold Your compassion from me; Your constant love and truth will always guard me. For troubles without number have surrounded me; my sins have overtaken me; I am unable to see. They are more than the hairs of my head, and my courage leaves me. LORD, be pleased to deliver me; hurry to help me, LORD. . . . Though I am afflicted and needy, the Lord thinks of me. You are my help and my deliverer; my God, do not delay (vv. 11–13, 17).

My sins always catch up with me. There is a ripple effect with sin. Like a pebble dropped into the water that creates ever widening circles, an act of sin has expanding consequences. The Lord forgives and erases the guilt, but he does not change history. Much of my pain emanates from the effects of sin that have continued past the original act.

David too is hurting. Overwhelmed by the number of his sins ("more than the hairs of my head") and the extent of his troubles, he is about ready to give up, to throw in the towel. Yet he cries out for mercy and for the protection of God's loyal love and flawless truth.

David may be down about his own sin, but he's very much aware of the sins of others as well, and he still has energy left to pray about the enemies who pursue him relentlessly. He petitions the Lord for their confusion, shame, and disgrace (vv. 14–15). In contrast, he also prays for the salvation, help, and deliverance of those who seek the Lord. This dual theme reminds us that, above all, God alone is worthy to be exalted and magnified (v. 16).

Though I am poor and needy, like David I recognize that the Lord is my help and deliverance. David closes his exquisite "Sonatina of Sacrifice" by focusing on the majesty and glory of God.

Personal Prayer
Lord, may I seek you, rejoice and be glad in you, and may you always be exalted and magnified in my life and work.

A MADRIGAL ON MERCY

A FUNDAMENTAL PRINCIPLE STATED

∽ Psalm 41 ∽

Happy is one who cares for the poor; the LORD will save him in a day of adversity. The LORD will keep him and preserve him; he will be blessed in the land. You will not give him over to the desire of his enemies. The LORD will sustain him on his sickbed; You will heal him on the bed where he lies (vv. 1–3).

The message of these verses from Psalm 41 is found in miniature in Matthew 5:7 where the Lord Jesus says, "Blessed are the merciful, because they will be shown mercy." David asserts the maxim of God's moral law that he will deliver the person who shows regard for the weak.

It is encouraging to see a growing response to human need. Many musicians sometimes donate the proceeds of their concerts to the underprivileged in cities where they perform. When motivated by love for the Lord, these merciful acts will not go unrewarded.

In fact, David is specific about the four blessings the Lord bestows on the compassionate person: protection, security, strength, and good health. How practical and down-to-earth!

The Lord protects and preserves the life of the sympathetic and empathetic person. He also "blesses him in the land" and provides a profound sense of security. He further gives him strength over his foes; his enemies neither intimidate not dominate him. Finally, he heals those who show compassion to the poor and needy.

Personal Prayer

Lord, make me more sensitive to hurting people. Open my eyes and my heart to their needs, and let me be a channel of your blessing in their lives.

The Language of Music

Madrigal

A complex, polyphonic (many voices), unaccompanied vocal piece.

This form flourished from the fourteenth to seventeenth centuries.

A MADRIGAL ON MERCY
A FUNDAMENTAL PRINCIPLE SUPPORTED

❦ Psalm 41 ❦

I said, "LORD, be gracious to me; heal me, for I have sinned against You." My enemies speak maliciously about me: "When will he die and be forgotten?" When one [of them] comes to visit, he speaks deceitfully; he stores up evil in his heart; he goes out and talks. All who hate me whisper together about me; they plan to harm me. . . . Even my friend in whom I trusted, one who ate my bread, has lifted up his heel against me. But You, LORD, be gracious to me and raise me up; then I will repay them (vv. 4–7, 9–10).

Most highly creative, artistic people are a bit fragile. Beneath the surface is a sea of insecurity. I have seen some of the top people in the music industry demonstrate some pretty unchristlike characteristics when threatened by competition from within the ranks.

It's easy to understand why David is down in the pits again. Not only are his enemies hovering like vultures, just waiting for his death and denunciation, but he has just learned that he can't even count on his friends! Though they come to visit while he is on his sickbed, pretending concern, they spread malicious rumors about him the minute they leave. Even the friends with whom he has shared intimate confidences have betrayed him.

Though vengeance belongs to Jehovah alone, perhaps David is contemplating the punishment of traitors, one of the duties of a just monarch. David illustrates and supports God's principle that he will deliver those who are merciful. David believes his enemies have been held at bay because of his own integrity.

A glorious doxology concludes this madrigal on mercy and serves as a fitting close to the First Book of Psalms. It is a veritable outburst of praise comprising a double "Amen!"

Personal Prayer
Dear Lord, it's tough to forgive those
who deliberately set out to malign me.
But because you have been merciful to me,
I long to show mercy to others.
Give me the grace to do it!
Amen and Amen.

LONGING AND LAMENT
THIRSTING FOR GOD

∽ Psalm 42 ∽

As a deer longs for streams of water, so I long for You, God. I thirst for God, the living God. When can I come and appear before God? I remember this as I pour out my heart: . . . how I walked with many, leading the festive procession to the house of God, with joyful and thankful shouts (vv. 1–2, 4).

This ancient temple singer, perhaps exiled in the north, has a deep longing for God and his house. His longing takes the form of an insatiable thirst, much like that of a deer longing for water in a dry and arid land. He has been separated from God, estranged from the sanctuary, and is in desperate need of intimacy and fellowship.

His only solace is the memory of the great festivals in God's sanctuary. He remembers the pulsating excitement of public worship when throngs of worshipers filled the air with shouts of praise and songs of joy. He remembers being brought to the core of his own reality through his interaction with the Living God.

My life resonates to the song this Levite is singing. How many times have I attempted to fill the vacuum of my life with substitutes for God? How often have I felt emptiness deep inside my soul because I have become separated from Him? How typical of me to misuse God's precious gifts from a desire for sensual pleasure, only to block deep personal intimacy! And what am I left with? A profound thirst and longing for the living God. Only he can satisfy my deepest longings. All the rest is a disappointingly empty cup.

Personal Prayer
Lord, teach me to fill my life with you so that I will be fully satisfied.

A Beautiful Old Hymn

Satisfied

All my life long I had panted
For a drink from some clear spring,
That I hoped would quench the
    burning
Of the thirst I felt within.
Feeding on the husks around me,
Till my strength was almost gone,
Longed my soul for something better,
Only still to linger on.
Well of water ever springing
Bread of life so rich and free,
Untold wealth that never faileth
My Redeemer is to me.
Hallelujah! I have found Him
Whom my soul so long has craved!
Jesus satisfies my longings—
Through His blood I now am saved.
Words by Clara Tear Williams. Music by Ralph E. Hudson.

LONGING AND LAMENT
OVERWHELMED WITH DESPAIR—I

✑ Psalm 42 ✑

*Why am I so depressed? Why this turmoil within me? Hope in God, for I will
still praise Him, my Savior and my God. . . . Deep calls to deep in the roar of
Your waterfalls; all Your breakers and Your billows have swept over me.
The LORD will send His faithful love by day; His song will be with me in
the night—a prayer to the God of my life (vv. 5, 7–8).*

My soul is rooted in eternity, but my mind and body are often under
severe pressures of the here and now. It is difficult to sustain creative
energy over a long period of time. I live in fear of deadlines. I struggle with
balancing my priorities, with handling money wisely, with proper investment
of time, with handling difficult and demanding relationships. When I feel I'm
in over my head, this psalm brings consolation.

David knew the debilitating effect of depression and despair. In verse 7,
his mind must have been in turmoil as he portrays an alien scene. Perhaps
churned by a spring storm, the Jordan River rages. As the troubled waters hiss
and spew, the river becomes a metaphor for all that is overwhelming and
uncontrollable in David's life, and he feels that he has lost his footing and is in
danger of drowning.

Still his hope is in God. Verse 8 is the centerpiece, the psalmist's confession of faith. The one ray of light in the darkness is his confidence that the
Lord loves him. All of David's anxiety is channeled through prayer to the God
of his life. The song of the Lord is with him—and with me—even in the
deepest waters and through the darkest night.

Personal Prayer
*Lord, when I feel as if I'm sinking under unbelievable burdens,
teach me to sing, to pray, and to feel your inexhaustible love!*

LONGING AND LAMENT

OVERWHELMED WITH DESPAIR—II

∽ Psalm 42–43 ∽

Why am I so depressed? Why this turmoil within me? Hope in God, for I will still praise Him, my Savior and my God. . . . For You are the God of my refuge. Why have You rejected me? Why must I go about in sorrow because of the enemy's oppression? Send Your light and Your truth; let them lead me. Let them bring me to Your holy mountain, to Your dwelling place. Then I will come to the altar of God, to God, my greatest joy. I will praise You with the lyre, O God, my God (42:11; 43:2–4).

Just about the time I think I have gained the victory over some black mood, some writer's block, some unworthy goal, the whole thing comes crashing down around me, and I am back to square one. In this rut of defeat, my prayers sound very much like those of this psalmist: "Why have You rejected me? Why must I go about in sorrow because of the enemy's oppression?" (43:2).

David has a right to his depression. Ungodly people have accused him unjustly, and he prays to the Lord for vindication—for a declaration of his innocence.

But dark moods can give way to positive praying. Like the psalmist, I can't allow my mind to camp on negative ideas and feelings, but I can pray for God's light and truth to guide me. "Let them bring me to your holy mountain, to Your dwelling place" (43:3).

In the sanctuary, in the presence of my fellow believers, I'll praise the Lord with acoustic and electric instruments, with sophisticated rhythms, and innovative harmonies and soaring melodies—all reveling in the ineffable glory of God! In this way I, too, will be able to experience his transcending, transforming power.

Personal Prayer
Lord, in the darkness of my circumstances, help me to be aware that consummate joy and delight are centered in you.

LONGING AND LAMENT
OVERWHELMED WITH DESPAIR—III

✑ Psalm 43 ✑

Why am I so depressed? Why this turmoil within me? Hope in God, for I will still praise Him, my Savior and my God (v. 5).

Psalms 42 and 43 are actually one sadly beautiful poem. The two parts are unified by a plaintive refrain heard three times—42:5, 11; 43:5. It is the lament of a temple singer in the ancient world. Its bittersweet song is startlingly relevant to our situation today.

This psalmist knew how to pray. He expresses his feelings honestly, admitting that his inner life is restless and insecure. Some deep longings have gone unmet, and he doesn't pretend otherwise, skimming over the surface of his personal needs.

But he doesn't stop with this candid appraisal of his life, refusing to wallow in his hopelessness. He utters a full-throated confidence in God and vows that he will again praise the Lord and will turn his whole being to face him.

Unlike modern man, who gives up in despair or clings obstinately to some flimsy philosophy, this believer chooses to declare his faith in the one, true, living God of the universe. To pretend faith in an unworthy or imaginary object is foolishness. But to place our hope in God, no matter how uncertain and insecure we may be, is the path to praise.

Personal Prayer
O Elohim, I pray that my hope will be in you, even when I feel most helpless. May I never turn my face away from you!

Unfailing Love

THEN...

✑ Psalm 44 ✑

*God, we have heard with our ears—our forefathers have told us—the work You
accomplished in their days, in days long ago: to plant them, You drove out the nations
with Your hand; to settle them, You crushed the peoples. For they did not take the land
by their sword—their arm did not bring them victory—but by Your right hand, Your
arm, and the light of Your face, for You were pleased with them (vv. 1–3).*

This psalm begins with a rousing recital of past victories in the history of
Israel: Nations were driven out, peoples were crushed, enemies were
pushed back, soldiers were victorious, foes were trampled. Israel's ancestors
flourished as a theocracy—a nation united under the living God—in the
midst of paganism and idolatry.

The psalmist articulates the secret of the overwhelming success of the
armies of Israel: "For I do not trust in my bow, and my sword does not bring
me victory. But You give us victory over our foes and let those who hate us be
disgraced. We boast in God all day long; we will praise Your name forever"
(44:6–8). They fought in the name of the Lord. That name alone empowered
them!

Names or song titles are also pivotal in capsulizing the meaning and
power of a lyric. The chief musician, David, would have loved "How Great
Thou Art!" or "His Name Is Wonderful." There is incomparable force and
energy in the name of the Lord.

What is the secret of effectiveness and power for me today? I must choose
not to live independently of God but to make him central in my life. I must
resist an easy, casual commitment to Christ but reflect in my daily walk the
personality of the One whose name I bear. That name will give me the power
to withstand temptation, endure criticism, and witness boldly.

Personal Prayer

*O God, may I boast, not in my own gifts and abilities, but in you.
And may I praise your name forever!*

UNFAILING LOVE

NOW...

✑ Psalm 44 ✑

But You have rejected and humiliated us; You do not march out with our armies. You make us retreat from the foe, and those who hate us have taken plunder for themselves. You hand us over to be eaten like sheep and scatter us among the nations....
My disgrace is before me all day long, and shame has covered my face (vv. 9–11, 15).

*I*f ever there were a passage written in the minor key, it's this one. Hear the litany of defeat in the action words of these verses: *rejected, humbled, plundered, scattered, devoured.* Israel, God's favored nation, now faces demoralization and destruction.

Neighboring nations scoff and scorn; they gloat over the ill fortunes of Israel. They thumb their noses at these people who have apparently been abandoned by their God.

I heard my friend Dr. Chuck Swindoll give a moving message on integrity. In it he said that God tests his servants in two major ways—through adversity and through prosperity. Because we are children of the Heavenly Father, he sometimes disciplines or chastens us. That's tough love.

But how do we handle rejection and defeat? How do we react when our faith doesn't seem to be getting results? Is our relationship to God a hoax?

This psalm does not give us neat, tidy answers to those questions. The mystery of God's grand design looms in the distance. In the immediate situation God's people are suffering. Rather than causing them to forsake their faith, however, it drives them to their knees in profound prayer.

Personal Prayer

O God, in the reversals and discordant moments of my life, help me to hear your faithful love calling me to repentance and renewal.

Unfailing Love

WHY?

∾ Psalm 44 ∾

Wake up, LORD! Why are You sleeping? Get up! Don't reject us forever!
Why do You hide Yourself and forget our affliction and oppression? . . .
Rise up! Help us! Redeem us because of Your faithful love (vv. 23–24, 26).

Why me, Lord? The psalmist reflects my own present struggle to see God when the lights are turned out. The people of Israel are experiencing the crush of rejection, and they are as perplexed as I with the mysteries of my own life. Why has this happened? What have I done? I've been on the job, faithfully serving him, laboring in the place he's assigned to me. Doesn't he know I'm hurting? Doesn't he care? Is he asleep?

The history of God's people, both past and present, seems to fluctuate between periods of blessing and periods of defeat. At these times is God really withdrawing in wrath, or does he just refuse to be hurried? During a furious squall on the Sea of Galilee, as waves threatened to capsize the disciples' boat, Jesus slept peacefully on a cushion in the stern (Mark 4:37–38).

God's timetable is often different from ours. Suffering may not be a punishment, only a battle scar—the price paid for serving the Lord in a hostile environment, in a world at war with God.

When it seems as if the boat is sinking, we can cling to the reality of his unfailing love. "Who can separate us from the love of Christ? Can affliction or anguish or persecution or famine or nakedness or danger or sword? . . . No, in all these things we are more than victorious through Him who loved us" (Rom. 8:35, 37).

Personal Prayer
O God, may my impatience not prevent me
from constantly trusting in your steadfast love
no matter how bleak my circumstances appear.

THE LOVE SONG
VERSES FOR A KING

ᗡᗡ Psalm 45 ᗡᗡ

My heart is moved by a noble theme as I recite my verses to the king;
my tongue is the pen of a skillful writer (v. 1).

No writer should write until a fire burns deep inside. If one feels no strong conviction, no genuine emotion, no real compulsion, there is nothing to say!

This verse gives us a glimpse of the process of composition in the ancient world. In this messianic psalm, the inscription tells us the name of the tune— "Lilies." The composers are the sons of Korah; their subject, the wedding of the King of kings.

No wonder this musical artist's heart is stirred! Moved by the most noble theme of all times—the marriage of Christ to his bride, the church—the psalmist's words flow quickly and fluently. With consummate creativity he portrays Christ in all his beauty as a bridegroom arrayed for his bride.

Now deeply involved—intellectually, emotionally, and spiritually—the psalmist's tongue becomes "the pen of a skillful writer," and he articulates an eloquent lyric. As his heart responds and his thoughts are engaged, the sacrifice kindled upon his lips overflow upon the page. Truly this is an inspired work, and crafted with great artistry. Sincerity, especially among biblical writers, is never a substitute for skill.

What a mandate for a Christian artist! What a mission statement for the Christian writer! What goals to live for! What a target to shoot toward! And all centering in a depiction of the Messiah that is intensely personal, beautiful, and artistic.

Personal Prayer
Lord, give me a vision of your Son
that will set my heart on fire.
Then my songs and my writing
will burn with joy, praise, and beauty.

THE LOVE SONG

VERSES FOR THE GROOM

⚬ Psalm 45 ⚬

You are the most handsome of men; grace flows from your lips. Therefore God has blessed you forever. Mighty warrior, strap your sword at your side. In your majesty and splendor—in your splendor ride triumphantly in the cause of truth, humility, and justice. May your right hand show your awe-inspiring deeds. . . . You love righteousness and hate wickedness; therefore God, your God, has anointed you, more than your companions, with the oil of joy (vv. 2–4, 7).

When I read the words of this beautiful psalm, I'm reminded of my own marriage to Karen. July 14, 1963, was a spectacular day for an outdoor wedding on the lawn of Word of Life Inn. With Schroon Lake and the majestic Adirondack Mountains as our backdrop, we recited our vows from memory. This groom was typically nervous and apprehensive but anticipated a glorious future with his beautiful bride.

The warrior King described by the psalmist is the "most excellent of men," the model for all men of God. He is to ride forth in splendor and majesty, "in behalf of truth, humility, and righteousness."

His kingdom will be everlasting. It will be characterized by righteousness and justice. The King himself is incomparable. He is anointed with the oil of joy; his robes are scented; his house is adorned with inlaid ivory; and his rooms are filled with the glorious music of strings. His honored women are the daughters of kings, the chiefest of whom is the royal bride beautified in robes of gold.

Hebrews 1 shows us that this is God's Son, the "heir of all things" and the Creator of the universe. This King is the Son who is the "radiance of God's glory, the exact expression of His nature, and He sustains all things by His powerful word" (1:3). He is the model for all believers but particularly for all who would aspire to be men of God.

Personal Prayer

Lord, I worship you in all of your magnificence and transcendent beauty. Make me more like you in truth, humility, and righteousness.

The Love Song
Verses for the Bride

∽ Psalm 45 ∽

Listen, daughter, pay attention and consider: forget your people and your
father's house, and the king will desire your beauty. Bow down to him,
for he is your lord. . . . I will cause your name to be remembered for all generations;
therefore the peoples will praise you forever and ever (vv. 10–11, 17).

The dignity of biblically ordained marriage in the ancient world is certainly foreign to the psychology of many modern marriages. This scene from the royal wedding depicts clearly the parting with the old and the new beginning required of this princess bride. The husband too must make a break from his childhood home, separating both physically and emotionally from parents, in order to give himself fully to his wife (Gen. 2:24).

This is to be an all-encompassing relationship, and no sacrifice is too great to ensure its success. Karen, for example, left her home and family in Topeka, Kansas, to join me in New York. She then accompanied me to Dallas so I could further my education in both music and theology. She moved our young family to Grand Rapids, Michigan, and later to Nashville, Tennessee, to pursue various ministry opportunities the Lord opened up for us. None of these adjustments has been easy or problem free, but like her biblical sister, Sarah, she has chosen to honor her husband at great personal sacrifice (1 Pet. 3:6).

This evidence of her love supports me daily, but I recall that radiant young woman on our wedding day. I still have the newspaper clipping describing her gown. In my opinion it rivals that of the royal bride in David's psalm. "Of white, silk organza, the bride's gown was fashioned with Alencon lace and seed pearls around the portrait neckline of the molded bodice and on the skirt which fell into a full cathedral-length train. On her head she wore a Swedish crystal crown and carried a bouquet composed of yellow roses, daisies, lily of the valley, and ivy." Like that royal procession in David's psalm, Karen was accompanied by friends and approached our improvised altar "with joy and gladness."

In conclusion, new glories are promised to couples who are yielded to the Lord. David's bride and groom will be blessed with sons who will become princes to "perpetuate their memory through all generations." This is a foretaste of the Messiah who will bring "many sons to glory" (Heb. 2:10) and who will reign forever.

Personal Prayer

Lord, I thank you for Karen and for the beautiful relationship of marriage which
illustrates so clearly your relationship to your bride, the church.

A MIGHTY FORTRESS
GOD'S POWER OVER NATURE

∽ Psalm 46 ∽

God is our refuge and strength, a helper who is always found in times of trouble.
Therefore we will not be afraid, though the earth trembles and the mountains
topple into the depths of the seas, though its waters roar and foam and
the mountains quake with its turmoil. Selah (vv. 1–3).

How does one face the possibility of world catastrophe? How does one guard against internal disintegration of the personality in view of pressure to conform to the false standards of society? The answer is found in God alone, not in God plus anything else.

In our lifetime we may never personally experience earthquake, volcanic eruption, or tornadic winds—all evidences of the physical universe in turmoil. While these natural calamities are devastating, equally distressing and disrupting are the more common upheavals caused by marital conflict, financial reverses, illness, and death of friends or loved ones.

When that which seems unchangeable and impregnable falls, God is my stability. He is my *refuge*—"my shelter and protection from danger." He is my *strength*—"my vigor, mental and moral power, firmness and courage." He is my ever-present help in trouble.

As a high-strung, sensitive, emotional person, I need to be constantly reminded of these truths. Worry is an inappropriate response for God's child. Anxiety, mental distress, and emotional agitation yield to trust in the unshakeable, immutable, omnipotent God of the universe. He is the Master of all of nature, and I must make him the Master of my troubled soul.

Personal Prayer

O Lord, I praise you that I do not have to fear anyone or anything
because you are my Refuge and Strength.

A Hymn Lyric

A Mighty Fortress
A mighty fortress is our God,
A bulwark never failing;
Our helper He amid the flood
Of mortal ills prevailing.

Dost ask who that may be?
Christ Jesus it is He—
Lord Sabaoth His name,
From age to age the same,
And He must win the battle.
Words and music by Martin Luther.

A Mighty Fortress

GOD'S PROTECTION OF HIS CITY, PART 1

∽ Psalm 46 ∽

[There is] a river—its streams delight the city of God, the holy dwelling place of the Most High. God is within her; she will not be toppled. God will help her when the morning dawns. Nations rage, kingdoms topple; the earth melts when He lifts His voice. The LORD of Hosts is with us; the God of Jacob is our stronghold. Selah (vv. 4–7).

The city of God is a rich metaphor, a symbol of peace, tranquility, and contentment. It denotes Jerusalem, Zion, any place where God dwells. The New Testament vision is of a heavenly community, rather than an earthly locality, where believers praise the Lord forever. God fills that place with his glory and peace. Fear, darkness, and vulnerability will be foreign there.

But how do I live now with daily stresses and nightly fears that claw at my soul? How do I cope with anxieties and pressures that keep me restless and uneasy? I must latch on to the exciting reality that the Lord is with me *now!* The God of Jacob is my fortress *now!*

Personal Prayer
O Lord, may I catch a vision of that city of God
where there is no anxiety, no fear,
no stress and may I realize that
I may dwell with you now in peace.

A Mighty Fortress

GOD'S OMNIPOTENCE, PART 2

∽ Psalm 46 ∽

Come, see the works of the LORD, who brings devastation on the earth. He makes wars cease throughout the earth. He shatters bows and cuts spears to pieces; He burns up the chariots. "Stop [your fighting]—and know that I am God, exalted among the nations, exalted on the earth" (vv. 8–10).

Christ commanded the violent surging waters, "Peace, be still!" When the last chapter of world history has been written, in the same way God will put an end to violence, war, and to all of the effects of sin in the universe.

In this vision of the end of time, desolations have been brought on the earth, wars have ceased, and instruments of war have been eliminated. God's judgment has prevailed, and the world has become forcibly disarmed. At that time he will be exalted among the nations and in the earth. Man's hopes will be dashed, but God will be exalted in all of his majesty and glory.

What should be my response to this vision? Once fully aware that God is my fortress, my shelter, my protection, I must learn to be still and know that God is God and that he has provided our redemption through Christ.

In the end he is all that matters in time and eternity.

Personal Prayer

O Lord, as you will finally be exalted among the nations and in the earth, be exalted in my life now and help me to be still before you.

A Hymn Lyric

A Mighty Fortress, continued

For still our ancient foe,
Doth seek to work us woe—
His craft and power are great,
And armed with cruel hate,
On earth is not His equal.
Did we in our own strength confide
Our striving world be losing,
Were not the right Man on our side,
The Man of God's own choosing.
Words and music by Martin Luther.

EXULTATION!

∽ Psalm 47 ∽

Clap your hands, all you peoples; shout to God with a jubilant cry. . . .
God ascends amid shouts of joy, the LORD, amid the sound of trumpets. Sing praise
to God, sing praise; sing praise to our King, sing praise! (vv. 1, 5–6).

This psalm, a hymn to the Great King, gives us a graphic picture of drama in worship. These ancient believers allowed themselves to be caught up in worship. They praised the Lord with every aspect of their being—intellectually, emotionally, and physically. They learned how to worship God with each of the five senses—sight, sound, smell, taste, and touch. This psalm pulsates and resonates with excitement!

Note the verbs that give movement and power to this psalm: "Clap your hands!" "Shout to God with cries of joy!" "Sing praises!" (Note too that these verbs are in the imperative. Lackluster worship is not acceptable.) Why such jubilation? Because the King has "subdued nations" (v. 3). "He chooses our inheritance" (v. 4), and now he "has ascended amid shouts of joy" (v. 5).

This is a royal procession. As God ascends, accompanied by trumpet fanfares, the people form a great choir of highly involved worshippers, all praising the Lord in song and with musical instruments.

We need to attend church as dynamically involved worshippers rather than spectators. Church services are not sitcoms that couch potatoes view for entertainment. They should be dynamic encounters with God—challenging, convicting, and somewhat uncomfortable!

I want to lay aside personal inhibition and apathy and catch the spirit of these ancient worshippers. When I see God as they saw him, high and lifted up, I will be euphoric in my praise and will long to exalt him with every means at my disposal.

Personal Prayer
Dear Lord, I long to praise you with vigor and unrestrained passion.
Unfetter my personality, enhance my sensitivity, and enlarge my
creativity so that I can be profoundly involved in lifting you high!

CHORUS OF PRAISE
THE KING IN ZION

❧ Psalm 48 ❧

The LORD is great and is highly praised in the city of our God. His holy mountain, rising splendidly, is the joy of the whole earth. Mount Zion on the slopes of the north is the city of the great King. God is known as a stronghold in its citadels (vv. 1–3).

*T*he glory of the Lord ...
Something has happened that has inspired the psalmist to exude praise. Perhaps the Lord has once again miraculously delivered the nation from annihilation. He sings out lustily and full-throatedly, "Great is the Lord, and most worthy of praise!" What a motif for today!

The songwriter revels in encomiums of praise to Zion, the city of our God. Nothing less than the most majestic expressions of highest praise will suffice in this setting—a city that is lofty and magnificent, "the joy of all the earth." God himself is her fortress, her sure defense.

Why are all nations charmed by this city of Jerusalem? Why is it pivotal and strategic? Because it represents the place where God dwells. Blessings flow forth from her to all the earth.

What is here for me to learn today? First, that the best place for me is where God is. There I will discover my identity, security, and stability in him. Second, the source of personal blessing is God himself. I must allow him to become the hub, the center, the fulcrum of my life, just as Jerusalem is the spiritual crossroads of all nations on earth.

Personal Prayer
Dear Lord, you are most worthy of my praise. Nothing charms me like the irresistible picture of the New Jerusalem where I will someday dwell with you.

CHORUS OF PRAISE
THE NATIONS IN RETREAT

∽ Psalm 48 ∽

Look! The kings assembled; they advanced together. They looked, and froze with fear; they fled in terror. Trembling seized them there, agony like that of a woman in labor, as You wrecked the ships of Tarshish with the east wind. Just as we heard, so we have seen in the city of the LORD of Hosts, in the city of our God; God will establish it forever. (vv. 4–8).

The protection of the Lord . . .

Assyrian warriors were renowned for their iron courage and enormous strength. Yet, at the sight of Jerusalem, the city of God, Sennacherib's vassals trembled! Even with their awesome power, they were no match for this impregnable fortress, defended by God himself.

Strong metaphors describe their panic: "Pain like that of a woman in labor"; "like ships of Tarshish shattered by an east wind" (vv. 6–7). There is no rational explanation for such a disaster—only the terrible majesty and strength of God, who provided supernatural protection and providence for his people.

How frail I am in my humanity. I must not let myself be intimidated by minor fears or even by problems of more significant proportions. The same God who routed the Phoenician armies and battered their ships at sea is available to me today to set my anxious heart at rest. "If [that] God is for [me], who can be against [me]?" (Rom. 8:31).

Personal Prayer
O Lord, I come to you as a little child, thanking you once again for your protection and care.

CHORUS OF PRAISE

∽ Psalm 48 ∽

God, within Your temple, we contemplate Your faithful love. Your name, God, like Your praise, reaches to the ends of the earth; Your right hand is filled with justice. Mount Zion is glad. The towns of Judah rejoice because of Your judgments (vv. 9–11).

The praise of the Lord . . .

What a beautiful model for a praise song. The psalmist ponders the unfailing love of the Lord. The Hebrew word *hesed* is a magnificent Old Testament word for God's loyal, covenant love. Much like the Greek word *agape* in the New Testament, it describes the fact that God loves us no matter what, no strings attached. His love is unconditional and persistent.

In our self-centered society—where even love often must be earned through good performance, wealth, beauty, or status—it is refreshing to know that the real world of the spirit is governed by a God of grace and stubborn love.

Supporting me today are the pillars of God's loyal love and his eternal faithfulness. When I meditate on that, I am encouraged and strengthened. I have a choice. Either I can succumb to fears of rejection and failure, or I can lean against God's promises.

Personal Prayer

O God, I praise you for your great faithfulness and stubborn love, even when I am tempted to try to "earn" my place with you and with my peers.

A Contemporary Lyric

Stubborn Love

Funny me . . . just couldn't see
Even long before I knew You, You were
  loving me.
Sometimes I cry . . . You must cry too.
When You see the broken promises
  I've made to You.
I keep saying that I'll trust You,
  though I seldom do.
Yet You stay and say "I love you still"

Knowing someday I'll be like You
It's your stubborn love
That never lets go of me.
I don't understand how You could
  stay—
Perfect love embracing the worst in
  me.
I can't live without Your stubborn love.
Words and music by Amy Grant, Gary Chapman, Sloan Towner, Brown Bannister, Michael W. Smith © Meadowgreen Music Co. / Handrail Music.

CHORUS OF PRAISE
THE REVIEW OF ZION

∽ Psalm 48 ∽

Go around Zion, encircle it; count its towers, note its ramparts;
tour its citadels so that you can tell a future generation: "This God,
our God forever and ever—He will lead us eternally" (vv. 12–14).

The posterity of the Lord . . .
Because the Lord has delivered Israel, they celebrate and worship with exuberance. Having been confined within the walls of the city, they are now free to walk outside. There, in the exhilaration of newfound freedom, they behold and admire the city's undamaged towers, walls, and pristine palaces.

Reviewing the city, they are reminded that the Lord is their high tower forever. He will continually protect and deliver them and will guide them forever. More importantly, they are to "tell of [these things] to the next generation."

What a responsibility! Through the medium of music, I have God's mandate to share my faith and my gifts with those who will come after me.

New music inevitably builds on what has gone before. Bach, the epitome of artistic genius and craftsmanship in the Baroque period, has inspired many musicians centuries after his death. I praise the Lord for other church musicians who have been my mentors—Don Hustad, John W. Peterson, Ralph Carmichael, and others.

Now maybe it's my turn. There is a musical discipleship involved. I must contribute to the lives of younger composers, arrangers, and orchestrators. As a communicator seasoned in the faith and in the medium, I must pass the baton of God's truth and his values to generations to follow.

Personal Prayer
Dear Lord, help me to be faithful, through the witness of my music, to "tell . . . the next generation" of your protection and guidance all the days of their lives.

MEANING IN WEALTH?

∽ Psalm 49 ∽

*Hear this, all you peoples; listen, all who inhabit the world, both low and high, rich
and poor together. . . . Why should I fear in times of trouble? The iniquity of my foes
surrounds me. They trust in their wealth and boast of their abundant riches. . . .
For one can see that wise men die; the foolish and the senseless also pass away.
Then they leave their wealth to others. . . . But despite [his] assets, man
will not last; he is like the animals that perish (vv. 1–2, 5–6, 10, 12).*

The futility of trusting in wealth . . .

I've talked to a lot of secular musicians, and most of them say the same
thing: When success comes, big money is at first a turn-on; after that, it can be
real trouble. The Christian music scene also has suffered many excesses: inflated
budgets, out-of-control production expense, political hype, unreasonable contracts, and outrageous lifestyles. This psalmist agrees and shoots down the
theory that the acquisition of wealth guarantees happiness and immortality.

He begins with a solemn introduction in which he proposes to grapple
with this age-old problem of meaning in life. Then he asks a question: Why
should I fear an enemy who trusts in wealth? No man can buy human life. Life
is so valuable and the price so high that no amount of money can buy off death.
In the end all men, whatever their station, die and leave their accumulation of
possessions behind.

In our blatantly materialistic society, many of us expend a lot of time
and energy chasing the bucks while denying the reality of our own appointment with death. Since money cannot buy me life or happiness, I need to
discover the true Source.

Personal Prayer

*O Mighty One, Lord God, help me not to buy into the world view that money
and status bring meaning to life when that is Satan's lie, his counterfeit proposal,
camouflaging the profound truth that you are our only real meaning.*

MEANING IN WEALTH

∽ Psalm 49 ∽

This is the way of those who are arrogant, and of their followers, who approve of their words. Like sheep they are headed for Sheol; Death will shepherd them. The upright will rule over them in the morning, and their form will waste away in Sheol, far from their lofty abode. But God will redeem my life from the power of Sheol, for He will take me. (vv. 13–15).

The final end of those who trust in wealth ...

What a graphic picture of death the psalmist paints! Those who are trusting "in themselves"—in their own resources—for salvation are destined for the grave. At the moment of death, even wealthy, influential persons will be as helpless as sheep herded together. According to one poet, "death pastures them," and their ultimate resting place is "far from their princely mansions."

What a contrast with the godly and upright! I'm impressed by three promises in this passage: (1) The godly will have dominion—"the upright will rule over them" (v. 14). (2) The souls of the upright will be ransomed from the place of the dead—"God will redeem my life from the power of Sheol" (v. 15). (3) The Lord himself will receive the righteous—"He will take me" (v. 15). When phobias and fears about death assail me, these verses are a comfort and a lifeline.

Enoch walked with God on a regular basis, and one day he continued walking right into his presence. Elijah was caught up in a chariot of fire. Our Lord ascended into the clouds. One day each one of us who knows the Lord will walk through a door into eternity. We will be "out of the body and at home with the Lord" (2 Cor. 5:8).

Personal Prayer
*Lord, I thank you that because you have conquered death,
I don't need to live in fear of it. I'm looking forward
to the day when you will take me to yourself.*

Meaning in Wealth?

∽ Psalm 49 ∽

Do not be afraid when a man gets rich, when the wealth of his house increases.
For when he dies, he will take nothing at all; his wealth will not follow him down.
Though he praises himself during his lifetime—and people praise you when
you do well for yourself—he will go to the generation of his fathers;
they will never see the light. A man with valuable possessions but without
understanding is like the animals that perish (vv. 16–20).

The finite nature of wealth ...

I must admit that I, along with many others, have been charmed by Tinseltown. The accoutrements of success seem so appealing that it's pretty easy to fall for those less-than-subtle advertising ploys touting fancy foreign engineering or the architectural wonders of some luxury house. Even in church we sometimes focus on the trappings—lavish sanctuaries, fine pipe organs, plush carpeting. When materialism and personal pride fuse together, we're all in grave danger of neglecting or even forgetting God!

Thoughts of death and the prospect of eternity, however, can abruptly change one's focus, perspective, and priorities. The psalmist reminds us that, no matter how imposing the wealthy and powerful may appear, they can't take it with them.

In this life the wealthy often inspire awe, admiration, and praise. But this adulation will be short-lived. The possessions that are the basis of their pride and self-aggrandizement will not survive past the grave. Verse 20 describes the final state of the man who leaves God out of his life. Without understanding, he is like the beasts that perish. His power, influence, and wealth won't carry any weight in eternity.

Personal Prayer
Lord, may I learn to live always, not for this life only,
but with eternity's values in view.

TRUE WORSHIP

∽ Psalm 50 ∽

God, the LORD God speaks; He summons the earth from east to west. From Zion, the perfection of beauty, God appears in radiance. Our God is coming; He will not be silent! Devouring fire precedes Him, and a storm rages around Him. On high, He summons heaven and earth in order to judge His people. "Gather My faithful ones to Me, those who made a covenant with Me by sacrifice." The heavens proclaim His righteousness, for God is the judge (vv. 1–6).

The Lord appears . . .

Through the words of the psalmist, can we see the Lord in the beauty of his holiness? He is transcendent—beyond and above us. He is the Mighty One, who spoke the world into existence and orders the universe. He is the Perfect One. He is the Righteous One. He is also Yahweh, unchangeable and faithful. It is this One who is coming to judge the earth.

From Zion, the glorious place where God dwells, he comes, surrounded by fire and fierce energy. He does not remain silent, for he comes to judge his covenant people who have been negligent in their worship. He sees their hearts and knows that their practices have been deficient and their attitudes flippant.

Our worship practices, like our relationship with the Lord, should reflect both majesty and intimacy. Unfortunately, we usually emphasize one or the other. We worship God in his majesty but are not intimate with him, or we cultivate intimacy and neglect reverence. There is a holy balance toward which we should strive. In our services there should be times of fervor in which we may even loudly proclaim his praises with clapping of hands. At other times, deeply moved by God's holiness, we approach him in quiet meditation.

Our Lord is absolutely holy. He is also jealous. He covets genuine worship and praise. He is serious about his personhood and disdains my inattentiveness and casual approach to my relationship with him. As he addresses his people Israel, he is also speaking to me.

Personal Prayer

Dear Lord, help me to sense your absolute holiness and transcendence. And may this glorious vision of you lead me to fall at your feet in total adoration.

True Worship

∞ Psalm 50 ∞

"Listen, My people, and I will speak; I will testify against you, Israel. I am God, your God. I do not rebuke you for your sacrifices or for your burnt offerings, which are continually before Me. I will not accept a bull from your household or male goats from your pens, for every animal of the forest is Mine, the cattle on a thousand hills. . . . Sacrifice a thank offering to God, and pay your vows to the Most High. Call on Me in a day of trouble; I will rescue you, and you will honor Me" (vv. 7–10, 14–15).

The Lord speaks against empty liturgy . . .
I stand amazed in his presence! This transcendent Lord, this Sovereign God, who is beyond us and above us is also around us and within us and desires fellowship with us!

Ritualism can never take the place of relationship. Obedience, faithfulness, and calling on God in trouble all flow from an intimate relationship with him. Now God comes into court to arraign his own covenant people, intellectually strong and orthodox in their beliefs but faulty in their motives and attitudes.

While Israel has practiced sacrifice and observed the law, she has assumed that her offerings benefited God, as if he were somehow in debt to them. They have grown independent and cold, and their fervor has cooled, but God owns everything, including the cattle on a thousand hills.

Adoration of God is not scoring brownie points with him. He is eternally self-existent and does not need our puny offerings, our gifts, our talents. But wonder of wonders, he longs to have us know him well, closely, intimately, and to worship him—not for what he gets out of it but because he is waiting to bless and deliver us!

Personal Prayer
*O Lord, you are high and holy, yet you invite me into your presence.
You tell me to call on you in trouble. Lord, you are my Friend!*

TRUE WORSHIP

∽ Psalm 50 ∽

But God says to the wicked: "What right do you have to recite My statutes and to take My covenant on your lips? You hate instruction and turn your back on My words. . . . You unleash your mouth for evil and harness your tongue for deceit. . . . You have done these things, and I kept silent; you thought I was just like you. But I will rebuke you and lay out the case before you. "Understand this, you who forget God, or I will tear you apart, and there will be no rescuer. Whoever sacrifices a thank offering honors Me, and whoever orders his conduct, I will show him the salvation of God" (vv. 16–17, 19, 21–23).

The Lord speaks against hypocrisy . . .

Sometimes I'm guilty of going through the motions—responding automatically to expectations when my mind is preoccupied with other concerns.

But God's indictment against the people in this passage involved more than a warning against simple preoccupation. Israel was engaged in full-fledged disobedience! While Israel was giving verbal assent to the law, she was in reality breaking it right and left. In fact, she went beyond disobedience to the point where she defended dishonesty (v. 19), condoned adultery (v. 18), and participated in slander, speaking against their own brothers and sisters and despising familial ties (v. 20).

Because the Lord has been silent to this point, Israel assumed that he was satisfied with mere lip service. God's outlook isn't like man's. Man places a high premium on outward appearance, but God looks at the attitude of the heart.

It isn't enough for me to have a thorough knowledge of the truth. I must cultivate intimacy with the Lord. Otherwise, all I will have is an empty religion rather than a transforming relationship.

Personal Prayer

Dear Lord, transform my mind and heart.
May your truth not just spring automatically
from my lips, but may it transfigure my life.

FUGUE ON FORGIVENESS

SUBJECT: PRAYER OF CONFESSION

∽ Psalm 51 ∽

Be gracious to me, God, according to Your faithful love; according to Your abundant compassion, blot out my rebellion. Wash away my guilt, and cleanse me from my sin. For I am conscious of my rebellion, and my sin is always before me. Against You—You alone—I have sinned and done this evil in Your sight. So You are right when You pass sentence; You are blameless when You judge (vv. 1–4).

The background of this splendid poem on forgiveness is David's sin of adultery with Bathsheba (2 Sam. 11). Bold phrases showcase the intensity of David's confession: "blot out my rebellion" (v. 1); "wash away all my guilt" (v. 2); "cleanse me from my sin" (v. 2). David is crying out for full forgiveness. Aware that he does not deserve God's mercy, he nevertheless appeals to God's unfailing love and compassion.

David feels the crushing weight of his guilt. Further compounding the problem is the fact that he has been engaged in a cover-up for at least a year. The death of the child conceived out of wedlock and the prophet Nathan's confrontation are the catalysts for his confession, and David acknowledges that his sin is ultimately against God and God alone.

The thesis of this remarkable outpouring from the heart of a king is that anyone—man or woman, peasant or potentate—may appeal to God for forgiveness and be restored to a life of joy and service.

I too am painfully aware that intimacy with God comes only when I am brutally honest with the Lord about specific sins in my life. I start making headway when I give up self-deception and stop playing games with myself and the Lord. Reality, not rationalization, leads to growth.

Personal Prayer

Lord, deliver me from impotence and guilt. On the basis of your unfailing love and grace, set me free and fill my life with your joy.

A Pertinent Hymn

Are You Washed in the Blood?

Are you washed in the blood,
In the soul-cleansing blood of the Lamb?
Are your garments spotless?
Are they white as snow?
Are you washed in the blood of the Lamb?

Words and music by Elisha A. Hoffman.

FUGUE ON FORGIVENESS
COUNTER-SUBJECT: PRAYER OF PETITION

∽ Psalm 51 ∽

Purify me with hyssop, and I will be clean; wash me, and I will be whiter than snow. Let me hear joy and gladness; let the bones You have crushed rejoice. Turn Your face away from my sins and blot out all my guilt. God, create a clean heart for me and renew a steadfast spirit within me. Do not banish me from Your presence or take Your Holy Spirit from me. Restore the joy of Your salvation to me, and give me a willing spirit (vv. 7–12).

Nearly three thousand years after David's downfall, we don't have to look far to find his successors—fallen leaders dragged down by their sin nature into moral bankruptcy. Unfortunately this condition is no longer limited to the secular world. In the Christian arena too we have been concerned with image rather than reality. We have evaluated success on the basis of external symbols rather than on internal purity. We have some Christian leaders who look great on the outside but are dying inside.

In this personal petition to the Lord, David acknowledges that he can't possibly correct his basic sin nature. Only the God who created him can cleanse, renew, and restore. David's body, wracked with physical and emotional pain, must learn how to rejoice again. His crushed spirit longs to hear, once more, the music of God's joy and gladness. He asks to become a new creation, both psychologically and judicially, and prays, in this Old Testament context, that the Holy Spirit not be taken from him. Likely he is remembering Saul, who had lived as such an exile, deposed from God's blessing.

I also need a deep work of God in my life. Like David, I yearn for radical spiritual surgery—cleansing, restoration, a purified heart, the transforming power of the Holy Spirit, and the antidepressant of being filled with the joy of my salvation!

Personal Prayer
Lord, cleanse me from sin today and fill my crushed spirit with the joy of the Holy Spirit.

The Language of Music

Fugue
A polyphonic musical composition in which one or two themes are imitated by successively entering voices.

Themes are developed contrapuntally (one or more independent melodies added above or below a given melody).

FUGUE ON FORGIVENESS

ANSWER: PRAYER OF PRAISE

∞ Psalm 51 ∞

Then I will teach the rebellious Your ways, and sinners will return to You.
Save me from the guilt of bloodshed, God, the God of my salvation, and my tongue
will sing of Your righteousness. Lord, open my lips, and my mouth will declare
Your praise. You do not want a sacrifice, or I would give it; You are not pleased
with a burnt offering. The sacrifice pleasing to God is a broken spirit. God,
You will not despise a broken and humbled heart (vv. 13–17).

You can feel the beat of David's heart in this deeply personal interaction with the Lord. He has been locked into a pattern of deceit, God has allowed him to be crushed, and now he pleads for mercy and forgiveness.

Yet David knows that the justice and honor of the Heavenly Father demand nothing less than his child's utter brokenness. You can hear the resonant chords of his broken heart as he pleads, "Save me from the guilt of bloodshed, God, the God of my salvation" (v. 14).

In exchange for mercy and forgiveness, David pledges himself to three actions: (1) to teach sinners the ways of God so convincingly that they will repent; (2) to praise God in song—genuine praise always springs from honest, heart-wrenching lament; (3) to worship God through the sacrifice of contrition. David offers up his broken heart.

David concludes this magnificent fugue on forgiveness with a prayer for prosperity. He believes that meaningful worship leads to national prosperity, beginning with the purity and righteousness of its leaders.

Personal Prayer

Lord, my heart breaks when I consider my own willfulness and waywardness. Teach
me to teach others about you, to praise you, and to sacrifice. Above all, lead me into a
genuinely honest relationship with you. May sin not be a veil separating us.

A Contemporary Lyric
_____

Something Beautiful

Something beautiful, something good,
All my confusion He understood;
All I had to offer Him was brokenness and strife,
But He made something beautiful of my life.

Words by Gloria Gaither. Music by William J. Gaither.
© 1971 by William J. Gaither. All rights reserved. Used by permission.

FANTASIA ON FAITH
IN MINOR: DECEIT'S DISCORD

∽ Psalm 52 ∽

Why brag about evil, you hero! God's faithful love is constant. Like a sharpened razor, your tongue devises destruction, working treachery. You love evil instead of good, lying instead of speaking truthfully.... This is why God will bring you down forever.... The righteous will look on with awe and will ridicule him: "Here's the man who would not make God his refuge, but trusted in the abundance of his riches, taking refuge in his destructive behavior" (vv. 1–3, 5, 6–7).

This psalm was written because of the treachery of a man named Doeg (1 Sam. 21–22), who was an informer during the reign of David. Doeg's career as a terrorist was built on slander, deceit, and intrigue. The tongue of this self-satisfied, clever man revealed his evil, corrupt character. His words, sharp as a razor, were used to destroy people and bring disgrace to God.

God will not put up with this kind of behavior forever, then or now. The unsaved can learn a lesson from Doeg. Their ruin, like his, is inevitable. In an act of final judgment, God will bring them to "everlasting ruin" (v. 5), and they'll learn, too late, that great wealth, obtained at the expense of destroying others, will not buy a reprieve in the day of judgment.

Probing my own often deceitful heart, I find that his psalm stirs my conscience. I'm so often controlled by mixed motives and false goals. This affects my speech. How much easier it is for me to be critical rather than creative, to put down rather than to build up, to be a troublemaker rather than a peacemaker. Deceit always creates discord. Only a truthful tongue can sing in harmony!

Personal Prayer

*O Lord, purify and purge me of deceit.
Cleanse me on the inside
so that my tongue sings only truth.*

The Language of Music

Fantasia

Italian term meaning "fantasy."

As you would think, it is an instrumental piece involving "fantasy." This is accomplished in different ways: improvisation, romanticism, or use of rather free forms.

FANTASIA ON FAITH

IN MAJOR: FAITH'S FANTASY

∽ Psalm 52 ∽

But I am like a flourishing olive tree in the house of God; I trust in God's faithful love forever and ever. I will praise You forever for what You have done. In the presence of Your faithful people, I will place my hope in Your name, for it is good (vv. 8–9).

What a difference between Doeg, the traitor, and David, the man of faith! What bold contrasts exist in the psalms: the wicked versus the righteous, the transient versus the permanent, adversity versus prosperity.

David uses the metaphor of a flourishing olive tree to depict God's blessing on his life. His faith is strong because his roots go down deep into the soil of God's unfailing love. Because of this inner security, David is able to praise God *for what he has done.* He also is freed to praise God *for who he is,* for his incomparable attributes, his "good name." In that name David places his eternal hope.

I love David's last statement in this psalm: "I will praise you *in the presence of your saints*" (emphasis mine). For ancient worshippers, private praise always led to public worship. Individualism did not obliterate their sense of community.

So many of us are loners, but how we need one another! Isolation, alienation, and aloneness result in weakness. The fellowship of brothers and sisters in Christ lends strength. God doesn't want us to be spiritual Lone Rangers.

Personal Prayer

Your unending, unfailing love, O God, inspires me to proclaim my faith in you wherever your saints gather for worship.

SONATINA ON WICKEDNESS

❧ Psalm 53 ❧

The fool says in his heart, "God does not exist." They are corrupt, and they do vile deeds. There is no one who does good. . . . Will those who practice sin never understand? They consume My people as they consume bread; they do not call on God. . . .Oh, that Israel's deliverance would come from Zion! When God restores His captive people, Jacob will rejoice; Israel will be glad (vv. 1, 4, 6).

The fool says in his heart, 'There is no God.'" This recurring theme is hammered home in the irreverent lyrics of heavy metal and punk rock musicians as well as in the various pseudo-religious movements so prevalent today. And if it isn't blatant atheism, it is passively leaving God out of our lives. Many live today as if God didn't exist!

The thesis of this psalm, almost identical to Psalm 14, is that people are universally corrupt. (Paul further elaborates on this theme in Romans 4—his theological masterpiece.) What a contrast to modern-day humanism, which boasts of the inherent goodness of man!

In the first movement (vv. 1–3), David describes the human race as "fools," "corrupt," "vile," "turned away." He further grieves, "There is no one who does good, not even one" (v. 3). How refreshing to find many godly people in the music industry. One such musician is Steve Green, who is known not only for his soaring voice but also for his strong conviction and personal holiness. David wishes he could find "even one"!

The second movement (vv. 4–5) portrays the wicked as ultimately "overwhelmed with dread" and despised by God. David can't believe the ignorance of those who persecute the righteous.

In the third and final movement, David utters a plea for the salvation of Israel and declares his faith that God will restore the fortunes of his people. David has a deep, inner longing for the coming of God's kingdom.

As I think about the fact that Christ is coming back to this sinful world, my whole perspective changes. When people leave God out of their lives, they sour and become corrupt. I want to warn them that he may come today! But without spiritual reality at the core of my personhood, I too will sour and become corrupt. What will keep me pure and fresh today? Closeness and intimacy with the Lord and the eager expectation of his return.

Personal Prayer

O God, act as my preservation from corruption. As I interact with unbelievers in my world, may I be salt and light. Come, Lord Jesus!

Hymn
of Confidence

∞ Psalm 54 ∞

God, save me by Your name, and vindicate me by Your might! . . .
God is my helper; the Lord is the sustainer of my life (vv. 1, 4).

How do I respond under pressure? Am I paralyzed by fear? Do I panic? Do I try to escape? Do I withdraw? Do I become depressed?

David, hotly pursued by his enemies, knows that he is in mortal danger. He has been betrayed by the Ziphites—ungodly, ruthless men—and even threatened by one who has loved him, King Saul. With his life on the line, David doesn't panic but cries out to God.

His prayer is in two parts: "God, save me by Your name, and vindicate me by Your might!" In the second part of this hymn, David asserts his trust in God: "God is my helper; the Lord is the sustainer of my life."

Under fire, David faced the hard facts of his dilemma with confidence, but he was not alone. Nor does God abandon me to sort out my problems alone. The same Lord who delivered David "from all [his] troubles" is able to deliver me!

Personal Prayer

O God, when I am experiencing unbelievable pressure, help me to trust
in your name and in your power—not in human solutions.

BALLAD OF BETRAYAL
FIRST MOTIF: REJECTION

✑ Psalm 55 ✑

Now, it is not an enemy who insults me—otherwise I could bear it; it is not a foe who rises up against me—otherwise I could hide from him. But it is you, a man who is my peer, my companion and good friend! We used to have close fellowship; we walked with the crowd into the house of God (vv. 12–14).

One of the most painful experiences in life is betrayal by a close and trusted friend, one "with whom [you] once enjoyed sweet fellowship." Insult and persecution from enemies is to be expected; rejection by a beloved companion is almost unendurable! And this happens because human relationships are never free from impure motivations. It is human nature to use, exploit, and manipulate people for our ends. Often all of this is denied until the association sours, the communication ceases, and the friendship dies. Then, when we see this person in the mall, we turn and go the other way!

As a warrior, David was often in danger. He had learned to live with "the terrors of death" (v. 4), "horror" (v. 5), "violence and strife" (v. 9), "oppression and deceit" (v. 11). But the ultimate blow is the rejection rendered by an intimate friend.

Destructive forces are loose in the city of David. Anarchy and confusion are the result of the betrayal of his trusted confidant who has become a traitor. To make matters worse, David has even worshipped with this rogue!

What do I learn from David's desperate cry? I learn to expect the unexpected, to stand firm in my belief that the Lord is orchestrating my life—its highs and lows, its dissonance and consonance. Further, I learn from my own suffering and anguish something of what Christ endured for me and that redemption comes at a terribly high price.

Personal Prayer
*O God, help me to be honest with you about my feelings
of injustice and unfairness.
May times of persecution give me insight into
the compassion and suffering of my
Lord and Savior.*

BALLAD OF BETRAYAL

SECOND MOTIF: AFFIRMATION

∽ Psalm 55 ∽

Cast your burden on the LORD, and He will support you; He will never allow the righteous to be shaken. You, God, will bring them down to the pit of destruction; men of bloodshed and treachery will not live out half their days. But I will trust in You (vv. 22–23).

In the midst of his gut-wrenching betrayal by a close friend, David feels the affirming hand of God on his life. I am reassured today, knowing that God has not changed and that he ministers to me in the same ways.

He hears my cry of distress—morning, noon, and night (v. 17). He is able to save me just as he saved David (v. 16). He is aware of the violence of the wicked because "they do not change" (vv. 18–19). Even before I suspect treachery, the Lord knows the intent of the heart (v. 21).

The rich metaphors used in this psalm aptly depict a modern-day Judas. David's friend uses speech "as smooth as butter," but beneath the surface lies a ruthless, violent man. His words "more soothing than oil," are "drawn swords." This situation is not new to David, for he mentions it on at least three other occasions (57:4; 59:7; 64:3).

What a God! He will not forsake the righteous (v. 22). I can "cast my burdens" on the Lord and he will see me through my own Gethsemanes. David's final words in this psalm echo the song of my heart: "But I will trust in you!"

Personal Prayer

O God, help me not to get so wrapped up with the rejection that I miss the liberating power of your affirmation.

The Language of Music
_____

Ballad
From the Latin, <u>ballare</u> which means "to dance."
    A ballad is now a popular song involving romantic, adventurous, and narrative elements.

POLYPHONY
OF PRESSURE
DAVID'S PLIGHT

✑ Psalm 56 ✑

Be gracious to me, God, for man tramples me; he fights and oppresses me all day long. My adversaries trample me all day, for many arrogantly fight against me. When I am afraid, I will trust in You. In God, whose word I praise, in God I trust; I will not fear. What can man do to me? (vv. 1–4).

The publishing world is a pressure cooker. But all of modern life, whether in the corporate world or the kitchen, is a cauldron of frenetic activity, vigorous competition, and pressing decisions. We're all on the run. Seldom, however, are Christians in America running for their lives, though many are quietly dying inside.

In this psalm David is acutely aware of his fight for survival (see 1 Sam. 21 and Ps. 34). During a visit to Gath, he faces the possibility of daily attack. His enemies, all conspirators and killers, twist his words and plot to harm him. Simply speaking, David is on the run. He is a fugitive, living like a scavenger on the edge of society. He is fighting for his life. He even has to pretend insanity! But because of his intimate relationship to the Lord, his response isn't typical. Instead of giving into fear, he chooses faith.

As I face the stresses and tensions of modern life, I want to respond like King David. Instead of groveling in fear and intimidation, I choose to pray, to trust, to exercise faith, and to praise the Lord. How I respond under pressure reveals my true character. My neighbors are watching!

Personal Prayer

O God, may I not be intimidated by other people. When I'm afraid, let me learn to trust more in you, for "what can mortal man do to me?"

POLYPHONY
OF PRESSURE
GOD'S PROTECTION

∽ Psalm 56 ∽

You Yourself have recorded my wanderings. Put my tears in Your bottle. Are they not in Your records? Then my enemies will retreat on the day when I call. This I know: God is for me. In God, whose word I praise, in the LORD, whose word I praise, in God I trust; I will not fear. What can man do to me? ... For You delivered me from death, even my feet from stumbling, to walk before God in the light of life (vv. 8–11, 13).

*E*very tear we shed is recorded "on God's scroll"! What a comfort to David, whose back was to the wall! The king was a brilliant soldier and a military genius who exuded power and strength. But he wasn't afraid to cry!

Like a highly competent recording engineer who uses digital sampling, God accurately records every sigh, every whisper, every heartbeat, every tear—from the moment of my birth cry to the present. He knows me intimately. He is the complete and perfect Engineer, always attuned to my condition.

Though under severe stress, David is a real model for me. He places his complete trust in the Lord and in his Word. He is so confident of deliverance that he speaks in the past tense: "You *have delivered* my soul from death and my feet from stumbling" (v. 13).

David wasn't victimized by his circumstances. He didn't let pressure overwhelm him. His conscious choice made all the difference. He chose to praise the Lord and to trust his supernatural powers of protection. David's decision drove away his fear and enabled him to see his deliverance as an accomplished fact.

Personal Prayer

Father, I am moved not only by your vigilant protection but by your tenderness. Not a whisper goes unheard! What can I do but praise your name?

The Language of Music

Polyphony
Greek for "many voiced."

There are three basic musical textures: monophonic (a single, melodic line unaccompanied), homophonic (a single, melodic line accompanied), and polyphonic (two or more melodic lines). Polyphony is synonymous with counterpoint. (Romans 8:28 shows how God, the Master Composer, controls the counterpoint of our lives around the theme of His own glory.)

Triumphant Song
POWER OF DELIVERANCE

❦ Psalm 57 ❦

*I call to God Most High, to God who fulfills [His purpose] for me. He reaches
down from heaven and saves me, challenging the one who tramples me. God sends
His faithful love and truth. . . . God, be exalted above the heavens; let
Your glory be above the whole earth (vv. 2–3, 5).*

Again I see myself reflected in David. This time he has fled form King
Saul and is hiding in a cave (1 Sam. 22, 24). There are times when I feel
like escaping from the world and going into hiding "until the [present] disaster
has passed."

In fact, when I was attending a Christian high school, I was under pressure to be a campus leader. Secretly I wanted to blend in with the crowd or,
better still, to be left alone. I still struggle with feelings of shyness and social
ineptitude, so I can relate to David's cave.

Instead of giving up or giving in, David prays in that dark hiding place.
His prayer is a harmony in four parts.

Part 1: "Lord, have mercy!" He calls on the mercy of God and huddles
under "the shadow of His wings" (v. 1).

Part 2: He believes that God has a plan, uniquely designed for him, and
that he will "fulfill His purpose" (v. 2).

Part 3: He acknowledges his helpless state and describes his adversaries
as predators with teeth like "spears and arrows" and tongues like "sharp
swords" (v. 4).

Part 4: Seeing beyond his present plight, David looks forward to a time
when he will be vindicated and avenged and to that day when the Lord will
establish his righteousness and glory over the earth! (v. 5).

When David finds himself in hot water, he prays. When he is between
a rock and a hard place, he prays. When he is under extreme pressure, he
prays. I'd like to be more like this warrior who prayed!

Personal Prayer
*My prayer, O God Most High, is that your purpose will be fulfilled in my life
and that your glory may shine through my personality.*

TRIUMPHANT SONG

PRAYER CELEBRATING GOD'S LOVE AND FAITHFULNESS

∞ Psalm 57 ∞

My heart is confident, God, my heart is confident. I will sing, I sing praises. Wake up, my soul! Wake up, harp and lyre! I will wake up the dawn. I will praise You, Lord, among the peoples; I will sing praises to You among the nations. For Your faithful love is as high as the heavens; Your faithfulness reaches to the clouds. God, be exalted above the heavens; let Your glory be over the whole earth (vv. 7–11).

David is counting on victory, so he celebrates God's love and faithfulness. As the chief musician in Israel, he can't conceive of a better way to adore his Lord than through music and song. Because his faith is steadfast, he feels no fear but plans to "awaken the dawn" with singing. How interesting, since depression and despair are most acutely felt by many people in the early morning hours.

On a crescendo of praise, David's imagination soars as he exults in purest praise of his Lord. He vows to sing of him to all peoples. He eloquently proclaims the greatness of God's love and worshipfully celebrates his faithfulness which reaches to the skies. "God, be exalted above the heavens; let Your glory be above the whole earth" (v. 5).

David didn't bow down in defeat to his intolerable circumstances. Instead, he made an artistic choice to lift his voice in song, celebrating God's incomparable love and faithfulness!

Personal Prayer

O God, I praise you for giving me reason to awaken the dawn.
May I start each day with you, sharing the melody of your love
and faithfulness with others I meet today.

APPASSIONATA FOR JUSTICE
THE CHARGE

❦ Psalm 58 ❦

Do you really speak righteously, you mighty ones? Do you judge people fairly? No, you practice injustice in your hearts; with your hands you weigh out violence in the land. The wicked go astray from the womb; liars err from birth. They have venom like the venom of a snake, like the deaf cobra that stops up its ears, that does not listen to the sound of the charmers who skillfully weave spells (vv. 1–5).

Many of us struggle with bitterness over dishonesty, injustice, and unfairness in life. From the perspective of the immediate, life is often unfair. I know what it is like to be set up for humiliation in a public business meeting—to feel like a sheep among wolves because of the surprise element.

Our God is a God of righteousness and justice. Moses correctly assumes that "the Judge of all the earth" will do right (Gen. 18:25 NIV). On this basis David poses two critical questions: "Do you really speak righteously?" and "Do you judge people fairly?" (v. 1).

The questions are obviously rhetorical and intended to cause self-assessment in the hearers. A scathing denunciation follows. David's accusation rings out: "You practice injustice" (v. 2). "Your hands weigh out violence" (v. 2). [You] "speak lies" (v. 3). And there is more. These judges are as venomous as snakes and as indifferent to correction as cobras who pay no heed to their charmers.

David is right in denouncing these ancient judges. God places a high premium on justice since this is an aspect of his own character. Still, Jeremiah 17:9 reminds us that the human heart is desperately deceitful.

David's haunting questions linger in my mind like an unwelcome refrain. Am I honest and aboveboard in all my dealings? Am I a just executive? As a husband and father, do I give Karen and the kids a fair hearing? I'm glad our God is a just and merciful Judge!

Personal Prayer

Dear Lord, search my heart and, by the power of your Holy Spirit, point out any wicked way in me. I want to reflect your character with integrity.

The Language of Music

Appassionata
Italian for "impassioned."
It is the nickname for Beethoven's Piano Sonata in F minor, op. 57 (1806). It is the dark companion piece to the Waldstein Sonata. Beethoven wrote the most magnificent piano sonatas of all time.

APPASSIONATA FOR JUSTICE

THE VERDICT

∽ Psalm 58 ∽

God, knock the teeth out of their mouths; LORD, tear out the young lions' fangs. They will vanish like water that flows by; they will aim their useless arrows. Like a slug that moves along in slime, like a woman's miscarried [child], they will not see the sun. Before your pots can feel the heat of the thorns—whether green or burning—He will sweep them away (vv. 6–9).

I know just how David feels! How often have I been tempted to judge others as they have judged me. It's especially easy to spot a weakness in someone else when I too am guilty—like knocking lack of discipline in overeating when I've put on a few pounds myself.

David doesn't check his emotions here. He pronounces his verdict on these unjust judges, using bold strokes and vivid imagery. He demands that their teeth be smashed and their fangs pulled out so they will not be able to communicate their lies. He hopes they will vanish like water on a hot day. He wants their words to be as ineffectual as blunted arrows. He desires that they simply melt away like slugs (snails) in a drought. He wants them to die suddenly like a stillborn child who never sees the light of day. He wants their destruction to be swift.

In anticipating the fulfillment of a geopolitical kingdom on earth, David expects that all enemies who threaten the establishment of God's kingdom on earth will be destroyed swiftly and violently. Here he savors the sweet taste of revenge.

The New Testament, however, gives us an entirely different perspective. We are to leave the final judgment of scoundrels to God and wait patiently for his kingdom to be established on earth. "Vengeance Belongs to Me," says the Lord (Heb. 10:30).

Personal Prayer

Lord, may I entrust the ultimate end of my enemies to you.
Remove from me the bitterness of revenge.

APPASSIONATA FOR JUSTICE
THE VINDICATION

∽ Psalm 58 ∽

The righteous will rejoice when he sees the retribution; he will wash his feet in the blood of the wicked. Then people will say, "Yes, there is a reward for the righteous! There is a God who judges on earth!" (vv. 10–11).

Immanuel Kant, noted German philosopher, believed that the universal notion of justice was proof of God's existence. He also believed it was proof of a literal heaven. Why? Because he didn't observe justice being fully fulfilled on this earth. It is also tacit evidence for a place of eternal punishment. Why? Because Hitler, for example, never got the punishment he deserved during his lifetime.

David is encouraged that God's justice will be carried out. In these verses he resorts to wild, strong imagery to carry the intensity of his thoughts. He longs to see the righteous "bathing their feet in the blood of the wicked." Such a military coup would bring him great satisfaction.

David also is convinced that injustice will not prevail forever. The righteous will be rewarded. Men will see that God does judge the earth finally and righteously. So ends David's passionate plea for justice and vindication.

What personal comfort and intellectual solace I can derive from the fact that God will someday set all things straight! The finale of a Beethoven symphony will seem inconsequential in comparison to this!

Personal Prayer
Dear Lord, I thank you that by definition you are just.
Help me to leave final judgments with you.

EIN' FESTS BURG
("A MIGHTY FORTRESS")
CONSPIRACY AND TREACHERY

◌ Psalm 59 ◌

Deliver me from my enemies, my God; protect me from those who rise up against me.
Deliver me from those who practice sin, and save me from men of bloodshed. . . .
I will keep watch for You, my strength, because God is my stronghold (vv. 1–2, 9).

As I read these hymns penned by David, the greatest warrior-king Israel ever produced, I'm reminded that my own life seems somewhat tame by comparison. While David, the shepherd boy, was stalking and killing fierce predators that threatened his flock, I struggle with fierce competition in life. Still a lad, he fought the giant Goliath with a slingshot, five smooth stones, and the name of the Lord. Some of the giants in my life loom large to me; but budgets hassles, contract negotiations, and balancing priorities are not so dramatic. Assuming manhood, David seemed forever engaged in the fight for survival, while I attempt to keep creative energy alive and wrestle with significance and meaning in life.

Inspired by yet another attempt on his life, this time by crazed and jealous King Saul, David prays for deliverance from the treachery of evildoers. As is so often the case in an assassination attempt, conspiracy is involved (v. 3). But David's wife, Michal, foils the plan, warns David, and helps him escape through a window.

In my daily routine, it isn't often fierce and "bloodthirsty men" who conspire against me and rob me of life and vitality but tight schedules, family crises, and creative dry spells. In these mundane moments too, God provides an "open window" of deliverance, a way out.

Personal Prayer
O God, I praise you for open windows and that you continue to stand as
my Strength and Fortress in every circumstance of my life.

Ein' Fests Burg
("A Mighty Fortress")
JUSTICE AND PEACE

❧ Psalm 59 ❧

Do not kill them; otherwise, my people will forget. By Your power, make them home-less wanderers and bring them down, O Lord, our shield. . . . But I will sing of Your strength and will joyfully proclaim Your faithful love in the morning. For You have been a stronghold for me, a refuge in my day of trouble. To You, my strength, I sing praises, because God is my stronghold—my faithful God (vv. 11, 16–17).

While David expects justice to be done, he is motivated by more than revenge and vindication. He longs for the punishment of his enemies to reflect God's sovereignty. Is this the same David who envisioned a blood-bath of the wicked (58:10) and exhorted God to defang the lions and blot them up like water that evaporates in the sun (58:6–7)?

Now the psalmist implores God to stay his hand of execution (v. 11) but allow his enemies to wander as fugitives so that "they will know to the ends of the earth that God rules over Jacob" (v. 13).

I pause to reflect: Do I desire that God be glorified . . . even more than I desire to see my competitors get their deserts? Am I motivated by pride to seek credit for peacemaking, or do I point others to him?

Notice that bold contrast in verse 16. David is carried away into paeans of praise. So moved is he by his Sovereign Lord that he promises to extol his virtues "in the morning." And, to emphasize his intent, David repeats his promise: "I will sing of Your strength, and will joyfully proclaim Your faithful love in the morning. For You have been a stronghold for me, a refuge in my day of trouble" (v. 16).

Personal Prayer
*O Lord God Almighty, You are King of kings, my All in all.
May I never be guilty of seeking revenge for injustices but desire
to point all people—even my opponents—to you.*

MILITARY MARCH

DELIVERANCE

❧ Psalm 60 ❧

You have given a signal flag to those who fear You, so that they can
flee before the archers. Save with Your right hand, and answer me,
so that those You love may be rescued (vv. 4–5).

*B*eing a passionate person, I'll have to admit that there have been times when
I've been angry with God. When bad things happen, when my goals are
blocked, when nothing seems to work out, I feel angry! In turn, my attitude is
displeasing to my Heavenly Father, and he deals with me like the obstinate
child I am.

David is keenly aware that God is sovereign and has absolute control over
victories and defeats. The big threat here is probably the nation of Edom, which
invaded Judah while David was fighting in the north (2 Sam. 8; 1 Kings 11;
1 Chron. 18).

This major defeat is the result of God's anger kindled against his people. The earth has been shaken, and David pleads with the Lord to "heal its
fissures" (v. 2). "You have been angry—now restore us!" he cries.

When God is angry with me and I have felt the earthquake of his displeasure, there is only one hope—to ask for restoration and renewal. Battling with
God is no contest. To withdraw or to move farther away is to prolong healing
and intimacy with him. "Let [me] draw near with a true heart in full assurance
of faith, [my] heart sprinkled clean from an evil conscience and [my] body
washed in pure water" (Heb. 10:22).

Personal Prayer

O God, continue to save me and help me with your right hand. I am so grateful
that your great love and mercy outweigh your anger.

Military March

TRIUMPH

∽ Psalm 60 ∽

God has spoken in His sanctuary: "I will triumph! I will divide up Shechem. I will apportion the Valley of Succoth. Gilead is Mine, Manasseh is Mine, and Ephraim is My helmet; Judah is My scepter. Moab is My washbasin; on Edom I throw My sandal. Over Philistia I shout in triumph" (vv. 6–8).

When I moved my family from Grand Rapids, Michigan, to Nashville, Tennessee, feelings of disorientation, dislocation, and disruption were almost overwhelming. Yet I felt the move was part of God's plan for our lives. Perhaps he wanted us to face our deepest soul longings that can only be fulfilled in him, not in friends or familiar surroundings. He puts us in the place where he wants us!

The psalmist reminds us that because the tribes of Israel belong to God, he will deliver his own and subjugate their enemies. They will be put in their place. God, the Lord of the manor, will parcel out the lands precisely as it suits him.

To Israel, he assigns the lands of Shechem, the Valley of Succoth, Gilead, Manasseh, Ephraim (his helmet of defense), and Judah (his place of rule).

Israel's enemies will become their slaves. Moab will be reduced to the level of a washbasin! God will toss his sandal on Edom! Philistia will hear God's shout of triumph!

Note that all of these lands already belong to God. The Israelites are merely sojourners, tenants, and stewards of all that the Lord has given to them. This gives them both security and an awesome responsibility.

Personal Prayer

O God, I thank you for providing our home, for which we are only tenants for the time you have given us on this earth. May I never forget that, whatever my address, my real dwelling place is with you!

MILITARY MARCH

TRUST

❧ Psalm 60 ❧

Who will bring me to the fortified city? Who will lead me to Edom? Is it not You, God, who have rejected us? God, You do not march out with our armies. Give us aid against the foe, for human help is worthless. With God we will perform valiantly; He will trample our foes (vv. 9–12).

In the ancient world David believes that supernatural power supercedes natural resources. Divine victory comes through trusting and praising God. Human defeat is the result of fearing man and cowering before him. The answers to David's problems almost always come through prayer and praise— a recognition of God's sovereignty.

This is a reminder to me when I'm intimidated by obstacles to success and tempted to depend solely upon human resources—my mind, my talent, the corporation, the weekly paycheck, the marketing team, the sales force, and the professional musicians with whom I work.

In this passage David asks some questions I might ask myself: "Who will lead me to this heathen, fortified city?" (*Am I intimidated by the size and strength of the opposition, or do I trust God to make up for my inadequacies?*) "Who will lead me to Edom?" (*Dare I face my competition without prayer for direction?*) "Is it not you, O God?" (*Are you on my side, Lord? Or, more importantly, Am I on your side?*)

David then declares that human help is worthless and ends this military psalm by pleading with God for aid against the enemy. His faith is strong. God *will* give the victory.

Technology and human ingenuity are no match for the incomparable power of God. Without his inspiration, no matter how well trained or gifted or knowledgeable I may be, I'll fail. Under his banner I march to sure and certain victory!

Personal Prayer

Lord, help me neither to trust in my own abilities and connections nor to flinch in the face of overwhelming obstacles but to depend on your supernatural power.

HIDING IN THEE

LEAD ME TO THE ROCK THAT IS HIGHER THAN I

∽ Psalm 61 ∽

God, hear my cry; pay attention to my prayer. I call to You from the ends of the earth when my heart is without strength. Lead me to a rock that is high above me, (vv. 1–2).

*F*ar from home David is feeling overwhelmed, inadequate, and insecure. Isolation makes one an easy target for discouragement and depression.

From time to time, I've felt this way on a business trip. Differences in time zones, jet lag, and unfamiliar surroundings exacerbate those feelings. And calling home isn't always the answer since problems crop up there too! It's not easy to be God's man in today's world.

Nor was it easy for David. But he didn't allow himself the luxury of sliding into despair. He called on God who "neither slumbers nor sleeps" (see Ps. 121:4). He asked the Lord to lead him to a place of safety, a high refuge—one that he could never attain by himself. Only then will he feel truly safe.

Though I may travel to "the ends of the earth" on business for my company, I'm as close to my Lord as my next prayer.

Personal Prayer

*Lead me today, Father to
"the Rock that is higher than I"!*

A Gospel Hymn Lyric

Hiding in Thee

O safe to the Rock that is higher than I,
My soul in its conflicts and sorrows would fly;
So sinful, so weary—Thine, Thine would I be:
Thou blest "Rock of Ages," I'm hiding in Thee.
Hiding in Thee, Hiding in Thee,
Thou blest "Rock of Ages," I'm hiding in Thee.
Words by William O. Cushing. Music by Ira D. Sankey.

Hiding in Thee

I LONG TO DWELL IN YOUR TENT FOREVER

∞ Psalm 61 ∞

For You have been a refuge for me, a strong tower in the face of the enemy. I will live in Your tent forever, take refuge under the shelter of Your wings. God, You have heard my vows; You have given a heritage to those who fear Your name (vv. 3–5).

There are times when even strong men feel weak and undone. Some time ago, a series of losses changed my life radically and decimated my emotional energy.

David candidly admits his weakness—both physically and emotionally. Now he simply wishes to retreat for a time into the sanctuary of the tent of the Lord. He is likely referring to the tabernacle, that magnificent portable temple of God, built of acacia wood overlaid with gold and hung with blue, purple, and scarlet curtains of finest linen. It was here that God's shekinah glory dwelt in the holy of holies, his presence abiding with David's forebearers during their sojourn in the wilderness. Now, so far from home, David longs for such a physical manifestation of his Lord.

David has made his vows before God, just as I dedicated my life to his service on Word of Life Island when I was a kid. I share David's spiritual inheritance—unlimited and inalienable. In reality, then, I already possess the power of God's attributes, if I lay claim to them, confessing my own unworthiness and weakness.

In these times of retreat, when I'm at the end of myself, I find him in a fresh experience of worship. These episodes had the positive effect of causing me to reevaluate my life critically and forcing me to face "false gods" squarely. It was the beginning of a turning point in my ministry!

Personal Prayer
O God, may I dwell in your place of safety forever.
There may I experience the profound fulfillment of my deepest longings.

HIDING IN THEE

INCREASE THE DAYS OF THE KING'S LIFE

∽ Psalm 61 ∽

Add days to the king's life; may his years span many generations. May he sit enthroned before God forever; appoint faithful love and truth to guard him. Then I will continually sing of Your name, fulfilling my vows day by day (vv. 6–8).

When David prays, "Increase the days of the king's life, his years for many generations," I understand his concern. America is a nation preoccupied with aging.

It's uncomfortable to age. Because I have prematurely silver hair, some people think Karen is my daughter instead of my wife! Even my Dad liked to tell people that he was my brother. Not only that, but I'm surrounded by highly talented, young musicians in an industry dominated by youth.

While much of Western society worships at the shrine of youth, touting wrinkle creams, beauty spas, and fitness clubs as the secret to its preservation, King David knows that there is only one lasting solution. I know it too. To abide in the presence of God forever is to enjoy eternal life—both in duration and in quality. What an answer to deep personal fears and insecurities!

Since this psalm most likely also alludes to the coming Messiah, these blessings will be fulfilled to overflowing in the person of the King of kings and Lord of lords!

No wonder David's intense emotion erupts in exuberant praise. "Then I will continually sing of Your name" (v. 8). He pledges his faithfulness "day after day." The mandate for the believer is a deep, abiding sense of the Lord's love and faithfulness.

Personal Prayer

O Lord, you have numbered my days. Don't let me be so concerned with my own aging process that I miss the blessings of intimate relationship with you, now and in the life to come.

Hymn in Three Stanzas

FIRST STANZA: WAITING IN SILENCE

∽ Psalm 62 ∽

I am at rest in God alone; my salvation comes from Him. He alone is my rock and my salvation, my stronghold; I will not be greatly shaken. How long will you threaten a man? Will all of you attack as if he were a leaning wall or a tottering stone fence? They only plan to bring him down from his high position. They take pleasure in lying; they bless with their mouths, but they curse inwardly (vv. 1–4).

David's life wasn't a bed of roses. He faced an inordinate amount of adversity. He learned, however, to be still under stress—to rest in the Lord.

Rests in music are crucial. A musical rest is a sign that, for a specified time, the music ceases. Contrasts in the arts are highly significant; hence, rests are often as important as the notes. Intervals of silence between tones enhance the beauty and texture of the music. So, also, in life!

The psalmist's calm security and implacable stability come from God. David perceives his Lord as his Rock, his Salvation, his impregnable Fortress. Therefore, he cannot be moved or distracted by the taunts of the wicked.

His enemies, of course, see him in a different light. They view him as vulnerable—"a leaning wall," "a tottering stone fence" (v. 3). Shouting curses and lies, they will attempt to topple David from his lofty position.

Unbelievable strength is drawn, however, in rest—waiting in silence which implies utter trust that the rope will hold, the fortress will stand, the walls won't cave in. No only does salvation come from God, but he gives me those still moments when I gain strength for the battle.

Personal Prayer

O God, I thank you for intervals of silence when, if my soul really listens, I can hear, not the mockery of the world, but your still, small voice.

The Language of Music

Stanza

A stanza is a verse, measure, or refrain.

Songs are made up of stanzas. David is called "Israel's singer of songs" (2 Sam. 23:1 NIV).

HYMN IN THREE STANZAS
SECOND STANZA: TRUSTING IN GOD

✑ Psalm 62 ✑

Rest in God alone, my soul, for my hope comes from Him. He alone is my rock and my salvation, my stronghold; I will not be shaken. My salvation and glory depend on God; my strong rock, my refuge, is in God. Trust in Him at all times, you people; pour out your hearts before Him. God is our refuge (vv. 5–8).

David has a personal relationship with God. This intimacy is observed in his use of the pronoun *my*. Note the phrases: *"my soul," "my hope," "my rock," "my salvation," "my fortress," "my honor," "my strong rock,"* and *"my refuge."* God was not an abstract theological concept to David but his source of hope, safety, deliverance, and unshakeable faith.

On the basis of his experiential knowledge of God, David pleads with other believers to trust in God, to pour out their hearts to him, and to rely on him as their shelter from danger.

This biblical picture of a man is in sharp contrast to the bleak portrait painted by secular existentialism. Yes, *apart from God,* I am fragile and vulnerable. But *in union with God,* I am complete and fulfilled!

Personal Prayer

O God, my Rock and my Refuge, once again I express my trust in you. I pour out my heart to you. I thank you for filling the vacuum of my soul with the hope of your salvation.

A Beloved Gospel Hymn

Rock of Ages

Rock of Ages, cleft for me,
Let me hide myself in Thee;
Let the water and the blood,
From Thy riven side which flowed
Be of sin the double cure,
Cleanse me from its guilt and power.

Nothing in my hands I bring,
Simply to Thy cross I cling;
Naked, some to Thee for dress,
Helpless, to look to thee for grace;
Foul, I to the fountain fly,
Wash me, Savior, or I die!
Words by Augusta M. Toplady. Music by Thomas Hastings.

HYMN IN THREE STANZAS

THIRD STANZA: EXPECTING HIS REWARD

∽ Psalm 62 ∽

Men are only a vapor; exalted men, an illusion. On a balance scale, they go up; together they [weigh] less than a vapor. Place no trust in oppression, or false hope in robbery. If wealth increases, pay no attention to it. God has spoken once; I have heard this twice: strength belongs to God, and faithful love belongs to You, LORD. For You repay each according to his works (vv. 9–12).

I have a tendency to be impressed with a person's status, his level of achievement, her impeccable credentials. David shows us how futile it is to place too much emphasis on human accomplishment. Why? Because all people, regardless of rank or position, are "but a breath."

Another common fallacy in affluent America is our fascination with money-making. We have only to watch the stock market to see that money is an inadequate object for our faith. In a roller-coaster economy, a person who sets his heart on getting rich is skating on thin ice. Both human ingenuity and material prosperity are meaningless when weighted against the majesty and might of God.

Where, then, is the real power in life, the real reward? David shows us the answer in two facets of God's diamondlike character: "You, O God, are strong.... You, O Lord, are loving." On the basis of these two attributes, he will control events so that perfect justice prevails in the end. We can trust that kind of God to reward us accordingly.

Personal Prayer

O God, I thank you that, though I am so weak, you are strong. Even more astounding is that you love me and are planning to reward me "according to what [I have] done."

A Contemporary Lyric

Secret Ambition

Young man on the hillside
Teaching new ways,
Each word winning them over;
Each heart a kindled flame.
Some say, "Death to the radical
He's way out of line!"
Some say, "Praise be the miracle!
God sends a blessed sign—
A blessed sign for troubled times!"
Nobody knew his secret ambition,

Nobody knew his claim to fame;
He broke the old rules steeped in
   tradition,
He tore the holy veil away.
Questioning those in powerful
   position,
Running to those who called his name;
But nobody knew his secret ambition,
Was to give his life away.

Words by Amy Grant and Wayne Kirkpatrick. Music by Michael W. Smith.
© 1988 by O'Ryan Music, Emily Booth, and Fred & Ethel.

PLAIN SONG OF PRAISE
MY SOUL THIRSTS FOR YOU

✑ Psalm 63 ✑

O God, You are my God; I eagerly seek You. My soul thirsts for You; my body faints for You in a land that is dry, desolate, and without water (v. 1).

The desert sands are hot, the heat excruciating, the land parched and dry. David is thirsty. His mouth is as dry as a potsherd. This experience prompts him to reflect on his deep thirst for God.

This first verse of his song is an affirmation of David's faith: "O God, You are my God." The prayer that follows is expressed in three motifs: "I eagerly seek You." "My soul thirsts for You." "My body faints for you." His whole being is in touch and in love with God. Nothing that "dry and desolate land" can provide will satisfy the driving hunger and thirst of his soul.

Much like David's my song "Longing for God" was born out of the hunger and thirst of my soul.

Personal Prayer
Dear Lord, my whole being longs for you today. Please come and let me drink deeply of the living water.

The Language of Music

Plainsong
A form of monophonic, unaccompanied liturgical music.
Also called "plainchant" or "Gregorian chant." Without strict meter, the plainsong is mellifluous, serene music. An example is the Christmas carol, "O Come, O Come, Emmanuel."

A Contemporary Lyric

Longing for God
Like a dry and thirsty land,
I long for you, O Lord!
My parched and hungry soul
Longs for your quenching Word!
May I find you in sweet fellowship,
May I see you in great preaching;

May my heart be moved with your
    love,
May your Spirit work in teaching!
In the shadow of your wings
I sing songs in the night;
In the darkness of this world
I cling to you for light.
Words and music by Don Wyrtzen. © 1980 Singspiration Music.

Plain Song of Praise

I WILL PRAISE YOU AS LONG AS I LIVE

❧ Psalm 63 ❧

*So I gaze on You in the sanctuary to see Your strength and Your glory. My lips will
glorify You because Your faithful love is better than life. So I will praise
You as long as I live; . . . You satisfy me as with rich food; my
mouth will praise You with joyful lips. . . . because You are my help;
I will rejoice in the shadow of Your wings (vv. 2–4a, 5, 7).*

Once David had beheld the power and glory of his Lord, he was never the
same again. Deeply moved by the presence of God in the sanctuary, he was
inspired to write some of the loftiest and most sublime praise music ever written.

Because the love of God also means more to me than life itself, I will
praise him "as long as I live."

Like David, I know the deep satisfaction of composing praise music—
a satisfaction much like that of rich food that satisfies physical hunger.

I long for the kind of divine obsession that drove David to meditate on
the name of the Lord through the watches of the night. As my soul clings to
him, whether in the sanctuary or in the shadows of my life, I pray that my
music will be a reflection of his power, glory, and love.

Personal Prayer

*Dear Lord, I want to praise you as long as I live!
Kindle in me a fire of passion until the
words and music flow through my purified soul.*

A Contemporary Lyric

As Long As I Live

As long as I live, he will be supreme,
As long as I live, he will be my theme;
As long as I live, this will be my dream—
Jesus, the Source of lasting joy.
Jesus, the Source of lasting joy,
Giving life abundantly;
Jesus, the Source of lasting joy,
He's my only security.
Words and music by Don Wyrtzen. © 1982 Singspiration Music.

Plain Song of Praise

THEY WHO SEEK MY LIFE WILL BE DESTROYED

∽ Psalm 63 ∽

But those who seek to destroy my life will go into the depths of the earth.
They will be given over to the power of the sword; they will become the jackals'
prey. But the king will rejoice in God; all who swear by Him will boast,
for the mouths of liars will be shut (vv. 9–11).

There is more than one way to "destroy" life. A sarcastic comment can cut like a sword. When it is premeditated, the wound is even deeper. Gossip, often without basis in fact, can be a lethal weapon. "The tongue is a small part of the body.... Consider how large a forest a small fire ignites" (James 3:5).

It's much easier to be a critic than a creator—to pick apart someone's work rather than to put together something new. How insidious we are with our criticism! "So and so is terrific, *but . . .*" These negative evaluations tear down those who are made in God's image and destroy the creative process as well. The church needs to become much more tolerant of creative people. Art doesn't flourish in the harsh winds of criticism. A bitter spirit can't break forth into beautiful song.

King David knew all about verbal sword play as well as physical attack. His enemies were ever lurking in the shadows. In this psalm he has been personally absorbed in praising God until some incident or memory triggers his thoughts about his enemies, and he is forced to contemplate the judgment of the wicked. The destroyers will themselves be destroyed and swallowed up into the depths of the earth. They will be devoured by the sword, and their bodies will be thrown to the jackals. "The mouths of liars will be shut" (v. 11). It seems a fitting punishment for the crime.

What a contrast for King David and contemporary Christians as well! We, who have been delivered, spontaneously burst forth into affirmations of belief in God's name and songs of praise. When the Lord meets our needs, as he works in our lives, when he defuses the venomous words and deeds of our critics, we praise him!

Personal Prayer

Dear Lord, I rejoice in your holy name and thank you for helping me deal with criticism. Turn the words of my critics into praises to you!

DRONE-PIPE OF JUDGMENT

DRONE OF COMPLAINT

∽ Psalm 64 ∽

God, hear my voice when I complain. Protect my life from the terror of the enemy. Hide me from the scheming of the wicked, from the mob of evildoers, who sharpen their tongues like swords and aim bitter words like arrows, shooting from concealed places at the innocent. They shoot at him suddenly and are not afraid. They encourage each other in an evil plan; they talk about hiding traps and say, "Who will see them?" They devise crimes [and say,] "We have perfected a secret plan." The inner man and the heart are mysterious (vv. 1–6).

A drone-pipe is the lowest tone on the bagpipe, used for accompaniment. It is often used as a pedal point—a long, sustained bass note against which changing harmonies sound.

Like so many of David's psalms, my prayers often take on the monotonous tone of complaint. Here David is overwhelmed by the malicious schemes of that "noisy crowd," the wicked. "They shoot from concealed places at the innocent!" (v. 4). What a natural tendency it is to counterattack—to "sharpen [our] tongues like swords" and to "aim [our] words like arrows" (v. 3).

Yet beneath the apparent bitterness and complaining is a ground bass, an insistent pedal point: "Hear me, O God. . . . Hear me, O God. . . . Hear me, O God." David's emphasis is not on his grumbling but on God!

Caught in the cross fire of slanderous speech and hidden snares, he acknowledges the Sovereign Lord as his ultimate Arbiter, the supreme Peacemaker. David may drone on indefinitely about his woes, but he always turns to the Lord for protection and justice.

Personal Prayer

Hear me, O God! If I must be monotonous, let it be in singing your praises!

The Language of Music

Drone-Pipe

The lowest tone used for accompaniment on the bagpipe.

It can refer to any long sustained bass note. It is often used as a pedal point (a long-held bass note against which changing harmonies sound). God's judgment is like a drone-pipe underneath the rapidly changing textures of human history.

DRONE-PIPE OF JUDGMENT
PROPHECY OF PRAISE

✍ Psalm 64 ✍

But God will shoot them with arrows; suddenly, they will be wounded. They will be made to stumble; their own tongues work against them. All who see them will shake their heads. Then everyone will fear and will tell about God's work, for they will understand what He has done. The righteous rejoice in the LORD and take refuge in Him; all the upright in heart offer praise (vv. 7–10).

When I'm tempted to question certain inequities in my world, I need to be reminded that the administration of a just God promises perfect objectivity and lack of prejudice . . . *someday.* Such a God can be counted on to balance the scales.

Ironically the people who are bringing me the most grief, those who dare to wage war against God, will be brought down by their own words and schemes. God is in control!

Over and over again, I read the psalmist's litany of grievances, his pleas for protection, and, at last, his songs of praises. I've wondered, sometimes, just why God felt it necessary to be so repetitious in recording his Word.

In music, repetition is vital! Beethoven was a master at taking a little bit of material—sometimes just one short theme—and repeating it in a kaleidoscope of musical variations. The psalmists did the same thing. They hammered away at similar motifs and themes repeatedly. Perhaps the ancient Israelites were like us—slow learners! Like the ocean, music is cyclical—it thrives on thematic repetition, development, and variety.

God is teaching me—pounding out the truth in every heartbeat, in every rhythmic cycle of nature, in the echoes of his love—that he is the Sovereign Lord of my life. *Someday* he will be feared and respected by all mankind because of his swift enactment of justice. *Someday* all the righteous will rejoice and take refuge in him. *Someday* "at the name of Jesus every knee [will] bow . . . and every tongue should confess that Jesus Christ is Lord" (Phil. 2:10–11).

Personal Prayer

O Lord, I rejoice in you today. My heart leaps in recognition of another continuous theme—the insistent, steady reminder of your love!

CONCERTO OF GRATITUDE

HIS BLESSING

∽ Psalm 65 ∽

Praise is rightfully Yours, God, in Zion; vows to You will be fulfilled. All humanity will come to You, the One who hears prayer. Iniquities overwhelm me; only You can atone for our rebellions. How happy is the one You choose and bring near to live in Your courts! We will be satisfied with the goodness of Your house, the holiness of Your temple (vv. 1–4).

God is so good; God is so good; God is so good . . . He's so good to me." The words of this chorus reflect the view of ancient believers who celebrated this life-sustaining affirmation in conjunction with the barley harvest (Lev. 23). This psalm holds the key to the "utter fulfillment, blissful happiness, and complete contentment" available to modern-day believers as well.

In meditation, I review God's blessings on my life—salvation, answered prayer, Christian fellowship. I'll never forget the night, when I was seven, my mom led me to the Lord. I was afraid and upset. She comforted me with Christ's words in John 6:37: "All the Father giveth me shall come to me; and him that cometh to me I will in no wise cast out" (KJV). Upon accepting that promise, peace and serenity displaced my childish fears. Since then, I have felt God's hand of provision. Once when Karen and I were down to our last nickel, an unexpected royalty check put food on our table!

Finally, like the temple worshippers, I have been chosen and brought near to life in his courts! What sublime happiness awaits me for the rest of my life and through all eternity. All the good things of his house are mine! Where will I experience real happiness and a rich, inner satisfaction? Only in the presence of the Lord.

Personal Prayer

O God, my Savior, thank you for saving me, for sustaining me, and for giving me all the good things of your house.

CONCERTO OF GRATITUDE

HIS POWER

∽ Psalm 65 ∽

You answer us in righteousness, with awe-inspiring works, God of our salvation, the hope of all the ends of the earth and of the distant seas; You establish the mountains by Your power, robed with strength; You silence the roar of the seas, the roar of their waves, and the tumult of the nations. Those who live far away are awed by Your signs; You make east and west shout for joy (vv. 5–8).

We Americans are obsessed with power. We want to climb higher, run farther, move faster than any other generation in history. Our psychologists delve into the recesses of inner space, while our scientists explore outer space. All America held its breath when Neil Armstrong stepped onto the moon! Sometimes, when I take the express elevator to the top of the Sears Tower in Chicago, I wonder if we are even guilty of erecting our own twentieth-century towers of Babel.

As a kid I used to watch the Atlantic Ocean roar off the New Jersey coastline. I've observed Niagara Falls many times from different vantage points, including the excursion boat at the foot of the Falls! And I've peered into the crater atop Mt. St. Helens via videotape, helicopter, and television. God's omnipotence evidenced in nature dwarfs even the most splendid of man's puny achievements.

But this God of might and majesty is also intensely personal. He is intimate as well as infinite. He who "formed the mountains" and "stilled the roaring of the seas" hears every whispered prayer.

Such a God inspires me to hope. He "calls forth songs of joy" from my soul until I can hardly wait to transcribe them to paper!

Personal Prayer

O God, my Savior, thank you for your power, which not only formed the world but also keeps my spirit alive with joy!

CONCERTO OF GRATITUDE
HIS PROVISION

∽ Psalm 65 ∽

You visit the earth and water it abundantly, enriching it greatly. God's stream is filled with water, for You prepare the earth in this way, providing [people] with grain. You soften it with showers and bless its growth, soaking its furrows and leveling its ridges. You crown the year with Your goodness; Your ways overflow with plenty. The wilderness pastures overflow, and the hills are robed with joy. The pastures are clothed with flocks, and the valleys covered with grain. They shout in triumph; indeed, they sing (vv. 9–13).

Human striving and struggle to attain is often disappointing. Always wanting more and never being satisfied feeds on itself and produces greed, lust, and discontentment. What a waste of energy!

In these exalted verses the psalmist tells us a simpler way to be happy. He points us to God who answers prayer not in the abstract but specifically and in intricate detail. Look at the exquisite lines in verses 9 through 13. He waters the land, enriches it abundantly, drenches its furrows, levels its ridges, softens it with showers, and blesses its crops. The carts are filled to overflowing with grain. Even the desert flourishes, and the hills are "clothed with gladness."

God is not only the consummate Husbandman; he knows all about the music business too! He knows what it takes to take a song from its germ idea—often a title, sometimes a "hook," a chorus, or a musical phrase—through the various stages of development. Fine craftsmanship is imperative. Then comes reevaluating, rewriting, polishing.

Whatever my need—whether shepherding a single song through the recording process, developing a major new recording artist, or fulfilling my role as husband and father—my God has all the answers. His concern for every minute detail of my work and existence prompts me to shout for joy!

Personal Prayer
O God, my Savior, thank you for caring about every aspect of my life and answering my smallest prayer with your bounty.

The Language of Music

Concerto
A musical composition for solo and orchestra.

The soloist is usually a pianist or violinist. The form is similar to the classical sonata. Tchaikousky's B-Flat Major Concerto and Rachmaninoff's Second Piano Concerto are notable examples.

CALL TO REMEMBRANCE
"COME AND SEE WHAT GOD HAS DONE!"

∽ Psalm 66 ∽

Shout joyfully to God, all the earth! Sing the glory of His name; make His praise glorious. . . . Come and see the works of God; His acts toward mankind are awe-inspiring. . . . For You, God, tested us; You refined us as silver is refined. You lured us into a trap; You placed burdens on our backs. You let men ride over our heads; we went through fire and water, but You brought us out to abundance (vv. 1–2, 5, 10–12).

"Come and see what God has done," exhorts the psalmist. Israel is encouraged to remember past victories and to join in a song of deliverance. Strong verbs signal the personal involvement of surrounding nations: "Shout with joy!" "Sing to the glory of his name!" "Make his praise glorious!"

Israel has reason to rejoice. God has performed "awesome works"—the parting of the Red Sea, the routing of rebels, the overthrow of dangerous enemies, the provision of his presence in times of severe testing and trial. The Israelites have come through a painful process of purification much like the refining of silver. "You, God, tested us; You refined us as silver" (v. 10). To remove impurities the smelter must fire his furnace to at least 1,761 degrees F. According to Pliny in his *Hostiria Naturalis,* "the ore was washed and sieved five times, fused with lead, and then cupelled for pure silver."

God is faithful to lead us through the fire and water to a place of "abundance" (v. 12). Jesus says, "I have come that they may have life and have it in full" (John 10:10). I find a place of fullness and intimacy with my Lord when I follow where he leads.

Personal Prayer

Dear Lord, I praise you for walking with me through the fire and water of purification so that I may enjoy you forever in the "place of abundance."

A Song Borne of Grief

When Thou Passest Through the Waters

When thou passest through the waters, I will be with thee,
When thou passest thru the waters,
I will be with thee;

And thru the rivers, they shall not overflow thee,
When thou walkest thru the fire,
thou shalt not be burned.
When thou passest thru the waters,
I will be with thee.

Words and music by Don Wyrtzen. © 1979 by Singspiration Music. (From Isa. 43:2.)

CALL TO REMEMBRANCE

"COME AND LISTEN!"

∽ Psalm 66 ∽

*Come and listen, all who fear God, and I will tell what He has done for me. I cried
out to Him with my mouth, and praise was on my tongue. If I had been aware of
malice in my heart, the Lord would not have listened. However, God has listened;
He has paid attention to the sound of my prayer. May God be praised! He has
not turned away my prayer or turned His faithful love from me (vv. 16–20).*

What did an Old Testament believer do when he was in the furnace of
God's testing, when he was on a "guilt trip"? He fulfilled his vows to the
Lord. He went to the temple to present burnt offerings, animals "without spot
or blemish," as a sacrifice for sin. Why? Because "without the shedding of
blood there is no forgiveness" (Heb. 9:22).

Karen and I once had an interesting conversation with a well-known
songwriter. He was having a hard time accepting the gospel. The Old
Testament blood sacrifices seemed primitive and barbaric to him, and he
could not conceive of a loving God sacrificing his own Son!

Each time a choice animal was killed and the white wool was stained
crimson with its life's blood, the worshipper received a graphic message of sub-
stitutionary death. God's refrain echoed again and again: "I love you. I love
you. I love you." Because of God's great love, that ancient believer saw with his
own eyes the staggering cost of sin and the amazing grace that guarantees our
redemption.

God's full forgiveness follows *sincere* repentance. "If I had been aware of
malice in my heart, the Lord would not have listened" (v. 18). But the Lord does
listen to the psalmist's heartfelt confession and pours out his love in response.

Twenty-one centuries later you and I have the benefit of the gospel message
that was foretold in those Old Testament rites: "For God so loved the world in
this way: He gave His One and Only Son, so that everyone who believes in Him
will not perish but have eternal life" (John 3:16). Therefore, I am filled with joy
and thanksgiving because I am forgiven, cleansed, and absolved from guilt! I am
now free to accept myself because the Lord accepts my prayer and does not
withhold his love from me.

Personal Prayer
*O Lord, I can't keep silent! You inspire me to write and to sing
songs of thanksgiving for the miracle of your love and forgiveness!*

SHINE ON ME

∾ Psalm 67 ∾

*May God be gracious to us and bless us; look on us with favor
so that Your way may be known on earth, Your salvation among all nations.
Let the peoples praise You, God; let all the peoples praise You (vv. 1–3).*

The LORD bless you and keep you;
the LORD make his face shine upon you
 and be gracious to you;
the LORD turn his face toward you
 and give you peace (Num. 6:24–26).

So Aaron and his sons blessed the Israelites in ancient times. This familiar benediction has been blessing people for generations.

In this passage the composer uses the metaphor of light: "May God . . . make his face shine upon us" (v. 1), followed by a trio of eternal themes: God's grace (vv. 1–2), praise of the peoples (vv. 3–5), and God's blessing (vv. 6–7).

I can envision a scenario in which the worship leaders, the congregation, and God all play vital roles. See it with me. It could go something like this:

Pastor or worship leader: O God, may your unmerited favor rest upon us, and may the light of your countenance flood our hearts and minds with all spiritual understanding. Then we can be your witnesses, your living letters, bringing proof of your salvation and love to all nations on earth.

Congregation: In this praise gathering, we lift our voices to you, O God! We are but one tribe, one nation among many who rejoice to see justice and perfect leadership. We express the utmost joy and gladness in you today.

God's blessing: "If my people, who are called by my name, will humble themselves and pray and seek my face and turn from their wicked ways, then will I hear from heaven and will forgive their sin and will heal their land" (2 Chron. 7:14 NIV).

God is speaking. We must listen. As he shines upon us, we'll reflect his glory.

Personal Prayer
Joyful, joyful, I adore you, God of glory, Lord of light!

CELEBRATION OF CONQUEST

EXTOLLING GOD

⊱ Psalm 68 ⊰

But the righteous are glad; they rejoice before God and celebrate with joy. Sing to God! Sing praises to His name. Exalt Him who rides on the clouds—His name is Yahweh—and rejoice before Him. A father of the fatherless and a champion of widows is God in His holy dwelling. God provides homes for those who are deserted. He leads out the prisoners to prosperity, but the rebellious live in a scorched land (vv. 3–6).

The more intimately I come to know God, the more I am awed by his grace and goodness. Through David's eyes, I see even more clearly God's compassionate nature as well as his majesty and power.

This song accompanied a ritual procession celebrating God's conquests and victories on behalf of Israel. David begins by praying that God will show his awesome power to the wicked by "blowing them away" (v. 2). Then he moves almost immediately to praise, urging his followers to honor and extol the Lord for his tender care. He is the Father of the fatherless, the Defender of the widows, the Caring One who sets the lonely in families, the Deliverer of prisoners.

I have a dad whom I respect and admire, so I don't know what it's like to be fatherless. But my friend, Margaret Clarkson, hymn writer par excellence, never knew her father, and I can read the depth of her pain in her lyrics. I will never be a widow, but my mother-in-law, Ruth Parr, lost her husband some time ago. I don't know exactly how she feels, but I hear her crying sometimes. I have a friend who has been in prison; and, while I haven't served a jail sentence, I imprison myself sometimes behind bars of isolation and remoteness, even with my family around me! But I know our Heavenly Father can meet every one of these needs and so many more, if we let him, for he is our source of consummate security, shelter, and safety.

> **The Language of Music**
>
> ## Celebration
> The public performance of sacraments or ceremonies with appropriate rites.
>
> A festive, religious ceremony or worship service where the Lord is acclaimed and extolled.

When I experience God in his gentleness, I am compelled to join in the chorus of praises to his name. He is my Father, my Defender, my Provider, my Redeemer!

Personal Prayer

O God, I rejoice before you today. May I continue to see you not only as the omnipotent Rider of the clouds but as the tender Shepherd.

CELEBRATION OF CONQUEST
REMEMBERING THE CONQUEROR

∽ Psalm 68 ∽

Mount Bashan is God's towering mountain; Mount Bashan is a mountain of many peaks. Why gaze with envy, you mountain peaks, at the mountain God desired for His dwelling? The LORD *will live [there] forever! God's chariots are tens of thousands, thousands and thousands; the Lord is among them in the sanctuary as He was at Sinai. You ascended to the heights, taking away captives; You received gifts from people, even from the rebellious, so that the* LORD *God might live [there] (vv. 15–18).*

Sometimes I need to step back and take a look at where I've been before I can discern where I'm going or how I'm going to get here. These times of inventory are not always preplanned, but it occurs to me that midway through the year is a natural time to take stock.

David must have felt much the same way since so many of his psalms review Israel's glorious history—from her trek through the wilderness to her conquest of the promised land (vv. 7–10). The psalmist then describes the occupation of Canaan where wicked kings were routed and driven out (vv. 11–14).

This psalm brings to mind some of my own wilderness wanderings. It's easy to get lost on the pilgrim journey when you tend to live in a fog. Creative people are like that. Maybe I'm too laid back, not decisive enough. Or maybe I don't always discipline myself enough. But I'm thankful that even at these times my Lord knows the way!

The climax of the passage comes in the form of exquisite poetry (vv. 15–18), depicting God ascending Mt. Zion, a mighty conqueror with "thousands and thousands" (v. 17) of chariots, and "taking away captives" (v. 18). The apostle Paul uses this metaphor to illustrate the spiritual victory that believers experience in Christ (Eph. 4:8). This song also recalls the siege of Jerusalem by David's army and his establishing the ark of the covenant there.

My life gains fresh perspective when I count my victories, not my losses, and focus on the Conqueror. God himself has escorted me through the wastelands, has cared for me tenderly when I was troubled and tired, and has even conquered death (vv. 19–20) as a guarantee of my eternal life in him. Such a conquering Savior demands my highest praise and adoration!

Personal Prayer

O God, thank you for reminding me of your comforting presence through some tangled times. I praise you, my Savior, for rescuing me and leading me to the mountaintop where I will dwell with you forever!

CELEBRATION OF CONQUEST
ASSESSING HIS VICTORY

∽ Psalm 68 ∽

People have seen Your procession, God, the procession of my God, my King, in the sanctuary. Singers lead the way, with musicians following; among them are young women playing tambourines. Praise God in the assemblies; [praise] the LORD from the fountain of Israel. . . . God, You are awe-inspiring in Your sanctuaries. The God of Israel gives power and strength to His people. May God be praised! (vv. 24–26, 35).

I love a parade! I remember taking our kids, D. J. and Kathy, when they were small to the Fourth of July parade in Cascade, a suburb of Grand Rapids, Michigan. There were homemade floats, decorated bikes with streamers in the wheels, and even an old fire tender with water spewing forth in all directions. Parades are exciting!

God's triumphal entrance into Zion is pictured as a victory parade, complete with singers, dancers, and musicians. Led by the little tribe of Benjamin, they all are praising God in the assembly.

David ends this celebration psalm with a moving call to praise the God "who rides in the ancient, highest heavens" and "thunders with His powerful voice" (v. 33). God's power is awesome, and he bestows strength on his people.

May my vision of the Lord increase to the magnitude of David's vision! May I resonate with the awareness that if I open up to him and cultivate spiritual receptivity, I will receive more of his awesome power and strength in my life. Praise be to God!

Personal Prayer

O Lord, I join the artists, musicians, and singers of the ancient world in worshipping you in all of your power, majesty, and glory!

A Contemporary Praise Song

El Shaddai

El Shaddai, El Shaddai,
El Eloy na Adonai
Age to age You're still the same
By the power of the name;
Er kanka na Adonai—
We will praise and lift You high,
El Shaddai
Thru Your love and thru the ram

You saved the son of Abraham,
Thru the power of Your hand
You turned the sea into dry land;
And by Your might You set Your Children free.
Your most awesome work was done
Thru the frailty of Your Son,
I will praise You till I die,
El Shaddai.

Words by Michael Card. Music by John W. Thompson.
© 1981 and arr. © 1983 Whole Armor Publishing Company.

ODE TO HOPE

THE LORD HEARS

✍ Psalm 69 ✍

I will praise God's name with song and exalt Him with thanksgiving. That will please the LORD more than an ox, more than a bull with horns and hooves. The humble will see it and rejoice. You who seek God, take heart! For the LORD listens to the needy and does not despise His own who are prisoners (vv. 30–33).

Our Lord is like the shepherd who knows each individual sheep intimately and by name. He is also like the symphony conductor who not only hears the grand ensemble of the orchestra but can also single out each individual part.

The ear of the Lord is tuned to the hearts of his people. "When he cries out to me, I will hear, for I am compassionate" (Exod. 22:27 NIV).

David is counting on that compassion. He comes before the Lord with singing, knowing that the sounds of thanksgiving will be more pleasing than burnt offerings, "an ox . . . [or] a bull with horns and hooves" (v. 31). In turn, this sacrifice of praise will be heard by all in the assembly, and the hearts of the people will be encouraged.

As the psalmist gains personal strength and hope in the process of praising the Lord, he urges others to join him in the glad chorus. All is not lost! We are not alone in our pain and distress. He hears! He hears!

Personal Prayer
O God, you know the sounds of my distress.
You hear me when I sing your praises.
May I never fail to hear your voice—
comforting, guiding, instructing, warning.

ODE TO HOPE

DAVID FEELS LOW . . .

ᴥ Psalm 69 ᴥ

Save me, God, for the water has risen to my neck. . . . I am weary from my crying; my throat is parched. My eyes fail, looking for my God. Those who hate me without cause are more numerous than the hairs of my head; my deceitful enemies, who would destroy me, are powerful. Though I did not steal, I must repay (vv. 1, 3–4).

There is nothing more disconcerting than being unjustly accused, since denial is the weakest form of defense. David finds himself in just such a no-win situation in this psalm.

His enemies, some of whom are important city officials, despise him, and even his own relatives have disowned him. He feels like a drowning man! "The waters has risen to my neck" (v. 1); "I sink in the mud" (v. 2); "I have come into deep waters, the flood sweeps over me" (v. 2). His enemies sing cynical songs about him and mock him.

What's significant here is that David is suffering not because of sin but as a consequence of zealously following the Lord. He puts on sackcloth, signifying mourning, and pours out his heart to the Lord.

Music is probably the richest of all art forms because it speaks to all levels of the personality simultaneously. One doesn't relate to a powerful piece of music cognitively only, but emotionally and physically as well. Hence we use music to speak the unspeakable, to express the inexpressible—sorrow, discouragement, anger, bitterness, joy. And we use it when words are not enough.

David uses poetic lament to vent his sense of personal injustice. I'm encouraged by his honesty. I am made aware again that not all suffering is the result of sin. Christ himself suffered the greatest injustice of all, precisely because he was pure and righteous. Following him sometimes leads me into uncomfortable circumstances, but I'm in good company!

Personal Prayer
*Dear God, teach me how to embrace your sufferings
so I can share in the delights of your kingdom,
and may I use the gift of music to share
the secrets of your caring with others.*

ODE TO HOPE

DAVID PRAYS . . .

♋ Psalm 69 ♋

But as for me, LORD, my prayer to You is for a time of favor. In Your abundant, faithful love, God, answer me with Your sure salvation. . . . Answer me, LORD, for Your faithful love is good; in keeping with Your great compassion, turn to me. Don't hide Your face from Your servant, for I am in distress. Answer me quickly! Draw near to me and redeem me; ransom me because of my enemies (vv. 13, 16–18).

No one has ever prayed with more fervor than David. His intensity is equal to his need, graphically described in these phrases: "Rescue me from the miry mud; don't let me sink, Let me be rescued. . . . Don't let the floodwaters sweep over me or the deep swallow me up; don't let the pit close its mouth over me" (vv. 14–15).

Ninety-nine out of a hundred persons will not go through the hard work of letting the Lord excise the pain from their lives. Denial, changing external behaviors, and maintaining proper images are attempted shortcuts to maturity for most people.

David refuses to resort to that kind of evasive maneuver. He is facing reality here, and I can learn something from his prayer. He appeals to the Lord on the basis of (1) his timing, "in the time of favor" (v. 13); and (2) his purposes, "your sure salvation" (v. 13). Yet his overriding desire seems to be that God's justice prevail (v. 18). Maybe this is the secret to power in prayer. When selfish desires are yielded to the Lord, his name is glorified and his purposes fulfilled.

Often I try to hurry God or attempt to manipulate him for my own ends. I need to be aware that I limit his work in my life when I confine him to the present moment rather than the time span of eternity. When I'm in trouble, I need to pray for his name to be magnified through my circumstances, in his timing, for the salvation of souls.

Personal Prayer
Dear Lord, you are the Giver of life, but you are also my Lifesaver in times of deep trouble.

Petition

O GOD, SAVE ME!

ᔆ Psalm 70 ᔆ

God, deliver me. Hurry to help me, Lord! Let those who seek my life be disgraced and confounded; let those who wish me harm be driven back and humiliated. Let those who say, "Aha, aha!" retreat because of their shame (vv. 1–3).

For years I've dreaded deadlines. Enormous pressure builds when there is a full symphony recording session booked for tomorrow and the scores aren't done even though there has been pacing and discipline. Often there is only time for a hasty "Help, Lord!"

David is again in dire straits. His life is in danger and his reputation at stake (v. 2). God must act quickly, or David's adversaries will press their advantage. With his enemies breathing down his neck, he cries, "O God, save me!"

The apostle Peter had a similar experience in New Testament times. Like his Lord, he walked on water. "But when he saw the wind, he was afraid and, beginning to sink, cried out, 'Lord, save me!'"

Along with David and Peter, I can praise the Lord for responding to life's emergencies with his grace and deliverance.

Personal Prayer

Hurry, Lord! I need the strength of your presence right now . . . this hour . . . this minute! And hasten the coming of your kingdom on earth, as it is in heaven.

PETITION

LET GOD BE EXALTED!

✍ Psalm 70 ✍

Let all who seek You rejoice and be glad in You; let those who love Your salvation continually say, "God is great!" But I am afflicted and needy; hurry to me, God. You are my help and my deliverer; LORD, do not delay (vv. 4–5).

There is no trumped-up worship experience here, no empty ritual or phony program. David is brutally honest with himself and with God in facing the reality of his plight. But he doesn't stay in the doldrums. He shifts his focus from problems to praise.

He revels in exalting the Lord and in expressing the love he feels for him. The Lord is his Help and Deliverer. Though David is poor and needy, surely the Lord will come to his aid without delay.

As I actively seek the Lord, I find great joy in him. I delight in my salvation, in the help and deliverance he offers. Thank you, Lord.

Personal Prayer

O God, may you be lifted to the highest position of praise, honor, and power in my life!

A Song of Praise

Praise My Soul, the King of Heaven

Praise my soul, the King of heaven.
To His feet thy tribute bring;
Ransomed, healed, restored, forgiven,
Evermore His praises sing.
Praise Him for His grace and favor
To our fathers in distress;
Praise Him, still the same as ever,
Slow to chide, and swift to bless.
Fatherlike, He tends and spares us;
Well our feeble frame He knows;
In His hands He gently bears us,
Rescues us from all our foes.
Words by Henry F. Lyte. Music by Henry Smart.

LIFESTYLE OF DEPENDENCE

CONFIDENCE

❧ Psalm 71 ❧

LORD, I seek refuge in You; never let me be disgraced. In Your justice, rescue and deliver me; listen closely to me and save me. Be a rock of refuge for me, where I can always go. Give the command to save me, for You are my rock and fortress. Deliver me, My God, from the hand of the wicked, from the grasp of the unjust and oppressive (vv. 1–4).

This psalmist is most likely an older person who has experienced the marvelous faithfulness of God for a lifetime. He knows his Psalter well, for he quotes Psalms 22, 31, 35, and 40, and vows to continue praising God. He also asks for deliverance from the wicked men who seek to harm him and who mock him for his faith.

He has supreme confidence in the Lord's ability to save. He pictures the Lord as his Refuge, his Rock, and his Fortress. He knows that the only reliable place of safety and security is with the Lord.

I have observed some benefits of growing older in the Lord. For example, there is nothing so full of character as the time-worn, wrinkled face of one of God's prayer warriors, glowing with a radiance that no cosmetic on earth can bestow. The practice of praise produces inner beauty, seasons the spirit, develops prayer muscle. Older saints have learned the paradox that dependence on the Lord is the secret to perfect freedom! Like the great hymns of the faith, these dear men and women of God grow more precious as time goes by.

Personal Prayer

O Lord, you are my Refuge, my Rock, and my Fortress.
May I learn to lean on you more completely.

LIFESTYLE OF DEPENDENCE
HOPE

∽ Psalm 71 ∽

*For You are my hope, Lord GOD, my confidence from my youth. I have leaned on You
from birth; You took me from my mother's womb. My praise is always about You.
I have become an ominous sign to many, but You are my strong refuge. My mouth
is full of praise and honor to You all day long. Don't discard me in my old age:
as my strength fails, do not abandon me (vv. 5–9).*

This psalmist believes in the sovereignty of God—that the Lord, the Supreme Ruler of the universe, has everything under his control. Not only is he sovereign, but he sustains. From birth, through youth, into the middle years and beyond, the psalmist has felt his sustaining grace.

In music we use the fermata (musical pause or hold) to indicate that a note is to be sustained or held. Breaking the rhythmic pace of a piece adds texture and variety. Sustained notes have emphasis because of their staying power. A person can likewise exhibit strong character through endurance, persistence, and continuance in habits of holiness.

Now that the psalmist is growing older, however, he is afraid. He fears losing his strength (v. 9). He fears his enemies (v. 10). He even fears the possibility that the Lord will forsake him (v. 11). Still, he is honest and forthright about his anxieties and cries out to God who has always been his safe haven. He prays for "staying power" as he faces the challenges of aging.

As I grow older, I need to build my confidence on my own life history with the Lord. He has never failed to meet my needs. He has always taken care of me. He has proven himself faithful and has been my confidence and hope "since my youth." I know I can rely on him to take care of me today . . . and tomorrow.

Personal Prayer
*O Lord, you are fully trustworthy. I rest myself in you for the
remaining days of my life and into all eternity!*

LIFESTYLE OF DEPENDENCE

PRAISE

∽ Psalm 71 ∽

Therefore, with a lute I will praise You for Your faithfulness, my God; I will sing to You with a harp, Holy One of Israel. My lips will shout for joy when I sing praise to You, because You have redeemed me. Therefore, my tongue will proclaim Your righteousness all day long, for those who seek my harm will be disgraced and confounded (vv. 22–24).

Repetition teaches and reinforces. This psalmist has learned how to praise the Lord by praising—repeatedly, continually, for a lifetime. He revels in the subject of his praise—God's faithfulness and righteousness (v. 16). He delights in the act of praise—"with a harp" (v. 22); "with a lute" (v. 22); with "my lips" (v. 23); and "my tongue" (v. 24).

Musicians have a divine mandate to live a lifestyle of praise. I thrill to the variety of musical instruments mentioned in the book of Psalms and to the parts of the body used in praising the Lord. Hands clap and strum; lips shout; vocal cords resonate and sing; tongues confess and testify; feet dance! Our bodies are created to perform a symphony of praise! As temples of the Holy Spirit, our bodies are sacred sanctuaries, to be used for his glory, not for our selfish desires. Worship begins with the imagination and the heart, but it must expand outward until our nerve endings tingle with praise.

The longer I live, the more evidence I gather of God's grace and glory. As I practice praise, I become more proficient in expressing my love and gratitude to him. Like the elderly psalmist, I've experienced some dissonant moments, when it appeared there was no resolution, only to find that God was orchestrating these events for my good. "We know that in all things work together for the good of those who love God: those who are called according to His purpose" (Rom. 8:28).

Personal Prayer

O Lord, teach me how to praise you and remind me to practice until my heart sings in perfect harmony with your will.

SOLOMON'S SONG

HIS JUSTICE

❧ Psalm 72 ❧

God, give Your justice to the king and Your righteousness to the king's son.
He will judge Your people with righteousness and Your afflicted ones
with justice. . . . May he vindicate the afflicted among the people, help
the poor, and crush the oppressor. May he continue while the sun endures,
and as long as the moon, throughout all generations (vv. 1–2, 4–5).

Solomon most likely composed both Psalm 72 and Psalm 127. In this first psalm, he is probably describing his reign as well as the millennial reign of Christ, for he speaks of righteousness, peace, and long-term prosperity.

While he has the good judgment to ask God's blessing on his own administration, "God, give Your justice to the King" (v. 1), it seems clear that Solomon is referring also to the coming messianic kingdom that "will endure as long as the sun, as long as the moon, through all generations" (v. 5).

What can I learn from Solomon? First, I admire his verbal artistry. "He [Jesus] will be like rain that falls on the cut grass, like spring showers that water the earth. May the righteous flourish in his days, and prosperity abound till the moon is no more" (vv. 6–7).

But I also am deeply moved by Solomon's personal ethics. "He will judge Your people with righteousness. . . . He will defend the afflicted among the people and save the children of the needy; he will crush the oppressor" (vv. 2, 4). Solomon is worthy of emulation in my business dealings and in the practice of my faith.

Without Christ's love in my heart, I might be tempted to lapse into neglect of the talented people who come through my office. But I operate my work on Christian principles, nurturing musical gifts for the glory of God, not for selfish gain. I look for opportunities to hear the unheard and to stand firmly against outside influences that would dilute the Christian message of our music. Living a life of integrity may not promote material rewards, but it promises spiritual prosperity!

Personal Prayer

Lord, reign in my heart and bring your justice and
righteousness to every area of my life!

SOLOMON'S SONG

HIS RULE

∽ Psalm 72 ∽

And let all kings bow down to him, all nations serve him. For he will rescue the poor who cry out and the afflicted who have no helper. He will have pity on the poor and helpless and save the lives of the poor. He will redeem them from oppression and violence, for their lives are precious in his sight (vv. 11–14).

Solomon's reign was lengthy and far-reaching, extending "from sea to sea and from the Euphrates to the ends of the earth" (v. 8). He received tribute from "the kings of Tarshish" and gifts from "the kings of Sheba and Seba" (v. 10). He was widely worshipped and revered.

One might imagine that mighty Solomon would have become corrupted and drunk with pride because of his great power and influence. Instead he had a heart of compassion for the needy, the afflicted, and the helpless. He rescued them from oppression and violence. Motivated by a lofty concept of the worth of the individual, he was a great king with a servant heart much like that of One who came much later—our Savior, who knelt to wash his disciples' feet (John 13:5).

I would love to be remembered for several things: some of the songs I've written; the passion with which I approach music; attempts at soaring melodies, sophisticated harmonies, and unusual voicings. I love to communicate, to feel as if I'm playing an audience like a Stradivarius. But to be known as a competent musician with a servant's heart would be the highest accolade of all!

Personal Prayer

O Lord, may I lay aside my hang-ups with success and model myself after you, who willingly laid down your crown and took up a cross . . . for me!

SOLOMON'S SONG

HIS ADORING SUBJECTS

⨯ Psalm 72 ⨯

May he live long! May gold from Sheba be given to him. May prayer be offered for him continually, and may he be blessed all day long. . . . May his name endure forever; as long as the sun shines, may his fame increase. May all nations be blessed by him and call him blessed. May the LORD God, the God of Israel, be praised, who alone does wonders. May His glorious name be praised forever; the whole earth is filled with His glory. Amen and amen (vv. 15, 17–19).

I barely remember the coronation of Queen Elizabeth II of England, only that there was a lot of pomp and pageantry and that some magnificent music was played in Westminster Abbey. I loved the majesty of the pipe organ, combined with brass fanfares and undergirded by the strength and power of rolling timpani and clashing cymbals. And I'll never forget seeing the telecast showing the smiling faces and waving flags of the English subjects who lined the streets to celebrate her coronation day.

King Solomon was held in the highest esteem. He was blessed with personal gifts, agricultural prosperity, an enduring reputation, and the respect of his peers. The Queen of Sheba alone brought him massive amounts of gold (1 Kings 10:10). The common folk praised him for paving the way for flourishing trade, peaceful alliances with neighboring nations, and the blessing of God on their land, which yielded unprecedented crops and herds.

Solomon's response to all of this takes the form of a majestic doxology. It is the second doxology in the book of Psalms and is a fitting close for Book II (Pss. 41–72). "May the LORD God, the God of Israel be praised, who alone does wonders. May His glorious name be praised forever; the whole earth is filled with His glory. Amen and amen" (vv. 18–19).

In 1741, at the London premiere of Handel's *Messiah*, King George II rose to his feet during the glorious "Hallelujah Chorus," in worshipful recognition of his supreme Sovereign. Later Queen Victoria said, "Someday it shall be my joy to lay my crown at his feet!"

Personal Prayer

*Lord, whatever honors or accolades come to me in this life
I will gladly lay at your feet!*

PRELUDE TO
TRUE PROSPERITY

STATING THE PARADOX

✥ Psalm 73 ✥

God is indeed good to Israel, to the pure in heart. But as for me, my feet almost slipped; my steps nearly went astray. For I envied the arrogant; I saw the prosperity of the wicked. They have an easy time until they die, and their bodies are well-fed. They are not in trouble like others; they are not afflicted like most people (vv. 1–5).

If the Christian life promises blessing, why do godly people struggle while unbelievers enjoy prosperity? Some, in attempting to answer that question, have considered turning away from God.

Sheldon Vanauken, noted author of *A Severe Mercy*, was tempted to disown God when his wife was dying of cancer. My dad had a friend, a highly articulate, gifted evangelist who abandoned his ministry after becoming disillusioned. And when I was in college, I too experienced some disharmony between mind and spirit and came close to a decision to get along without God in my life.

This psalm wrestles with those issues poignantly and poetically. Asaph, one of the chief singers, percussionists, and ministers in the ancient temple, almost walked away from God. He was one of the Lord's major spokesmen and a charismatic leader; yet he seriously considered packing it all in.

I believe spirituality begins with honesty. Part of that is being objective about one's true feelings. This psalm is a beautiful catharsis for Asaph. He pours out his hurting soul before his Heavenly Father. The Lord, in his marvelous mercy and incomprehensible grace, hears.

Personal Prayer

O Father, how can I ever be objective about my feelings? I'm hurting, confused, and frustrated. Please minister to me out of your vast storehouse of grace.

PRELUDE TO TRUE PROSPERITY

VIEWING LIFE FROM WHAT IS SEEN

✑ Psalm 73 ✑

Therefore, pride is their necklace, and violence covers them like a garment. Their eyes bulge out from fatness; the imaginations of their hearts run wild. They mock, and they speak maliciously; they arrogantly threaten oppression.... Therefore His people turn to them and drink in their overflowing waters. They say, "How can God know? Does the Most High know everything?" (vv. 6–8, 10–11).

Has the Lord called us to happiness or to holiness? Is it possible to have harmony in life without dissonance? Asaph, in attempting to come to grips with adequate answers to those questions, is tempted to wander away from the Lord.

First, he draws his view of life from what he sees: The wicked are prospering, and the godly are afflicted. To Asaph and to many modern worshippers, this seems contrary to the moral teachings of the Scriptures, since the Law and Proverbs boldly promise blessing for obedience (Deut. 28; Prov. 3). The more Asaph observes these apparent contradictions, the more his faith is shaken.

I too suffered from cognitive dissonance while in college. I believed what I saw—that the external symbols of success equated success itself. Nor did I observe enough internal consistency and reality in Christendom. (It's easier to build a flourishing Christian empire than to nurture a sensitive, beautiful marriage, for example.) Behavioral conformity without spiritual renewal leads to performance without intimacy, breeds doubt rather than faith, and stresses illusion rather than reality.

Secular society and the media can also impact our Christian beliefs. For many people, newspapers and television—indeed the whole non-Christian milieu—carry more clout than God's Word! Yet the Scriptures present the big picture, the long-term view. My own limited perspective often leads to an incorrect translation of God's meaning for my life. I don't want to be guilty of making the mistake Asaph almost made—selling the Lord short.

Personal Prayer

O Father, help me to have complete confidence in the authority of your Word even if it seems to contradict what I see with my eyes. You alone know my tomorrows and how the minor chords of my life can be used to produce a pleasant and harmonious melody.

PRELUDE TO
TRUE PROSPERITY

BECOMING CONSUMED BY ENVY

✑ Psalm 73 ✑

Look at them—the wicked! They are always at ease,
and they increase their wealth (v. 12).

H ow perplexing! Asaph takes the second step down the ladder of faith when he allows envy to dominate his thoughts. How easy to be drawn into this tangled web spun by the master deceiver. Sometimes the grass *does* seem greener on the other side of the fence!

Envy is sin. It's as simple as that. Yet I know of no more subtle addiction to which Christians, living in a highly commercialized world, can fall prey. We see the same ads as the wicked—the posh luxury resorts, the high-tech cars and gadgets, the designer clothing—and wonder why some who seem so undeserving get all the breaks, particularly when prosperity for obedience was promised in the law! We might as well admit, along with Asaph, that we don't have it all together. Some things just don't add up!

In Isaiah 55:8–9, I receive a gentle rebuke: "For my thoughts are not your thoughts, neither are your ways my ways. . . . As the heavens are higher than the earth, so are my ways higher than your ways, and my thoughts than your thoughts." The apostle Paul echoes this truth and adds the dimension of his own reaction: "We are pressured in every way but not crushed; we are *perplexed* but not in despair" (2 Cor. 4:8).

Apparently the proper response to perplexity, at least for the Christian, is to trust in the Lord . . . anyway!

Personal Prayer

O Father, I bring my perplexities and unresolved conflicts to you. Help me not to envy the unrighteous who prosper but to put my trust in you.

PRELUDE TO
TRUE PROSPERITY
ALMOST DROPPING OUT

✑ Psalm 73 ✑

*Did I purify my heart and wash my hands in innocence for nothing? For
I am afflicted all day long, and punished every morning (vv. 13–14).*

What's the use? I can almost hear Asaph's rationale as he takes the third step down the ladder of faith to defection: "I am afflicted all day long, and punished every morning" (v. 14). "But as for me, my feet almost slipped; my steps nearly went astray" (v. 2).

In Hebrew, the word *foot* includes the area from the knee to the sole. The picture is this: "My knees nearly buckled. My steps almost slipped out from under me." In effect, Asaph is saying, "I can't take it anymore!" He's about to take matters into his own hands and remove the Lord from the throne of his life.

In some ways, John DeLorean was the paradigm of the modern American man. One of the "beautiful people," he was bright, pragmatic, energetic, and innovative. But without Christ at the helm of his life, without his sights set on Christian values, without a proper perspective of the value of people, his empire came crashing down.

Fortunately for John, Asaph, and me, God is "merciful and longsuffering, not willing that any should perish, but that all should come to repentance" (2 Pet. 3:9 KJV).

Personal Prayer
*O Father, when everything in me screams,
"I can't take it any more," help me to hold on!*

PRELUDE TO
TRUE PROSPERITY
RETURNING TO THE LORD

❧ Psalm 73 ❧

*If I had decided to say these things [aloud], I would have betrayed Your people.
When I tried to understand all this, it seemed hopeless until I entered God's
sanctuary. Then I understood their destiny (vv. 15–17).*

Asaph now begins his journey back to the Lord by pondering "all this" (v. 16)
and rejecting materialism—what is seen. Materialism is seriously flawed.
It can put food *on* the table but will never guarantee fellowship *around* the table.
It can provide a *house*, but not a *home*. It can adorn a woman with fine jewels but
never promises love. Materialism generates the notion of loving things and using
people; Christianity produces love for people and subordinates things.

Asaph takes a second run up the ladder of faith when he enters the sanctuary (v. 17). In that place of shelter and serenity, he experiences fellowship
and hears God's Word. With the temple as his support system, he's no longer
trying to go it alone.

All Christians, including leaders, speakers, writers, and recording artists,
need that kind of support. Since true prosperity is spiritual in nature, we find
it only in fellowship with other "becomers." In concert, we give and receive
empathy, accountability, inquiry, and care. The enemy would love to encourage
the "star syndrome," which places the "star" in a class by himself, above the limitations and restrictions governing everyone else. When that person becomes
isolated in an ivory tower, when he believes his own stuff, when he becomes
charmed by the press releases and his own notoriety, he is set for a big fall.
There is only one Superstar, the Lord Jesus Christ.

Asaph too begins to get the picture when he encounters God. The terminology used in this magnificent psalm stresses God's holiness, his "everlastingness," his transcendence. When Asaph finally sees God as he really is,
the stunning revelation gives him a whole new perspective on life.

Personal Prayer
*O Father, give me a fresh revelation of yourself. May I not neglect my worship
experience but gladly seek the fellowship of other believers in your sanctuary.*

PRELUDE TO
TRUE PROSPERITY

ENCOUNTERING THE LIVING GOD

✑ Psalm 73 ✑

When I became embittered and my innermost being was wounded,
I was a fool and didn't understand; I was an unthinking animal toward You.
Yet I am always with You; You hold my right hand. You guide me with Your
counsel, and afterward You will take me up in glory. Whom do I have in heaven
but You? And I desire nothing on earth but You (vv. 21–25).

After Asaph's encounter with the living God, he sees himself as he is:
"embittered ... a fool ... an unthinking animal," hardly the picture of success as we know it. That's always the case. Meeting God and coming to know
him intimately expose our limitations, our inadequacies, our weaknesses.

And now Asaph begins to understand the ultimates of life. Because he
has caught a glimpse of God in his glory, his perspective is changed on everything, including death. "And afterward You will take me up in glory" (v. 24).
The alternative is to see life as the brutes or animals who are locked by instinct
into the material world.

Asaph then commits his life to God. He invites God to meet his needs for
love and meaning. "My flesh and my heart may fail, but God is the strength of
my heart, my portion forever" (v. 26). He concludes by fully committing himself to the Lord. In turn, God stamps upon Asaph his own character, heart,
and mind.

Personal Prayer

O Father, give me your thoughts, your mind-set, and your perspective on my life. Please
meet my profound longings for meaning and love as I commit myself fully to you.

An Old Hymn

Come Thou Fount of Every Blessing
O to grace how great a debtor
Daily I'm constrained to be!
Let Thy goodness like a fetter
Bind my wandering heart to Thee.
Prone to wander—Lord, I feel it—
Prone to leave the God I love;
Here's my heart—O take and seal it,
Seal it for Thy courts above.
Words by Robert Robinson. Music by John Wyeth.

ASAPH'S LAMENT

DEVASTATION: NO LEADERS IN THE LAND

∞ Psalm 74 ∞

Why have You rejected [us] forever, God? Why does Your anger burn against the sheep of Your pasture? Remember Your congregation, which You purchased long ago and redeemed as the tribe for Your own possession. [Remember] Mount Zion where You dwell....
They set Your sanctuary on fire; they utterly desecrated the dwelling place of Your name. They said in their hearts, "Let us oppress them relentlessly." They burned down every place throughout the land where God met with us. We don't see any signs for us. There is no longer a prophet. And none of us knows how long this will last (vv. 1–2, 7–9).

No prophets are left...." This mournful theme delivers Asaph's message of devastation. A nation or an individual without prophets' spiritual counsel is a prime target for the enemy. What Israel needed most was Solomon's dictum: "Plans fail when there is no counsel, but with many advisors they succeed" (Prov. 15:22).

Asaph groans over the fate of his people, who are suffering at the hands of enemy invaders. He describes, in graphic detail, the demolition of the sanctuary, the seat of worship and God's dwelling place. The aggressors have roared in like renegade lumbermen raping a forest (v. 5). They have "smashed all the carved paneling," looted, and pillaged. The final act of blasphemy is the burning of the sanctuary and the dispersion of the prophets. God's Word is not heard in the land, and no one knows how long the devastation will continue.

Though our church buildings are not in imminent danger of being razed at this time in our history, we might well ask ourselves why our pulpits and our people are not evidencing more power. Is it because we fail to lift up our spiritual leaders in our prayers? Do we criticize instead of encourage? Or is it that so many of our churches are Laodicean, "neither hot nor cold" (Rev. 3:15)? We coast along apathetically, satisfied with the status quo.

What is needed? Honest, courageous facing of our sin as God's people—individually and corporately. Repentance—crying out to God with contrite hearts. Forgiveness—accepting the covering of Christ's precious blood shed on the cross. Renewal—allowing his Spirit to change our lives to conform to his image. Witness—sharing the gospel with the unsaved world.

God's dwelling place in my neighborhood is safe. No marauding army has invaded it. But when we fall in any one of these areas, then we might as well post a "closed" sign on the door.

Personal Prayer

O God, may I be faithful to be in your house, worshipping, praising, thanking you for our freedom to gather. Anoint your servant, my pastor, with your grace and blessing.

ASAPH'S LAMENT

DISORIENTATION: GOD'S TEMPO OR MINE?

∽ Psalm 74 ∽

God, how long will the foe mock? Will the enemy insult Your name forever? Why do You hold back Your hand? Stretch out Your right hand and destroy [them]! God my king is from ancient times, performing saving acts on the earth (vv. 10–12).

Unlike the impotent gods of the ancient world, Asaph's God is fully involved, fully in control of his creation. Still, he doesn't move fast enough to suit the psalmist, for God does not bow to man's demands or adhere to his timetable.

We are often like the trumpet player in an orchestra who wants to set his own tempo instead of following the conductor. We'd like for God to work presto (at a rapid rate) when the tempo of his plan may be largo (slow and dignified). A major aspect of being a world-class conductor, such as Herbert Von Karajan or George Solti, is to be in perfect control of the orchestra, setting the appropriate tempo to enhance the master score. As a virtuoso percussionist in Israel, Asaph should have known that.

But Asaph has had it with waiting on God. "Why do You hold back Your hand?" (v. 11) he complains. He'd be much happier if the Lord would assert himself and destroy the adversary quickly and decisively.

As if to refresh his memory, Asaph outlines God's sovereign acts of the past: You split open the Red Sea; you broke the heads of sea monsters; you crushed Leviathan (a reference to Egypt); you opened up springs for the Israelites; you set all the boundaries of the earth (vv. 13–17). Asaph wonders how such an active God can sit passively by and why he doesn't strike back on behalf of his people with dramatic force and energy.

But God always moves to accomplish his purposes ... with precise timing. What Asaph needed to learn, and what I need to remember, is that God's tempo is perfect. "But when the completion of the time came, God sent His Son, born of a woman, born under the law, to redeem those under the law, so that we might receive adoption as sons" (Gal. 4:4–5).

Personal Prayer

O God, forgive my impetuous nature, my desire to rush things. Teach me that the greatest gifts come to those who wait patiently for you.

ASAPH'S LAMENT

DELIVERANCE: THE GRAND FINALE

✑ Psalm 74 ✑

Remember this: the enemy has mocked the LORD, and a foolish people has insulted Your name. Do not give the life of Your dove to beasts; do not forget the lives of Your poor people forever. Consider the covenant, for the dark places of the land are full of violence. Do not let the oppressed turn away in shame; let the poor and needy praise Your name. Arise, God, defend Your cause! Remember the insults that fools bring against You all day long. Do not forget the clamor of Your adversaries, the tumult of Your opponents that goes up constantly (vv. 18–23).

*E*verything in this psalm is building to a grand finale, a glorious resolution of the woes of these prophetless people.

The glory of a finale was mastered by Beethoven. He was able to build enormous tension before the final ending. He would often seesaw back and forth between tonic and dominant, throwing in a neopolitan sixth to build even more intensity. All of the energy set up an incredibly satisfying final chord. Asaph's lament is moving toward such a climax here.

Pleading the cause of Israel, Asaph pours out his soul before God. He asks the Lord to remember his promise to his covenant people, "Your dove," who have suffered affliction. He argues a strong case in defense of the poor, the needy, and the oppressed. When God hears, defends, and delivers them from disgrace, then his people will be able to praise his name.

The apostle James reminds us that "the intense prayer of a righteous is very powerful" (James 5:16). Asaph is such as man, interceding for the helpless children of Israel. A note of triumph soars high above Asaph's lament, heralding God's grand finale of deliverance.

Personal Prayer
O God, I take my stand with Asaph,
a musician who interceded for his people.
Deliver us from the clamor and uproar of sin
in our lives as we anticipate your glorious finale!

VICTORY CELEBRATION

PRAISE TO GOD

⟶ Psalm 75 ⟵

We give thanks to You, God; we give thanks to You, for Your name is near. People tell about Your wonderful works. . . . As for me, I will tell about Him forever; I will sing praise to the God of Jacob. "I will cut off all the horns of the wicked, but the horns of the righteous will be lifted up" (vv. 1, 9–10).

Asaph's cup is overflowing. He is profuse in his praise and his thanksgiving, singling out the nearness of God's name and his wonderful deeds as cause for celebration. In fact, in his ecstasy he vows to praise the God of Jacob forever!

It is possible that God himself is speaking in verse 10. He promises to cut off the defiance of the wicked and to lift up and exalt the righteous. Those of us who feel the sting of injustice and inequality understand the job of God's intervention in our relationships.

I learn a couple of crucial things from these verses. First, I need to praise the name of the Lord regularly. Second, I need to give thanks to him for his sovereign acts in my life. Third, I need to rest in the fact that God will judge evil. Things are not careening out of control. My Lord, the Divine Arbiter, is the eternal evaluator of all things.

A Contemporary Hymn

Celebrate

Look and see in awesome wonder
People coming without number
From ev'ry tribe and nomad band,
From ev'ry sea and bound'ried land:
See them marching, singing, swaying!
Can't you hear the people saying,
"Salvation is our God's alone,
The Lamb is now upon the throne."
Ev'ry tongue and ev'ry nation
They will join our celebration,
Our God is great!
So celebrate, celebrate!
Words by John E. Walvoord. Music by Don Wyrtzen.
© 1971 by Singspiration Inc.

Personal Prayer

O Lord, I adore you and find exquisite comfort in the security of knowing you have everything under control.

VICTORY CELEBRATION

JUDGMENT OF GOD

∽ Psalm 75 ∽

"When I choose a time, I will judge fairly. When the earth and all its inhabitants shake, I am the One who steadies its pillars. I say to the boastful, 'Do not boast,' and to the wicked, 'Do not lift up your horn. Do not lift up your horn against heaven or speak arrogantly.'" Exaltation does not come from the east, the west, or the desert, for God is the judge: He brings down one and exalts another. For there is a cup in the Lord's hand, full of wine blended with spices, and He pours from it. All the wicked of the earth will drink, draining it to the dregs (vv. 2–8).

When you're on a roll it's easy to take the credit and forget the One who wrote the music!

The Lord despises arrogance! Caught up in their own self-importance, the proud are pictured in this passage as animals who strut about, lifting up their horns in stiff-necked rebellion.

God himself will judge our performance. It is he who promotes and demotes, exalts and diminishes. It is only by his touch that any life produces the kind of music that is pleasing to his ear. Those who are consistently "out of tune" will find themselves confronting his wrath. It will be administered like a cup of strong, foaming wine, which they will be forced to drink to the last dregs!

At the "appointed time," every person will stand before this righteous Judge. He shows no favoritism. He will judge "uprightly," with absolute integrity.

Personal Prayer

O Lord, I will never stop speaking of you. I will never stop singing of you. And I'm grateful that you will judge my performances in this life with utter fairness.

A Contemporary Lyric

Lord of Everything

I give thanks to You, O Lord,
I give thanks to You!
I want to proclaim how great You are,
I want to tell of all the wonderful things You have done.
I will never stop speaking of You
And I'll never stop singing my praise to You,
For You are my Eternal King,
The Lord of everything.

Words and music by Don Wyrtzen. © 1988 Singspiration Music.

PSALM OF SOVEREIGNTY

∽ Psalm 76 ∽

God is known in Judah; His name is great in Israel. His tent is in Salem, His dwelling place in Zion. There He shatters the bow's flaming arrows, the shield, the sword, and the weapons of war. You are resplendent and majestic [coming down] from the mountains of prey (vv. 1–4).

In these stirring lines, Asaph plays on two physical characteristics of the countryside to describe God—the "resplendent light" of the desert sun and the "majestic" mountains surrounding Jerusalem.

God's majesty and light have inspired hymnists through the ages. Think of the lexicon of praise hymns used in our worship: "Joyful, Joyful, We Adore Thee," "The Lord Is My Light and My Salvation," "Praise, My Soul, the King of Heaven," "How Great Thou Art," "Sing Praise to God Who Reigns Above," "Praise the Lord! Ye Heavens, Adore Him," "The Light of the World," "My Tribute," "Bless His Holy Name," and on and on. We can never exhaust the majesty and glory of his name.

God displays his majestic power in his sovereign judgment of the wicked; "He shatters the bow's flaming arrows, the shield, the swords" (v. 3). "The bravehearted . . . sleep their final sleep" (v. 5). "Both chariot and horse lay still" (v. 6). What a prophecy! One day all weapons of war will be obsolete (Isa. 2:4).

I am moved by reverent awe for this God of ours to vow my allegiance to him. He is capable of using his terrible might and majesty to chasten his children as well as to rout the enemy. But there is another reason. He is also a God of infinite and unconditional love, dazzling radiance and light, and my only place of shelter is in the shadow of his mountain.

Personal Prayer

How majestic is thy name, O Lord! Light the dark corners of my life and give me a fresh vision of your majesty!

A SONG IN THE NIGHT

FEELING ABANDONED

∽ Psalm 77 ∽

In my day of trouble I sought the Lord. My hands were lifted up all night long;
I refused to be comforted. At night I remember my music (vv. 2–6a).

Why is it that one's troubles seem so much worse at night? There have been times when I've been so disturbed I couldn't sleep. Tossing and turning, I've asked the same questions the psalmist asked so long ago: Does God still love me? Has he forgotten me? Can he hear my prayer? Is he mad at me? Has he turned his back on me forever?

Asaph feels utterly abandoned by God and cries out but finds no comfort for his churning emotions. Recalling times in the past when God has acted in his behalf, he is puzzled now by God's silence. The Lord seems distant, remote, even angry. Asaph is experiencing deep, personal pain and begins a downward spiral on a decrescendo of depression (vv. 7–9).

Rejection breeds deep inner fear that can hold the spirit in a vicelike grip. In my midnight hours, irrational emotions sweep over me like waves in a turbulent sea.

My fellow musician did the right thing in venting his feelings. Asaph was learning some of the deep mysteries of life in God's school of suffering. He was learning to wait patiently for the Lord. He was learning that honesty precedes spirituality, and that lament almost always precedes praise.

Personal Prayer

Lord, I'm hurting. Right now, in the soul-deep darkness of my night,
I cry out for relief. Let me hear some note of hope.

A Poem of Remembrance

Then I Remembered

Troubled, I couldn't speak
Worried, I couldn't sleep;
Rejected, unloved, my longings were
  unfulfilled.
I prayed to God for help,
"O Lord, Don't You hear me?"
Distressed, I reached out my hands
  to Him,
His voice said, "Peace be still!"

Then I remembered how He touched
  me
And He made me His heir,
How He's led me like a Shepherd
I'm a wonder of His care;
When I remembered all He had done
  for me,
I was lifted from despair—
He heard me, He touched me
And He answered my prayer.

Words and music by Don Wrytzen. © 1988 Singspiration Music.

A Song in the Night

REMEMBERING GOD'S MIRACLES

∽ Psalm 77 ∽

So I say, "It is my sorrow that the right hand of the Most High has changed."
I will remember the LORD's works; yes, I will remember Your ancient wonders.
I will reflect on all You have done and meditate on Your actions. God, Your
way is holy. What god is great like God? You are the God who works
wonders; You revealed Your strength among the peoples (vv. 10–14).

Asaph's deliverance from despair comes when he remembers that his God is a God of miracles, past and present. Asaph's joy erupts in his penetrating question: "What god is great like God?" (v. 13).

He recalls the astonishing events of the Exodus: Rain cascades in sheets; thunder rumbles; lightening rips the sky; the earth quakes; the waters writhe and convulse and are at last swept back into trembling walls, forming a conduit for the teeming masses of Israelites escaping Egyptian tyranny (vv. 16–20).

Meditation on these miracles prompt him to praise God for his incomparable holiness and majesty.

Asaph's conclusion is based on a critical evaluation of the past. The Lord has consistently met the needs of his people. The implication is that he will again rescue and deliver them. Hence, Asaph moves from a diatribe of despair to a doxology of hope.

Personal Prayer

O Lord, why do I ever worry and fret? Yesterday you died for me.
Today you live for me. Tomorrow you come for me.

Yesterday, Today, and Tomorrow

Yesterday He died for me, yesterday, yesterday,
Yesterday He died for me, yesterday,
Yesterday He died for me, died for me—
This is history.
Today He lives for me, today, today,
Today He live for me, today,
Today He lives for me, lives for me—
This is victory.
Tomorrow He comes for me, He comes, He comes,

Tomorrow He comes for me, He comes,
Tomorrow He comes for me, comes for me—
This is mystery.
O friend do you now Him? know Him? know him?
O friend do you know Him? know Him?
O friend do you know Him? you know Him?
Jesus Christ the Lord.

Words by Jack Wrytzen. Music by Don Wrytzen. © 1966 Singspiration Music.

CHORDS OF REBELLION
DISOBEDIENCE

∽ Psalm 78 ∽

He established a testimony in Jacob and set up a law in Israel, which He commanded our fathers to teach to their children so that a future generation—children yet to be born—might know. They were to rise and tell their children so that they might put their confidence in God and not forget God's works, but keep His commandments (vv. 5–7).

Teach the children "so the next generation would know them . . . and they in turn would tell their children."

Hundreds of generations after God gave that command to teach the children, my parents obeyed! Mom taught us most of the time, since Dad was a traveling evangelist. But when he was home, we kids got the whole nine yards—Bible reading, Scripture memory, singing, and prayers around the world!

Just as my parents warned me, Asaph now warns his audience about personal rebellion against God and disobedience of his law. He tells of ancestors who forgot God and were slain in the wilderness because of his anger. He also tells of a nation graciously delivered when its people learned to obey.

As an example of disobedience, he relates the case history of the tribe of Ephraim. They broke God's covenant and spurned his law. Intoxicated by self-confidence and human independence, they forgot God's miracles and spurned his law. Though armed to the teeth with bows and arrows, in battle they turned back.

What is the message for me from these verses? Once committed to the Lord, I must not turn back or I set myself up for personal disaster. If I rebel, he will crush me. If I allow a pattern of disobedience to develop, God will respond in anger—not because he has the right as my Creator but because he cannot bear to see me destroy myself. I must go all the way with him—the whole nine yards!

Personal Prayer

Dear Lord, so soon I forget your wonderful works. Forgive my poor memory, my rebellion, and my disobedience. Don't let me stray from your side.

A Gospel Song

Trust and Obey

Trust and obey—
For there's no other way
To be happy in Jesus
But to trust and obey.
Words by John H. Sammis. Music by Daniel B. Towner.

CHORDS OF REBELLION

DISLOYALTY

✺ Psalm 78 ✺

He worked wonders in the sight of their fathers, in the land of Egypt, the region of Zoan. . . . But they continued to sin against Him, rebelling in the desert against the Most High. They deliberately tested God, demanding the food they craved. . . .But they deceived Him with their mouths, they lied to Him with their tongues, their hearts were insincere toward Him, and they were unfaithful to His covenant (vv. 12, 17–18, 36–37).

So often I'm like these willful wanderers of Israel. Instead of being grateful for God's gracious provision in the wilderness, they griped!

When they demanded food, "He rained down manna for them to eat, he gave them the grain of heaven. . . . He sent them all the food they could eat. . . . He rained meat on them like dust. . . . They ate and were completely satisfied, for He gave them what they craved" (vv. 24–25, 27, 29).

Despite all this, the children of Israel behaved like spoiled brats. They were negative, critical, and rebellious. When God chastised them, they returned to him briefly before lapsing back into flattery and deceit. Yet he was merciful and chose not to destroy them, remembering "that they were only flesh, a wind that passes and does not return" (v. 39).

Yet who am I to condemn? I'm as ambivalent as they. The Lord calls me to consistency, but my walk with him is cluttered with behavioral highs and lows. He asks that I be thankful for unexpected mercies and daily gifts of grace, but I demand more. Lord, forgive me!

Personal Prayer

Father, deliver me from the sins of ingratitude and greed.
Above all, don't let me take your goodness for granted!

CHORDS OF REBELLION

DESERTION

✐ Psalm 78 ✐

But they rebelliously tested the Most High God, for they did not keep His decrees. They treacherously turned away like their fathers; they became warped like a faulty bow. They enraged Him with their high places and provoked His jealousy with their carved images. God heard and became furious; He completely rejected Israel. . . . He chose David His servant and took him from the sheepfolds; He brought him from tending ewes to be shepherd over His people Jacob—over Israel, His inheritance. He shepherded them with a pure heart and guided them with his skillful hands (vv. 56–59, 70–72).

Asaph continues to describe his rebellious people. They put God to the test, did not keep his statutes, and engaged in idolatry and spiritual adultery. Their Heavenly Father reacted in anger and rejection. He abandoned the tabernacle of Shiloh and allowed the ark (covenant box) to be captured by the enemy. Young men were killed in war, leaving eager maidens with no one to marry; priests died violently, and widows were not able to mourn.

Then the Lord awoke "as from sleep" and saved them. He rejected the tribes of Joseph, Manasseh, and Ephraim in favor of Judah's Zion for the place of his sanctuary. He also reached down into the sheep pens and chose the country boy, David, to shepherd people instead of sheep. The young man was chosen because of two outstanding personality traits—skill and integrity. His hands were proficient, and his heart was pure.

What a model King David is for me! I covet the delicate balance between a high level of professional skill and a deep sense of personal integrity. I admire his roots, his country values, and his poet's vision, which he took with him all the way to the throne of Israel!

Personal Prayer
*Dear Lord, bless my life with skill and integrity so that
I can aspire to leadership with distinction.*

LAMENTATION
OVER JERUSALEM
THE HOLY CITY DEFILED

∽ Psalm 79 ∽

God, the nations have invaded Your inheritance, desecrated Your holy temple, and turned Jerusalem into ruins. They gave the corpses of Your servants to the birds of the sky for food, the flesh of Your godly ones to the beasts of the earth. They poured out their blood like water all around Jerusalem, and there was no one to bury [them]. We have become an object of reproach to our neighbors, a source of mockery and ridicule to those around us (vv. 1–4).

Despite the animated promises of modern media evangelists, life sometimes delivers blows instead of blessings, even for the godly.

This psalm recaps the theme of Psalm 74—the devastation of the Holy City. The temple had been defiled. Saints had been slaughtered, the corpses left to be scavenged by the birds of the air. Blood was flowing like water around Jerusalem, and there was no one left to bury the dead. The heathen nations, filled with profane people, mocked and blasphemed the name of God.

Moved by the plight of his people, Asaph prayed with deep feeling that the Lord would not remember their sins but would come to their aid once again. This was not a time of booming prosperity but a time of national agony and personal suffering. The only hope was God's supernatural intervention.

This very day I can expect to encounter at least three obstacles that cause pain or distress—from mild discomfort and irritation to deep, personal anguish. And I will probably compound the trauma by adding guilt. It encourages me to learn that Asaph faced trouble, just as I do, yet was faithful to his commitment to the Lord.

Personal Prayer
O God, my life is a mess! I've come to the end of myself, and I don't know which way to turn. But I know that wherever I might go, you are there!

LAMENTATION
OVER JERUSALEM
PRAYER AND PRAISE

✑ Psalm 79 ✑

How long, LORD? Will You be angry forever? Will Your jealousy keep burning like fire?
Pour out Your wrath on the nations that don't acknowledge You, on the kingdoms that
don't call on Your name, for they have devoured Jacob and devastated his homeland. . . .
Why should the nations ask, "Where is their God?" Before our eyes, let vengeance for
the shed blood of Your servants be known among the nations. Let the groans of the
prisoners reach You; according to Your great power, preserve those condemned to
die. . . . Then we, Your people, the sheep of Your pasture, will thank You forever;
we will declare Your praise to generation after generation (vv. 5–7, 10–11, 13).

Asaph is fed up! I sympathize with his frustration over the heathen nations who mock God. Christians in the marketplace constantly hear such complaints from skeptical colleagues and neighbors: "Where was God when the stock market crashed?" "How can a loving God let innocent people suffer?" Or even from Christians themselves: "Why did the Lord let this happen to me . . . after all I've done for him?"

Still, Asaph doesn't lose faith here. He implores God to hear the "groans of the prisoners" and "avenge the outpoured blood of [his] servants" (vv. 10–11). This plea is not motivated by duty but out of a sense of "desperate need." He longs to see the Lord glorified *through the affliction of the people.*

Joni Eareckson Tada is physically disabled because of a diving mishap when she was a teenager. She is paralyzed from the neck down. Yet the Lord has graced Joni with profound insight and faith and has given her a far-reaching ministry that she didn't have before the accident. She's a special person whose life has touched literally millions around the world!

This is the kind of answer Asaph and I long to hear from the Lord. Crippled by painful loss, emotional and psychological trauma, lack of love and acceptance, we cry out for ourselves and other sufferers: "Lord, I am weak, but you are strong!"

Personal Prayer

O Lord, help me to hear your voice above the din of human confusion. Teach me
that your strength is made perfect in my weakness and let me praise you forever.

Refrain
of Restoration
PLEASE LISTEN!

✑ Psalm 80 ✑

Listen, Shepherd of Israel, who guides Joseph like a flock; You who sit enthroned on the cherubim, rise up at the head of Ephraim, Benjamin, and Manasseh. Rally Your power and come to save us. Restore us, God; look [on us] with favor, and we will be saved (vv. 1–3).

A choir containing one person singing off-key is distracting and displeasing to the ear. But when the "out of tuneness" is between an individual and God, the melody of life is destroyed!

For too long the children of Israel have been off-key with the Lord. They have lost their reference point and have strayed into some atonal musical wilderness. Now the psalmist pleads for his people to be restored to God's favor. "Hear us! . . . Wake up! . . . Restore us, O God!" he cries out in spiritual agony. "Bring us back to our former condition with you!"

Hope is implied in the psalmist's plaintive refrain. While Asaph is addressing the eternal God who "sits enthroned between the cherubim," he perceives him also as the tender "Shepherd of Israel."

Shepherds often soothed their restless flocks with music. David himself got his start singing his folk songs to sleepless sheep out in the desert on many Mediterranean nights.

Asaph and I long to hear harmony restored once more in the life of the flock and in our own hearts.

Personal Prayer
Shepherd of Israel, please listen! And let me hear the tender melody of your love so I can tune my life to your perfect pitch.

The Language of Music

Refrain
A regularly recurring phrase or verse repeated at the end of each stanza.

Similar to "chorus," the basic structure is: (a, v, b, v, c, v . . .) or verse-chorus.

REFRAIN
OF RESTORATION
PLEASE DON'T BE ANGRY!

∽ Psalm 80 ∽

Lord God of Hosts, how long will You be angry with Your people's prayers? You fed them the bread of tears and gave them a full measure of tears to drink. You set us at strife with our neighbors; our enemies make fun of us. Restore us, God of Hosts; look [on us] with favor, and we will be saved (vv. 4–7).

I like the emotional openness of these verses, since I tend to deny a lot of emotion. Like my ancient brothers and sisters, I need to become more transparent and vulnerable. Toughing it out with the aid of denial and pretense is dishonest and self-defeating. Beyond that, it's not biblical.

Here, in stunning hyperbole, Asaph portrays the response of Israel to the disciplining hand of God. "You fed them the bread of tears and gave them a full measure of tears to drink" (v. 5)!

Though I seldom cry, I know that tears are often therapeutic. They give emotional release. They also cleanse and lubricate the ducts of the eye, and they can even dislodge foreign objects. Perhaps the faithless children of Israel are dislodging the foreign object of sin from their hearts as they weep tears of repentance. As a result of their penitent state, God will not be angry forever but will restore them to full favor (v. 7).

When I recall that even "Jesus wept" (John 11:35), I am encouraged to allow the healing tears to flow!

Personal Prayer
Shepherd of Israel, please don't be angry with me! Open me up emotionally and show me how my deepest needs can be met in you.

REFRAIN
OF RESTORATION
PLEASE RESTORE PROSPERITY!

∽ Psalm 80 ∽

It was cut down and burned up; They perish at the rebuke of Your countenance.
Let Your hand be with the man at Your right hand, with the son of man You
have made strong for Yourself. Then we will not turn away from You; revive
us, and we will call on Your name. Restore us, Lord God of Hosts; look
[on us] with favor, and we will be saved (vv. 16–19).

In this psalm the metaphor of a flourishing vine is used to picture Israel. At one time the vine was so abundant that it spread to the southern mountains, to the northern cedars of Lebanon, to the eastern Euphrates River, and to the western Mediterranean Sea. But now it has withered and died after being trampled by wild beasts and boars.

For the third time Asaph reiterates the refrain, "Restore us, Lord God of Hosts; look [on us] with favor, and we will be saved" (v. 19). He promises faithfulness in exchange for restoration and salvation.

I need to remember that prosperity finds its genesis in the Lord. Secular success, apart from God's hand on my life, it a hollow victory. Without his blessing, life has no meaning. I want to be aware of how much my personal effectiveness depends on him.

Personal Prayer
Shepherd of Israel, please prosper my soul
and make my life a flourishing vine.

MUSIC FOR THE FEAST OF TABERNACLES

LET'S CELEBRATE!

∽ Psalm 81 ∽

Sing for joy to God our strength; shout in triumph to the God of Jacob. Lift up a song—play the tambourine, the melodious lyre, and the harp. Blow the horn during the new moon and during the full moon, on the day of our feast. For this is a statute for Israel, a judgment of the God of Jacob (vv. 1–4).

This psalm celebrates God's miraculous deliverance of his people from Egyptian bondage. In the wilderness he had met every need. On one occasion he had answered out of a thundercloud (Exod. 16:10). On another he tested his people at Meribah (Num. 20).

Now Asaph calls the people to a glorious festival that will memorialize these events. He commands them to sing joyfully and loudly. The choir is to be accompanied by an orchestra of tambourines, melodious harps, and lyres. The ram's horn will deliver its fanfare at the new moon to usher in the feast. God himself has decreed this worship service as an ordinance and statute.

What do I learn from this joyous festival? I learn that part of my worship should memorialize God's supernatural acts in my life, such as the most recent time his truth set me free in my inner person. I learn that I need to get creatively involved in praising the Lord—reading Scripture aloud, praying the Word back to the Lord, or sharing the work of the Holy Spirit in my life with another person.

And one of the best ways to do this is through music.

Personal Prayer

God of Jacob, teach me to make music for your glory today.
Set me free to play skillfully, to sing worshipfully,
and to dance joyfully.

MUSIC FOR THE FEAST OF TABERNACLES
HEAR, O MY PEOPLE

✆ Psalm 81 ✆

Listen, My people, and I will admonish you. O Israel, if you would only listen to Me!
There must not be a strange god among you; you must not bow down to a foreign
god. I am Yahweh your God, who brought you up from the land of Egypt. Open your
mouth wide, and I will fill it. "But My people did not listen to Me; Israel did not
obey Me. So I gave them over to their stubborn hearts to follow their own plans.
If only My people would listen to Me and Israel would follow My ways, I would
quickly subdue their enemies and turn My hand against their foes" (vv. 8–14).

Without the responsive ear of the listener, there is no music! There is a marked difference between passive hearing and active listening. Music depends on involved listeners: Choir members must hear their director's instructions; soloists must listen for their musical cues; symphony conductors must listen critically to create balance and ensemble in their orchestras. Audiences too must learn how to listen.

In this psalm God is saying, "Listen, my people, let me warn you." But the people are willful and independent. *They will not listen!* And God "gave them over to their stubborn hearts to follow their own devices" (v. 12).

What Israel missed by refusing to listen is parallel to my own loss if I miss God's cues for my life: freedom from enemies (v. 14), food for the table (v. 16). In fact, if I worship God in an exclusive relationship, I will be abundantly blessed with "the best of wheat ... with honey from the rock" (v. 16).

Unfortunately for the Israelites, God's hands were tied. Because of their stubborn rebellion, he could not bring the prosperity and peace they craved. How sad that so often I too go unrewarded because I don't listen.

Personal Prayer
God of Jacob, I'm much like those other people of yours in my stubbornness
and refusal to listen to your instructions for abundant life. Speak loudly
so your servant will hear and obey.

PSALM OF JUSTICE

GOD INDICTS HUMAN JUDGES

∽ Psalm 82 ∽

*"How long will you judge unjustly and show partiality to the wicked?
Provide justice for the needy and the fatherless; uphold the rights of the
oppressed and the destitute. Rescue the poor and needy; save them from
the hand of the wicked." They do not know or understand; they wander
in darkness. All the foundations of the earth are shaken (vv. 2–5).*

God is speaking here. And when God speaks, we'd do well to listen! The
question he asks probes my own conscience: "How long will you judge
unjustly and show partiality to the wicked? . . . Rescue the poor and needy!"

Though God is addressing the legal magistrates he himself has appointed
over Israel, I need to assess my own attitudes and actions toward the oppressed,
the weak, the fatherless, and the poor. As I encounter these needs in my daily
life, do I turn a deaf ear, or do I respond with compassion and mercy?

It is the rare person who really shows compassion for needy, hurting
people. In this society we're programmed to expect a person to shape up, take
control, solve his or her own problems. We applaud self-reliance and scorn any
show of dependence.

God's structure of law and order is undermined when his people don't
respond to the needs of others; his kingdom is advanced when they do!

I may not be an elected official, but I am God's official representative
within my own sphere of influence. And I'm accountable to him to reflect not
only his justice but also his mercy.

Personal Prayer

*O God, I thank you for allowing me the privilege of representing
you in my world. Help me to emulate your righteousness
and kindness to all I meet.*

PSALM OF JUSTICE
GOD IS THE ONLY RIGHTEOUS JUDGE

∽ Psalm 82 ∽

God has taken His place in the divine assembly; He judges
among the gods: . . . Rise up, God, judge the earth, for all
the nations belong to You (vv. 1, 8).

God is the Judge of human judges. He created justice, equity, and objectivity. Judges who practice law deceitfully, without awareness of God's solemn appointment, will perish. It is the Lord who presides in the great assembly.

Not only will God come down on the heads of human judges, but he will also judge all the earth. The nations of the world belong to God, who holds the inhabitants responsible for their ethics and conduct.

All of this confirms that I am not just a statistic in a cold, indifferent universe or merely part of the flow in an environment resulting from chance. I am a human being who fits into God's plans for all eternity. Therefore, I have rare value. Because I am precious to him, my behavior has significance. I am responsible, so I must learn to live responsibly. Beyond that, I am unique because I am made in God's image. He has created me, saved me, and sealed me with his Spirit. What encouraging thoughts for today!

Personal Prayer
O God, I thank you that you are impartial and just
and that I can rest my case with you.

Asaph's Lament for Judah

O GOD, DO NOT KEEP SILENT!

✑ Psalm 83 ✑

*God, do not keep silent. Do not be deaf, God; do not be idle. See how
Your enemies make an uproar; those who hate You have acted arrogantly.
They devise clever schemes against Your people; they conspire against
Your treasured ones. They say, "Come, let us wipe them out as a nation so
that Israel's name will no longer be remembered" (vv. 1–4).*

Groaning is good! One of the keys to dispelling pain is to face it head on.
Pain almost always precedes praise.

Asaph is in pain. Troubled by a coalition of disgruntled nations who are
plotting to overthrow tiny Judah, he takes his complaints to God once again.
Edomites, Ishmaelites, Moabites, Ammonites, Amalekites, and Philistines
have allied themselves and, with the support of mighty Assyria, are threatening to roll over Judah like a tidal wave. Total annihilation is their objective.

The psalmist doesn't mince words. He wants God to get involved: "Do
not keep silent! . . . Do not be deaf; . . . Do not be idle." In reverse order he
seems to be saying, "It's your move, Lord. Don't just speak to our enemies.
Shout if you have to!"

Still, Asaph has pled before, and his words alone seem impotent to produce the desired effect.

In facing personal pain, I've learned that when words fail me I can trust
the Holy Spirit to help me. "[I] do not know what [I] ought to pray, but the
Spirit himself intercedes for [me] with groans that words cannot express"
(Rom. 8:26 NIV).

Personal Prayer

*Holy Spirit, speak for me. My own words are weak and powerless, but your
groans on my behalf will be heard and interpreted by the Father.*

ASAPH'S LAMENT FOR JUDAH

DO IT TO THEM!

∽ Psalm 83 ∽

*Deal with them as [You did] with Midian, as [You did] with Sisera and Jabin
at the Kishon River. They were destroyed at En-dor; they became manure for
the ground. Make their nobles like Oreb and Zeeb, and all their tribal leaders
like Zebah and Zalmunna, who said, "Let us seize God's pastures for ourselves."
. . . Let them be put to shame and terrified forever; let them perish in disgrace.
May they know that You alone—whose name is Yahweh—are the
Most High over all the earth (vv. 9–12, 17–18).*

Asaph is a consummate lyricist. He uses vivid, picturesque imagery to
express his feelings. What haunting Israeli melody accompanied this
powerful lament? We can only imagine what it sounded like—plaintive, vigorous, intense!

The angrier Asaph grows, the more moving and dramatic his imagery!
His lyric captures the intensity of his lament to the Lord: "Do to them as you
did to Midian . . . to Sisera and Jabin at the river Kishon . . . to Oreb and Zeeb,
Zebah and Zalmunna." Here Asaph is referring to specific historical events:
When the Lord delivered the Midianites into Gideon's hand (Judg. 7), when
Sisera met a grisly death through Deborah and Barak (Judg. 4–5), and when
Oreb and Zeeb (Midianite warriors) and Zebah and Zalmunna (Midianite
kings) were crushed because they dared to oppose him (Judg. 8).

The next phrases shimmer with excitement. Asaph asks God to make the
enemy hosts "like tumbleweed . . . like straw before the wind. As fire burns a
forest, as a flame blazes through mountains, so pursue them with Your tempest and terrify them with Your storm" (vv. 13–15).

The God I worship is the God of fire and storm as well as green pastures
and still waters. He alone inspires the intricate composition of my life, and it
involves tension along with release.

Personal Prayer

*O God, with the power of Asaph's pen I would compose rhapsodies to your name.
I want the world to know that you alone are the Most High over all the earth!*

PILGRIM'S SONG

LONGING FOR GOD

❧ Psalm 84 ❧

How lovely is Your dwelling place, LORD of Hosts. My soul longs, even languishes, for the courts of the LORD; my heart and flesh cry out for the living God. Even a sparrow finds a home, and a swallow, a nest for herself where she places her young—near Your altars, LORD of Hosts, my King and my God. How happy are those who reside in Your house, who praise You continually. Happy are the people whose strength is in You, whose hearts are set on pilgrimage. As they pass through the Valley of Baca, they make it a source of springwater; even the autumn rain will cover it with blessings. They go from strength to strength; each appears before God in Zion (vv. 1–7).

How easy it is for contemporary society to accept the view that this life is all there is! We tend to put down as many roots as possible and pretend that this world is really our home.

The writer of this psalm has discovered his permanent roots. Driven by a deep, inner compulsion to know God, he is drawn to the temple. He longs to make his home in the place where God is. Just as the lark and the swallow—birds known for their sweet songs—have found nests for themselves, this unknown psalmist desires to nestle near the altar close to his God, where he can sing his praises continually.

Other believers, in pilgrimage to Jerusalem, must pass through the Valley of Baca, a once-arid region where the Lord has caused springs of water to flow. Refreshed and strengthened, these pilgrims move on to complete their journey.

I too must remember that I'm only a pilgrim. "This world is not my home." Instead of putting down roots in a particular city or community or vocation, I must keep in mind my eternal destination. My roots are in eternity, not in this life. But I need frequent renewal in God's refreshing springs and the fellowship and loving support of other pilgrims. I love the church because it is my place of stability, security, and sustenance as I continue the journey.

Personal Prayer

O Lord Almighty, help me to love your place and your people. May I draw strength from my fellow pilgrims, my brothers and sisters in Christ.

PILGRIM'S SONG

PRAYING TO GOD

✑ Psalm 84 ✑

LORD *God of Hosts, hear my prayer; listen, God of Jacob. Consider our shield, God; look on the face of Your anointed one. Better a day in Your courts than a thousand [anywhere else]. I would rather be at the door of the house of my God than to live in the tents of the wicked. For the* LORD *God is a sun and shield. The* LORD *gives grace and glory; He does not withhold the good from those who live with integrity.* LORD *of Hosts, happy is the person who trusts in You! (vv. 8–12).*

These verses are both a comfort and a challenge. I know I've been set apart to Christian service in the ministry of music, but sometimes low-grade motivation obscures my vision. The enchantment of conducting a professional orchestra for the first time, seeing my first published song, listening to my first record has faded, and I'm faced with the daily grind. I must work harder to keep the excitement and creative-energy level high.

The psalmist has no such fears or insecurities. His rock-solid devotion to God supercedes all other concerns. He knows he has been set apart ("anointed") by the Lord, and he is utterly committed to his calling (v. 9). In fact, if necessary, he is willing to serve in some menial position (a doorkeeper) in the house of the Lord rather than to live in the lavish tents of the wicked (v. 10).

In verse 11 we learn the reason for such devotion. The Lord is pictured as a "sun and shield." He offers warmth, blessing, protection, and prosperity. He does not withhold anything good from those whose walk with him is *blameless*—"a spotless walk, conduct ordered according to God's will, and a truth-loving mode of thought."

Now that the musical honeymoon is over, I need to be more committed, to persist and persevere in practicing my craft. I need to exercise discipline as I'm enjoying inspiration. I also need to follow the example of my ancient colleague—turn to my Source and spend more time in meaningful interaction with his people. Out of the rich texture of meaningful human relationships come songs that touch the heart.

Personal Prayer

O Lord, today I rededicate my life to your service. Be my Sun and Shield, and give me the satisfaction of knowing that my walk is worthy of my calling.

RHAPSODY ON RENEWAL

PRAYER FOR REVIVAL

∽ Psalm 85 ∽

LORD, *You showed favor to Your land; You restored Jacob's prosperity. You took away Your people's guilt; You covered all their sin. You withdrew all Your fury; You turned from Your burning anger. Return to us, God of our salvation, and abandon Your displeasure with us. Will You be angry with us forever? Will You prolong Your anger for all generations? Will You not revive us again so that Your people may rejoice in You? Show us Your faithful love,* LORD, *and give us Your salvation (vv. 1–7).*

*L*ife is often difficult and discouraging for me. Work and family priorities go askew. I feel stressed out, disoriented, unbalanced. Why? Because I'm trying to make it on my own, taking God for granted, failing to follow his master score.

In art, as in life, balance and symmetry of form are crucial both in the creation and the reception of the work. Sir Georg Solti, former maestro of the Chicago Symphony, is a master at juggling the intricacies of complex works and fashioning them into a glorious musical mélange. Our lives need to be lived as art forms for God's glory.

This psalm, written by the Sons of Korath, begins by reciting ways in which the Lord has restored Israel—he has forgiven and covered their sins; he has set aside his wrath and turned from (changed his mind about) his anger toward them (v. 3).

The people need revival once again. They have failed to stay in tune with his will. They are out of sync with his plan. They need to right themselves, to shift their position until they are restored to harmony and balance in him.

No one needs revival more than I. When the Lord dominates and controls my life, then and only then will I feel his incredible love and lasting joy ... again!

Personal Prayer

O God my Savior, let me experience a renewal of my soul today so that your love breaks out in every word and action of my life.

A Gospel Hymn

Revive Us Again

Revive us again—fill each heart with
  Thy love;
May each soul be rekindled with fire
  from above.

Hallelujah, Thine the glory!
Hallelujah, amen!
Hallelujah, Thine the glory!
Revive us again.
Words by William P. Mackay. Music by John J. Husband.

RHAPSODY ON RENEWAL
HARVEST TIME

✑ Psalm 85 ✑

I will listen to what God will say; surely the LORD will declare peace to His people, His godly ones, and not let them go back to foolish ways. His salvation is very near those who fear Him, so that glory may dwell in our land. . . . Also, the LORD will provide what is good, and our land will yield its crops. Righteousness will go before Him to prepare the way for His steps (vv. 8–9, 12–13).

When a dying church is rekindled, when a spirit is revived, when harmony is restored—a blend of elements produces a symphony of grace. "Faithful love and truth will join together, righteousness and peace will embrace" (v. 10).

Though I have a tendency to pretend that pain doesn't exist in my close relationships, when the Holy Spirit convicts me of some sinful attitude and I'm willing to repent, I know the ecstasy of freedom and release.

The psalmist is looking forward to this kind of answered prayer because he knows God always keeps his promises. For those who choose faith instead of folly, he will grant "harvest." Blessing is the effect of God's character colliding with culture (v. 12).

This kind of harmony is perfectly illustrated in the life of Christ. As God in human flesh, he dwelt among us "full of grace and truth" (John 1:14). Further, he was a walking revelation of God's glory and lives today in repentant hearts.

Presently, my spirit wrestles with many hindrances to lasting revival—among them, a powerful and sometimes shaky ego. I need to let go and let God take full control. I need to be a "miniature Christ," reflecting his glory. When I die to self, he will assume his rightful place as Conductor of my life, and I will hear the full symphony of his favor, promised to the faithful!

Personal Prayer

O God, my Savior, reflect your glory in me today. May my ego decrease as your attributes increase in my life today!

DAVID'S PRAYER

FOR MERCY

✑ Psalm 86 ✑

Listen, LORD, and answer me, for I am poor and needy. Protect my life, for I am faith-
ful. You are my God; save Your servant who trusts in You. Be gracious to me, Lord,
for I call to You all day long. Bring joy to Your servant's life, since I set my hope
on You, Lord. For You, Lord, are kind and ready to forgive, abundant in faithful
love to all who call on You. LORD, hear my prayer; listen to my plea for mercy.
I call on You in the day of my distress, for You will answer me (vv. 1–7).

I really admire David. Here is a man who doesn't mind admitting his weaknesses, and in doing so, demonstrates his strength. Three times in these few
verses, the verb "call" is used (vv. 3, 5, 7). David doesn't just pray; he calls to
God "all day long."

When I'm under intense pressure, I tend to question God rather than call
out to him. My life gradually becomes layered with anxiety. Before long, fear
has a firm grip on my soul, and my prayer is more a pathetic whimper than a
strong plea.

Not David! He speaks to the Lord with all the authority of his convictions and in the expectation of an affirmative answer, "for You will answer me."
He thanks the Lord for his kindness and forgiveness, his abounding love and
his tender mercy.

David's song is a perfect balance of petition and praise. This form provides a
model, not only for my meditations, but for the full measure of my days. How
simple! How profoundly rewarding!

Personal Prayer

Hear my prayer, O Lord, as you heard King David's. Give me the same
bold conviction, the same simple faith, the same childlike trust. May
I never petition until I've taken time to praise!

DAVID'S PRAYER
FOR AN "UNDIVIDED" MIND

✎ Psalm 86 ✎

Lord, there is no one like You among the gods, and there are no works like Yours.
All the nations You have made will come and bow down before You, Lord,
and will honor Your name. For You are great and perform wonders; You alone are
God. Teach me Your way, LORD, and I will live by Your truth. Give me an undi-
vided mind to fear Your name. I will praise You with all my heart, Lord my God,
and will honor Your name forever. For Your faithful love for me is great, and
You deliver my life from the depths of Sheol (vv. 8–13).

Though David sometimes prays and writes in bold strokes, this passage has an almost ethereal quality. How magnificently he expresses God's sovereignty! How tenderly he caresses the name of the Lord who loves him and preserves his life!

In these lines I hear traces of the impressionists—Debussy, Ravel, Delius; I hear muted strings and harp glissandi. I hear transparency, sheen, and range of mood, from turbulence to serenity.

With all the verbal artistry at his command, David pours out his love song to the Lord. But for me the climax of the piece comes in verse 11, when he prays, "Give me an undivided mind."

Suddenly I am startled out of my reverie, brought up short, reduced to tears. I, who never cry! "An undivided mind"! I know that line—that hauntingly familiar refrain. I understand so well how a mind can be ripped open and laid bare, fragmented, broken. Yet I rarely share this kind of intimate pain but bury it beneath a façade of cool indifference.

So David knows that agony too! Yet there is no hint of self-pity. From the heights of ecstasy to the "depths of the grave," he keeps on singing!

Personal Prayer
Hear my prayer, O Lord. Make my life an artistic statement that magnifies and
glorifies your name and celebrates your incomparable greatness.

DAVID'S PRAYER
FOR STRENGTH

∽ Psalm 86 ∽

God, arrogant people have attacked me; a gang of ruthless men seeks my life. They have no regard for You. But You, Lord, are a compassionate and gracious God, slow to anger and abundant in faithful love and truth. Turn to me and be gracious to me. Give Your strength to Your servant; save the son of Your female servant. Show me a sign of Your goodness; my enemies will see and be put to shame because You, LORD, have helped and comforted me (vv. 14–17).

I must admit I'm sometimes morose and unpredictable. David too is a man of many moods. Like most creative people, he shifts quickly from passion to pathos, from biting sarcasm to tender lyricism.

Harmony directly affects the emotions. Try watching a suspenseful program on television . . . with the sound turned down! Much of the edge, the drama, is lost. John Williams, composer of the scores for *Star Wars, E.T.,* and *Superman,* is a master of film scoring. Here is a lyric full of potential for a Christian composer.

Forte—In loud and positive terms, David, here profiles the "ruthless" enemies who oppose him and defy everything for which he stands. Not only do these "arrogant" men attack David, they have utter contempt for the Lord as well (v. 14).

Affetuoso—The mood changes to one of warmth and affection as David catalogs the virtues of his Lord—compassion, grace, slow to anger, love, faithfulness, mercy, strength, goodness. Such a God will not fail him in this time of imminent danger (vv. 15–16).

Spiritoso—With rising vigor and a sense of urgency, David cries out for mercy and for "a sign . . . my enemies will see and be put to shame" (v. 17).

Rallentando—As the tempo slows, there is implicit trust in David's final words; "You, LORD, have helped and comforted me" (v. 17). Whether David was anticipating God's early response to his request or whether he is reflecting on past favors, he's confident that God acts on his behalf.

Personal Prayer

My Lord and my God, I bow in acknowledgment of your mercies. Come to my rescue today and deliver me as much from myself as from false friends and enemies.

PROCESSIONAL TO ZION

∽ Psalm 87 ∽

His foundation is on the holy mountains. The LORD loves the gates of Zion more than all the dwellings of Jacob. Glorious things are said about you, city of God ... Singers and dancers alike [will say], "All my springs are in you" (vv. 1–3, 7).

I love to hear people really sing—so that the walls vibrate and the air currents get moved around! I remember hearing some kids sing like I'd never heard before. About a hundred of them were jammed into a small, white-brick chapel at Hampden DuBose Academy. Under the baton of Miss Dorothy Hill and accompanied by two grand pianos, they lifted the roof! There have been other memorable times and places . . . the Praise Gathering in Indianapolis, Indiana . . . Christian Artists' Retreat at Estes Park, Colorado.

But the music we'll hear in the celestial city will far surpass anything we'll ever hear on this earth. The "city of God" mentioned in these verses written by the Sons of Korah is both a geographical location—Jerusalem—and a symbolic one—heaven.

Zion, which encompasses Jerusalem and surrounding hills, was the earthly dwelling place of God—the chosen object of his love (Ps. 78:68). With its towers, gates, bulwarks, and palaces, it stood as proof of eternal reconciliation with God. The enemies who pursued David most of his life—Rahab (Egypt), Babylon, Phillistia, Phoenicia, Tyre—will be recorded by the Lord himself in his register (v. 6).

In the New Jerusalem, that heavenly city, the population will be composed of peoples from all nations and ages. Music will be the language of praise!

As a Christian whose name is recorded in the Lamb's Book of Life, I look forward to that glorious reunion. I will become part of the music and dancing of eternity. I will sit down with the saints at God's banquet table. Today I march onward and upward to Zion!

A Rousing Gospel Hymn

We're Marching to Zion
We're marching to Zion,
Beautiful, beautiful Zion;
We're marching upward to Zion,
The beautiful city of God.
<small>Words by Isaac Watts, Chorus: Robert Lowry. Music by Robert Lowry.</small>

Personal Prayer

O Lord, keep my eyes firmly fixed on my future home. Don't let the hindrances and strongholds of the enemy rob me of rewards and joy in that great day when I will see you face-to-face.

SONG OF SUFFERING

HEMAN'S COMPLAINT

✑ Psalm 88 ✑

O LORD, God of my salvation, I cry out before You day and night. May my prayer reach Your presence; listen to my cry. For I have had enough troubles, and my life is near Sheol. I am counted among those going down to the Pit. I am like a man without strength, Abandoned among the dead. I am like the slain lying in the grave, whom You no longer remember, and who are cut off from Your care. . . . You have distanced my friends from me; You have made me repulsive to them. I am shut in and cannot go out. My eyes are worn out from crying (vv. 1–5, 8–9a).

Physical suffering, the irrational emotions that accompany it, and the seeming injustice of "bad things happening to good people" is a bewildering reality. Sensitive scholars have grappled with these questions. (See *The Problem of Pain* by C. S. Lewis; *Why Me, Lord?* by Warren Wiersbe; *Where Is God When It Hurts?* by Phillip Yancey.)

This psalmist isn't afraid to ask hard, penetrating questions. Heman the Ezrahite, a gifted and sensitive musician (1 Chron. 25:1), has composed one of the saddest passages in all the Bible. Since youth he has been afflicted with some kind of debilitating disease that has not only sapped his strength (v. 4) but has separated him from the comfort of his closest friends. He is actually "repulsive to them" (v. 8). In his lonely isolation he feels like a forgotten man.

He handles his pain by praying day and night. "O LORD, the God of my salvation, . . . listen to my cry!" (vv. 1–2).

I'm reminded of another man who suffered not only physical torture but also bore the weight of my sin. He too cried out in his pain: "My God, My God, why have You forsaken Me?" (Mark 15:34). Jesus, though sinless and perfect, experienced unimaginable shame and agony for me.

Personal Prayer

Father, when I'm called upon to suffer, may I cry out to you in patient prayer. Deliver me from bitterness and remind me always of the One who suffered so cruelly on my behalf!

SONG OF SUFFERING
HEMAN'S CONCLUSION

✐ Psalm 88 ✐

LORD, I cry out to You all day long; I spread out my hands to You. Do You work wonders for the dead? Do departed spirits rise up to praise You? ... But I call to You for help, LORD; in the morning my prayer meets You. LORD, why do You reject me? Why do You hide Your face from me? From my youth, I have been afflicted and near death. I suffer Your horrors; I am desperate (vv. 9b–10, 13–15).

Like many a modern-day counterpart, this ancient psalmist is full of mind-boggling questions about his condition: If I die, can I praise God from the grave? Why have I suffered so long? Is God deaf? Why have my friends and loved ones been taken from me?

This deeply emotional psalm is a mini-version of the book of Job. As in that masterpiece, Heman's questions are left unanswered. Yet I'm convinced that Job—and perhaps Heman too—found comfort in the process of prayer. Job concluded, "Though he slay me, yet will I hope in him" (Job 13:15 NIV)! Not being in control, they were driven to trust in God's sovereignty.

God alone knows the answers to the puzzling circumstances of life, though prayer itself, as an act of worship, does bring a measure of relief. *Personal introspection* is not the total answer. *Personal projection* in faith toward the Lord is the beginning of divine resolution.

Personal Prayer
O Lord, I thank you for the release I find in prayer and for the fact that I am not overwhelmed by my pain in any final sense. Help me continually to choose to exercise faith in you ... even when I see no visible solutions.

COVENANT–MAKER

GOD'S PROMISES

❧ Psalm 89 ❧

I will sing about the LORD's faithful love forever; with my mouth I will proclaim Your faithfulness to all generations. . . . [The LORD said,] "I have made a covenant with My chosen one; I have sworn an oath to David My servant: 'I will establish your offspring forever and build up your throne for all generations.'" . . . If his sons forsake My instruction and do not live by My ordinances, if they dishonor My statutes and do not keep My commandments, then I will call their rebellion to account with the rod, their sin with blows. But I will not withdraw My faithful love from him (vv. 1, 3–4, 30–33a).

In one of the greatest contracts ever written, the agreement is between two parties, God and his servant David. "I have made a covenant with My chosen one," God says. "I have sworn an oath to David My servant: 'I will establish your offspring forever and build up your throne for all generations'" (vv. 3–4).

In legal parlance the party of the first part is God; the party of the second part is David and his descendants. Still, a contract is only as valid as the integrity of the persons negotiating it. God is faithful and trustworthy (v. 1), while he acknowledges that the human weakness of David and his line will cause them to be capable of violating the terms of the agreement. Further promises in the form of warnings are made: "If his sons forsake My instruction and do not live by My ordinances, . . . I will call their rebellion to account with the rod, . . . But I will not withdraw My faithful love from him [David]" (v. 30, 32–33). This covenant of love, faithfulness, and blessing is inviolable, eternal, and based on God's holiness.

Ethan, the wise man who wrote this psalm, grapples with one apparent contradiction in God's contract with King David. God has promised blessing to future generations, yet the king is in imminent danger of death from his enemies almost daily! The succession does not appear secure.

The psalmist moves quickly to remind the Lord of his own nature and character. In essence he said, "Lord, I believe you are loving and faithful. You haven't delivered David from his enemies *yet*, but I believe you will!" (v. 1).

If only my faith could soar on such wings! "Lord, you haven't answered all my prayers yet, but I believe you will!"

Personal Prayer
O Lord, I cling to your precious promises, fully confident that you who made the promises are able to keep them!

COVENANT–KEEPER
GOD'S FAITHFULNESS

∽ Psalm 89 ∽

For I will declare, "Faithful love is built up forever; You establish Your faithfulness in the heavens." . . . LORD, the heavens praise Your wonders—Your faithfulness also—in the assembly of the holy ones. For who in the skies can compare with the LORD? Who among the heavenly beings is like the LORD? . . . who is strong like You, LORD? Your faithfulness surrounds You. . . . "But I will not withdraw My faithful love from him or betray My faithfulness. I will not violate My covenant or change what My lips have said. Once and for all I have sworn an oath by My holiness; I will not lie to David. His offspring will continue forever, his throne like the sun before Me, like the moon, established forever, a faithful witness in the sky" (vv. 2, 5–6, 8b, 33–37).

Contracts are no longer taken seriously. Legal loopholes are found and exercised every day. Marriage vows are violated and families ripped apart. Promises between friends are broken.

Only One can be counted on to keep his Word. "His [David's] offspring will continue forever, his throne like the sun before Me, like the moon, established forever, a faithful witness in the sky" (vv. 36–37). Even the heavens bear witness to his faithfulness!

The Lord doesn't approve of broken promises and casual contracts. I long to uphold my part of his covenant of grace and follow him faithfully.

Personal Prayer
O Lord God Almighty, may I honor all vows and keep all contracts, remembering that you consider such agreements sacred and binding.

A Wonderful Gospel Hymn

Great Is Thy Faithfulness

Great is Thy faithfulness, O God my Father,
There is no shadow of turning with Thee;
Thou changest not, Thy compassions, they fail not;
As Thou has been Thou forever wilt be.

Great is Thy faithfulness!
Great is Thy faithfulness!
Morning by morning new mercies I see;
All I have needed Thy hand hath provided;
Great is Thy faithfulness, Lord, unto me!

Words and music by Thomas O. Chisholm.
(Based on Lam. 3:22–23.)
© 1923. Renewal 1951 (ext.) by Hope Publishing Co.

COVENANT–BREAKER

GOD'S MEMORY

∽ Psalm 89 ∽

How long, LORD? Will You hide Yourself forever? Will Your anger keep burning like fire? Remember how short my life is. Have You created everyone for nothing? What man can live and never see death? Who can save himself from the power of Sheol? Lord, where are the former acts of Your faithful love that You swore to David in Your faithfulness? Remember, Lord, the ridicule against Your servants— in my heart I carry [abuse] from all the peoples—how Your enemies have ridiculed, LORD, how they have ridiculed every step of Your anointed. May the LORD be praised forever. Amen and amen (vv. 46–52).

There are times when I'm tempted, like the writer of this psalm, to wonder if God has forgotten his promises. Surely the Lord will remember his covenant to King David, Ethan agonizes, though it seems doubtful at the moment. Despite God's promises, the king has suffered humiliating defeat— rejection, anger, renunciation, plunder, scorn, and shame.

Ethan, the Levite musician renowned for his remarkable wisdom, writes of divine wrath and holy anger. He is moved by the futility of life and the inevitability of the grave. He appeals to God's infinite love and great faithfulness. He asks God to honor His word, then ends his prayer with a moving doxology that concludes Book III (Ps. 73–89).

If I take only the immediate point of view, life often appears unfair and futile. But if I appeal to God's love and faithfulness, I begin to approach life from the divine perspective. The final step is to follow Ethan's lead in praising God for everything that happens. "May the LORD be praised. Amen and amen."

Personal Prayer

O Lord God Almighty, I know you keep your promises, but time passes, and I can't always see the answer to my prayers. Give me steadfastness and faith to believe in your perfect faithfulness. The only covenant-breakers are your people!

MOSES' MASTERPIECE

CONTRASTING IMAGES: TRANSITORY MAN VERSUS THE EVERLASTING GOD

✑ Psalm 90 ✑

Lord, You have been our refuge in every generation. Before the mountains were born, before You gave birth to the earth and the world, from eternity to eternity, You are God. You return mankind to the dust, saying, "Return, descendants of Adam." For in Your sight a thousand years are like yesterday that passes by, like a few hours of the night. . . . You have set our unjust ways before You, our secret sins in the light of Your presence. For all our days ebb away under Your wrath; we end our years like a sigh. Our lives last seventy years or, if we are strong, eighty years. Even the best of them are toil and sorrow; indeed, they pass quickly and we fly away. . . . Teach us to number our days carefully so that we may develop wisdom in our hearts (vv. 1–4, 8–10, 12).

When I was just a little kid, I enjoyed blowing those bubbles made of soapsuds. They would appear in the atmosphere like iridescent Christmas ornaments, only to disappear a second later. I had a similar experience with cotton candy. With great expectation I would bite into the tantalizing pink bouquet of candy, only to have it dissolve in my mouth almost immediately. I learned early how many things in life are merely beautiful illusions, quickly passing away.

In this masterful blend of contrasting images, Moses teaches us that our earthly existence is like that sparkling bubble or that frothy confection. Human beings are "dust" that is soon swept away in "the sleep of death" or new grass that springs up in the morning but withers away by nightfall (v. 5).

Though mankind is transitory, God is eternal. "Before the mountains were born, ... You are God" (v. 2). Many may be finite, but God is infinite, "from eternity to eternity" (v. 2). Nor does he measure time as we do, for "a thousand years are like yesterday that passes by, like a few hours of the night" (v. 4).

Moses pleads with his fellow mortals to recognize the fleeting quality of life, "to number our days" (v. 12). Since the normal life span is generally only seventy or eighty years at most, each moment is precious. Wisdom comes with an objective awareness of time that results in a changed perspective.

I must reorder my priorities and plan strategically so that every moment of every day will be spent wisely and in preparation for the glorious life to come!

Personal Prayer

Lord, I praise you for your infiniteness and constancy. I thank you that, even though my days on this earth are brief, I will sing your praises for eternity!

MOSES' MASTERPIECE

CONTRASTING IMAGES: AFFLICTION VERSUS AFFIRMATION

✒ Psalm 90 ✒

LORD—how long? Turn and have compassion on Your servants. Satisfy us in the morning with Your faithful love so that we may shout with joy and be glad all our days. Make us rejoice for as many days as You have humbled us, for as many years as we have seen adversity. Let Your work be seen by Your servants, and Your splendor by their children. Let the favor of the Lord our God be upon us; establish for us the work of our hands—establish the work of our hands! (vv. 13–17).

The human mind can only conceive of things in contrasts. For example, love would be unintelligible if there were no such thing as indifference. Francis Schaeffer, noted theologian, used to refer to "a" and "non-a," or the law of contradiction. The arts use contrasts in a similar fashion. The tension between unity and diversity produces high art.

In the same way, we can't fully appreciate the splendor of a sunrise without the darkness of night (v. 14), or vibrant good health without a little pain (v. 15), or the satisfaction of a job well-done without some failures (v. 17).

Living out the changing textures of my life, I discover new depth in my growing relationship with my Lord. As he meets my deepest needs for love and acceptance, for healing, for relief from persecution, for meaningful work, I find inspiration for music-making. Out of a heart filled with gladness and gratitude, I will write, sing, and play songs of praise to him.

When I am plagued by uncertainty about the future, insecurity about the present, and guilt about the past, I need to focus on the unchanging nature of God. My moods may shift like quicksilver, but God remains ever the same—omnipotent, infinite, and eternal. I rest on these granite peaks of his personality.

Personal Prayer

O Lord, I long to compose a masterpiece to you.
Against the drab backdrop of my own sin, sickness, and despair,
I am inspired to write of your everlasting, unfailing love!

SONG OF
SHELTER AND SECURITY
PROMISE OF PROTECTION

✤ Psalm 91 ✤

The one who lives under the protection of the Most High dwells in the shadow of the Almighty. I will say to the LORD, "My refuge and my fortress, my God, in whom I trust."... For He will give His angels orders concerning you, to protect you in all your ways. They will support you with their hands so that you will not strike your foot against a stone. You will tread on the lion and the cobra; you will trample the young lion and the serpent. Because he is lovingly devoted to Me, I will deliver him; I will exalt him because he knows My name. When he calls out to Me, I will answer him; I will be with him in trouble. I will rescue him and give him honor. I will satisfy him with a long life and show him My salvation (vv. 1–2, 11–16).

Because I live in a fallen world, I am constantly exposed to violence, corruption, and raw, ugly evil. If it's not the blatant assault of the temporal world on my five senses, it's a more subtle blitz of Satan on my spirit. Seen and unseen dangers lurk in every shadow.

This magnificent psalm is a testimony to the security found only in the "Most High," the Sovereign God of the universe. The Creator has posted a guard of angels around the psalmist to protect him "in all [his] ways" (v. 11).

Some angelic beings are created to praise God continually (i.e., seraphim). Whole choirs of angels, like those who appeared to the shepherds on the night of Christ's birth, sing "Holy, holy, holy" (see Isa. 6:3; Rev. 4:8; 5:9–12). Others are assigned to guard duty (Ps. 91:11). Still others serve God as agents of his mighty works (Job 38:7; Acts 7:53). Some are ministering spirits sent to defend God's people (Ps. 34:7). Another special ministry of angels is to assist the saints at the time of death. Angels carried Lazarus to Abraham's bosom (Luke 16:22).

What security in knowing about these practical ministries of angels! I can heave a big sigh of relief. I'm safe in him!

Personal Prayer

O Most High, the Almighty, help me to become fully aware that I have complete safety and security because you are my hiding place and I dwell in the shadow of your wings.

A Beautiful Swedish Hymn

More Secure Is No One Ever
(Tryggare Kan Ingen Vara)

More secure is no one ever
Than the loved ones of the Saviour—
Not yon star on high abiding
Nor the bird in homenest hiding.

Translated from Swedish by Lind Sandell Berg.
Music—Swedish folk melody.

Song of Shelter and Security
Freedom from Fear

∽ Psalm 91 ∽

He Himself will deliver you from the hunter's net, from the destructive plague. He will cover you with His feathers; you will take refuge under His wings. His faithfulness will be a protective shield. You will not fear the terror of the night, the arrow that flies by day, the plague that stalks in darkness, or the pestilence that ravages at noon. Though a thousand fall at your side and ten thousand at your right hand, the pestilence will not reach you. You will only see it with your eyes and witness the punishment of the wicked. Because you have made the LORD—my refuge, The Most High—your dwelling place, no harm will come to you; no plague will come near your tent (vv. 3–10).

Can it be true? As a believer, will I really be spared suffering? Will the "destructive plague" pass over my house and strike my unsaved neighbor? Can I avoid the "hunter's net"—those insidious attempts to damage my reputation—just because I'm a Christian? How do I trust in the Lord when pain and death and treachery are real?

The key to my understanding lies in verses 4 and 5: "He will cover you with His feathers; you will take refuge under His wings.... You will not fear...."

Does this passage mean, then, that I will never suffer pain or loss? I don't think so, though I choose to believe the truth of this psalm. Through the power of the Holy Spirit, I believe that if I take refuge in the Lord, I will not be afraid *in spite of my circumstances.* I become aware that the deep inner core of my personality—the real me—cannot be touched or harmed by evil unless I permit it. Pressure and pain also give me an opportunity to flex my spiritual muscles. I can choose to trust the Lord to deliver me from fear, or I can be victimized by it.

In time I experience the miracle of triumph through my tears, peace in the midst of the storm.

Personal Prayer

O Most High, the Almighty, I praise you for protecting my real self—the part of me that will live forever—from all danger including death. I can live unafraid, knowing that you are with me always.

DOXOLOGY OF PRAISE
DECLARATION

∽ Psalm 92 ∽

It is good to praise the LORD, to sing praise to Your name, Most High, to declare Your faithful love in the morning and Your faithfulness at night, with a ten-stringed harp and the music of a lyre. For You have made me rejoice, LORD, by what You have done; I will shout for joy because of the works of Your hands. How magnificent are Your works, LORD, how profound Your thoughts! (vv. 1–6).

This psalm is music to a musician's ears! The psalmist declares that it is good to praise the Lord, from morning till night (v. 2). I am to make music to his name, an outpouring of praise to be accompanied by the ten-stringed lyre and the melody of the harp.

A contemporary song that grew out of two hearts united in praise to their Lord is often performed in concert on the synthesizer, to the beat of drums and fanfares of brass. But it is equally effective for a great choir, accompanied by a symphony orchestra with a full string section. What motivates me to praise is the impact of the Lord's works—not only his acts in history but also his personal supernatural work in my life. I don't need to play semantic games or to psych myself into a fake piety or phony joy. The Lord really has done profound and amazing things! His thoughts are infinite and astonishing. I want my life to be captivated by his greatness and grandeur. What cause for singing, playing, and dancing!

Personal Prayer
*Great are you, Lord! I want to make
music to your name all day long!*

A Contemporary Lyric

Great is the Lord
Great is the Lord,
He is holy and just,
By His power we trust
In his love.
Great is the Lord,
He is faithful and true,
By His mercy He proves
He is love.

Great is the Lord
And worthy of glory.
Great is the Lord
And worthy of praise.
Great is the Lord—
Now lift up your voice!
Now lift up your voice!
Great is the Lord!
Words by Deborah D. Smith.
Music by Michael W. Smith.
© 1982 Meadowgreen Music.

DOXOLOGY OF PRAISE

EXALTATION

℘ Psalm 92 ℘

But You, LORD, are exalted forever. For indeed, LORD, Your enemies—indeed, Your enemies will perish; all evildoers will be scattered. You have lifted up my horn like that of a wild ox; I have been anointed with oil. My eyes look down on my enemies; my ears hear evildoers when they attack me. The righteous thrive like a palm tree and grow like a cedar tree in Lebanon. Planted in the house of the LORD, they thrive in the courtyards of our God. They will still bear fruit in old age, healthy and green, to declare: "The LORD is just; He is my rock, and there is no unrighteousness in Him" (vv. 8–15).

Can you imagine "winter without Christmas"? That's exactly how C. S. Lewis described the state of the unsaved. The enemies of God have nothing to look forward to!

Boldly contrasting with this bleak metaphor is the eternal condition of the believer. The righteous will flourish like a stately palm tree or like a cedar of Lebanon, remaining "healthy and green" into old age and still bearing fruit.

So life is perceived in simple, basic terms. I can choose to live solo—apart from God, independent and autonomous. Or I can draw near him and develop a finely tuned intimacy, vulnerability, and dependence. He lets me play my instrument in my own style. But as I follow him, the Master Conductor, I become part of his score.

One person follows the path of self-destruction; another follows the way to mature, productive faith and exquisite harmony!

Personal Prayer

O Lord, Most High, you are exalted forever. I confess my utter dependence and vulnerability before you. Satisfy my thirst for you today.

Doxology

Praise God, from whom all blessings flow;
Praise Him, all creatures below;
Praise Him above, ye heavenly host;
Praise Father, Son, and Holy Ghost.
Amen!

From the Genevan Psalter. Music attr. to Louis Bourgeois.. Words by Thomas Kerr.

OUR GOD REIGNS

❧ Psalm 93 ❧

The LORD reigns! He is robed in majesty; The LORD is robed, enveloped in strength. The world is firmly established; it cannot be shaken. Your throne has been established from the beginning; You are from eternity. The floods have lifted up, LORD, the floods have lifted up their voice; the floods lift up their pounding waves. Greater than the roar of many waters—the mighty breakers of the sea—the LORD on high is majestic. LORD, Your testimonies are completely reliable; holiness is the beauty of Your house for all the days to come (vv. 1–5).

I remember being overwhelmed the first time I heard Beethoven's "Hallelujah" from *The Mount of Olives* when I was still in high school. I'll never forget the power, the majesty, the dignity of that piece. I wondered if the music of heaven would sound like that!

Psalm 93 echoes that immortal music, celebrating the day when the Lord will reign forever and ever. This poetic form—the enthronement psalm or theocratic psalm—was used in temple worship to extol God's sovereignty. It soars majestically to the Lord, "robed in majesty" and "enveloped in strength" (v. 1), whose throne is high above the oceans.

The ancients—the Canaanites in particular—were terrified of the sea. Baal, their god, was authenticated by struggling with and overcoming Yam, the sea god in Canaanite mythology. But in verses 3–4 the sea is a metaphor of God's strength and might—"pounding waves," "the roar of many waters," "the mighty breakers of the sea."

I can live today in anticipation of his future reign on this earth when final justice will prevail. In the meantime I need to have no fear of the awe-inspiring forces of nature, but I can exult in them as evidence of the power of Almighty God. Such incredible beauty and might are but a reflection of his character and strength.

Personal Prayer

Dear Lord, I worship you whose voice thunders above the crashing waves and rolling breakers. Please focus your power on solving my small problems today as I wait in eager expectation of that day when all nature sings.

Soliloquy on Security

MY INHERITANCE—GOD'S AWARE

❧ Psalm 94 ❧

Lord, God of vengeance—God of vengeance, appear. Rise up, Judge of the earth; repay the proud what they deserve. . . . The One who instructs nations, the One who teaches man knowledge—does He not discipline? The Lord knows man's thoughts; they are meaningless. Lord, happy is the man You discipline and teach from Your law to give him relief from troubled times until a pit is dug for the wicked. The Lord will not forsake His people or abandon His heritage, for justice will again be righteous, and all the upright in heart will follow it (vv. 1–2, 10–15).

It is with great ambivalence that I attend award ceremonies. Admittedly, it's a thrill to be nominated and win. After all, peer approval is something to be appreciated at any age! But if I don't win, or worse, if I'm not even nominated, I feel a certain rejection.

It seems so innocent—this compulsion we have to prove ourselves, to earn recognition, to accumulate awards. Yet at the root of these ambitions is that subtle and seductive monster, pride, that seeks to elevate self rather than God.

Selfish ambition has no place in the life of the believer, nor is it necessary, for I am already guaranteed a precious legacy. As Christ's coheir, I will share in his glory (Rom. 8:18). Instead of gold medallions and lavish trophies conferred by my peers, I'd rather work for the "prize promised by God's heavenly call in Christ Jesus" (Phil. 3:14). On that day of judgment and reward, I want to receive his "Well done!" Such a commendation will far surpass all the tarnished gold the world has to offer.

Personal Prayer

Dear Lord, forgive my preoccupation with trivialities—the recognition of my peers and the acclaim of the world. Crush any proud place in me and help me focus on receiving an award of merit from you, bestowed after the grand finale of time.

SOLILOQUY ON SECURITY
MY CONSOLATION—GOD'S LOYAL LOVE

∽ Psalm 94 ∽

Who stands up for me against the wicked? Who takes a stand for me against evildoers? If the LORD had not been my help, I would soon rest in the silence [of death]. If I say, "My foot is slipping," Your faithful love will support me, LORD. When I am filled with cares, Your comfort brings me joy (vv. 16–19).

I can relate to this psalmist whose "foot is slipping" and whose knees are buckling beneath him. He is weighted down with performance pressure and negative criticism. At such times even the godly can stumble.

I remember vividly the first time I had a memory lapse in a public performance. I was playing Mendelssohn's "Rondo Capriccioso" as a piano solo at Word of Life Island. Up to that time I'd never gone blank in my life! But here, before an audience of five hundred people, I forgot the notes. That sinking sensation came flooding back as I watched Debi Thomas one time stumble on the ice during the Olympic figure-skating competition. It takes a lot to be able to get up and go on with your career after that kind of public embarrassment!

In this psalm the psalmist is outnumbered and overpowered. Human resources are inadequate. He has no backup....

In music, backup is critical. Once, while conducting several hundred Baptist teenagers in John Peterson's and my musical, *I Love America*, to the accompaniment of a tape track, someone accidentally kicked out the plug! I was mortified, but we continued *a cappella.*

At last the psalmist remembers the Lord—his help (v. 17), his love, (v. 18), his comfort (v. 19). Belief in one's own ability alone produces a false sense of security. Faith in God results in consolation, comfort, and inner strength.

Personal Prayer
Dear Lord, I thank you for lifting me up when I stumble. When I'm filled with anxiety and stage fright, I'm a prime candidate for your comfort!

INVENTION OF PRAISE
FIRST PART—PRAISING GOD'S SOVEREIGNTY

∽ Psalm 95 ∽

*Come, let us shout joyfully to the LORD, shout triumphantly to the rock
of our salvation! Let us enter His presence with thanksgiving; let us
shout triumphantly to Him in song. (vv. 1–2).*

The psalmist almost explodes with praise in this stirring enthronement
psalm. He sings for joy to the Lord and worships the One who provides
security and deliverance. He moves on to celebrate God's marvelous, wide-
ranging creativity. For he is the "great King above all gods" (v. 3) who made the
mountain peaks, the sea, and the depths of the earth.

Moved by the same great theme, I composed this song of praise:

O come, let us sing to the Lord
The Rock of our salvation;
With joyous shouts of love and praise
We'll sing a psalm for endless days:
In vibrant jubilation,
Come, let us sing to the Lord!
We come to him, the Creator,
The one Illuminator;
He made the sea and formed the land,
And he shaped the earth with his mighty hand:
With songs of appreciation,
Come, let us sing to the Lord!

<small>Words and music by Don Wyrtzen © 1974 by Singspiration.</small>

In the tradition of Abraham and other spiritual forefathers, I am compelled
to fall facedown before my Lord. Merely bowing or kneeling will just begin to
express my heart's adoration in the presence of such majesty. Yet he is also my
tender Shepherd and desires to have intimacy with the people of his pasture.

Personal Prayer

*O Great King and Gentle Shepherd, I can scarcely believe that you who created
the world desire fellowship with one of your lowly sheep. Praise your name forever!*

INVENTION OF PRAISE
SECOND PART—WARNING AGAINST UNBELIEF

⨏ Psalm 95 ⨏

Today, if you hear His voice: "Do not harden your hearts as at Meribah, as on that day at Massah in the wilderness where your fathers tested Me; they tried Me, though they had seen what I did. For 40 years I was disgusted with that generation; I said, 'They are a people whose hearts go astray; they do not know My ways.' So I swore in My anger, 'They will not enter My rest'" (vv. 7–11).

As the first movement in this symphony of praise ends, bringing the believer to his knees in worshipful adoration, there is an abrupt change of pace.

I can almost hear the rich, somber tones of the horns here. God is issuing a stern ultimatum: "Do not harden your hearts!" He is referring, of course, to the obstinate children of Israel who had murmured in the wilderness, sounding like the random notes of an orchestra tuning up. But his warning has my name on it. I often become critical and negative, and my whining sounds like a kid learning to play the violin!

The names of key geographical locations in Israel tell the story: "Meribah" (strife—like the fuzzy tones on an electric guitar); "Massah" (testing—like the critical shaping of the oboe's double reed). At those memorable sites, his rebellious children pushed the Lord to the limits of his patience. As a result, they never made it to the promised land. This whole episode feels romantic, German, and Wagnerian to me—so intense, so sad, so earthy.

Suddenly I hear a trumpet fanfare signaling God's desires for me: "Be warned! I will give you abundant opportunity to follow where I lead, but you must obey—instantly and without argument or complaint!"

This warning, in stark and striking measures, climaxes the symphony, and the lingering cadences resonate in my heart and mind: Unbelief and resistance cost the children of Israel their promised rest in the land flowing with milk and honey. Will I be faithful to the end? Will my performance disintegrate, or will I reach the finale?

Personal Prayer

O Great God King, soften my heart toward you and turn my murmurings into a melody of praise.

The Language of Music

Invention
A form of imitative counterpoint used by Bach.

Bach wrote two sets of keyboard pieces (circa 1723): 15 two-part inventions and 15 three-part.

Great Is He

ALL THE EARTH PRAISES HIS MAJESTY

∽ Psalm 96 ∽

Sing a new song to the LORD; sing to the LORD, all the earth. Sing to the LORD, praise His name; proclaim His salvation from day to day. Declare His glory among the nations, His wonderful works among all peoples. For the LORD is great and is highly praised; He is feared above all gods. For all the gods of the peoples are idols, but the LORD made the heavens. Splendor and majesty are before Him; strength and beauty are in His sanctuary (vv. 1–6).

What makes a song publishable? The content first must be fresh and biblical—presenting God's truth in a new way. Too many songs are imitative and derivative and seem to be cloned from secular sources.

A wonderful song should be eternal, dealing with a universal theme that has cosmic significance and is presented in a form that is contemporary and natural.

Certain themes are especially pleasing to the Lord: salvation (v. 2), his glory (v. 3), his wonderful works (v. 3). Thematically, in both life and music, we must declare his attributes and his acts, reflect his majesty, and celebrate history—*his* story!

Pondering his majesty, splendor, strength, and glory should lead us to spiritual ecstasy. *Our Lord made the heavens and spun the galaxies into space!* Out of this should come art that is worthy of his praise. The alternative is the lifeless, toneless sound of the pagan world.

Powerful, life-changing music will never be initiated by monetary concerns or ego needs, for human genius without a focus on God is sterile. Until he does a deep work in our lives, we really don't have anything to write about!

Personal Prayer

I worship you, Sovereign Lord, with all the creativity at my command. Inspire me to write and sing your praises and to live my song!

GREATER IS HE

NATIONS AND NATURE PRAISE HIS MAJESTY . . .

✑ Psalm 96 ✑

Say among the nations: "The LORD reigns. The world is firmly established; it cannot be shaken. He judges the peoples fairly." Let the heavens be glad and the earth rejoice; let the sea and all that fills it resound. Let the fields and everything in them exult. Then all the trees of the forest will shout for joy before the LORD, for He is coming— for He is coming to judge the earth. He will judge the world with righteousness and the peoples with His faithfulness (vv. 10–13).

When I was still in graduate school, I had a marvelous opportunity to participate in a revival in Mexico City. The evangelist was Luis Palau, the Billy Graham of Latin America; the song leader was Bruce Woodman, the Cliff Barrows of that continent; the organist was yours truly. I can still hear those thousands of Latin people singing God's praises in their own language. Because I don't speak fluent Spanish, I recognized only a few phrases, but the name of "Je-sus" provided a common denominator. What a preview of the music of heaven!

The apostle Paul tells of a day, perhaps soon, when Christ will be exalted and every creature from every nation on earth will acknowledge him. Today's reading from the Psalms is the Old Testament counterpart of a magnificent passage in Philippians: "For this reason God also highly exalted Him and gave Him the name that is above every name, so that at the name of Jesus every knee should bow—of those who are in heaven and on earth and under the earth—and every tongue should confess that Jesus Christ is Lord, to the glory of God the Father" (2:9–11).

On that day the curse on nature will be lifted, and God will pour out his blessing. As harmony and balance are restored to the universe, the heavens and earth will be glad, and all of creation will tremble with joy and music. The sea and "all that fills it resound" (v. 11); the fields will be jubilant (v. 12), and "all the trees of the forest will shout for joy" (v. 12).

If even inanimate objects are moved to praise, how much more should my tongue be loosed to join in the universal chorus! It will be "love in any language"—Spanish, English, Russian, Chinese. . . .

Personal Prayer

Dear Lord, I sing your precious name, for "Jesus is the sweetest name I know!" I rejoice with people of all nations and with all of nature in the majesty and glory of that name.

EPIPHANY OF GLORY

VISION OF THE LORD'S GLORIOUS COMING

∽ Psalm 97 ∽

The LORD reigns! Let the earth rejoice; let the many islands be glad. Clouds and thick darkness surround Him; righteousness and justice are the foundation of His throne. Fire goes before Him and burns up His foes on every side. His lightning lights up the world; the earth sees and trembles. The mountains melt like wax at the presence of the LORD—at the presence of the Lord of all the earth. The heavens proclaim His righteousness; all the peoples see His glory (vv. 1–6).

Reading the prophetic words of this psalm excites my imagination. My Lord is coming again to rule and to reign! In light of that dynamic truth, all the petty frustrations of this life seem ridiculously unimportant.

The sublime poetry of these verses describe in figurative language the Lord's glory. In their broadest interpretation they also depict his coming reign and remind me of prophecies in both Old and New Testaments. When he comes, he will be surrounded by clouds (see Rev. 1:7). "Fire goes before him and consumes his foes" (see Isa. 66:15–16). Not only do men fear him, but nature trembles as well. "His lightning lights up the world" (see Luke 17:24). "The mountains melt like wax" (see Mic. 1:4). "The heavens proclaim His righteousness; all the peoples see His glory" (v. 6).

If I knew Jesus were coming one week from today, how would I change my life and ministry? I'd go on a crash course to know my Lord a lot better. I'd put house hunting on hold and wait for that mansion in glory! I'd double-check with certain relatives about their relationship with the Lord, and if necessary I'd share the gospel more honestly and passionately with them. I'd spend more time in the Word, allow the Holy Spirit to control me more completely, and draw closer to my brothers and sisters in Christ. If I had any extra time, I'd concentrate on making some music to the praise and glory of God!

Personal Prayer

*O Lord, I feel like a child at Christmas when
I anticipate your coming again! Order my priorities to conform to your plan
for my role in your kingdom. Give me a fresh vision!*

EPIPHANY OF GLORY
A CALL TO RIGHTEOUS LIVING AND FAITHFULNESS

∞ Psalm 97 ∞

All who serve carved images, those who boast in idols, will be put to shame. All the gods will worship Him. Zion hears and is glad, and the towns of Judah rejoice because of Your judgments, LORD. For You, LORD, are the Most High over all the earth; You are exalted above all the gods. You who love the LORD, hate evil! He protects the lives of His godly ones; He rescues them from the hand of the wicked. Light dawns for the righteous, gladness for the upright in heart. Be glad in the LORD, you righteous ones, and praise His holy name (vv. 7–12).

How do we define idolatry in contemporary terms? The "images" mentioned in biblical times refer to physical objects made with hands. But *idolatry* also means "clinging attachment or devotion." In Christian terms idolatry refers to anything or anyone that comes "between God and me." It takes many subtle forms—making heroes out of celebrities, getting carried away with my own gifts, being unduly impressed with personal status symbols, education, or expertise.

The emptiness and foolishness of idolatry is exposed when the radiant glory of God penetrates the fog. This superego that blinds us to our own sin and these works of our own hands are then laid bare, and we recognize the "Most High over all the earth" (v. 9).

With the Lord of glory as my reference point and his righteous reign as my context, I need to learn how to discern idolatry—especially in myself—and hate it as much as he does. I need to trust in his deliverance from wickedness, then rest secure because "he protects the lives of his godly ones."

On this—my birthday—I want to celebrate by creating a new work of praise to his glory. He is the Author of life, the Composer of the music of my days, my Songmaker!

Personal Prayer
Dear Lord, trample any idols I may have foolishly erected. As you crush them, may the sweet perfume of my love and gratitude rise before you and may the melody of my heart be a sacrifice of praise.

SING TO THE LORD
A NEW SONG

THE LORD HAS MADE HIS SALVATION KNOWN

⌘ Psalm 98 ⌘

Sing a new song to the LORD, for He has performed wonders; His right hand and holy arm have won Him victory. The LORD has made His victory known; He has revealed His righteousness in the sight of the nations. He has remembered His love and faithfulness to the house of Israel; all the ends of the earth have seen our God's victory (vv. 1–3).

When I read of God's covenant with Israel, his loyal love and faithfulness to his chosen people, I don't feel excluded, but rather I feel greatly blessed. Spiritually I too am Jewish—part of the spiritual seed of Abraham (Gal. 3:28–29)!

As that concept impacts my life, I am moved to make music to this God who has included me in his marvelous plan. Saved and sealed by his Spirit, I sing and proclaim his salvation to "all the ends of the earth." As nonbelievers overhear my songs of praise, they will be drawn to his irresistible love.

This psalm motivated Isaac Watts to write the familiar carol "Joy to the World" that is sung each Christmas to Frederick Handel's heroic melody.

Personal Prayer
O Lord, I long to compose carols of joy, celebrating the marvelous things you have done in my life.

A Song

Joy to the World

Joy to the world! The Lord is come!
Let earth receive her King;
Let every heart prepare Him room,
And heaven and nature sing.
Joy to the earth! The Savior reigns!
Let men their songs employ;
While fields and floods, rocks, hills, and plains
Repeat the sounding joy.

No more let sins and sorrows grow,
Nor thorns infest the ground;
He comes to make His blessings flow
Far as the curse is found.
He rules the world with truth and grace,
And makes the nations prove
The glories of His righteousness
And wonders of His love.

Words by Isaac Watts (adapted from Psalm 98).
Music adapted from George F. Handel.

SING TO THE LORD
A NEW SONG

HE WILL JUDGE THE WORLD IN RIGHTEOUSNESS

∽ Psalm 98 ∽

Shout to the LORD, all the earth; be jubilant, shout for joy, and sing. Sing to the LORD with the lyre, with the lyre and melodious song. With trumpets and the blast of the ram's horn shout triumphantly in the presence of the LORD, our King. Let the sea and all that fills it, the world and those who live in it, resound. Let the rivers clap their hands; let the mountains shout together for joy before the LORD, for He is coming to judge the earth. He will judge the world righteously and the peoples fairly (vv. 4–9).

There is nothing subdued or restrained about the message of this psalm! It's a toe-tapper! How can we be still when we are exhorted to "be jubilant" (v. 4), "shout for joy" (v. 4), and "with trumpets and the blast of the ram's horn shout triumphantly" (v. 6)!

My former neighbor, Dr. Bill Reus, has hunted long-horn rams on all the major continents of the world. When I first saw these fierce-looking horns mounted over his fireplace, I was reminded of the ancient orchestra. At the inauguration of Solomon's temple, 120 priests blew rams' horns, accompanied by other Levites singing and playing cymbals, harps, and lyres (2 Chron. 5). No wonder the Lord says, "Make a joyful noise!"

All of nature joins in a cacophony of sound and motion. "Let the sea resound. Let the rivers clap their hands; let the mountains shout together for joy" (vv. 7–8).

What inspires this explosion of joy? What induces this liberated worship in song? The Lord is coming! And when I think of all that will mean, I am inspired to mix all the rich colors available to me in this palette of praise and pour out my own "melodious song."

Personal Prayer
Dear Lord, unleash my spirit today and set me free to create music worthy of your praise. Let my imagination soar as I lift up your name!

A Contemporary Lyric

Sing to the Lord a New Song

Sing to the Lord a new song,
Sing to the Lord all day long;
Break out in praise and sing the refrain;
Our Lord will come to rule and reign.

Words and music by Don Wyrtzen © 1974 Singspiration Music.

HOLY, HOLY, HOLY

THE LORD IS HOLY

∽ Psalm 99 ∽

The LORD reigns! Let the peoples tremble. He is enthroned above the cherubim. Let the earth quake. The LORD is great in Zion; He is exalted above all the peoples. Let them praise Your great and awe-inspiring name. He is holy. The mighty King loves justice. You have established fairness; You have administered justice and righteousness in Jacob. Exalt the LORD our God; bow in worship at His footstool. He is holy (vv. 1–5).

Dr. Karl Menninger, internationally celebrated psychiatrist, has asked the question, "Whatever became of sin?"

The ugly reality of sin fades away when we love our vision of the dazzling holiness of God (Isa. 6). In our modern perception the shed blood seems cannibalistic and barbaric, the price of forgiveness is cheapened, and the good news is relegated to the religion section of the local newspaper.

This psalm inspires us to recover the truth of God's character. He alone is *holy*—"perfectly pure and worthy of profound reverence." This is the pillar— the *sine qua non*—upon which everything in Christianity rests!

Personal Prayer

Dear Lord, I praise your great and glorious
name because you alone are holy.

A Wonderful Old Hymn

Holy, Holy, Holy

Holy, holy, holy! Lord God Almighty!
Early in the morning our song shall rise to Thee;
Holy, holy, holy! Merciful and mighty!
God in three persons, blessed Trinity!
Holy, holy, holy! all the saints adore Thee,
Casting down their golden crowns around the glassy sea;
Cherubim and seraphim falling down before Thee,
Who wert and art and evermore shalt be.
Holy, holy, holy! Though the darkness hide Thee,
Though the eye of sinful man Thy glory may not see;
Only Thou art holy—there is none beside Thee,
Perfect in pow'r, in love and purity.
Holy, holy, holy! Lord God Almighty!
All Thy works shall praise Thy name in earth and sky and sea;
Holy, holy, holy! merciful and mighty!
God in three persons, blessed Trinity!
Words by Reginald Heber. Music by John B. Dykes.

HOLY, HOLY, HOLY

THE LORD ANSWERS PRAYER

ᗡ Psalm 99 ᗡ

Moses and Aaron were among His priests; Samuel also was among those calling on His name. They called to the LORD, and He answered them. He spoke to them in a pillar of cloud; they kept His decrees and the statutes He gave them. O LORD our God, You answered them. You were a God who forgave them, but punished their misdeeds. Exalt the LORD our God; bow in worship at His holy mountain, for the LORD our God is holy (vv. 6–9).

The Lord has dramatically steered my passage through life. In high school I wanted to attend a particular college, but God chose Moody Bible Institute. If I hadn't listened to his voice, I probably wouldn't have met Karen!

After Moody, I planned to study at Juilliard, but God wanted me at King's. If I hadn't obeyed, I probably wouldn't be involved in the world of Christian music.

After college I had my sights set on graduate school at Columbia University, but God led me to Dallas Theological Seminary. If I had followed my own inclination, I probably wouldn't have written this book!

These career turning points all came out of wrestling matches with the Lord. It is only as I look back that I can see the providential hand of God on our lives.

Our Lord has a history of answering the prayers of his saints. In ancient times Moses (Exod. 3–4), Aaron (Exod. 4:27–31; 7:6), Hannah (1 Sam. 2), Samuel (1 Sam. 3), and Nehemiah (Neh. 1) called on the name of the Lord, and he answered. They were rewarded for their obedience. Though God punished Israel for misdeeds, he also forgave them and regularly answered their prayer.

Why don't more people pray more often, believing that God really hears and answers? Maybe it's because they have bought into the system that claims we are self-sufficient beings, perfectly capable of taking care of ourselves, and, at the extreme, that we're even evolving into gods! Yet it only takes one turning point like mine, one gigantic crisis, one moment of unresolved conflict to realize how frail and vulnerable we are. We need him every hour!

Personal Prayer

Dear Lord, I know you hear and answer today just as you did in the days of Moses, Aaron, and Samuel. May I always call on you rather than relying on my puny human resources.

THE OLD ONE-HUNDREDTH

∽ Psalm 100 ∽

Shout triumphantly to the LORD, all the earth. Serve the LORD with gladness; come before Him with joyful songs. Acknowledge that the LORD is God. He made us, and we are His—His people, the sheep of His pasture. Enter His gates with thanksgiving and His courts with praise. Give thanks to Him and praise His name. For the LORD is good, and His love is eternal; His faithfulness endures through all generations (vv. 1–5).

A brilliant example of an ancient musician at his best is contained in this enduring psalm. Perhaps only the Twenty-third is more widely known and loved in all of Christendom.

The things that are most familiar to us, however, often lose their deepest meaning. To rediscover the rich mother lode of treasure in these verses, I've asked myself why this passage has remained one of the best loved in all the Bible.

There are at least five reasons: First, the Lord is God—Creator, Sustainer, Redeemer (v. 3). Second, he made me and I belong to him. My identity is in him. I'm not a faceless nonentity, floating through the impersonal cosmos, but a *child of God*, "the sheep of His pasture" (v. 3). Third, the Lord is good. He wishes me well, not evil (v. 5). Fourth, he loves me with an endless love because I am infinitely precious to him (v. 5). Finally, his covenant of love extends to my children—D. J. and Kathy—and to my grandchildren (v. 5).

Such good news fills me with joy and a desire to "enter His gates with thanksgiving and His courts with praise."

Personal Prayer

Dear Lord, help me to shout for joy today, to worship you with gladness, and to come before you with joyful songs.

A Contemporary Lyric

Sing Joyfully Before the Lord!

Sing joyfully before the Lord,
Obey Him gladly on the earth;
Rejoicing, take Him at His Word,
Before Him sing with joy and mirth!
Go through His open gates with joy,
Go to His courts with deepest praise;

Let grateful songs your tongue employ,
And bless His name for endless days!
Because the Lord is always good,
His faithfulness forever sure,
His truth for endless ages firmly stood,
And will for ages still endure.

Words and music by Don Wyrtzen © 1971 Singspiration Music.

PSALM OF INTEGRITY

✑ Psalm 101 ✑

I will sing of faithful love and justice; I will sing praise to You, LORD. I will pay attention to the way of integrity. When will You come to me? I will live with integrity of heart in my house. I will not set anything godless before my eyes. I hate the doing of transgression; it will not cling to me. . . . No one who acts deceitfully will live in my palace; no one who tells lies will remain in my presence. Every morning I will destroy all the wicked of the land, eliminating all evildoers from the LORD's city (vv. 1–3, 7–8).

I've given a lot of thought lately to personal and professional ethics. Rumors of corruption in government have always been rife; business empires crumble in the face of fraud and embezzlement at the level of top management; politicians and preachers alike succumb to greed and lust. How can I guard my own integrity in these perverse times?

David's psalm gives me some cues to managing my personal and professional life. Unique among the rulers of the ancient Near East, David was a man whose lifestyle and reign were marked by integrity. He was scarred, fallen, and flawed like the rest of us; yet he submitted to God's authority over his life. Here is the character by which he ruled.

First, he pledged himself to be "pay attention to the way of integrity," realizing that the attitude of one's heart dictates his actions (vv. 2–3). Second, he warned the people that he would tolerate no shady deals, no under-the-counter maneuvers, no ethical hanky-panky (vv. 4–6). More than that, he threatened to deal sternly with those who violated sound principles of moral conduct (vv. 7–8), and then God allowed David to experience the consequences of his own actions!

David chose justice over popularity, integrity over peace at any price. He boldly confronted evil in his empire and set the standard by his strong commitment to personal purity.

Nor can I abdicate my responsibility as God's man in my own world. He calls me to authenticity—not just image—both in the office and at home.

Personal Prayer
O Lord, keep me pure and blameless as I move from the realm of my business dealings to my God-ordained position as head of my home.

BALLAD OF BURNOUT
BURNED OUT

❧ Psalm 102 ❧

LORD, hear my prayer; let my cry for help come before You. Do not hide Your face from me in my day of trouble. Listen closely to me; answer me quickly when I call. For my days vanish like smoke, and my bones burn like a furnace. My heart is afflicted, withered like grass; I even forget to eat my food. . . . My enemies taunt me all day long; they ridicule and curse me. . . . My days are like a lengthening shadow, and I wither away like grass (vv. 1–4, 8, 11).

I know what it's like to run dry, both spiritually and creatively. The symptoms the psalmist describes in these verses are all too familiar. One day blends facelessly, into another, with nothing to show for it. Unbridled emotions produce almost physical pain before plunging me into a state of feeling almost nothing at all. I have no heart for my work, no inspiration. To top it all off, I suffer from periodic insomnia and, occasionally, even loss of appetite!

Psychologists diagnose this problem as "burnout." Authors call it the "blank page syndrome." Musicians sometimes refer to it as a creative dry spell. I call it low-grade motivation or no motivation at all. The psalmist feels that life itself is over.

But there's a flip side to this record of griefs. This afflicted believer is doing the only thing he knows to do, thereby setting the pace for every depressed believer who has ever lived. He calls on the Lord! He cries out to him and groans in his presence.

Inspiration for victorious living and for creative music-making have a common source—intimacy with the Lord. One way to nurture intimacy with him and beat the cycle of despair is to begin with an uninhibited outpouring of raw and honest emotion. To deny these overwhelming feelings is to concede defeat. Pretending is fantasy; honesty produces reality. The psalmist's way, though painful, is the only sure route to healing, wholeness, and renewed creativity.

Personal Prayer
Hear my prayer, O Lord. I'm burned out, dried up, and spiritually depleted. I turn to you—Savior, Fellow Sufferer, Songmaker.

BALLAD OF BURNOUT

WORN OUT

∞ Psalm 102 ∞

Then the nations will fear the name of the LORD, and all the kings of the earth Your glory, for the LORD will rebuild Zion; He will appear in His glory. He will pay attention to the prayer of the destitute and will not despise their prayer. . . . "Long ago You established the earth, and the heavens are the work of Your hands. They will perish, but You will endure; all of them will wear out like clothing. You will change them like a garment, and they will pass away. But You are the same, and Your years will never end. Your servants' children will dwell [securely], and their offspring will be established before You" (vv. 15–17, 25–28).

My wife Karen is an astonishingly beautiful lady whose clothes make an artistic statement. A person with a strong sense of style and color, her tastes run from sporty and classic to elegant and sophisticated. With her fair Nordic coloring, I love to see her in pink. In any gathering she stands out, and I'm always proud of her. Whatever the occasion she's always appropriately dressed.

But clothing, no matter how fine the fabric or how well constructed, eventually wears out or becomes outdated. In this passage the psalmist calls our attention to the fact that even the heavens, that vast canopy covering the earth, will "change them like a garment" (v. 26). The Lord will change them (heaven and earth) "like a garment" and "they will pass away" (v. 26).

Karen is no clotheshorse. While she enjoys dressing in good taste and with a kind of flair, she's a person of great spiritual sensitivity and depth. She knows as well as this psalmist that the only covering that will endure is Jesus Christ, who clothes us in his righteousness.

We can have confidence that the Lord knows the deepest needs and desires of our heart and will respond accordingly. Styles may change—in fashion and other art forms, including music! Only our great God remains the same, from generation to generation, world without end!

Personal Prayer

Lord, Karen and I bring our pitiful wardrobe to you. In your sight our garments are as filthy rags. We rejoice that we will be dressed in your righteousness throughout all eternity!

BLESS THE LORD, O MY SOUL!

PRAISING THE LORD FOR HIS BENEFITS

∞ Psalm 103 ∞

My soul, praise the LORD, and all that is within me, praise His holy name.
My soul, praise the LORD, and do not forget all His benefits. He forgives all
your sin; He heals all your diseases. He redeems your life from the Pit; He
crowns you with faithful love and compassion. He satisfies you with
goodness; your youth is renewed like the eagle (vv. 1–5).

This exalted work is the definitive answer to the problems so honestly enumerated in Psalm 102.

David's artistic soul erupts in uninhibited praise. From the core of his being, from the focal point of his soul, he praises the holy name of the Lord. And he has good reason to celebrate!

The Lord has given David a cornucopia overflowing with gifts of his grace. He has forgiven David's sins (v. 3). He has healed his sickness (v. 3). He has delivered David from the grave (v. 4). He has enriched David's life with gifts of loyal love and tender compassion (v. 4). He has satisfied David's deepest desires with good things (v. 5).

Instead of being grounded by despair, David can now soar like an eagle. Instead of a weak, anemic faith, he is blessed with vigorous spiritual health that vibrates in his songs of praise.

Personal Prayer

I praise you and thank you, O Lord, for all of your blessings to me: your forgiveness,
your healing, your deliverance, your love, your compassion, and for fully satisfying
my inner being with yourself.

BLESS THE LORD, O MY SOUL!

PRAISING THE LORD FOR HIS COMPASSION

✑ Psalm 103 ✑

The LORD executes acts of righteousness and justice for all the oppressed. He revealed His ways to Moses, His deeds to the people of Israel. The LORD is compassionate and gracious, slow to anger and full of faithful love. He will not always accuse [us] or be angry forever. He has not dealt with us as our sins deserve or repaid us according to our offenses. For as high as the heavens are above the earth, so great is His faithful love toward those who fear Him. As far as the east is from the west, so far has He removed our transgressions from us. As a father has compassion on his children, so the LORD has compassion on those who fear Him. For He knows what we are made of, remembering that we are dust. . . . But from eternity to eternity the LORD's faithful love is toward those who fear Him, and His righteousness toward the grandchildren of those who keep His covenant, who remember to observe His instructions (vv. 6–14, 17–18).

Whenever I read this psalm cataloging the virtues of God, I feel like Moses must have felt when standing in his presence on Mt. Sinai (Exod. 34:6–7). Moses was allowed to view the back of God, and in that intimate exposure the great man of God found out what our Lord is like!

He is compassionate and not only feels our pain and sorrow but also stands ready to alleviate it. He is gracious, choosing not to punish our sins in proportion to their seriousness (v. 10). He is loving and even tempered (vv. 7–8). He does not hold grudges (v. 9). His love is infinite; his forgiveness, totally effective and complete (vv. 11–12).

Of all these divine attributes, the one that resounds in my spirit like the clash of cymbals is his love. It is incomprehensible and inexhaustible. It is "wide and long and high and deep," and when I begin to grasp it, my inner being is strengthened by the Holy Spirit (Eph. 3:16–21). I am changed from the inside out.

My imagination fired, I want to write a concerto, using God's incomparable love as my theme!

Personal Prayer

I am grateful, Lord, that your mercy, love, and compassion temper the anger and judgment that should rightfully fall on me. Praise be to the Lord of love and grace!

Bless the Lord, O My Soul!

PRAISING THE LORD FOR HIS DOMINATION

∽ Psalm 103 ∽

The Lord has established His throne in heaven, and His kingdom rules over all. Praise the Lord, all His angels of great strength, who do His word, obedient to His command. Praise the Lord, all His armies, His servants who do His will. Praise the Lord, all His works in all the places where He rules. My soul, praise the Lord! (vv. 19–22).

At various stages of my life, I have exercised authority in a number of arenas. I have been a church music director, head of a music department in a Christian college, editor in chief of a music company, and lecturer in a theological seminary. Musicians and writers sometimes consult me for musical and theological advice. At home God has assigned me to the role of husband to Karen and father to D. J. and Kathy.

But God's domain has no such limitations or restrictions. The entire universe is under his dominion. All of creation is obligated to bow before him. "His angels of great strength, who do His word, obedient to His command. Praise the Lord, all His armies, His servants who do His will" (vv. 20–21).

If the whole creation is expected to worship the Lord, then I must bless the Lord in my personal life as well. Neglecting worship and praise will shrink my soul and reduce the margins of my life and influence. If I desire fullness, richness, and abundance, I'll spend my days adoring the King of the universe—the only One worthy of concentrated service and worship.

Personal Prayer

I praise you and thank you, O Lord, for your sovereignty and authority over all creation. I want to join the heavenly hosts in praising your name today. Teach me some "melodious sonnet."

His Glorious Creation
THE GLORY OF THE CREATOR

✑ Psalm 104 ✑

My soul, praise the LORD! LORD my God, You are very great; You are clothed with majesty and splendor. He wraps Himself in light as if it were a robe, spreading out the sky like a canopy, laying the beams of His palace on the waters [above], making the clouds His chariot, walking on the wings of the wind, and making the winds His messengers, flames of fire His servants. He established the earth on its foundations; it will never be shaken. You covered it with the deep as if it were a garment; the waters stood above the mountains. . . . He causes the springs to gush into the valleys; they flow between the mountains (vv. 1–6, 10).

Psalm 104 focuses on the glory of the Creator revealed in his majesty, his care of creation, and His rule.

The exalted poetry of these verses portray God as light. He wraps himself in a garment of radiance. The skies over the earth are envisioned as a tent, covering nomadic dwellers. His personal dwelling place is pictured above the waters of the sky, attended by the elements—winds and flames of fire.

God's glory is also observed in his perfect maintenance of creation. He waters the animals from freshly made springs. He provides grassy meadows for cattle to graze in and for men to cultivate. Out of the rich resources of the ground come wine, oil, and bread. He provides stately trees as homes for birds and majestic mountains as havens for wild goats.

He established the intricacies of the vernal equinox and the summer solstice, and marked out the precise pathway of all the stars. He allows the sun and moon to rule the days, the nights, and the seasons. The circadian rhythms of men and animals, predetermined by these heavenly bodies, give meaning and variety to life, and further indicate the glory and imagination of the Creator.

Personal Prayer

Praise the Lord, O my soul! I praise you for your majesty, your creativity, your care, and your rule. As the seasons change and as each day fades into night, I'm continually reminded of your glory in creation.

HIS GLORIOUS CREATION

THE GLORY OF HIS CREATION

❧ Psalm 104 ❧

How countless are Your works, LORD! In wisdom You have made them all; the earth is full of Your creatures. Here is the sea, vast and wide, teeming with creatures beyond number—living things both large and small. There the ships move about, and Leviathan, which You formed to play there. All of them wait for You to give them their food at the right time. . . . I will sing to the LORD all my life; I will sing praise to my God while I live. May my meditation be pleasing to Him; I will rejoice in the LORD. May sinners vanish from the earth and the wicked be no more. My soul, praise the LORD! Hallelujah! (vv. 24–27, 33–35).

The psalmist bursts into passionate praise, celebrating God's creation. An earth full of creatures, teeming seas, and overarching heavens were brought into being where nothing had existed before! Only God can do that.

Dr. Harold Best, former dean of Wheaton College Conservatory, says, "Creativity is the ability both to imagine (think up) something and to execute it." He feels that creativity, craftsmanship, technique, and skill often are confused. The *special quality* of creativity "lies in the thinking up, the *imagining.*"

Man takes raw materials that God has made and fashions them into useful items (i.e., trees become lumber; lumber becomes houses or furniture). In the same way a Christian musician uses the laws of nature (i.e., the harmonic series) to produce music. The composer must fashion the building blocks of music into ideas, themes, and melodies that become vehicles of praise.

The psalmist is so stirred by these lofty thoughts that he vows to sing praise to the Lord as long as he lives, *in a manner pleasing to the Lord.* I too want to please God—not my colleagues or my audience—through the works of my mind and my hands. Though I have written approximately four hundred anthems and songs, only those will endure that have been inspired by the heart of God.

I echo the psalmist who concludes with a mighty "Hallelujah!"

Personal Prayer

I praise you, Lord, for your creativity and your artistic control over creation. I, like every other living creature of earth, am totally vulnerable and dependent on you for inspiration and for life itself! Hallelujah!

HOW GREAT THOU ART!

HIS GREATNESS

∽ Psalm 105 ∽

Give thanks to the LORD, call on His name; proclaim His deeds among the peoples. Sing to Him, sing praise to Him; tell about all His wonderful works! Honor His holy name; let the hearts of those who seek the LORD rejoice. Search for the LORD and for His strength; seek His face always. Remember the wonderful works He has done, His wonders, and the judgments He has pronounced, O offspring of Abraham His servant, O descendants of Jacob—His chosen ones. He is the LORD our God; His judgments govern the whole earth (vv. 1–7).

Throughout the entire history of Israel, God has revealed his greatness through his loyal, covenant love. The psalmist inspires his audience to call on the name of the Lord and to give thanks. He urges them to proclaim to the nations the Lord's mighty miracles in history.

I need this kind of spiritual motivation. I need a stirring preacher to remind me that the Lord has worked miraculously on my behalf. Why? Because I tend to take for granted his continual intervention in my life and to get so wrapped up in myself that I forget how great he is!

Personal Prayer

Dear Lord, prod my memory when I forget your miracles!
Write them on my heart and stir me to
sing about your goodness!

A Glorious Gospel Song

How Great Thou Art

Then sings my soul, my Savior God, to Thee:
How great Thou art, how great Thou art!
O Lord my God, when I in awesome wonder
Consider all the world Thy hands have made,
I see the stars, I hear the rolling thunder,
Thy power throughout the universe displayed!
And when I think that God His Son not sparing,

Sent Him to die, I scarce can take it in—
That on the cross, my burden gladly bearing,
He bled and died to take away my sin!
When Christ shall come with shout of acclamation
And take me home, what joy shall fill my heart!
Then I shall bow in humble adoration
And there proclaim, my God, how great Thou art!

Words by Carl Boberg. Music—Swedish Folk Melody. (Arr. and trans. by Stuart K. Hine.) © 1953, 1955 by Manna Music, Inc.

HOW GREAT THOU ART!

HIS FAITHFULNESS

∽ Psalm 105 ∽

He forever remembers His covenant, the promise He ordained for a thousand generations—[the covenant] He made with Abraham, swore to Isaac, . . . Then He brought Israel out with silver and gold, and no one among His tribes stumbled. Egypt was glad when they left, for dread of Israel had fallen on them. He spread a cloud as a covering and [gave] a fire to light up the night. They asked, and He brought quail and satisfied them with bread from heaven. He opened a rock, and water gushed out; it flowed like a stream in the desert (vv. 8–9, 37–41).

Certain key words leap from the pages of the Psalms—words used repeatedly to speak of the enduring quality of God's covenant with his people—words and phrases such as "forever," "for a thousand generations," "everlasting" (vv. 8–10).

In this psalm the musician is praising the Lord for taking his promises seriously. Unfortunately, we contemporary Christians use these words and phrases pretty casually. They have a certain ring that makes them attractive to songwriters and poets. In fact, our list of synonyms is extensive: eternal, always, evermore, unending, endless, ceaseless, continual, perpetual. But do we really grasp the meaning of *forever?*

In reviewing this passage, I see again the "forever" faithfulness of God in keeping his covenant with Israel. First, he protected them as aliens in foreign lands, keeping his eye on Abraham wherever he went—Chaldea, Haran, Canaan, Egypt, and the Negev (vv. 12–15). Second, the Lord guided his people to Egypt and promoted Joseph to rule over them (vv. 17–22). Third, the lord blessed his oppressed people with productivity (v. 14). Fourth, the Lord used Moses and Aaron to deliver them from Egypt (vv. 26–36). Finally, the Lord was faithful in providing for them while they were in the wilderness (vv. 39–41). So even when Israel was "following afar off," God was faithful in meeting their needs (vv. 42–45).

If I were to trace the steps of my own pilgrimage, there would be many parallels because God's character never changes. It is this kind of endless love and provision he promises me today.

Personal Prayer

Dear Lord, I thank you for providing for Israel's needs in the ancient world. Because your character never changes, I know you will care for me unceasingly, always, forever!

HOW GREAT THOU ART!

FREEDOM

∽ Psalm 105 ∽

For He remembered His holy promise to Abraham His servant. He brought His people out with rejoicing, His chosen ones with shouts of joy. He gave them the lands of the nations, and they inherited what other peoples had worked for. [All this happened] so that they might keep His statutes and obey His laws. Hallelujah! (vv. 42–45).

This shrinking world of ours has given me a new appreciation for this passage from Psalm 105. America has never fallen into enemy hands, nor has any other nation stormed the streets of our cities and carried our people into captivity. Still, I read newspaper accounts and see telecasts of this kind of tyranny in the world today.

When the Lord remembered his "holy promise" to Abraham, he "brought His people out" from the bondage of Egypt to the security of the Holy Land "that they might keep His statutes and obey His laws" (v. 45). The bottom line of deliverance is freedom to obey him and praise his holy name.

How ironic that "captives" are often freer than many Americans who practice shallow and casual Christianity. Tatianà Goricheva, author of *Talking about God Is Dangerous: Diary of a Russian Dissident,* is an emigrant who claims, "My life only began when God found me." Even in atheistic Russia her faith was growing strong and vibrant before her arrival in this country. Upon viewing a Western TV evangelist for the first time, however, she observed, "What this man said on the screen was likely to drive more people out of the church than the clumsy chatter of our paid atheists. Dressed up in a posh way . . . he was a boring, bad actor with mechanical and studied gestures . . . For the first time I understand how dangerous it is to talk about God. Each word must be a sacrifice—filled to the brim with authenticity. Otherwise it is better to keep silent." God demands our praise, but it must be genuine!

Personal Prayer

O Lord, may every word I write and every song I sing be a sacrifice of praise to your holy name!

CHACONNE OF CONFESSION

CONFESSING INCONSISTENCY

∞ Psalm 106 ∞

*Hallelujah! Give thanks to the Lord, for He is good; His faithful love endures forever.
Who can declare the Lord's mighty acts or proclaim all the praise due Him? How
happy are those who uphold justice, who practice righteousness at all times. Remember
me, Lord, when You show favor to Your people. Come to me with Your salvation
so that I may enjoy the prosperity of Your chosen ones, rejoice in the joy of
Your nation, and boast about Your heritage (vv. 1–5).*

In Baroque music a composition consisting of the repetition of a short theme
or succession of harmonies in slow triple meter was called a "chaconne."
Johann Sebastian Bach said, "The end and goal of thorough bass is nothing but
the honor of God." Here we have the psalmist's chaconne of confession.

Musically speaking, confession is the ground bass around which this
psalm is structured. Far from being "righteousness at all times," Israel was
more often ungrateful and rebellious. The ancient prophets, including Ezekiel
and Isaiah, sounded a stern warning, urging her to confess and forsake her evil
ways (see Neh. 9; Isa. 63; and Ezek. 20).

The psalmist strikes a major chord by praising God's goodness and constancy, as evidenced in the mighty acts he has performed on Israel's behalf. On
that same note he moves on to pronounce a blessing on those who are consistently just and fair, progressing to a chord of concern for his personal accountability before the Lord.

Emotionally I'm capable of pretty severe mood swings, but I worship the
living God of the universe who never changes. Sunrise and sunset, summer
and winter, in adversity and prosperity, he parades past me the evidence of his
unchanging nature.

Personal Prayer

*I praise you today, Lord, for your con-
stancy. When all of life crumbles in
around me, I can count on your faithful
love to orchestrate a symphony of joy.*

The Language of Music

Chaconne

In Baroque music, a composition
consisting of the repetition of a short
theme in slow, triple meter.

The theme, rather than being a
tune, is a succession of harmonies
(i.e., I-IV-1$^{1/4}$–V) repeated many
times. Another term for chaconne is
"passacaglia."

CHACONNE OF CONFESSION

CONFESSING SIN

∽ Psalm 106 ∽

Both we and our fathers have sinned; we have gone astray and have acted wickedly.
Our fathers in Egypt did not grasp [the significance of] Your wonderful works or
remember Your many acts of faithful love; instead, they rebelled by the sea—the Red
Sea. Yet He saved them for His name's sake, to make His power known. . . . They
soon forgot His works and would not wait for His counsel. . . . They defiled them-
selves by their actions and prostituted themselves by their deeds (vv. 6–8, 13, 39).

It has been said that the curse of Christianity is a short memory! Why can't we learn? Why must we continue to make the same mistakes? Don't we know the consequences of following our spiritual ancestors who sinned in the same ways as their fathers before them?

Listen to the psalmist's litany of sins and feel deep empathy with those ancient brothers and sisters who stumbled through the wilderness. Over and over again—at the Red Sea, at Peor, at Meribah—they resisted God's guidance. How could they have made such arrogant demands to be fed, then complain when the menu never varied? How could they forget all those miracles so soon and begin their murmuring and complaining? Moses himself was no paragon of virtue. His disobedience cost him the dream of his life—entering the promised land.

Pride, arrogance, complaining, disobedience. Guilty as charged—my spiritual forebears . . . and me! I stand condemned before the God of Abraham and Moses "without one plea, but that thy blood was shed for me."

Personal Prayer

I'm just like my fathers, Lord! Those people just couldn't learn. Neither can I. My soul
is also a litany of disobedience and rebellion, but I'm glad 1 John 1:9 is still in the Book!

A Beloved Hymn

Just As I Am

Just as I am, and waiting not,
To rid my soul of one dark blot,
To Thee whose blood can cleanse each spot,
O Lamb of God, I come! I come!
Just as I am, Thou wilt receive,
Wilt welcome, pardon, cleanse, relieve,
Because Thy promise I believe,
O Lamb of God, I come! I come!
Words by Charlotte Elliott. Music by William B. Bradbury.

CHACONNE OF CONFESSION

SEEKING FORGIVENESS

❧ Psalm 106 ❧

Therefore the Lord's anger burned against His people, and He abhorred His own inheritance. He handed them over to the nations; those who hated them ruled them. Their enemies oppressed them, and they were subdued under their power. He rescued them many times, but they continued to rebel deliberately and were beaten down by their sin. When He heard their cry, He took note of their distress, remembered His covenant with them, and relented according to the abundance of His faithful love. . . . May the Lord, the God of Israel, be praised from everlasting to everlasting. Let all the people say, "Amen!" Hallelujah! (vv. 40–45, 48).

God is neither distant nor deaf. He did not turn his face from faithless Israel, nor does he fail to hear our cries of distress, though it may seem that way sometimes.

In his anger God turned Israel over to heathen nations for punishment. Under their foreign taskmasters the chosen people soon cried out for deliverance, and God answered.

Suddenly a majestic fanfare soars above the confessional—the harmonic changes for which I've been listening: "He remembered His covenant with them, and relented according to the abundance of His faithful love" (v. 45). Despite their stiff-necked rebellion and the pitiful waste of their lives, God still loved them and wouldn't let them go!

Time after time he sent judges to lead them back to him. Time after time they were faithful for a season and then fell back into their old ways. He was forced to discipline these delinquent children. "As many as I love, I rebuke and discipline" (Rev. 3:19).

At last! The great resolution! God will return the people to him, where they will remain in his presence "from everlasting to everlasting." The psalmist ends Book IV of the Psalter with a doxology of praise to the God of Israel. And all the people said, "Amen!"

Personal Prayer

O Lord my God, I thank you for not closing the door permanently when I sin. Like my ancient brothers and sisters, I can approach you with a contrite heart and find forgiveness and restoration.

DESCANT OF DELIVERANCE
A SIMPLE THEME

∽ Psalm 107 ∽

Give thanks to the Lord, for He is good; His faithful love endures forever. Let the redeemed of the Lord proclaim that He has redeemed them from the hand of the foe and has gathered them from the lands—from the east and the west, from the north and the south. Some wandered in the desolate wilderness, finding no way to a city where they could live. They were hungry and thirsty; their spirits failed within them. Then they cried out to the Lord in their trouble; He rescued them from their distress. . . . Let them give thanks to the Lord for His faithful love and His wonderful works for the human race. Let them offer sacrifices of thanksgiving and announce His works with shouts of joy (vv. 1–6, 21–22).

In hymn singing, a descant is a soaring countermelody, usually sung by a few sopranos as a decorative addition to the hymn. The moving theme of this passage is the simple declaration of God's goodness and enduring love.

Most likely God's people had been in exile in Babylon. Now back in their native land, they are praising him again.

Descant: He gathers his chosen people from all corners of the earth.

Theme: The Lord is good; his love endures forever.

Descant: He has redeemed us—paid our ransom, bought us back, covered our debt.

Theme: The Lord is good; his love endures forever.

Descant: He delivers us from distress.

Theme: The Lord is good; his love endures forever.

Descant: He leads us on level pathways to his holy city, where we will settle for eternity.

Theme: The Lord is good; his love endures forever.

Descant: He satisfies our hunger and thirst with living water and good things.

Theme: The Lord is good; his love endures forever.

Descant: He brings us out of darkness into his marvelous light.

Theme: The Lord is good; his love endures forever.

Descant: He heals all our diseases and rescues us from the grave.

Theme: The Lord is good; his love endures forever.

Descant: He will still every storm of life to a whisper and guide us to our haven of rest.

Theme: The Lord is good; his love endures forever!

Personal Prayer

Lord, I praise you for your unfailing love and incomparable deeds of kindness.

DESCANT OF DELIVERANCE

A SOARING DESCANT

∽ Psalm 107 ∽

He turns rivers into desert, springs of water into thirsty ground, and fruitful land into salty wasteland, because of the wickedness of its inhabitants. He turns a desert into a pool of water, dry land into springs of water. He causes the hungry to settle there, and they establish a city where they can live. . . . But He lifts the needy out of their suffering and makes their families [multiply] like flocks. The upright see it and rejoice, and all injustice shuts its mouth. Let whoever is wise pay attention to these things and consider the Lord's acts of faithful love (vv. 33–36, 41–43).

The southeastern region, where I now live, is in its fourth year of drought. Interestingly enough, weather fronts have skirted middle Tennessee many times, bringing storms and showers to neighboring counties, but not a drop to Nashville and Williamson County! There has been a great deal of speculation as to the reasons—our geographical configuration, changes in prevailing winds, even the ozone layer.

Wiser heads, seeking counsel from the Scriptures, have concluded that only God holds the answer, since he alone can "turn a desert into a pool of water and dry land into springs of water" (v. 35). The governor of a sister state suffering from the same drought called for a day of prayer for rain. Within twenty-four hours the whole state was enjoying the first good downpour in weeks!

The Lord gives and withholds blessing according to the faithfulness of his people. Since all products come from resources in the earth, all of humanity depends on God's providential care.

Just as he controls nature, he also is fully capable of ordering human experience. He may choose to humble the arrogant or to exalt the poor and needy. He can silence the wicked and inspire the redeemed to sing his praises. The psalmist suggests, "Let whoever is wise pay attention to these things and consider the Lord's acts of faithful love" (v. 43).

Personal Prayer

*As I meditate on your great love,
O Lord, I long for showers
of blessing on the barren soil of my life.*

The Language of Music

Descant

A soaring counter melody, usually sung by several sopranos.

Used as a decorative addition to a hymn, the descant is a very effective musical device that can leave listeners feeling exhilarated.

TOCCATA OF TRIUMPH
CELEBRATING HIS LOVE AND FAITHFULNESS

∽ Psalm 108 ∽

My heart is confident, God; I will sing; I will sing praises with the whole of my being. Wake up, harp and lyre! I will wake up the dawn. I will praise You, Lord, among the peoples; I will sing praises to You among the nations. For Your faithful love is higher than the heavens; Your faithfulness reaches the clouds. Be exalted above the heavens, God; let Your glory be over the whole earth (vv. 1–5).

I love to improvise on the piano—to sit down at the keyboard and freely associate musically, to wing it! The term *toccata* comes from the Italian *toccare*, "to touch" (the keys), and is an early keyboard form designed to showcase the resources of the instrument, the ingenuity of the composer, and the technical virtuosity of the performer.

Part of the extraordinary body of King David's creative work is this toccata of triumph in praise of the Lord's loyal love of Israel. The theme is repeated for emphasis from Psalm 57:7–11.

Being the virtuoso he is, David is not interested in a dull, lifeless recital as he worships, but he brings his whole being into the experience. He begins the day with a spontaneous outburst of song, depending not on prepared material but on the flow of the Spirit to inspire both words and melody.

David's theme is the unsurpassed greatness of God's love which is "higher than the heavens," and his marvelous faithfulness which "reaches the clouds." He exalts his Lord who dwells in the heavens and desires that his glory will pervade the earth.

King David possessed not only a healthy mind-set but the fullness of God in the deep recesses of his being. Because he was in touch with eternity, he was able to interpret reality and to live his life with freedom and authenticity. He beautifully fulfilled and pre-lived Christ's words in John 10:10: "A thief comes only to steal and to kill and to destroy. I have come that they may have life and have it to in abundance."

Personal Prayer

O God, I want to sing and make music with all my soul today. I lift my worship to you because of your great love and faithfulness.

The Language of Music

Tocatta

From the Italian term <u>tocarre</u> "to touch" (the keys).

Early keyboard form involving improvisation, fugue, and virtuosity desired to show off the resources of the instrument, the ingenuity of the composer, and the virtuosity of the performer.

TOCCATA OF TRIUMPH

PLEADING FOR GOD'S HELP

∽ Psalm 108 ∽

Save with Your right hand and answer me so that those You love may be rescued.
God has spoken in His sanctuary: "I will triumph! I will divide up Shechem.
I will apportion the Valley of Succoth. Gilead is Mine, Manasseh is Mine, and
Ephraim is My helmet; Judah is My scepter. Moab is My washbasin; on Edom
I throw My sandal. Over Philistia I shout in triumph." Who will bring me to
the fortified city? Who will lead me to Edom? (vv. 6–10).

Our do-it-yourself society has developed another dimension over the past few decades—professions geared to helping us do it ourselves. All of these professionals—financial advisors, tax consultants, career counselors, psychologists, family and children's service personnel, marriage counselors—are in business for the primary purpose of adding input to our decision-making. These advisors, especially if they are Christians, are generally motivated by genuine concern for people, and we benefit from their training and expertise.

Solomon, the wisest man who ever lived, said, "Plans fail when there is no counsel, but with many advisers they succeed" (Prov. 15:22). There are times when tragedies, crises, or life changes create tension in an individual or a family. Professional Christian counselors who listen with empathy and a strong commitment to confidentiality can help untangle our knotty problems.

But David sounds a warning note: "Have You not rejected us, God? . . . Give us aid against the foe [fear, financial reverses, family crises], for human help [godless] is worthless" (vv. 11–12).

The Lord is the source of all personal strength and confidence and the ultimate answer to every problem we face in life. Sensitive counselors are often instruments of help and healing, but "with God we will perform valiantly" (v. 13).

Personal Prayer

O God, I thank you for your trained representative of personal healing and
deliverance, but may I never make the mistake of placing all my faith
in human counsel. Your right hand is my strength!

CHANT OF CURSES
CURSING THE WICKED

❧ Psalm 109 ❧

O God of my praise, do not be silent. For wicked and deceitful mouths open against me; they speak against me with lying tongues. . . . Set a wicked person over him; let an accuser stand at his right hand. When he is judged, let him be found guilty, and let his prayer be counted as sin. Let his days be few; let another take over his position. Let his children be fatherless and his wife a widow. Let his children wander as beggars, searching [for food] far from their demolished homes. . . . Let his forefathers' guilt be remembered before the Lord, and do not let his mother's sin be blotted out. Let their sins always remain before the Lord, and let Him cut off [all] memory of them from the earth (vv. 1–2, 6–10, 14–15).

David, the man "after God's own heart," is never seen in his true humanity more graphically than in this psalm. On the surface he appears vindictive and cruel. His rhetoric is sharp and his attitude toward his enemies is harsh. David minces no words in letting God know how to dispose of his persecutors. He wants them blotted off the face of the earth! Exterminated! X-ed out!

In explosive terms the psalmist describes the scenario as he'd like to see it played out. He asks that these wicked and deceitful men be opposed, accused, found guilty, condemned, yanked from positions of leadership, their families made fatherless and husbandless, and their children left to become homeless scavengers of society. As if that isn't punishment enough, David goes on to suggest that their sins be *remembered* while they themselves be *forgotten* as if they had never existed!

How do we mesh this diatribe with the New Testament imperative to "turn the other cheek"? (see Luke 6:29). One must bear in mind that David antici-pated a theocracy, an earthly kingdom dedicated to righteousness. He did not have the full biblical revelation we possess today. Heathen peoples in the ancient world were corrupt and licentious, and David's righteous stance stood in bold contrast to their debauchery. What we have here is bold, passionate poetry curs-ing sin and immorality and defending righteousness and morality. In short, David does not deny his angry feelings but freely vents them!

Personal Prayer

O God, I learn from David that, if I must let off steam about my circumstances, I can do it safely in your presence!

284

Chant of Curses

PRAYING FOR HELP

∽ Psalm 109 ∽

But You, God my Lord, deal [kindly] with me for Your name's sake; deliver me because of the goodness of Your faithful love. For I am poor and needy; my heart is wounded within me. . . . Help me, Lord my God; save me according to Your faithful love so they may know that this is Your hand and that You, Lord, have done it. . . . I will fervently thank the Lord with my mouth; I will praise Him in the presence of many. For He stands at the right hand of the needy, to save him from those who would condemn him (vv. 21–22, 26–27, 30–31).

The violent enemy David so vividly portrays here spews forth curses until he wears them like a black shroud about himself. I have a hard time condemning David for feeling the way he does about this guy! In fact, I admire his honesty.

David is in no condition to avenge or even to protect himself from further insult and injury. He simply doesn't have the resources, physically or emotionally. His body is weakening because of fasting and lack of appetite, and his gaunt appearance serves only to bring on more ridicule.

Realizing his helpless condition, David's prayer is upfront, candid, and forthright. He submits to the Lord's sovereignty, appealing to his goodness and love and asking for deliverance.

The key to his prayer resounds like the chord from a great organ echoing in an empty cathedral: "Let them know that it is *Your* hand and that *You*, LORD, have done it" (v. 27). Now David's true motives are clearly seen. By a super-natural work of the Lord, his enemies will know the Source of real power!

I am sometimes guilty of trying to crank up a worship experience without an intense awareness of any supernatural work of God in my life. An honest, vulnerable appraisal provides the rich soil for God to work creatively. I wonder how often my own self-deception, denial, and defensiveness have kept me from a deep work of God in my life. Real need motivates intense prayer. Passionate prayer prompts the Holy Spirit to produce miracles. When I experience a miracle—God's unmistakable touch on my life—I burst out in genuine praise!

Personal Prayer

O God, I too extol you. You work daily in my life and continually meet my needs, and I can't help bursting out in praise to your name!

MESSIANIC MASTERPIECE
HIS SOVEREIGNTY

∞ Psalm 110 ∞

The Lord declared to my Lord: "Sit at My right hand until I make Your enemies Your footstool." The Lord will extend Your mighty scepter from Zion. Rule over Your surrounding enemies. Your people will volunteer on Your day of battle. In holy splendor, from the womb of the dawn, the dew of Your youth belongs to You. The Lord has sworn an oath and will not take it back: "Forever, You are a priest like Melchizedek" (vv. 1–4).

This important psalm is quoted many times in the New Testament (Matt. 22:44; Mark 12:36; Luke 20:42; Acts 2:34–35; Heb. 1:13). From these references we learn that Jesus himself quoted this psalm often. We also learn that the Holy Spirit inspired it, David wrote it, and that it is definitely Messianic.

By "listening" carefully, I can "hear" the voice of God speaking to his Son, who would not be born for yet another thousand years! David says: "The Lord [Yahweh] declared to *my* Lord [David's LORD, the Messiah]: 'Sit at My [the Father's] right hand until I make Your [the Son's] enemies Your footstool.'" David could have written this amazing prophecy only by divine inspiration! In this conversation between God the Father and God the Son (Messiah), Messiah is seated at the right hand of God—the place of authority. At the end of time, the Messiah will wield his holy scepter, ruling all peoples righteously, and his enemies will consequently become his footstool. Vigorous young warriors, adorned in holiness, will fight in a massive battle against the forces of evil.

Yahweh has proclaimed that the Messiah will be an eternal Priest in the order of Melchizedeck (see Heb. 5–7). Priest and King will be united in One Person, Israel's true Messiah. As Priest, Christ became his own sacrifice when he died on the cross. As King, he is destined to rule and reign righteously at the end of time, the consummation of the ages.

In a few lines of exquisite Hebrew poetry, the Lord gives us a glimpse into some of the mysteries of his glorious plan of redemption. Old Testament history is full of motifs that will only find their fulfillment at the end of time in Messiah's reign.

Personal Prayer

Dear Lord, because of the sacrifice of your Son, I have eternal life. Because of his predicted rule and sovereign reign, my future is secure!

MESSIANIC MASTERPIECE

HIS CONQUEST

∽ Psalm 110 ∽

The Lord is at Your right hand; He will crush kings on the day of His anger. He will judge the nations, heaping up corpses; He will crush leaders over the entire world. He will drink from the brook by the road; therefore, He will lift up His head (vv. 5–7).

*F*rom my perspective there's something wrong with just about everything these days! But these verses assure me that someday soon everything will be set aright, the books will be balanced, and the enemies of God defeated once and for all!

Without the revelation of the New Testament, however, we would be in the dark about his passage. Later witness from God informs us that Christ will come again, accompanied by saints of all ages, to reign on the earth. At that time he will rule from his position of sovereign authority at the right hand of God, the Father. From that vantage point, he will crush kings and judge the nations (v. 5). He will drink from the brook by the road and lift up His head (v. 7).

These are lofty thoughts. What do I learn from all of this? I learn that wickedness will give way to righteousness, that suffering will succumb to good health, that war will be replaced by perennial peace, that unfairness will be supplanted by justice, and that righteousness will reign on the earth.

I derive enormous security from the fact that all conflicts—from international and national to relational and personal—will be finally and ultimately resolved. Only the Lord can do that. Bless his holy name!

Personal Prayer

Dear Lord, I look forward to the dawn of a new day, when you will make all things right. The glorious prospect of the future gives me hope as I face the frustrations of today.

PAEAN OF PRAISE
BECAUSE OF WHO HE IS

∽ Psalm 111 ∽

*Hallelujah! I will praise the Lord with all my heart in the assembly of the upright
and in the congregation. The Lord's works are great, studied by all who delight in
them. All that He does is splendid and majestic; His righteousness endures
forever. He has caused His wonderful works to be remembered. The Lord
is gracious and compassionate (vv. 1–4).*

U sing an artistically controlled art form—the acrostic—the psalmist celebrates the nature of God. Each line begins with a letter of the Hebrew
alphabet, extolling God's glory and majesty, his righteousness, his grace and
compassion.

Volumes have been written on knowing about God. We can know all
about someone yet never come to know that person intimately.

We can read about God, study about him, sing to him, even pray to
him—without really *knowing* him. But when we recognize him for who he
is—our Creator and Redeemer—then our spirits cry out, "Abba, Father!"

Personal Prayer
*I praise you, Lord, not just for the wonderful things you have done
in my life but because of who you are!*

A Contemporary Lyric

Because of Who You Are

You spoke the word and all the
worlds came into order,
You waved Your hands and planets
filled the empty skies,
You placed the woman and the man
inside the garden
And tho they fell they found compas-
sion in your eyes;
One holy night You brought Your
promise from a virgin,
And Promise grew as He revealed to
us Your heart;
Enduring love displayed throughout
His crucifixion,

And in the dark You tore the grave
and death apart.
Lord, I stand amazed at the wonder
of Your deeds,
And yet a greater wonder brings me
to my knees.
Lord, I praise You because of who
You are,
Not just for all the mighty things
that You have done;
And Lord, I worship You because of
who You are,
You're all the reason that I need to
voice my praise—
Because of who your are . . . Because
of who You are!

Words and music by Bob Farrell and Billy Smiley.
© 1982 by Paragon Music Corp.

Paean of Praise

BECAUSE OF WHAT HE DOES...

∽ Psalm 111 ∽

*He has provided food for those who fear Him; He remembers His covenant forever.
He has shown His people the power of His works by giving them the inheritance of
the nations. The works of His hands are truth and justice; all His instructions are
trustworthy. They are established forever and ever, enacted in truth and uprightness.
He has sent redemption to His people. He has ordained His covenant forever. His
name is holy and awe-inspiring. The fear of the Lord is the beginning of wisdom; all
who follow His instructions have good insight. His praise endures forever (vv. 5–10).*

The psalmist develops his theme specifically here. Our compassionate and
gracious Lord has expressed himself by helping his people—by providing a daily supply of food, by remembering his covenant and keeping his
promises to make them victorious in conquest, by bequeathing to them the
heathen lands around them, by revealing his power. And wonder of wonders,
when they continued to grumble and complain against him, he provided a way
back to him—a plan of redemption and forgiveness!

My Lord is no less active in my life today. He provides for my basic
needs—food, shelter, clothing—by allowing me to serve him through meaningful and fulfilling work. He has blessed me with rich personal relationships
with my family and intimate friends. To guide me in facing the hassles of daily
living, he has sent his Holy Spirit, and I find myself clinging to him every day.

The conclusion of this psalm reminds me of Proverbs 1:7: "The fear
[awesome respect] of the Lord is the beginning of knowledge." It seems that
following his precepts in obedience should be the obvious outcome of my
gratitude for all he's done for me!

Personal Prayer

*I pray that you will find me with an awesome respect for you, Lord, so that it will
be the most natural thing in the world to obey your rules for right living!*

PORTRAIT OF A
GODLY PERSON

WHAT DOES A GODLY PERSON LOOK LIKE?

✷ Psalm 112 ✷

*Hallelujah! Happy is the man who fears the Lord, taking great delight in
His commandments. His descendants will be powerful in the land; the generation
of the upright will be blessed. Wealth and riches are in his house, and his
righteousness endures forever (vv. 1–3).*

God has always sought out strong individuals who are willing to commit
themselves to courageous leadership. The need has never been more desperate than now! Psalm 112 suggests the prototype for this kind of leader.

What does this person look like?

First, you can usually spot a godly man or woman by his or her *happy* countenance. I don't mean a perpetual ear-to-ear grin or some kind of slaphappy
euphoria, but a stillness, a serenity, a relaxing of the facial muscles that is rare in
this world of uptight urbanites. Only the indwelling Spirit of God can bring that
unearthly peace and joy—a joy that is promised to the one who takes "great
delight in [passionate love for] His [the Lord's] commandments" (v. 1).

C. S. Lewis, internationally celebrated author said, "God cannot give us happiness and peace apart from Himself because it is not there. There is no such
thing." Peace is found in a cause or a person greater than oneself. Christ is that
quintessential Person.

Second, the godly person is *prosperous* (vv. 2–3). This Old Testament
promise for Israel suggests that this godly leader's children will make their
mother and father proud, that the family will enjoy agricultural prosperity,
and that right living will result in long life.

Our contemporary culture defines prosperity more narrowly in terms of
money and financial independence only. I want to be God's man, but I limit
the Lord's blessings if I anticipate a financial windfall. I'll take any blessing He
chooses to give me—family harmony, spiritual growth, effectiveness in ministry, knowing Him more intimately!

Personal Prayer

*O Lord, let me be a godly person in a hostile world. Don't let me settle for our cultural
definition of prosperity, but open my spiritual eyes to see that Your desires for me are
infinitely more satisfying than my limited dreams.*

PORTRAIT OF A GODLY PERSON

HOW DOES A GODLY PERSON ACT?

✑ Psalm 112 continued ✑

Light shines in the darkness for the upright. He is gracious, compassionate, and righteous. Good will come to a man who lends generously and conducts his business fairly. . . . The wicked man will see [it] and be angry; he will gnash his teeth in despair. The desire of the wicked will come to nothing (vv. 4–5, 10).

Whenever I think of a man of God, I inevitably think of my Dad. A man marked by conviction, consistency, and energy, he has been my greatest role model.

A man of great strength and generosity, he derives enormous pleasure from being involved with people. He has stood behind my music and has been a real encouragement to me. He is living proof of the paradox in Christianity that, when you give much, it will be multiplied to you (Luke 6:38). His happiness is in direct relation to his active caring for others.

Dad has rock-solid faith. Even when my Mom died, he was unflappable. So deep were his spiritual roots that, when the winds of adversity blew, the branches of that mighty oak swayed, but the taproot held firm. "He will not fear bad news" (v. 7). Because his faith is steadfast, his security system could not be taken away. He is acutely aware that the Lord has already conquered the worst possible thing that can happen. His phobias and icy fears melt in the warm sunshine of God's love. Unlike secular man who "will gnash his teeth in despair" (v. 10), my Dad is part of the unshakable kingdom.

The French have an interesting word, *creneau*. It means "hole" or "opening." To be successful, a businessman has to look for holes or openings in the marketplace. There is a huge *creneau* in the Christian marketplace for godly leaders who have the strength to be role models. The world desperately needs such persons—joyous and prosperous (effective), compassionate and generous, stable and secure. These attributes belong to the kingdom man!

Personal Prayer

Lord, I want to be a kingdom man! I'd like to model for others what my father has modeled for me.

ANTHEM OF ANGELS
CALL TO WORSHIP

∞ Psalm 113 ∞

Hallelujah! Give praise, servants of the LORD; praise the name of the LORD. Let the name of the LORD be praised both now and forever. From the rising of the sun to its setting, let the name of the LORD be praised (vv. 1–3).

Musically inclined or not, have you ever pictured yourself in heaven, singing with the angelic choir? You may not be able to carry a tune now, but if you're a believer, your voice will blend one day with countless millions of others in a glad "hallelujah!"

The word *hallelujah* comes from two beautiful Hebrew words: *hallel*, "praise," and *jah*, referring to "Yahweh," Jehovah. *Hallelujah* means "praise the Lord." Taken from the *hallel*, a collection of songs sung at the great Jewish festivals—Passover, Pentecost, and Tabernacles—Psalms 113–118 are music for a heavenly choir performance. Our Lord joined in shortly before his death (Mark 14:26).

This psalm begins and ends with an exhilarating call to worship. Praising the Lord is a divine imperative, not an option for the servants of God. You can't plead a case of laryngitis or skip rehearsal. The command is clear. Praise the Lord—"now and forevermore" from "the rising of the sun to its setting" (vv. 2–3).

Only Yahweh—whose name was too sacred even to be uttered aloud by ancient worshippers—is worthy of continual praise. Yet how blithely and flippantly we speak that glorious name. As we moved toward colloquial speech in our prayers, sermons, and lyrics, we need to guard against irreverence and disrespect. We need to speak his sacred name as if we were breathing a prayer.

Am I praising him continually—by every action of my life as well as with my vocal chords? Am I praising him in front of my children as well as in private moments of meditation? It's time for the angelic choir rehearsal to begin! He's coming soon!

Personal Prayer
Beginning now, O Lord, keep me accountable for my praise to you. Let it be unending . . . beginning now!

Anthem of Angels

CAUSE FOR PRAISE

∞ Psalm 113 ∞

The LORD is exalted above all the nations, His glory above the heavens. Who is like the Lord our God—the One enthroned on high, who stoops down to look on the heavens and the earth? He raises the poor from the dust and lifts the needy from the garbage heap in order to seat them with nobles—with the nobles of His people. He gives the childless woman a household, [making her] the joyful mother of children. Hallelujah! (vv. 4–9).

In this descriptive praise psalm, two great themes will echo for eternity through the halls of heaven: God's greatness (vv. 4–5) and his grace (vv. 6–9).

God is great. There is no lord like our Lord. He is unique, over all, above all. He sits enthroned on high (literally: "who makes high with respect to sitting"). In this context, study the magnificent lyric poetry of Isaiah 40:12–41:4. Our view of man tends to be overblown and our view of God to be disproportionately small. When our vision of God enlarges, our problems will shrink to size.

God is grace (unmerited favor). He manifests grace to us in three ways:

First, from his exalted position in the heavens, he stoops to survey all of creation. The greatest act of divine stooping would come when God the Father "emptied Himself by assuming the form of a slave, taking on the likeness of men" (Phil. 2:6–7).

Second, God honors the poor and seats them with the nobility. Our position in the heavenly community will not depend on earthly status or recognition by our peers but on his grace.

Third, God settles the barren woman in her home "as a happy mother of children." Sarah's miraculous pregnancy was the joy of the ancient world (Gen. 18, 21). Hannah's humiliation was transformed into jubilation (1 Sam. 2). These great ladies were the motifs preparing for the grand theme of Mary, the Jewish peasant girl, who bore the Messiah. This psalm links the song of Hannah (1 Sam. 2:1–10) with the Magnificat of Mary (Luke 1:46–55).

The psalm concludes with a final hallelujah—praise the Lord! God's glory differs sharply from man's glory. Who is like the Lord, our God? He is unique—equally at home above the heavens or at the side of the lowliest and loneliest creature.

Personal Prayer

I praise you, Lord, for stooping to lift me up, for seating me at your banquet table, and for settling me forever in your home in glory.

CELEBRATION
OF DELIVERANCE
THE EARTH TREMBLES

✑ Psalm 114 ✑

Why was it, sea, that you fled? Jordan, that you turned back? Mountains, that you skipped like rams? Hills, like lambs? Tremble, earth, at the presence of the Lord, at the presence of the God of Jacob, who turned the rock into a pool of water, the flint into a spring of water (vv. 5–8).

The psalmist doesn't attempt to answer the questions posed in verses 5 and 6. Instead, he commands the earth to tremble in the presence of the Lord, the God of Jacob. Why? Because only he can turn desert rocks into refreshing pools of water. Only he can transform inanimate stones into wells of gushing water. Only he can take my parched, meaningless life and restore it with springs of living water!

The revelation of God's power over nature was the only thing that encouraged Job when he was hurting. God led him through a painfully revealing process of counseling through such questions as:

Do you know the laws of the heavens?
Can you set up God's dominion over the earth?
Can you raise your voice to the clouds
and cover yourself with a flood of water?
Do you send the lightning bolts on their way? ...
Who endowed the heart with wisdom
or gave understanding to the mind?
Who has the wisdom to count the clouds?
Who can tip over the water jars of the heavens
when the dust becomes hard
and the clods of earth stick together? (Job 38:33–38 NIV).

The Lord has sovereign control over nature. Man can't lift a finger to influence nature. It's unruly, violent, and disobedient; it can only be manipulated and rearranged. But if God can, even on a whim, control the forces of nature, he can exert control over my seemingly unpredictable life. When I am helpless and lack courage and confidence, I can place unwavering trust in his incomparable power and might.

Personal Prayer
O God of Jacob, refresh and renew my life today. Lead me out of the barren desert to an oasis of your care!

CONTRASTS

SPIRITUALITY VERSUS IDOLATRY

∽ Psalm 115 ∽

Not to us, LORD, not to us, but to Your name give glory because of Your faithful love, because of Your truth. Why should the nations say, "Where is their God?" Our God is in heaven and does whatever He pleases. Their idols are silver and gold, made by human hands. They have mouths, but cannot speak, eyes, but cannot see. They have ears, but cannot hear, noses, but cannot smell. They have hands, but cannot feel, feet, but cannot walk. They cannot make a sound with their throats. Those who make them are just like them, as are all who trust in them (vv. 1–8).

While heathen nations ask, "Where is their God?" our Lord is going about doing whatever he pleases.

Pagan idols are inanimate—having never possessed life—and obviously impotent. Made by man from the metals of the earth, they are unable to see, to hear, to smell, to feel, to speak, or to move about. God himself is responsible for the raw materials from which they are molded! Interestingly, the psalmist observes that the artisans who make idols, as well as those who trust in them, will be "like them"—powerless and useless.

We tend to become "like" the people we idolize, the environment we live in, even the music we hear! We absorb like a sponge the personalities and mannerisms of the people we admire. As mentors and models, they dramatically alter and influence our lives. It's also true that our minds are somewhat like computers. If we program them with junk, junk comes out! And if any of these people or things become more important to us than God, then we become idolators!

In short, there is only one authentic, infinite, personal God of the universe. Counterfeit gods are not only disappearing, but dead. What a pathetic waste when a person bestows his allegiance on worthless pieces of junk— whether they be carved images or compact discs! We must focus on the things that are excellent (see Phil. 4:8).

Personal Prayer

O Lord, not to us, but to Your Name
be the glory and honor.

CONTRASTS
LIFE VERSUS DEATH

∽ Psalm 115 ∽

May the LORD add to [your numbers], both yours and your children's. May you be blessed by the LORD, the Maker of heaven and earth. The heavens are the LORD's, but the earth He has given to the human race. It is not the dead who praise the LORD, nor any of those descending into the silence [of death]. But we will praise the LORD, both now and forever. Hallelujah! (vv. 14–18).

Why don't we sing? The Maker of heaven and earth has given us everything to delight us, but so many people move through the measure of their days like marionettes, with painted smiles and no music in their hearts.

Why don't we sing? There are three primary reasons.

First, the pressures and complexities of modern life can take the song right out of the heart. Contemporary lifestyles often destroy intimacy, the soil in which artistry grows.

Next, we are overexposed to music, especially "elevator music." Second-rate sounds flood the airwaves at home, in the car, in the office, in restaurants. It's like musical wallpaper, so we become spectators rather than participants.

Third, "it is not the dead [persons without the Lord]" who praise him. The psalmist tells us that they go to a place of *silence* (v. 17). There is no singing there!

Against the backdrop of pagan idolatry, the psalmist pleads with the house of Israel, the house of Aaron, and all who fear the Lord, to place their trust in the Lord and to lift their voices in praise. "We will praise the LORD, both now and forever" (v. 18).

Personal Prayer

O Lord, help me to trust and praise you endlessly. May I personally and with full self-awareness experience your blessing.

A Contemporary Lyric

Endless Praise

I sing the wonder of Your power,
I give the glory due Your name;
I see the splendor of Your holiness,
I marvel that forever You're the same.
I praise You for You alone are worthy,
I bless You for Your love and grace;
My soul finds refuge in Your mercy
And for endless days I'll sing Your endless
   praise!

Words and music by Phil and Lynne Brower © 1985 Singspiration.

Personal Song
of Thanksgiving

DELIVERANCE FROM DEATH

∽ Psalm 116 ∽

*I love the LORD because He has heard my appeal for mercy. Because He has turned His
ear to me, I will call [out to Him] as long as I live. The ropes of death were wrapped
around me, and the torments of Sheol overcame me; I encountered trouble and sorrow.
Then I called on the name of the LORD: "LORD, save me!" ... For You, [Lord,]
rescued me from death, my eyes from tears, my feet from stumbling. I will
walk before the LORD in the land of the living (vv. 1–4, 8–9).*

I'll never forget the day I discovered that our senior editor at Singspiration
Music, Norman Johnson, was terminally ill. I watched him cope with the
vicissitudes of suffering for eight years as he battled Lou Gehrig's disease.
About a week before he died, he called and asked me to represent the music
industry in making some comments at his funeral. He died while listening to
Handel's *Messiah*. The "Hallelujah Chorus" was beautifully and victoriously
rendered at his memorial service in an arrangement he penned. My dear friend
Norm went out in a blaze of glory!

Once you've stared death in the face, it is no longer the fearsome specter
that lurks in childhood dreams. In fact, at that moment, God's reality and
ultimate victory over death is never more evident.

The bad news of this psalm is that the psalmist, nearing death, was overcome with self-pity and defeat. Briefly, during this episode, life was the pits.
The good news is that he didn't rely on human resources to pull him through.
Though there is a place for medicine and Christian ministry to the hurting,
this psalmist went beyond all such aid and directly into the presence of the
Great Physician, the Wonderful Counselor. Furthermore, the Lord heard and
answered, choosing to demonstrate his graciousness and compassion (v. 8–9).

A certain responsibility accompanies great deliverance. For the rest of his
life, this psalmist won't forget God's loving mercy. Adversity has enriched
his life. Suffering has purged him of superficiality. Like Job, he can say, "But he
knows the way that I take; when he has tested me, I will come forth as gold"
(Job 23:10 NIV).

Personal Prayer

*O Lord, I don't have to experience serious illness to know your mercy and grace.
You are the Lord of my life ... and the Victor over death!*

PERSONAL SONG
OF THANKSGIVING
PROMISE TO PRAISE

✂ Psalm 116 ✂

How can I repay the LORD all the good He has done for me? I will take the cup of salvation and worship the LORD. I will fulfill my vows to the LORD in the presence of all His people. In the sight of the LORD the death of His faithful ones is costly. LORD, I am indeed Your servant; I am Your servant, the son of Your female servant. You have loosened my bonds. I will offer You a sacrifice of thanksgiving and will worship the LORD. I will fulfill my vows to the LORD, in the very presence of all His people, in the courts of the LORD's house—within you, Jerusalem. Hallelujah! (vv. 12–19).

How can I repay the LORD for all the good He has done for me?" This question asked by my ancient colleague rings true to me today. He answers with four "I wills." First, *I will pray.* "I will take the cup of salvation and worship the LORD" (v. 13). Second, *I will praise the LORD publicly.* "I will fulfill my vows to the LORD in the presence of all His people" (v. 14). Third, *I will offer sacrifice.* "I will offer You a sacrifice of thanksgiving" (v. 17). True worship doesn't come cheap. The psalmist concludes by repeating, "*I will fulfill my vows to the LORD in the very presence of all His people,*" (v. 18) adding "in the courts of the LORD's house—within you, Jerusalem" (v. 19).

He is overwhelmed that the Lord has delivered him from his miserable existence and from death. He is conscious of his servanthood and his sonship. He has become unshackled—freed from the confinement of his chains. He is filled with joy in the awareness that the Lord cares about the death of his saints (v. 15). God's children are safe and secure even at this ultimate moment.

"How can I repay the Lord for all his goodness to me?" I can pray, praise, and offer my life as a living sacrifice. The only fitting conclusion is again, "Hallelujah! Praise the Lord!"

Personal Prayer
Thank you, Lord, that I can trust you to be with me and take care of me in life . . . and in death.

ALL GLORY, LAUD, AND HONOR

∾ Psalm 117 ∾

Praise the Lord, all nations! Glorify Him, all peoples! For great is His faithful love to us; the Lord's faithfulness endures forever. Hallelujah! (vv. 1–2).

I've never been invited to the White House. President Gerald Ford, how-ever, was presented a copy of our musical, *I Love America*, and wrote a wonderful letter, extolling that patriotic work.

Psalm 117 is a miniature invitation to people everywhere. The purpose is praise; the place wherever God's people gather. The reasons for this adulation are given in verse 2. The Lord is to be praised because of his great love and his abiding faithfulness.

The Lord is to be worshipped for who he is—for his character, for his attri-butes. His covenant love (*hesed*) is loyal and eternal; it is not subject to mood swings and emotional vacillation. His faithfulness is based on truth (*emet*). Because the Lord's Word is true or reliable, he is faithful. Loving and faithful. What an apt description of our Lord! The psalmist's response is again, "Hallelujah! Praise the Lord!"

Whatever my mood today, I know my Lord is *loving and faithful*. Whatever adverse circumstances I face today, I know my Lord is *loving and faithful*. Whatever rejection may come my way today, I know my Lord is *lov-ing and faithful*. Whatever physical ailment I experience today, I know my Lord is *loving and faithful*. Whatever business reverses occur today, I know my Lord is *loving and faithful*. Whatever domestic tension I feel today, I know my Lord is *loving and faithful*. Why worry and fret? He invites me to remember that he is loving and faithful. Praise the Lord!

Personal Prayer

Lord, I may be unpredictable and moody, but you can be counted on to be loving and faithful . . . no matter what!

FESTAL PROCESSION
PRAISING HIS LOYAL LOVE

∽ Psalm 118 ∽

Give thanks to the LORD, for He is good; His faithful love endures forever.
Let Israel say, "His faithful love endures forever." Let the house of Aaron say,
"His faithful love endures forever." Let those who fear the LORD say,
"His faithful love endures forever" (vv. 1–4).

The ancient Israelites sang this psalm—the final song in the "Hallel"—as they marched to the sanctuary to worship the Lord. It was used during the Passion Week of our Lord (Matt. 21:9), and it may have been sung in the Upper Room (Matt. 26:30). It was God's loyal love that energized the Israelite army to defeat the surrounding nations.

The wording suggests that these first few verses were either spoken or sung antiphonally. If we read the passage that way, the phrases spring to life:

Congregation: "His love endures forever."
Worship leader: "Let Israel say . . ."
Congregation: "His love endures forever."
Worship leader: "Let the house of Aaron say . . ."
Congregation: "His love endures forever."
Worship leader: "Let those who fear the Lord say . . ."
Congregation: "His love endures forever."

Though I can't understand how this truth meshes with the obvious injustices in the world today, I know that God is loving and good. Though I see only a small slice of history, I know that God's wisdom encompasses all of time and eternity. I'm learning to accept by faith his mysteries. "His love endures forever!"

Personal Prayer
Lord, this psalm causes me to consider how your loyal love extends to our nation,
to the Wyrtzen household, and to all the community of believers who fear your name.
I praise you for your enduring love!

FESTAL PROCESSION

ACKNOWLEDGING HIS DELIVERANCE FROM DISTRESS

∽ Psalm 118 ∽

I called to the LORD in distress; the LORD answered me [and put me] in a spacious place. The LORD is for me; I will not be afraid. What can man do to me? With the LORD for me as my helper, I will look in triumph on those who hate me. It is better to take refuge in the LORD than to trust in man. It is better to take refuge in the LORD than to trust in nobles (vv. 5–9).

The stunning thought occurs to me that I've already made most of the major decisions I'll make in this life—choice of spouse, education, profession, Lord and Savior.

The psalmist is in the same boat. He can either trust his friends, or he can take refuge in the Lord. He can even consult with "princes" (authorities and experts), or he can cry out to the Lord in his dilemma. Human resources or divine power? Which shall it be?

I can trust in secular philosophy, humanistic psychology, and modern science and technology. I can cast my lot with the scholars and experts of human opinion. Or I can take the often unpopular stance of placing my faith in the Lord. When I choose the Lord, he erases past error and teaches me to sing again!

Personal Prayer

Lord, I'm so prone to human error without your constant watch care. Help me always to look to you—not to man-made systems—to define my life and to bring back the music when I falter.

A Contemporary Lyric

Teach Me to Sing Again

In my wandering, my heart hardening,
In such little things I made the wrong choice;
And for many days, in such little ways,
My life went astray from Your still, small
  voice.
Ever straying, disobeying,
Rarely praying, not judging right from wrong!
Needing closeness, not remoteness
I almost lost the joy of Your priceless song.
Teach me to sing again, light up my face again,
Help me trust again, dear Lord, today;
Teach me to sing again, lifting my praise
  again,
Free me to love again, dear Lord, I pray.
Words and music by Don Wyrtzen © 1985 by Singspiration.

FESTAL PROCESSION
EXULTING IN CONFIDENCE, TRIUMPH, AND JOY

❧ Psalm 118 ❧

You pushed me hard to make me fall, but the LORD helped me. The LORD is my strength and my song; He has become my salvation. There are shouts of joy and victory in the tents of the righteous: "The LORD's right hand strikes with power! The LORD's right hand is raised! The LORD's right hand strikes with power!" (vv. 13–16).

The psalmist is down for the count! Heathen nations swarm around him like bees, ready to crush and destroy. They have pushed him back until he is ready to fall.

The mighty conjunction *but* signals a dramatic change. "*But* the LORD helped me" (v. 13). Three times this psalmist has called on the name of the Lord. The Lord's response is to "cut them off." The Hebrew terminology is pretty graphic here. "Cut them off" means to "circumcise them" (vv. 10–12). Our Lord is not namby-pamby nor squeamish in dealing with evil. Now the shouts of victory can resound throughout the "tents of the righteous" (v. 15).

A hard-won battle isn't something you can keep to yourself! It's natural to exclaim and exult when a victory is won. This ancient colleague grows eloquent in his praise: "The LORD is my strength and my song; He has become my salvation" (v. 14). I felt much the same way when I wrote "Jesus Is My Music!"

Personal Prayer
Lord, help me to go forth in your name.
You are my strength, my salvation and my song!

A Contemporary Lyric

Jesus Is My Music
My life was out of tune and happiness eluded me,
My life was dissonant and missing inner harmony;
But then I met the Savior and received His gift of grace,
And now my heart sings melody.
Jesus is my music, Jesus is my song,
Jesus is my music, I want to sing His praises all day long.
Words and music by Don Wytzen © 1978 by Singspiration.

FESTAL PROCESSION
ANTICIPATING THE COMING KINGDOM

✧ Psalm 118 ✧

Open the gates of righteousness for me; I will enter through them and give thanks to the LORD. This is the gate of the LORD; the righteous will enter through it. I will give thanks to You because You have answered me and have become my salvation. The stone that the builders rejected has become the cornerstone. This came from the LORD; it is wonderful in our eyes. This is the day the LORD has made; let us rejoice and be glad in it (vv. 19–24).

Karen and I experienced the excitement that is Israel on our trip to the Holy Land. We were deeply moved to see Gethsemane, Golgotha, the Lord's tomb, and so many other biblical settings and scenes. One of the greatest thrills of the trip was entering Jerusalem through one of the many gates in the wall surrounding the ancient city. In fact, we even walked on the walls. While the present wall and buildings were erected in the sixteenth century AD, the pilgrim feels a sense of expectancy upon seeing those gates!

The topmost stone of each Gothic or Romanesque arch is called the "cornerstone"—a vital piece of architecture that knits the rest of the stones together. In this psalm the "stone" takes on a symbolic meaning. "The stone that the builders rejected [Jesus Christ, the Messiah] has become the cornerstone" (v. 22). The builders symbolize the Jewish leaders who not only rejected him but schemed to have him put to death (Matt. 26:3–5). The psalmist, overjoyed with this new development, bursts into song: "This is the day the LORD has made; let us rejoice and be glad in it" (v. 24).

Most of us try to fill the crowning point of our lives with people or things, but it can only be adequately fulfilled by one Person and that is Jesus Christ. Things, in time, prove to be worthless. Relationships often are broken or grow routine. Achievement may seem meaningless. Only Jesus, our cornerstone, can hold our lives together and give them eternal significance.

Personal Prayer
Lord, you are the Stone which the builders rejected, but I want you to be the cornerstone of my life.

PRAISE FOR THE WORD OF GOD

TRUST AND OBEY

∽ Psalm 119 ∽

ALEF

*How happy are those whose way is blameless, who live according to the law of the LORD!
Happy are those who keep His decrees and seek Him with all their heart. They do nothing
wrong; they follow His ways. You have commanded that Your precepts be diligently kept.
If only my ways were committed to keeping Your statutes! Then I would not be ashamed
when I think about all Your commands. I will praise You with a sincere heart when
I learn Your righteous judgments. I will keep Your statutes; never abandon me (vv. 1–8).*

Psalm 119 is a *magnum opus,* a mighty hymn of praise for the Word of God. The writer of this psalm lived under a lot of pressure—both internal and external. Men of earthly consequence persecuted him and ridiculed his beliefs. The severe test of his faith only strengthened him in his inner man. He became strong and resilient because he placed his faith in the Word of God and meditated on it day and night. The Word became his comfort and his ultimate resource for emotional strength.

This work is also an artistic masterpiece. Its structure is simple, elegant, and precise. This is the consummate alphabet psalm in which each line of each paragraph of eight verses starts with the same letter of the Hebrew alphabet. Verses 1–8 begin with the first letter of the Hebrew alphabet; verses 9–16 begin with the second, etc.

As he celebrates the value, worth, and magnificence of the law, the psalmist almost runs out of words—*commandment, statute, judgment, precept, testimony, way, path.*

The person who trusts in God's Word and obeys it is happy (vv. 1–2). Obedience brings stability and leads to righteousness.

The secular environment or worldly system we live in is diametrically opposed to the Word of God. Its philosophy and value system are poles apart from Christian beliefs, yet even believers are far more influenced by our materialistic culture than they realize. This psalm stops me short: Am I more deeply affected by the world or by the Word?

Personal Prayer

*Dear Lord, forgive me for not trusting and obeying you. My lack of faith has
caused pain and unhappiness for myself and others. As I meditate again on
your Word, fill me with deep joy and peace.*

PRAISE FOR THE WORD OF GOD

MEMORIZING THE WORD

∽ Psalm 119 ∽

BET

How can a young man keep his way pure? By keeping Your word. I have sought You with all my heart; don't let me wander from Your commands. I have treasured Your word in my heart so that I may not sin against You. Lord, may You be praised; teach me Your statutes. With my lips I proclaim all the judgments from Your mouth. I rejoice in the way [revealed by] Your decrees as much as in all riches. I will meditate on Your precepts and think about Your ways. I will delight in Your statutes; I will not forget Your word (vv. 9–16).

How can a young person in this decadent society hope to lead a pure life? How can one avoid wandering from the truth? How can one be protected from committing sin? By mastering God's Word. By allowing it to control his or her life. The way to master the Word is to memorize it—just the way a good symphony conductor memorizes a score. Then, when the spiritual battles come, the sword of the Spirit can be wielded at a moment's notice, without fumbling for words!

The psalmist asks the Lord's help in learning the divine decrees, then publicly recites God's magnificent law. He rejoices in following the Lord's statutes as one exults in great riches. At work during the day or in his bed at night, he runs these precepts through his mind. He doesn't intend to neglect them because God's law is his delight!

The Word has impacted this psalmist's mind-set. He has not programmed his mind with trash and pornographic material that feed lust and lead to unhealthy fantasizing. He doesn't have to live with the pressure and pain caused by an unbalanced, sick mental attitude. His life is pure because his thoughts are pure.

Personal Prayer

O Lord, don't let me neglect your Word. As I hide it away in my heart like nuggets of gold, I am enriched. As I follow its precepts, I'm strengthened for the battle.

PRAISE FOR THE WORD OF GOD

OPEN MINE EYES

∞ Psalm 119 ∞

GIMEL

*Deal generously with Your servant so that I might live; then I will keep Your word.
Open my eyes so that I may see wonderful things in Your law. I am a stranger on
earth; do not hide Your commands from me. I am continually overcome by longing
for Your judgments. You rebuke the proud, the accursed, who wander from Your
commands. Take insult and contempt away from me, for I have kept Your decrees.
Though princes sit together speaking against me, Your servant will think about Your
statutes; Your decrees are my delight and my counselors (vv. 17–24).*

Living is not just a meaningless vacuum for this author-composer. The goal
of his life is to keep God's Word. Is this legalism—a slavish adherence to
the letter of the law? No! The psalmist depends on God's truth for strength
and sustenance. This Word is supporting him like a life raft would support a
drowning man on a storm-tossed sea. This concept is repeated often in this
psalm (vv. 24, 37, 40, 50, 77, 88).

He prays that his eyes will be opened to behold "wonderful things" out of
the law. He prays for insight and illumination so that God's commandments
will not be hidden from him. So intensely involved is he in this quest that his
soul "is consumed with longing" for the Law "at all times" (v. 20).

What "wonderful things" do I find for living life in this troubled century?
I love to read the Word aloud; it gets my ear involved as well as my eye.
Recently, I read the whole book of Ephesians aloud in one sitting. Often, I put
outstanding passages on three-by-five-inch cards and carry them around with
me for ready reference. Second Corinthians 12:9 helps me with feelings of
inadequacy and incompetence. Jeremiah 29:11 helps me regarding uncertainty about the future. First Chronicles 28:20 gives me encouragement in my
work. Occasionally I make Scripture songs out of these key concepts. Then
the Scripture, combined with music, comforts and sustains me.

Personal Prayer

*O Lord, open my eyes that I may behold
"wonderful things" from your Word today.*

PRAISE FOR THE WORD OF GOD

SONG OF THE SOUL SET FREE

⌘ Psalm 119 ⌘

DALET

My life is down in the dust; give me life through Your word. I told You about my life, and You listened to me; teach me Your statutes. Help me understand the meaning of Your precepts so that I can meditate on Your wonders. I am weary from grief; strengthen me through Your word. Keep me from the way of deceit, and graciously give me Your instruction. I have chosen the way of truth; I have set Your ordinances [before me] I cling to Your decrees; LORD, do not put me to shame. I pursue the way of Your commands, for You broaden my understanding (vv. 25–32).

Rich in contrasts, this passage displays the positive against the negative. First, a mournful tone is heard: "My life is down in the dust"; "I am weary"; "Keep me from the way of deceit"; "Do not put me to shame" (vv. 25, 28, 29, 31).

Then on a rising crescendo, the psalmist realizes the possibilities available to him through God's Word—renewal, strength, truth, freedom! As he begins to understand these precepts, he is filled with wonder.

Jesus articulated this truth in John 8:30–32: "Jesus said to the Jews who had believed Him, 'If you continue in My word, you really are My disciples. You will know the truth, and the truth will set you free.'"

Personal Prayer
O Lord, set my heart free as I adhere to your truth and hold fast to your commands.

A Contemporary Lyric

The Day That I Met Jesus

The day that I met Jesus
My life was torn with grief and pain,
My soul had longed for something new in life—
Then I believed, and Jesus came.
That day that I met Jesus
My life was changed—my sins were gone,
The Lord has won Himself a trophy of grace,
For Jesus lives, He lives within my heart.
If I could be the one
To tell you what the Lord has done;
If you would just believe Him
And at this hour receive Him
If you would only let Him conquer you!

Words and music by Don Wyrtzen © 1964 by Singspiration.

PRAISE FOR THE WORD OF GOD
NOT FOR SELFISH GAIN

✑ Psalm 119 ✑
HE

Teach me, LORD, the meaning of Your statutes, and I will always keep them. Help me understand Your instruction, and I will obey it and follow it with all my heart. Help me stay on the path of Your commands, for I take pleasure in it. Turn my heart to Your decrees and not to material gain. Turn my eyes from looking at what is worthless; give me life in Your ways. Confirm what You said to Your servant, for it produces reverence for You. Turn away the disgrace I dread; indeed, Your judgments are good. How I long for Your precepts! Give me life through Your righteousness (vv. 33–40).

What drives me? What hidden desires motivate me to perform? What goals beckon me? Part of being imperfect, human, and fallen is the struggle with mixed motives. I want my life to bring glory to God, but I also want some other things—personal fulfillment, meaningful work, the recognition of my peers, financial success, domestic tranquility. O how easy it is to be deceived, to rationalize, to be a self-preservationist! I want to be "in the world but not of it," yet, to be honest, secular culture carries a punch that the Word often doesn't.

This psalmist puts me to shame! He observes the law wholeheartedly (vv. 33–35), then begs God to purge him of any unworthy motives—"material gain,""worthless things" (vv. 36–37). Then he gives us the key to proper motivation for the study of God's Word as well as for all other endeavors undertaken by the believer. "Help me stay on the path of Your commands" (v. 35). With divine direction the psalmist knows he can't miss a beat.

If I live to fulfill my own goals and desires or even to satisfy the expectations of others—no matter how worthy—I'll miss the greater blessing of living my life to please God. Obeying his Word is the premiere goal that drives me now!

Personal Prayer
O Lord, turn my heart toward your statutes today. May I not live my life for selfish gain but to please you!

Praise for the Word of God

I WILL SPEAK OF YOUR STATUTES

∽ Psalm 119 ∽
Vav

Let Your faithful love come to me, Lord, Your salvation, as You promised. Then I can answer the one who taunts me, for I trust in Your word. Never take the word of truth from my mouth, for I hope in Your judgments. I will always keep Your law, forever and ever. I will walk freely in an open place because I seek Your precepts. I will speak of Your decrees before kings and not be ashamed. I delight in Your commands, which I love. I will lift up my hands to Your commands, which I love, and will meditate on Your statutes (vv. 41–48).

Down through the ages some have dared to proclaim the Word of God at the risk of endangering their lives or reputations. In 1521, Martin Luther was excommunicated by Pope Leo X. Charles V, emperor of the Holy Roman Empire, ordered him to appear before the Diet (meeting) of princes, nobles, and clergymen at Worms, Germany. They demanded that Luther recant his beliefs, but he refused.

> Unless I am convinced by the testimony of the Scriptures or by clear reasons (for I do not trust either in the pope or in councils alone, since it is well-known that they have often erred and contradicted themselves), I am bound by the Scriptures . . . and my conscience is captive to the Word of God. I cannot and I will not retract anything!

This psalmist vows to "speak of [Your] statutes before kings" (v. 46). In his day that would have been a dangerous thing to do, as it is in some parts of the world today. People like Georgi Vins and my friends, Earl Poysti and Bark and Carleen Fahnestock, boldly proclaim the Word in hostile environments and under adverse circumstances.

Several other bold personal assertions are made in these verses: "I trust in Your word" (v. 42). "I hope in Your judgments" (v. 43). "I will always keep Your law" (v. 44). "I delight in Your commands which I love" (v. 47).

Here is a person with a passion for God's Word. He is obsessed with it. He thinks about it constantly. As the Word dominates his thoughts, it changes his life and frees him to face life unafraid.

Personal Prayer
O Lord, let me become so immersed in your Word that I share it freely wherever I go—whether in the company of colleagues or kings!

PRAISE FOR THE WORD OF GOD
PRECIOUS PROMISES

∞ Psalm 119 ∞
ZAYIN

Remember [Your] word to Your servant, through which You have given me hope. This is my comfort in my affliction: Your promise has given me life. The arrogant constantly ridicule me, but I do not turn away from Your instruction. LORD, I remember Your judgments from long ago and find comfort. Rage seizes me because of the wicked who reject Your instruction. Your statutes are [the theme of] my song during my earthly life. I remember Your name in the night, LORD, and I keep Your law. This is my [practice]: I obey Your precepts (vv. 49–56).

"Your decrees are the theme of my song!" What a mandate for the Christian musician! What a mission statement for a godly artist! As Christopher Smart said in 1763, "Glorious the song, when God's name the theme." The content of our art must be the magnificence of God's truth. Yet it is so easy to water it down, leave it out, or yield to the temptation to explore other areas of thought that are more appealing, more commercial.

This servant had discovered the rock of God's truth during a particularly painful time of suffering and opposition. The precious promises contained in God's Word had given him hope and comfort. Even in the depths of his dark night, he remembered these promises and recited them. The habits of holiness he had developed sustained him at the time of his greatest need. Therefore, because God's Word has been tried and tested in his life, these precepts now occupy all of his thought. There is no room for lesser interests!

My theme song is that which consumes me because it has been tested and proved. As I experience the truth of God's Word daily and am convicted by its power, my goal or mandate is to set God's truth to music in simple, powerful form.

Personal Prayer
O Lord, your promises preserve my life and comfort me.
May your decrees be the theme of my song for the rest of my days.

PRAISE FOR THE WORD OF GOD

WITH ALL MY HEART

∽ Psalm 119 ∽

KHET

The LORD is my portion; I have promised to keep Your words. I have sought Your favor with all my heart; be gracious to me according to Your promise. I thought about my ways and turned my steps back to Your decrees. I hurried, not hesitating to keep Your commands. Though the ropes of the wicked were wrapped around me, I did not forget Your law. I rise at midnight to thank You for Your righteous judgments. I am a friend to all who fear You, to those who keep Your precepts. LORD, the earth is filled with Your faithful love; teach me Your statutes (vv. 57–64).

I remember my high school days, when under pressure to produce and perform, I wanted to be left alone. The result was an unfulfilled inner life, a personal emptiness, and a passionless Christianity. I followed at a distance because there was little delight and joy in my relationship with the Lord.

This psalmist is committed, dedicated, passionately involved. "I have sought Your favor *with all my heart*" (v. 58), he declares. Nothing lackadaisical about this man's approach to Bible study! In fact, we'd say that this person is "on fire for the Lord." So strong is his devotion that even if the wicked were to bind him with ropes, he will not forget the law (v. 61).

Not only does he make all kinds of declarations about what he plans to do in the future, but he already has put feet to his intentions. He takes stock of his actions and chooses to follow God's law (v. 59). He prays, giving thanks for the good guidance of God's Word (v. 62). He befriends fellow believers who share his love and reverence for the Lord (v. 63).

Where is this level of commitment and dedication today? Which of us, living in the midst of a secular society, gives this kind of intense devotion and concentration to spiritual matters? We wake in the middle of the night, besieged with worries and anxieties. The psalmist wakes up and praises the Lord with all his heart!

Personal Prayer

O Lord, help me to seek your face with all my heart!

Praise for the
Word of God

It Was Good for Me to Be Afflicted

❧ Psalm 119 ❧
Tet

Lord, You have treated Your servant well, just as You promised. Teach me good judgment and discernment, for I rely on Your commands. Before I was afflicted I went astray, but now I keep Your word. You are good, and You do what is good; teach me Your statutes. The arrogant have smeared me with lies, but I obey Your precepts with all my heart. Their hearts are hard and insensitive, but I delight in Your instruction. It was good for me to be afflicted so that I could learn Your statutes. Instruction from Your lips is better for me than thousands of gold and silver pieces (vv. 65–72).

What kind of man is this psalmist? He thanks God for adversity and affliction! He must be sadomasochistic!

Reading on, I understand. "Before I was afflicted I went astray, but *now* I keep your word" (v. 67). The painful consequences of sin have driven him to the Word of God, and now he considers "instruction from Your lips . . . better for me . . . than thousands of gold and silver pieces" (v. 72).

We contemporary Christians prefer simple answers to complex issues. We seem to think there must be an easier way to personal depth and spiritual maturity. But the nature of reality is like a tapestry with knots underneath, a symphony containing dissonance, or a play enhanced by dramatic tension. When I wonder why life with the Lord can't be easier, I am reminded of the song, "No Easier Way," that I wrote with Claire Cloninger.

Personal Prayer

O Lord, let me learn to praise you for the hard times that drive me to my knees, and to remember that your suffering paid the price of my eternal security!

A Contemporary Lyric

No Easier Way

Why can't I live my life without losing it?
Why can't I grow without pain?
Why can't I live for You, Lord, without dying?
There must be an easier way!
There was no easier way for You,
There was no easier thing You could do;
The cost of my life
Was the cross and the grave,
There was no easier way!

Words by Clair Cloninger and Don Wyrtzen. Music by Don Wyrtzen. © 1984 Singspiration.

Praise for the Word of God
LIVING THE LAW

ꙮ Psalm 119 ꙮ
YOD

Your hands made me and formed me; give me understanding so that I can learn Your commands. Those who fear You will see me and rejoice, for I hope in Your word. I know, LORD, that Your judgments are just and that You have afflicted me fairly. May Your faithful love comfort me, as You promised Your servant. May Your compassion come to me so that I may live, for Your instruction is my delight. Let the arrogant be put to shame for slandering me with lies; I will meditate on Your precepts. Let those who fear You, those who know Your decrees, turn to me. May my heart be blameless regarding Your statutes so that I will not be put to shame (vv. 73–80).

This ancient believer-musician places his complete hope in the Word, since the Lord has delivered him from pain and has made of him an example and encouragement to other believers.

He is acutely aware that his life has come from God. Infinitely powerful hands have made and formed him. He is not a product of chance. Now he requests understanding to learn God's law so that others will be filled with joy when they observe his life.

The staggering truth dawns that I am the only Bible some people will ever read! Am I living its precepts faithfully so that unbelievers "rejoice when they see me and rejoice," or are the pages of my life so marred with my own errors that they are difficult to read? Is the music of my life flat, dull, and boring?

I cry out to the Lord for compassion! I need another chance to live out his Word before the world so I will point others to him.

Personal Prayer
Thank you, Lord, for forming me, for forgiving me, and for sending me as your love letter to the world. May the words and music of my life be consistent with your truth.

Praise for the Word of God

A WINESKIN IN THE SMOKE

✍ Psalm 119 ✍

KAPH

I long for Your salvation; I hope in Your word. My eyes grow weary [looking] for what You have promised; I ask, "When will You comfort me?" Though I have become like a wineskin [dried] by smoke, I do not forget Your statutes. How many days [must] Your servant [wait]? When will You execute judgment on my persecutors? The arrogant have dug pits for me; they violate Your instruction. All Your commands are true; people persecute me with lies—help me! They almost ended my life on earth, but I did not abandon Your precepts. Give me life in accordance with Your faithful love, and I will obey the decree You have spoken (vv. 81–88).

I've felt like "a wineskin [dried] by smoke"—empty and shriveled and useless. I've felt pressure like the thousands of pounds of tension on the strings inside a grand piano. What an encouragement this section is to me!

With dramatic imagery the psalmist compares himself to "a wineskin [dried] by smoke." In the heat of severe persecution and harassment, his soul is shriveling like a goatskin, and his eyes, "looking for what You had promised," grow red and watery.

Then he states, "They almost ended my life on earth" (v. 87). Arrogant persecutors are digging his grave in anticipation of an early death.

Even if all of this is taken figuratively, the metaphors are stunning. In these unbelievably adverse circumstances, the psalmist's faith in God's Word is immovable. He continually voices his hope and trust in God's trustworthy "commands," his "precepts," and "statutes." The emphasis is on God's Word—not on the wrongs that have been committed.

I can understand this ancient musician's impatience. I have experienced deep hurt, searing anger, and dark despair. I've sometimes wondered where I fit in and where God is when I've needed him. I've even rebelled and come awfully close to dropping out. Yet, when I allow God to perform on the keys of my life, music comes forth! Like the psalmist, I choose to put my hope in the Word, to honor the Lord, and to wait patiently for him to work more obviously and directly in my life.

Personal Prayer

O Lord, help me, even when under intense pressure and pain, to learn to wait for you to do your deep work in my life.

PRAISE FOR THE WORD OF GOD
IN ALL PERFECTION I SEE A LIMIT

✑ Psalm 119 ✑
LAMED

LORD, Your word is forever; it is firmly fixed in heaven. Your faithfulness is for all generations; You established the earth, and it stands firm. They stand today in accordance with Your judgments, for all things are Your servants. If Your instruction had not been my delight, I would have died in my affliction. I will never forget Your precepts, for You have given me life through them. I am Yours; save me, for I have sought Your precepts. The wicked hope to destroy me, but I contemplate Your decrees. I have seen a limit to all perfection, but Your command is without limit (vv. 89–96).

I'm a perfectionist by nature. I probably use perfectionism defensively in uncomfortable situations to distance myself from other people. We use all kinds of devices like armor to protect ourselves—humor (being too funny), intellectualization (being too smart), superficiality (being too sweet). Sometimes achievement is an attempt to prove ourselves worthy in the eyes of others and ourselves.

This psalmist has a more realistic view. He promotes the faithfulness of God and his eternal Word. It's settled in heaven, therefore he can stake his life on its immutable perfection. These qualities of the Word have supported the struggling psalmist in persecution and affliction. Through it all, he's clung to the one sure thing he knows—the Word of God. It has become his delight, his salvation, and his stable reference point.

This section ends with a beautiful, original insight. "I have seen a limit to all perfection" (v. 96). No matter how high the level of excellence one might attain, the product of human creativity is short-lived at best. Works of art, clever creations, powerful empires—all are temporal. Only the Word is perfect, boundless, and eternal!

Personal Prayer
O Lord, I praise you for the absolute reliability of your Word. Help me to recognize the short-term duration of any work I may accomplish, including songwriting. May I look to your Word for perfection and not to myself.

PRAISE FOR THE WORD OF GOD

I HAVE MORE INSIGHT THAN ALL MY TEACHERS

∽ Psalm 119 ∽

MEM

How I love Your teaching! It is my meditation all day long. Your command makes me wiser than my enemies, for it is always with me. I have more insight than all my teachers because Your decrees are my meditation. I understand more than the elders because I obey Your precepts. I have kept my feet from every evil path to follow Your word. I have not turned from Your judgments, for You Yourself have instructed me. How sweet Your word is to my taste—[sweeter] than honey to my mouth. I gain understanding from Your precepts; therefore I hate every false way (vv. 97–104).

I can recall some teachers and professors who profoundly impacted my life at critical turning points. Mrs. Lillian Gearhart taught me piano; Jay Ciser and Carl Hamilton taught me art; Dr. Charles Horne taught me apologetics; Dr. Howard Hendricks taught me Bible study methods; Dean Arlton taught me music history; Dr. Bruce Waltke taught me the Psalms and Hebrew; Dr. Charles Ryrie taught me theology; Dr. Francis Schaeffer taught me about culture.

But this psalmist claims that he has more "insight" than all his teachers (v. 99), "understands more than the elders" (v. 100), for "You Yourself [the Lord] have instructed me" (v. 102)!

I too have learned that reading the Word with my intellect alone is inadequate. I graduated from Dallas Theological Seminary, and even though I studied at the feet of the fine theologians and Bible scholars I have mentioned, I learned that it is the Holy Spirit who does the real teaching! As R. A. Torrey said:

> No amount of mere human teaching, no matter who our teachers may be, will ever give us a correct and exact and full apprehension of the truth. . . . We must be taught directly by the Holy Spirit. The one who is thus taught will understand the truth of God better, even if he does not know one word of Greek or Hebrew, than the one who knows Greek and Hebrew thoroughly . . . but who is not taught of the Spirit.

I also must submit to the Holy Spirit as my teacher. I need his comfort and counsel. Otherwise, the undertow of secular society may pull me down.

Personal Prayer
O Lord, your Word is sweeter than honey. Feed me by your Holy Spirit so I may know the truth.

Praise for the Word of God

YOUR WORD IS A LAMP UNTO MY FEET

ᕲᕲ Psalm 119 ᕲᕲ

NUN

Your word is a lamp for my feet and a light on my path. I have solemnly sworn to keep Your righteous judgments. I am severely afflicted; LORD, give me life through Your word. LORD, please accept my willing offerings of praise, and teach me Your judgments. My life is constantly in danger, yet I do not forget Your instruction. The wicked have set a trap for me, but I have not wandered from Your precepts. I have Your decrees as a heritage forever; indeed, they are the joy of my heart. I am resolved to obey Your statutes to the very end (vv. 105–112).

How well I remember taking my son, D. J., on a camping trip to northern Michigan. Just the two of us, a small tent, a crackling fire, some fishing poles, and a raft! Wanting to spend quality time with my son, I left my books at home. But just before we went to sleep, D. J. pulled out a flashlight and a book he had brought along! In the pitch dark the glow of the campfire and the beam from the flashlight gave us all the light we needed.

Without the searchlight of God's Word, we'd be left to flounder in the dark, looking for the way. But his law points out the snares of the wicked, and we can avoid stumbling into their traps.

The psalmist continues to take his life in his hands; but he has vowed to follow God's righteous decrees, so there is nothing to fear from visible or invisible foes. While the darkness closes in, he has the enlightenment of the Word and cannot stray from these rocklike precepts (v. 110).

Not only does this ancient one have light for his present difficulties, but God's statutes are his "heritage forever." He can look forward to life in the light now and throughout eternity. As a result, he offers the "willing offerings of praise" of his mouth (v. 108) and obedience to the Word "to the very end" (v. 112).

What the psalmist did not have was an intimate relationship with the Light of the world, who came to banish darkness forever. I walk in the increased illumination of the Messiah!—the prophecy fulfilled!

Personal Prayer

O Lord, I thank you for sending Christ, the living Word, who walks with me to point out hidden dangers and to shepherd me through the canyons and ravines of my life.

PRAISE FOR THE WORD OF GOD

I STAND IN AWE

∽ Psalm 119 ∽

SAMEK

I hate the double-minded, but I love Your instruction. You are my shelter and my shield; I hope in Your word. Depart from me, you evil ones, so that I may obey my God's commands. Sustain me as You promised, and I will live; do not let me be ashamed of my hope. Sustain me so that I can be safe and be concerned with Your statutes continually. You reject all who stray from Your statutes, for their deceit is a lie. You remove all the wicked on earth as if they were dross; therefore, I love Your decrees. I shudder in awe of You; I fear Your judgments (vv. 113–120).

*A*wesome! If I've heard that word once, I've heard it a thousand times. I've become convinced that this word is the cornerstone for the vocabulary of young America. They handle greatness with undue familiarity!

Still, *awesome* is a perfectly good word. It's in the dictionary as well as in the Bible itself. The dictionary defines the word as "characterized by awe—an overwhelming feeling of reverence, admiration, and fear produced by that which is grand, sublime, extremely powerful, or the like." I could use this word to describe Brahm's Fourth Symphony. And the psalmist certainly feels this kind of reverence for God's laws.

This psalmist isn't gullible enough to believe that he is immune to the seductive wiles of the wicked and prays earnestly for strength to stay true to God's awesome decrees. He actually trembles in God's presence!

I'm wondering if believers in this modern world don't often try to be too cozy, too familiar with God. We sing superficial songs and engage in cliché-ridden, repetitive prayers. Many of us know the *traditions* but have never been moved by the *truth*. We've never felt our flesh quiver in awe—holy respect—as we behold the majesty of God's eternal Word!

Personal Prayer

O Lord, when I open your Word, I'm standing on holy ground.
Teach me to tremble in your presence!

PRAISE FOR THE WORD OF GOD
I AM YOUR SERVANT

℘ Psalm 119 ℘
AYIN

I have done what is just and right; do not leave me to my oppressors. Guarantee Your servant's well-being; do not let the arrogant oppress me. My eyes grow weary [looking for] Your salvation and for Your righteous promise. Deal with Your servant based on Your faithful love; teach me Your statutes. I am Your servant; give me understanding so that I may know Your decrees. It is time for the Lord to act, [for] they have broken Your law. Since I love Your commandments more than gold, even the purest gold, I carefully follow all Your precepts and hate every false way (vv. 121–128).

Most of us living in affluent America know little about servanthood. We expect excellent and efficient service from others and accept it as our due. It is so much more human to desire stardom than servanthood!

Three times in this passage, however, the psalmist—likely a person of honor and prestige in the community—professes his status as a lowly servant before God: "Guarantee *Your servant's* well-being" (v. 122). "Deal with *Your servant*" (v. 124). "I am *Your servant*; give me understanding" (v. 125). He isn't too proud to admit his need to be educated in the royal decrees or to seek divine wisdom for decision-making.

Ancient believers, overcome by the greatness of God and their own worthlessness, often prostrated themselves before the Lord in abject humility (Ps. 5:7). We do well to get on our knees once in awhile.

Yet Jesus, God incarnate, willingly left the glories of heaven to walk the dusty pathways of this earth. He owned no property, sought no public office, accumulated no possessions. "The Son of Man did not come to be served, but to serve, and to give his life as a ransom for many" (Matt. 20:28). He came to serve . . . and to die for my sins!

Such love compels me to fall on my face. "I am Your servant; give me understanding so that I may know your decrees" (v. 125).

Personal Prayer
Speak, Lord! Your servant is listening!

PRAISE FOR THE WORD OF GOD

YOUR WORD IS WONDERFUL

∞ Psalm 119 ∞

PE

Your decrees are wonderful; therefore I obey them. The revelation of Your words brings light and gives understanding to the inexperienced. I pant with open mouth because I long for Your commands. Turn to me and be gracious to me, as is [Your] practice toward those who love Your name. Make my steps steady through Your promise; don't let sin dominate me. Redeem me from human oppression, and I will keep Your precepts. Show favor to Your servant, and teach me Your statutes. My eyes pour out streams of tears because people do not follow Your instruction (vv. 129–136).

God's Word is wonderful—marvelous, extraordinary, remarkable! The word *wonderful* literally means "to generate wonder." Even the simple, the unintelligent, the uneducated can grasp its truth when instructed by the Holy Spirit. Its inspiration exceeds that of Shakespeare, Mozart, Milton, Bach, and the greatest poets and composers who have ever lived.

So amazing is the power of these statutes and commands that the psalmist opens his mouth and "pants" for understanding. His deep personal longing for the truth is like gasping for breath after running the Boston Marathon.

As I read these verses, I'm reminded of "Wonderful Words of Life," Dad's theme song for the Word of Life Hour. I grew up hearing it.

Personal Prayer

O Lord, teach me to love your truth and see the wonder of your words!

A Wonderful Gospel Song

Wonderful Words of Life

Sing them over again to me,
Wonderful words of life;
Let me more of their beauty see,
Wonderful words of life.
Words of life and beauty,
Teach me faith and duty:
Beautiful words, wonderful words,
Wonderful words of life.
Words and music by Philip P. Bliss.

PRAISE FOR THE WORD OF GOD
YOUR WORD IS RIGHTEOUS

⤜ Psalm 119 ⤛
TSADE

You are righteous, LORD, and Your judgments are just. The decrees You issue are righteous and altogether trustworthy. My anger overwhelms me because my foes forget Your words. Your word is completely pure, and Your servant loves it. I am insignificant and despised, but I do not forget Your precepts. Your righteousness is an everlasting righteousness, and Your instruction is true. Trouble and distress have overtaken me, but Your commands are my delight. Your decrees are righteous forever. Give me understanding, and I will live (vv. 137–144).

The psalmist is filled with deep love and reverence for the law. Because the Lord is righteous, his Word is also fully trustworthy. The Lord's promises are fully reliable because they have been thoroughly tried, tested, and proven.

But all is not well here. The psalmist is almost worn out with zeal. His enemies ignore the Word of God. He is feeling lowly and despised. Arnold Schoenberg said, "Dissonances are more difficult to comprehend than consonances." Horace labeled it "harmony in discord." The psalmist is alluding to the "discordant harmony" of his existence.

But his depression cannot obliterate his memory of the law. Continual trouble and distress do not snatch away his ingrained delight in the Lord's commands. No matter how lonely or how oppressed he feels, God's Word stands unaffected.

What a comfort to know beyond a shadow of a doubt that the Word of God is absolutely trustworthy and reliable! May we not let technological change, moral relativism, scientific advances, or intellectual pride rob us of our confidence in God's eternal Word!

Personal Prayer
O Lord, I praise you and thank you for your flawless Word!

PRAISE FOR THE WORD OF GOD

LONG AGO I LEARNED FROM YOUR STATUTES

∽ Psalm 119 ∽

OOF

I call with all my heart; answer me, Lord. I will obey Your statutes. I call to You; save me, and I will keep Your decrees. I rise before dawn and cry out for help; I hope in Your word. I am awake through each watch of the night to meditate on Your promise. In keeping with Your faithful love, hear my voice. LORD, give me life, in keeping with Your justice. Those who pursue evil plans come near; they are far from Your instruction. You are near, LORD, and all Your commands are true. Long ago I learned from Your decrees that You have established them forever (vv. 145–152).

Some of the Scripture songs I learned as a kid have supported me in times of crisis such as those described by this psalmist (i.e. "Thy Word Have I Hid in My Heart," "Thy Word Is a Lamp unto My Feet"). My Mom taught me that music comforts. I remember her singing around the house some of Norman Clayton's songs: "Now I Belong to Jesus" and "We Shall See His Lovely Face."

As trouble sweeps in like a flood, the psalmist gets up before daybreak to pray. Then at night, restless and sleepless, he meditates on God's promises, likely committed to memory when he was younger. Because he knows the Word, the psalmist can call on it instantly for help in any emergency. He promises to "keep Your decrees" (v. 146), "to hope in Your word" (v. 147), and "keeping with Your faithful love . . . Your justice" (v. 149). This musician feels close to the Lord because God's Word is lodged firmly in his mind and heart!

Scripture songs are like tapes that play over and over in our minds. Because more of our senses are involved in learning them, they bring God's truth to the forefront of our consciousness. What a glorious wedding when the Word is united with music!

Personal Prayer

O Lord, thank you for my mom who taught me hymns and gospel songs when I was young. Now these Scripture songs and biblical promises hold me steady in times of trouble.

Praise for the Word of God

YOUR COMPASSION IS GREAT, O LORD

✑ Psalm 119 ✑

RESH

Consider my affliction and rescue me, for I have not forgotten Your instruction. Defend my cause, and redeem me; give me life, as You promised. Salvation is far from the wicked because they do not seek Your statutes. Your compassions are many, Lord; give me life, according to Your judgments. My persecutors and foes are many. I have not turned from Your decrees. I have seen the disloyal and feel disgust because they do not keep Your word. Consider how I love Your precepts; LORD, give me life, according to Your faithful love. The entirety of Your word is truth, and all Your righteous judgments endure forever (vv. 153–160).

How prone we human beings are to panic when the pressure builds. Our faith shrinks and we're even tempted to avoid unpleasant confrontations at all costs—in other words, to run in the other direction!

The ancient songwriter must have known that trapped feeling. Three times he reminds the Lord of his promise to renew and preserve life: "Give me life, as You promised" (v. 154). "Give me life, according to Your judgments" (v. 156). "Give me life, according to Your faithful love" (v. 159).

Suddenly the theme of this song sounds above the discord of defeat like the clear, sweet note of a lark: "Your compassions are many, LORD!" (v. 156). The Lord not only knows the feelings of our infirmities and sympathizes with us, but *he desires to alleviate the pain or remove its cause altogether!*

I can't begin to comprehend the love and compassion of the Lord. Under intense emotional pressure, I either abandon it or forget it. Yet he is faithful to supply his mercies in rich abundance if I follow the example of my ancient counterpart and ask for it!

Personal Prayer

O Lord, I thank you for your great love and compassion. Revive my life on the basis of your truth today!

PRAISE FOR THE WORD OF GOD

I REJOICE IN YOUR PROMISE

∞ Psalm 119 ∞

SIN/SHIN

Princes have persecuted me without cause, but my heart fears [only] Your word. I rejoice over Your promise like one who finds vast treasure. I hate and abhor falsehood, [but] I love Your instruction. I praise You seven times a day for Your righteous judgments. Abundant peace belongs to those who love Your instruction; nothing makes them stumble. LORD, I hope for Your salvation and carry out Your commands. I obey Your decrees and love them greatly. I obey Your precepts and decrees, for all my ways are before You (vv. 161–168).

What a sunny, bright, and joyful passage! The psalmist has the distinction of having both loved and kept the law. Now the music in his heart spills across the page in a lilting progression of praise: "I rejoice over Your promise" (v. 162). "I hope for Your salvation" (v. 166). "I obey Your decrees and love them greatly" (v. 167). I'm reminded of the tumbling, dancing counterpoint in a Bach invention or fugue.

This musician has taken his stand for God's law and has consequently suffered persecution at the hands of heathen rulers. He is not driven by selfish ambition, nor is he achievement oriented. He is not experiencing a midlife crisis. Rather, he's exulting in the "great spoil" he has found in God's Word. This "find" far surpasses earthly treasures—masterpieces of art and literature, wealth and possessions, even great music! God's Word has turned his life inside out.

I long to be radically changed—to know the psalmist's peace and stability, his patience and personal obedience. I want to love and follow the Word so that I'll be turned inside out!

Personal Prayer

O Lord, may my heart rejoice in your Word! Let me learn to love you with an intensity that is reflected in everything I do or write or sing!

PRAISE FOR THE WORD OF GOD

MY LIPS OVERFLOW WITH PRAISE!

✑ Psalm 119 ✑

TAV

Let my cry reach You, Lord; give me understanding according to Your word. Let my plea reach You; rescue me according to Your promise. My lips pour out praise, for You teach me Your statutes. My tongue sings about Your promise, for all Your commandments are righteous. May Your hand be ready to help me, for I have chosen Your precepts. I long for Your salvation, LORD, and Your instruction is my delight. Let me live, and I will praise You; may Your judgments help me. I wander like a lost sheep; seek Your servant, for I do not forget Your commands (vv. 169–176).

This magnificent psalm ends with a beautiful but humble prayer, encompassing a cluster of pleas for insight and help. Its tone is "the grace of thankfulness."

Five requests rise before the Lord like Berlioz's "Symphonie Fantastique," each of the five movements more beautiful than the last: "Let my cry reach You, LORD" (v. 169). "My lips pour out praise" (v. 171). "My tongue sings about Your promise" (v. 172). "May Your hand be ready to help me" (v. 173). "May Your judgments help me" (v. 175).

The psalmist, awed by the magnitude and depth of the divine revelation, recognizes his own need for renewal and revival.

In some ways I'm like that other musician. He knows he's not out of danger yet. He's like a sheep that has strayed from the shepherd's side (v. 176). Lost, he longs to be found and restored to the fold. At least he knows his weakness, and that's the beginning of the strength.

The psalm concludes at the end of the Hebrew alphabet, but the song plays on . . . in overflowing praise to God for his exquisite, awe-inspiring, magnificent law!

Personal Prayer
*O Lord, may my lips overflow with praise today,
and may my tongue sing of your Word!*

IMPERIAL MARCH
WAR

❧ Psalm 120 ❧

In my distress I called to the LORD, and He answered me: "LORD, deliver me from lying lips and a deceitful tongue." What will He give you, and what will He do to you, you deceitful tongue? A warrior's sharp arrows, with burning charcoal! (vv. 1–4).

Why does our Christian pilgrimage seem to be uphill so much of the time? It was the same for the early believers, who faced a tough climb, literally as well as symbolically.

This "pilgrim song" was sung by ancient Israelis as they journeyed up to Jerusalem for their annual feast days. Psalms 12–134 are also identified as "songs of ascent."

The psalmist has been "burned" by lying lips and deceitful tongues. This personal verbal attack made by warlike adversaries is probably only the beginning of more direct assaults. Still, the sting of a slanderous tongue is enough to launch full-scale war.

In verse 3 he addresses his foes with a question: "What will He do to you, you deceitful tongue?" then answers with vibrant imagery. The wicked will be slain with a "warrior's sharp arrows" and "with burning charcoal" (v. 4). The broom tree is mentioned because its excellent firewood burns bright, long, and hot!

From these verses I learn that God does not deal lightly with untamed tongues. He hates slander, lying, deceit, and gossip! Because individuals are made in the image of God, they are to be treated with dignity and respect, and we are not allowed to speak in an unrestrained manner about them. How typical it is to run rough-shod over God's precious children! Paul speaks against "obscenity, foolish talk or coarse joking" (Eph. 5:4). He tells us they are out of place for the Christian and ought to be replaced by thanksgiving talk!

Personal Prayer
Bridle my tongue, Lord, and keep me from speaking irreverently or thoughtlessly. Keep a song on my lips rather than shallow speech.

IMPERIAL MARCH
PEACE

∽ Psalm 120 ∽

What misery that I have stayed in Meshech, that I have lived among the tents of Kedar! I have lived too long with those who hate peace. I am for peace; but when I speak, they are for war (vv. 5–7).

War and peace have long been the topic of lively discussions among political analysts, writers, and thinkers of all generations. But even in peacetime, believers are not at home in this world. Until Jesus comes, there will be, at best, an uneasy truce between the forces of good and evil.

The psalmist laments that he dwells among people with whom he has nothing in common. Meshech, located southeast of the Black Sea, was a remote, barbaric tribe (Gen. 10:2). Kedar, south of Damascus in the Syrian desert, was about as far from Meshech as one could get. He was saying, in effect: "I'm surrounded by warlike, nomadic Ismaelites!" He has lived with these vexing people for too long and ends his song in clashing discord: "I am for peace; but when I speak, they are for war" (v. 7).

If we are to be salt and light in a hostile world, we can expect the same kind of opposition. But we have the consolation of a Friend who walks and talks with us and will make us special, distinctive, and unique as we live in our secular culture.

Personal Prayer

Lord, as I dwell in "Meshech" and "among the tents of Kedar," may I keep quiet appointments with you for strength and solace in this foreign land.

A Contemporary Lyric

I'll Walk and Talk with Him Today

This world is not my permanent place—
A barren desert land;
But trav'ling this wasteland by His grace,
I'll hold His mighty hand.
This life can be a crowded arcade—
A busy thoroughfare;
Yet quiet appointments can be made
With Jesus anywhere.
I'll walk and talk with Him today
Relating as friend to Friend;
My Lord will lead me thru life's way
As I walk and talk with Him today.

Words and music by Don Wyrtzen © 1975 Singspiration.

PILGRIM SONG
OF ASSURANCE
THESIS: THE LORD IS MY HELP

❧ Psalm 121 ❧

I raise my eyes toward the mountains. Where will my help come from? My help comes from the LORD, the Maker of heaven and earth (vv. 1–2).

A while back, while on vacation in New York state, I decided to climb Mt. Colden, one of the steepest peaks in the Adirondacks. Along with several relatives, I started out, and by late afternoon we had covered approximately ten miles to the top and back! Even though I could barely walk for the next three days, the exhilarating rush of achievement and the view from the top of the mountain were worth a little temporary discomfort!

Mountains were significant in the life of Israel. Not only did they provide natural fortifications against invading armies, but the mountains were places of comfort and security. Since Jerusalem rested on a cluster of hills, the whole area came to be associated with the Holy City—the dwelling place of Yahweh.

On his way to Jerusalem, this pilgrim observes the surrounding mountains. "Where will my help come from?" (v. 1) he asks, then answers his own question: "My help comes from the LORD, the Maker of heaven and earth" (v. 2). Part of that creation was the thrusting up and heaving of the earth to form the rounded hills and majestic mountains. Noticing his dramatic creation prompts us to remember the Creator.

Vicarious exposure to nature doesn't take the place of being there. Watching National Geographic documentaries on TV or videotape will never produce the same heady effect as breathing in fresh, clean air and seeing the view from the top! We need these reminders of the permanence of God's creative care and his help.

Personal Prayer
Precious Lord, remove the cataracts from my eyes. May I be reminded of your comfort and security when I behold the grandeur of your mountains.

PILGRIM SONG
OF ASSURANCE
DEVELOPMENT: HELPING IN ALL EVENTUALITIES

∽ Psalm 121 ∽

He will not allow your foot to slip; your Protector will not slumber. Indeed, the Protector of Israel does not slumber or sleep. The Lord protects you; the Lord is a shelter right by your side. The sun will not strike you by day, or the moon by night. The Lord will protect you from all harm; He will protect your life. The Lord will protect your coming and going both now and forever (vv. 3–8).

The divine Watchman! This psalm of assurance gives me a fresh glimpse of God as the One who keeps watch over his children night and day. In the words of the old spiritual, "He never sleeps, he never slumbers."

Perhaps a Levite priest, accompanying the pilgrim on his journey, is speaking here. Note the change in pronouns from *I* and *my* to *you*. He reassures the traveler of the Lord's divine protection as he walks the rugged terrain. The priest also suggests that God—unlike the Canaanite fertility gods—never goes off duty or takes a nap on the job.

The Lord himself guards us—not some common soldier on night watch! He "watches over" every aspect of our lives—our "comings and goings," our times of rest and recreation. He whose eye is on the sparrow promises to keep an eye on me!

Personal Prayer
Precious Lord, thank you for your watch care in all circumstances at all times. I can rest, knowing you neither slumber nor sleep.

A Song of God's Care

His Eye Is on the Sparrow
Why should I feel discouraged?
Why should the shadows come?
Why should my heart be lonely
And long for heav'n and home
When Jesus is my portion?
My constant friend is He:

His eye is on the sparrow.
And I know He watches me.
I sing because I'm happy,
I sing because I'm free;
His eye is on the sparrow,
And I know He watches me.
Words by Mrs. C. D. Martin. Music by Charles H. Gabriel.

PILGRIMAGE TO JERUSALEM
THE SPLENDOR OF THE HOLY CITY

✑ Psalm 122 ✑

I rejoiced with those who said to me, "Let us go to the house of the LORD." Our feet are standing within your gates, Jerusalem—Jerusalem, built as a city [should be], solidly joined together, where the tribes, the tribes of the LORD, go up to give thanks to the name of the LORD. (This is an ordinance for Israel.) There, thrones for judgment are placed, thrones of the house of David (vv. 1–5).

D o we drag our heels on Sunday morning or look forward to worship services? Do we expect to meet God there, or do we fail to find him in our empty ritual and meaningless form?

David has an entirely different attitude as he approaches the gates of Jerusalem. His heart is filled with joy and expectancy. "I rejoiced with those who said to me, 'Let us go to the house of the LORD'" (v. 1). He loves the capital city and looks forward to participating in one of the great festivals of worship there.

Located within the walls are the royal palace, administrative buildings, and sturdy homes of prominent citizens. The entire complex is solidly and compactly constructed. The psalmist also praises it as a civic and spiritual center, where justice is administered and the tribes congregate to praise the name of the Lord.

Jerusalem, teeming with people and activities of all kinds, was an exciting place to visit. One day the new Jerusalem will be the gathering place of peoples of all nations, and the Lord will be glorified forever! For a look at the new Jerusalem, turn to Revelation 21 and read about the Holy City "coming down out of heaven from God, prepared like a bride adorned for her husband" (v. 2).

Personal Prayer

Lord, make your house an exciting place for me to visit. May our worship together become an enriching, exhilarating experience.

PILGRIMAGE TO JERUSALEM

PRAYER FOR PEACE

✑ Psalm 122 ✑

Pray for the peace of Jerusalem: "May those who love you prosper; may there be
peace within your walls, prosperity within your fortresses." For the sake of my
brothers and friends, I will say, "Peace be with you." For the sake of the house
of the LORD our God, I will seek your good (vv. 6–9).

Ancient Israelis were not only to take pride in their capital city but also to pray for its security. Jerusalem has been a focal point, a hot spot, for centuries. Here David prays for the welfare of his beloved city and for the personal security of others who love her. He prays that there will be peace within the walls and security within the citadels—the two outside limits of the city.

More important than the city or its inhabitants, however, is the house of the Lord. David prays for its prosperity. The King James Version phrase, "I will seek thy good" (v. 9), is rendered by Luther, "I will seek what is best for you."

We live in a rootless society. Many factors contribute to rootlessness—mobility, industrialization, domestic upheaval, isolation, and alienation. The foundations are crumbling. We have downplayed community and stressed individualism. Our identities are threatened. We feel lost. We have become a society of vagabonds!

David's roots were in his Lord, his nation, his city, his family. He was not a loner—isolated from culture and tradition, nor was he insulated from regular interaction with people. He was part of a congregation of believers, and his unselfish prayer stretches beyond the bounds of his day to embrace believers of all generations. We are reminded to pray for the peace of Jerusalem!

Personal Prayer
Lord, as I pray for the peace of Jerusalem,
fill me also with your serenity and security.

SONG OF THE SLAVE
SUBMISSION TO GOD

⟡ Psalm 123 ⟡

I lift my eyes to You, the One enthroned in heaven. Like a servant's eyes on His master's hand, like a servant girl's eyes on her mistress's hand, so our eyes are on the LORD our God until He shows us favor (vv. 1–2).

Maclaren, internationally celebrated Scottish pulpiteer, called this psalm "a sigh and an upward gaze and a sigh!"

In this brief passage a slave lifts his eyes to God and cries out for mercy and deliverance from contempt. He places himself in complete submission to God with the faith that the One who sits enthroned in the heavens can help him. He finds his confidence in the exalted majesty of God. As a slave looks to his master and as a maid looks to her mistress, so also do "our eyes are on the LORD our God, until He shows us favor" (v. 2).

One of Mom's favorite songs was "There Is No Problem." When I play it, I think of her and of her loving counsel.

Personal Prayer
*May I lift up my eyes to you, today, O Lord,
and lay my burdens at your throne.*

A Contemporary Lyric

There Is No Problem

There is no problem
that Jesus cannot solve,
And not a need
He cannot satisfy;
There is no heartache
He cannot understand,
He is omniscient
and knows the reasons why.
CHORUS
So I can trust Him
when I'm hurting deep inside—
And I can pray to Him
in whom I may confide;

There is no pain
my Lord has never known
Because He's Lord,
I lay my burdens at His throne.
There is no valley
where Jesus has not been,
And not a test
that He has ever failed;
There is no conflict
He cannot comprehend—
He is the Savior
Who on a cross was nailed.

Words and music by Don Wyrtzen © 1981 by Singspiration.

SONGS OF THE SLAVE

RELEASE FROM CONTEMPT

∽ Psalm 123 ∽

Show us favor, LORD, show us favor, for we've had more than enough contempt. We've had more than enough scorn from the arrogant [and] contempt from the proud (vv. 3–4).

This is an earnest plea for deliverance from contempt and ridicule. Wounded and hurting, the author cries out, "LORD, show us favor!" (v. 3).

At times an agonized cry for mercy is the only recourse we can take. Christians, in all walks and circumstances of life, have had to take it on the chin for their faith.

The apostle Paul had more than his share:

Five times I received from the Jews forty lashes minus one. Three times I was beaten with rods. Once I was stoned. Three times I was shipwrecked. I have spent a night and a day in the depths of the sea. On frequent journeys, I faced dangers from rivers, dangers from robbers, dangers from my own people, dangers from Gentiles; dangers in the city, dangers in the country, dangers on the sea ... labor and hardship, many sleepless nights, I hunger and thirst, often without food; cold, and lacking clothing (2 Cor. 11:24–27).

This missionary martyr suffered for *doing* God's will; he didn't suffer for *not doing* God's will. Under abnormal stress and pressure, he reached unscaled heights of achievement, exploits, and excellence—not the least of which was writing almost half of the New Testament!

For it was Paul who also said, "I consider that the sufferings of this present time are not worth comparing with the glory that is going to be revealed in us" (Rom. 8:18).

The Lord must laugh at our complaints. We're soft! We need to toughen up and learn how to take anything the enemy can dish out because "the One who is in you is greater than the one who is in the world" (1 John 4:4).

Personal Prayer

O Lord, I'm ashamed when I read the recital of injustices and wrongs committed against the great saints of the ages. Help me to shape up as your man in my own hostile environment.

DELIVERANCE IN THE DORIAN MODE
FIRST MOTIF: PROTECTION

∽ Psalm 124 ∽

If the LORD had not been on our side—let Israel say—If the LORD had not been on our side when men attacked us, then they would have swallowed us alive in their burning anger against us. Then the waters would have engulfed us; the torrent would have swept over us; the raging waters would have swept over us (vv. 1–5).

The Dorian Mode is a musical scale that sounds somewhat like the minor scale. Melodies written in this mode have a somber feeling. David has narrowly escaped grave danger, and his song gives the impression that he is still gasping for breath! If the LORD had not delivered him, the surrounding nations would have "swallowed us alive" (v. 3).

Not only is David's life in jeopardy, but the entire nation of Israel is at risk. Enraged heathen nations pursue God's precious jewel like a flash flood that can swiftly destroy everything in its path.

These verses comprise more than a footnote in ancient history. This is a crisis of major proportions—a situation in which an entire nation can be obliterated from the earth! But God intervened and protected them.

I haven't yet been asked to put my life on the line for my faith, but I have felt the floodwaters of emotional pressure engulfing me. I know what it's like to feel pain from crisis in close personal relationships and from trauma related to upheaval in the circumstances of life. These verses are a reminder to me that God is always with me to sustain and uphold me. Since the Lord is on my side, I will never be swallowed up or destroyed. Nothing and no one can harm me. I'm safe!

Personal Prayer

I praise you for being on my side and for your protection in all kinds of danger— internal and external.

The Language of Music

Dorian Mode

The church modes were a medieval system of scales.

The first authentic mode (scale) is called Dorian (the white keys on the piano from D to D). The mood is dark, melancholy, and somber. It is the basis for much folk music.

DELIVERANCE IN
THE DORIAN MODE

SECOND MOTIF: HELP

∽ Psalm 124 ∽

Praise the LORD, who has not let us be ripped apart by their teeth. We have escaped like a bird from the hunter's net; the net is torn, and we have escaped. Our help is in the name of the LORD, the Maker of heaven and earth (vv. 6–8).

I probably don't realize just how spiritually destitute I am! To add more stress, I sometimes ponder the uncertainty of the future. What in the world can give me hope and help?

David's metaphor of the bird in the hunter's net is so appropriate. Israel was that "bird" enmeshed in the strands of the net, ripe to be torn by the teeth of wild animals (v. 6). The Lord broke the framework and allowed the bird to fly free, suggesting the utter helplessness of the trapped one and the need for radical intervention from the outside.

No wonder David bursts forth with thanksgiving and praise! "Praise the LORD" (v. 6) who has marvelously revealed his power to come to the aid of the weak. Because he is the great Creator of heaven and earth, he is also competent to sustain his creation and to hear the helpless cries of his creatures.

David ends his song with a simple declaration of faith. I return to my own original question: What in the world can give me hope and help? Maybe that's just it! True intervention and help don't exist in the world! David's overwhelmingly satisfying answer is good enough for me: My "help is in the name of the LORD, the Maker of heaven and earth" (v. 8). I claim that promise!

Personal Prayer
*May I place complete confidence in your ability to help me today,
O Lord, whatever I may be facing.*

HYMN OF TRUST
SECURITY

∽ Psalm 125 ∽

Those who trust in the Lord are like Mount Zion. It cannot be shaken; it remains forever. Jerusalem—the mountains surround her. And the LORD surrounds His people, both now and forever. The scepter of the wicked will not remain over the land allotted to the righteous, so that the righteous will not apply their hands to injustice (vv. 1–3).

This is a beautiful hymn about the inner security of believers—both in the time of David and for today.

The nation Israel was in grave danger of being dominated by foreign powers, but the Lord promises his people that he will not allow this scepter of wickedness to remain over them as long as they place their trust in him (v. 3). A New Testament quotation comes to mind: "God is faithful and He will not allow you be tempted beyond what you are able, but with the temptation He will also provide a way of escape, so that you are able to bear it" (1 Cor. 10:13).

If Israel will just trust in the Lord, they will be blessed with a deep sense of inner security and unshakability. They will be like Mount Zion, which is solid and immovable. They will be like a mountain rooted deeply in the bedrock of the earth. The Lord's protective care will encircle them at all times like the mountains surrounding Jerusalem. He will be for them an impregnable wall of defense.

My sense of security cannot be based on quality in human relationships or the relative stability of life's circumstances. It must rest squarely on the Lord himself who is immutable and unchanging. He is my mountain! I must believe that, apart from the irrationality of my feelings. Then I will be secure—regardless of how I feel!

Personal Prayer
I thank you, Lord, that my security is like Mount Zion, unshakable and deeply embedded in your attributes.

HYMN OF TRUST
PRAYER FOR PERSONAL INTEGRITY

✑ Psalm 125 ✑

Do good, LORD, to the good, to those whose hearts are upright. But as for those who turn aside to crooked ways, the LORD will banish them with the evildoers. Peace be with Israel (vv. 4–5).

The term *falsetto* refers to "an unnaturally or artificially high-pitched voice or register, especially in a man." In early music, prior to 1600, singers especially trained in falsetto sang the high parts of masses and motets. These tones, tending to be nasal and weak, are mostly used today for comic effect.

Here the psalmist contrasts the "upright" (straight as an arrow, honest, unswerving in principle) with the "crooked" (bent, devious, dishonest, untrue). God calls me to "be real" in my relationship with him. He expects me to stay true and not deviate from the course he has assigned me. Genuine godliness will be blessed, while those who bend his rules or adopt a falsetto approach to life will "banish them with the evildoers" (v. 5).

I struggle to remain perfectly true to my calling as a Christian musician in a world that loves artificiality and pretense. The applause of the crowd, while sweet to the ear, is short-lived. On the other hand, God's reward for arrow-straight, true-pitch living is eternal life in his presence and his "well done!"

Personal Prayer
Give me a vision of you, Lord—unshakable, unchangeable, and secure.
Keep me true and straight!

A Meaningful Lyric

To Be What You Want Me To Be

To be what You want me to be, dear Lord,
I'll live for eternity;
To be more like Your Son, dear Lord—
I've only just begun.
To be what You want me to be, dear Lord,
I'll live for eternity;
To be more like Your Son, dear Lord,
Until the race is won.
To be what You want me to be, dear Lord,
I'll live so the world can see
The image of Your Son, dear Lord—
Unite our hearts as one.

Words and music by Don Wyrtzen © 1972 Singspiration.

A BRIEF JUBILATE
JOY AND RESTORATION

✂ Psalm 126 ✂

When the LORD restored the fortunes of Zion, we were like those who dream. Our mouths were filled with laughter then, and our tongues with shouts of joy. Then they said among the nations, "The LORD has done great things for them." The LORD had done great things for us; we were joyful (vv. 1–3).

Anyone who has ever experienced the loss of a loved one, financial reverses, serious illness, or imprisonment of any kind will treasure this psalm! The first few verses vibrate with the sheer joy of deliverance after long years of burden-bearing and captivity!

Most likely the psalmist is referring to the time immediately after the return of the nation Israel from its exile in Babylon (537 BC). Happiness and exuberance reign supreme. God's people probably have to pinch themselves to believe they are really free! Laughter comes easily. Jubilant shouting is heard often. The Israelites, in typical Oriental abandonment, release their pent-up feelings in a flood of healing, restorative praise.

The Gentile outsiders looking on say in amazement, "The LORD has done great things for them" (v. 2). No nation has ever been restored after deportation! It is as incomprehensible to these ancient people.

It is this euphoric sensation of delight and joy that should seize me every time I meditate on all the great things the Lord has done for me. If I spent more time dwelling on God's major triad—"the great things"—there would be less time for the minor irritations and frustrations of life!

The Language of Music

Jubilate
From the Latin imperative, "jubilare."
Refers to the 100th Psalm in the Authorized Version ("Make a joyful noise unto the Lord . . ."). It also refers to a joyous song or outburst.

Personal Prayer
Remind me, O Lord, of the major triumphs you have accomplished in my behalf—my salvation, my eternal security, my constant protection— and don't let my song lapse into a minor mode!

A Brief Jubilate
HOPE AND FULL DELIVERANCE

∽ Psalm 126 ∽

Restore our fortunes, Lord, like watercourses in the Negev. Those who sow in tears will reap with shouts of joy. Though one goes along weeping, carrying the bag of seed, he will surely come back with shouts of joy, carrying his sheaves (vv. 4–6).

Unless you know something of the topography of Israel, you can't fully understand the faith demonstrated by the psalmist in this prayer.

The Negev—the desert south of Judah—contains many wadis that are bone-dry eleven months of the year. But in the twelfth month, during the rainy season, these dry streambeds quickly fill with water and become raging torrents. This psalm cries out for that kind of dramatic change in the history of Israel as the captives flow back to their native land.

The second metaphor is equally graphic. Before irrigation, sowing and reaping in this barren part of the world were extremely difficult. Seed was often sown with little prospect of harvest. Yet the ancient musician believes that God will send life-giving rains and, even after long neglect, that the desert will bloom once more. The weeping sowers will return "with songs of joy" to greet the returning captives.

What a comfort to know that the Lord can take my dried-up, unproductive life and drench it with his showers of blessing! All the self-improvement courses and how-to books in the world combined with Herculean human effort cannot begin to match the incomparable grace and mercy of God!

Personal Prayer
Lord, change the dry, barren riverbeds of my life into raging streams in the desert.

A Gospel Song

There Shall Be Showers of Blessing
There shall be showers of blessing;
This is the promise of love;
There shall be seasons refreshing,
Sent from the Savior above.
Showers of blessing.
Showers of blessing we need:
Mercydrops around us are falling,
But for the showers we plead.
Words by Daniel W. Whittle. (Based on Ezek. 34:26.)
Music by James McGranahan.

SOLOMON'S PILGRIM PSALM

FUTILITY OF WORK APART FROM GOD

✑ Psalm 127 ✑

Unless the LORD builds a house, its builders labor over it in vain; unless the LORD watches over a city, the watchman stays alert in vain. In vain you get up early and stay up late, eating food earned by hard work; certainly He gives sleep to the one He loves (vv. 1–2).

Solomon, the wisest man who ever lived and one of the greatest kings of Israel, teaches us that it is useless to attempt anything without God's approval and blessing whether we are building a house, making a home, guarding a city, earning a living, or even trying go get a decent night's sleep!

There is a simple interdependence in all of life—a basic theme that underlies the complex movements of our daily existence. That theme is the sovereignty of God—the fact that as Number One in the universe, he has everything under his control.

A building contractor can erect a house; but, whether he acknowledges it, he's dependent on the Lord for the right weather conditions, raw materials for building supplies, and the strength to build. A couple can get married and start a family; but unless they practice faith in the Lord, there is less than a 50 percent chance that their marriage will survive. An army can be mustered to defend cities and countries, but true peace comes only from God. Inspiration for worthwhile artistic achievement is God's gift. The ability to earn a living—both talent and drive as well as health and stamina—are his gifts. And even relief from one's labors—refreshing sleep—comes from the hand of a loving Father.

Diligence without divine blessing is an exercise in futility. For me to attempt anything without God's help is like trying to get my sailboat to tack by blowing into the sail. I have to wait for the breath of God!

Personal Prayer

Lord, I confess my utter dependence on you. Teach me to wait on inspiration from you in all my endeavors.

A Footnote on Solomon

Solomon's name in Hebrew is shalmoh, "peaceable." He was the third and last king of a united Israel. He built the kingdom to its greatest strength in terms of material prosperity, geographic extension, and military might. Though very wise and intelligent, Solomon in his later years lost his spiritual discernment. His life style became political, amoral, voluptuous, and apostate. This formerly wise king brought the nation to the brink of dissolution.

SOLOMON'S PILGRIM PSALM

REWARD OF CHILDREN SENT FROM GOD

✑ Psalm 127 ✑

Sons are indeed a heritage from the LORD, children, a reward. Like arrows in the
hand of a warrior are the sons born in one's youth. Happy is the man who has
filled his quiver with them. Such men will never be put to shame when they
speak with [their] enemies at the city gate (vv. 3–5).

Many young couples in our society seem to be content to remain childless. Their two-paycheck incomes buy a lot of convenience and a lot of "stuff." But few of them realize how children can enrich life by forcing us outside our self-centered routines. Few of them understand that children stretch our horizons and prompt us to higher goals. Few of them ever consider how lonely they'll be in old age. And almost nobody ever mentions the importance of bringing up godly children to build a dynamic Christian community that can impact our culture and civilization!

Part of the current erosion of the family is simply that children are undervalued. They often are viewed as excess baggage, an inconvenience. They seem to get in the way of career aspirations and create pressure on the woman, robbing her of youth and beauty and sapping her energy. They are considered, by some, as more of a liability than an asset.

How different from the Oriental point of view! Children were seen as "a heritage from the LORD" (v. 3), a reward, and tokens of his grace. Furthermore, the possibility of becoming the mother of the Messiah was the coveted goal of young Hebrew women.

To the Hebrew man, adult children were regarded as a means of defense—"arrows in the hands of a warrior" (v. 4) and support—"when they speak contend with [their] enemies at the city gate" (v. 5). Cases were tried and business was transacted at the gates of the city, and if a man were to encounter difficulty, he could count on his grown sons to lend strength to his argument.

Those who were childless or who had lost a child expressed their grief openly (Gen. 30:1; 1 Sam. 1:3–17). Infertile couples now have some medical options to improve the chances of pregnancy, or, failing that, they might consider adoption. Still, God sets aside special people who will neither get married nor have children because of their unique calling. God has not placed us on an assembly line. He loves to handcraft Rolls Royces!

Personal Prayer

Dear Lord, I thank you for D. J. and Kathleen and
for the love and support they give me.

COUNT YOUR MANY BLESSINGS

PRESENT BLESSINGS

∽ Psalm 128 ∽

*How happy is everyone who fears the LORD, who walks in His ways! You
will surely eat what your hands have worked for. You will be happy, and it
will go well for you. Your wife will be like a fruitful vine within your house,
your sons, like young olive trees around your table. In this very way
the man who fears the LORD will be blessed (vv. 1–4).*

*B*lessed (supremely happy) is the person who has meaningful work and a
fruitful family." This paraphrase of Psalm 128 reduces the abundant life to
its simplest terms. Yet many in our contemporary society, including Christians,
take such humble gifts for granted and expect more!

Solomon, in all of his brilliance and wisdom, takes us back to the basics.
Fearing God (reverencing and obeying him) will bring blessing, he states.
Then he enumerates the gifts of grace that follow: food to sustain life, produc-
tive work, and family. The wife and mother is depicted as a "fruitful vine"; the
children, "like young olive trees" (v. 3). This metaphor of a bountiful table is
God's true picture of prosperity and happiness, not material wealth.

Personal Prayer

*Lord, help me to fear you and walk in your way today.
Give my wife and children a special touch of your grace so they
may bask in the happiness of your presence with them.*

A Gospel Song

Count Your Blessings

Count your blessings—name them one by one;
Count your blessings—see what God hath done;
Count your blessings—name them one by one;
Count your many blessings—see what God hath done.
When you look at others with their lands and gold,
Think that Christ has promised you His wealth untold:
Count your many blessings—money cannot buy
Your reward in heaven nor your home on high.
Words by Johnson Oatman Jr. Music by Edwin O. Excell.

COUNT YOUR MANY BLESSINGS

FUTURE BLESSINGS

∞ Psalm 128 ∞

May the LORD bless you from Zion, so that you will see the prosperity of Jerusalem all the days of your life, and will see your children's children! Peace be with Israel (vv. 5–6).

The psalmist moves now from individual happiness in the context of a single family to national prosperity within the context of the nation of Israel. He longs to see Jerusalem, the City of Zion, prospering and flourishing all the days of his life. From her blessing will flow out to all nations on earth.

The young father pictured earlier in the psalm is now a grandfather, observing the blessings of the Lord falling on many generations. We make much of the sins of the fathers being visited on future generations but fail to speak of the blessings of the righteous filtering down through the generations (vv. 3–4, 6).

I remember well my paternal grandparents. They both died when I was seven years old. However, since they lived in our home during their latter years, they left an indelible impression of security and godliness.

The psalmist concludes with a lovely benediction: "Peace be with Israel!" Thus, he expresses for all of us the deepest longing of our hearts—peace. Deep personal peace doesn't come from things. It flows from warm, intimate relationships and from a close walk with God.

Personal Prayer

Dear Lord, as we learn to walk more consistently by your side, give us the peace that passes human understanding. If you don't come soon, may I live to hear my grandchildren singing your praises!

Opus of Oppression
DELIVERANCE

◌ Psalm 129 ◌

Since my youth they have often attacked me—let Israel say—Since my youth they have often attacked me, but they have not prevailed against me. Plowmen plowed over my back; they made their furrows long. The LORD is righteous; He has cut the ropes of the wicked (vv. 1–4).

We desperately need to grapple with a theology of suffering. Many Christians are surprised and even shocked when they're called upon to experience any degree of pain. This leads to a feeling of displacement, dislocation, even disinheritance. We may be confused and feel a profound sense of injustice. We may feel that more was promised than was delivered. Our doubt, anger, and resentment may even shake the foundations of our faith.

This psalmist laments, in a kind of summary, all of the national disasters that have befallen his people and prays for the overthrow of their enemies. Israel has suffered indignity, ignominy, and hostility for generations. She has been besieged continuously by the Canaanites, the Aramaeans, the Ammonites, the Edomites, the Philistines, the Assyrians, and the Chaldeans. He remembers many such attacks from his youth, but he also recalls that the enemy has never prevailed against him for long.

The literary figure is gripping! Israel is pictured as a poor wretch lying facedown on the ground as plowmen cut deep furrows in the tender flesh. This gives us some idea of the extreme suffering and severe pain that was commonplace for that nation.

But the psalmist does not dwell on these inhumane acts. He praises the righteous Lord who has delivered his people. He has "cut the ropes of the wicked" (v. 4).

Perhaps we need to learn about adversity from ancient Israel. Perhaps we need to remember that suffering is part of being human in a fallen world, that ungodly people suffer too. And perhaps we need to remind ourselves that our God is a righteous God. Justice will ultimately prevail. He has promised victory and deliverance—if not immediately—then in the world to come!

Personal Prayer
I thank you, Lord, for your righteousness. I pray that you will execute justice in my life and by your mercy cut me free from the ropes of wickedness.

OPUS OF OPPRESSION

VINDICATION

✑ Psalm 129 ✑

Let all who hate Zion be driven back in disgrace. Let them be like grass on the rooftops, which withers before it grows up and can't even fill the hands of the reaper or the arms of the one who binds sheaves. Then none who pass by will say, "May the LORD's blessing be on you." We bless you in the name of the LORD (vv. 5–8).

Why does it seem as if the nonbelievers in this world get all the breaks and have all the fun? They live fast, hard, and, it appears, free!

But we can take great comfort in the promise of this psalm. No matter how it may seem, the wicked are doomed to failure (see Ps. 37:1–2). This psalmist has the big picture, and our confusion stems from our limited and cloudy vision.

Still, my ancient colleague covers all his bases and prays for the vindication of his people. He pictures the Israel-haters as tufts of grass on a Palestinian roof. They wither even before the owner has a chance to pluck them. They're not worth the time it takes to weed them out! He'll leave them to the blazing sun of God's wrath.

The psalm ends with a strong suggestion to fellow Israelites to withhold blessing from passersby on the street. It has always been customary in Israel to greet people by invoking God's blessing on their lives. In this case the passionate musician/poet holds out for silence: "Then none who pass will say, 'May the LORD's blessing be on you'" (v. 8).

When Karen and I visited Israel, the people often greeted us with a friendly "Shalom"—"Peace be unto you." They're still looking for the fulfillment of that prophecy. Justice will prevail in the end, and Israel will be utterly and finally vindicated. It also follows that, if I am suffering unjustly, I can expect satisfaction from a just God. In the meantime I need to concentrate on my Savior, whose suffering I will never be able to imagine or comprehend in this life (Rom. 8:18)!

Personal Prayer

I thank you, Lord, that you are the answer to all injustice and inhumanity in this world and that you are still in control. Help me to trust in the fulfillment of that prophecy just as my Israeli neighbors do.

The Language of Music

Opus

A Latin term meaning "work."

An opus is a musical composition or set of compositions.

MOTET OF MERCY

FORGIVENESS

∽ Psalm 130 ∽

*Out of the depths I call to You, LORD! Lord, listen to my voice; let Your ears be
attentive to my cry for help. LORD, if You considered sins, Lord, who could stand?
But with You there is forgiveness, so that You may be revered (vv. 1–4).*

When I think of God's accounting ability, I cringe, much like the author of
this psalm. Suppose every unkind word I have ever spoken, every lie
I have ever told, every shortcut I have ever taken, every word of gossip that ever
passed my lips, every lustful thought I have ever entertained, every sin I've ever
committed were recorded on audio and videotape to be played back at will?

My fellow musician sums it up succinctly: "Who could stand?" (v. 3).

Though I am saved by grace, I am constantly engaged in a wrestling match
between the old sin nature and the new man. As the apostle Paul complained:
"I know that nothing good lives in me, that is, in flesh. For the desire to do what
is good is with me but there is no ability to do it. For I do not do good that
I want to do, but I practice the evil that I do not want to do" (Rom. 7:18–19).

There is a way out, however. It's a one-word answer: forgiveness. In his
infinite mercy, God chooses to pardon the penitent sinner (Isa. 55:6–7). If he
did not, we would all be destroyed by his judgment. Because we have been
forgiven much, we are able to respond in grateful praise. We will be moved to
revere and respect him, to worship and adore him, to follow and obey him!

Personal Prayer

*I cry out of the depths to you for mercy, O Lord!
I need your forgiveness again and again.*

Motet of Mercy

HOPE

∽ Psalm 130 ∽

I wait for the LORD; I wait, and put my hope in His word. I [wait] for the Lord
more than watchmen for the morning—more than watchmen for the morning.
Israel, hope in the LORD. For there is faithful love with the LORD, and with Him is
redemption in abundance. And He will redeem Israel from all its sins (vv. 5–8).

There are several musical terms for "pause" or "rest." Pauses in music, the cessation of sound, affect the flow of a piece and create variety and diversity. Delay, anticipation, buildup are all crucial in musical dynamics.

This pilgrim psalmist understands the value of patient waiting. Thoroughly familiar with the holy writings of the Old Testament prophets, he trusts the Lord for ultimate fulfillment of his promises—God's unfailing love and his full redemption. Lawrence Richards, in his work, *Expository Dictionary of Bible Words*, says, "It is striking to note that in all the Old Testament's exploration of the meaning of *padah* ('redeem or ransom'), only in Psalm 130:7–8 is this concept associated with redemption from sin." His sovereign hand is not forced by human entreaties unless the time is right. He hears prayer, then acts according to his own schedule.

In ancient times watchmen were posted atop the broad gates of Jerusalem to sound the alert if signs of imminent danger were observed. The night watches were long and arduous. If the watchmen could make it until the first rays of the rising sun, they could rejoice in their security for yet another night. Waiting in darkness merely emphasized the glory of the sunrise!

As I wait in the darkness of uncertainty and human inadequacy, I rest in the fact of his sunrise that is surely coming ... tomorrow!

Personal Prayer

Lord, I'm waiting as patiently as I know how. And in the process of waiting,
I find a blessing, for I am looking forward to your glorious coming
and to an eternity spent in your presence!

HARMONY OF HUMILITY

∽ Psalm 131 ∽

LORD, my heart is not proud; my eyes are not haughty. I do not get involved with things too great or too difficult for me. Instead, I have calmed and quieted myself like a little weaned child with its mother; I am like a little child. Israel, hope in the LORD, both now and forever (vv. 1–3).

David's reign as Israel's greatest king was matched by his contributions to art and literature, including the most profound psalm lyrics ever written. While he extended Israel's borders to their limit, made Jerusalem the capital city, and founded an eternal dynasty of which our Lord, the Messiah, descended, he was also a virtuoso harpist and led a sweeping renaissance of Israelite culture. He accomplished this through building instruments, teaching music, and composing the temple liturgy.

With all his worldly "success," David was a humble man with a childlike faith in God. His soul was calm and quiet (v. 2) because he was not neurotically driven by selfish ambition. He wrote: "He lets me lie down in green pastures; He leads me beside quiet waters" (Ps. 23:2). As a weaned child no longer needs its mother's milk, he learned to receive his nurture from the Lord: "You prepare a table before me" (Ps. 23:5). His value system was founded on God's eternal principles, not on ego-driven materialism.

The Bible stresses humility. To the humble, God gives salvation (Ps. 18:27), sustenance (Ps. 147:6), and grace (Prov. 3:34). The Lord hates arrogance and pride, which result in overwhelming self-confidence and insensitivity to others. This attitude is self-destructive. David is the consummate model of a creative artist and successful entrepreneur who didn't let his fame go to his head. Trusting in the Lord is the opposite of pride and the only route to deeply satisfying human fulfillment.

Personal Prayer

O Lord, "lead me beside quiet waters" and give me rest from my obsessive behavior. I'm tired of the pressure I impose on myself. Help me to trust in you today for everything I need.

RECITATIVE
OF REMEMBRANCE
REMEMBERING DAVID

∽ Psalm 132 ∽

LORD, remember David and all the hardships he endured, and how he swore an oath to the LORD, making a vow to the Mighty One of Jacob: "I will not enter my house or get into my bed, I will not allow my eyes to sleep or my eyelids to slumber until I find a place for the LORD, a dwelling for the Mighty One of Jacob" (vv. 1–5).

It is impossible to overestimate the contribution made by Bill and Gloria Gaither to the gospel music field. Bill's down-to-earth wisdom, combined with Gloria's reflective lyricism, has produced some of our best contemporary songs and hymns: "Because He Lives," "Something Beautiful," "There's Something about That Name," "The Family of God," "Let's Just Praise the Lord," and hundreds more. I love the reality of their lives and the passion they bring to their work. Bill has been a friend, advisor, and encourager to me.

David was such a leader, and this psalm celebrates his devotion to the nation he served and the Lord he worshipped. The nation had been restored from exile in Babylon, and its people were keenly aware of David's legacy.

He evidenced his commitment by swearing an oath that he would not rest until he found a place of worship in which the Lord could dwell. This oath most likely referred to David's intense desire to build the temple (2 Sam. 7). So fervent was this desire that he vowed neither to enter his house nor to sleep until his mission was accomplished (vv. 3–5). Because of this single-minded devotion, God made a covenant (contract) with David. This covenant, with future implications, was extremely significant, particularly during the leadership of Ezra and Nehemiah.

What a mentor David is to me! His commitment to the Lord resulted in concrete action. David was much more than a sentimental, romantic leader; he was serious and committed, and God dealt with him accordingly.

Personal Prayer

O Lord, deepen my commitment and conviction. I want to be deadly serious about your business and my relationship with you.

RECITATIVE
OF REMEMBRANCE
RESOLVING TO WORSHIP

ᗑ Psalm 132 ᗑ

We heard of [the ark] in Ephrathah; we found it in the fields of Jaar. Let us go to His dwelling place; let us worship at His footstool. Arise, LORD, come to Your resting place, You and the ark [that shows] Your strength. May Your priests be clothed with righteousness, and may Your godly people shout for joy. Because of Your servant David, do not reject Your anointed one (vv. 6–10).

Ephrathah? Jaar? What are these places with the strange-sounding names? They were towns where the ark (covenant box) rested in limbo until David moved it to Zion (2 Sam. 6). Ephrathah was an old name for Bethlehem, where our Lord was born. Jaar was also known as Kiriath Jearim—the "city of forests," one of the four leading cities of the Gibeonites (Josh. 9:17).

The ark was God's earthly dwelling, his footstool, in the sense that it was his earthly throne. Because it symbolized the awesome presence of God, the ark often went ahead of the Israeli army in battle.

The people are praying that God will reveal himself again to them, that their priests will be "clothe with righteousness," and that their saints will "shout for joy" (v. 16). The prayer concludes with a petition that David, the "anointed one," will not be rejected. The word *anointed* in Hebrew is *masiah* which is transliterated "Messiah, anointed one." Appearing only thirty-nine times in the Old Testament, this word is often a synonym for "royal office." It is used especially to identify the royal line of David (Ps. 2:2; 18:50; 24:9; 29:10; 132:10, 17).

These early saints were serious about their faith. Prayer and praise were not perfunctory, for worship was a priority in their lives. How human it is to take God for granted! Praise the Lord for the passionate leadership of King David!

Personal Prayer

Clothe me with righteousness today, O Lord, that I may shout for joy!

The Language of Music

Recitative
A rhythmically free declamatory vocal style for delivering a narrative text or a passage in this style.

RECITATIVE
OF RIGHTEOUSNESS
REITERATING THE LORD'S OATH

∽ Psalm 132 ∽

The LORD swore an oath to David, a promise He will not abandon: "I will set one
of your descendants on your throne. If your sons keep My covenant and My decrees
that I will teach them, their sons will also sit on your throne, forever." For the LORD
has chosen Zion; He has desired it for His home: "This is My resting place forever;
I will make My home here because I have desired it. I will abundantly bless its
food; I will satisfy its needy with bread. I will clothe its priests with salvation,
and its godly people will shout for joy. There I will make a horn grow for David;
I have prepared a lamp for My anointed one. I will clothe his enemies with
shame, but the crown he wears will be glorious" (vv. 11–18).

This psalm confirms that God's promises will be fulfilled no matter what the circumstances. God had made specific promises to King David about his dynasty—promises regarding the sanctuary and Mount Zion, which would be blessed with food for the poor, salvation for the priests, and joy for the saints (vv. 15–16). Under David's reign the tiny land expanded ten times over, became a powerful nation, and occupied almost all the land God had promised to Abraham.

The "burning lamp" is a word picture borrowed from the furnishings of the tabernacle and symbolizing the continuation of David's dynasty, which would come to a glorious culmination in David's greatest Son, the Messiah. The metaphor for the Messiah is the animal horn, an ancient symbol of strength and vigor. This horn, or powerful ruler, would sprout and flourish, In moving poetry the Lord reiterates his oath to David: From his line would come the Messiah, David's descendant and the coming One, the ultimate Priest and King of Israel! The Jewish people living in Jesus' time believed that the Messiah would be a Davidic ruler who would establish the long-promised kingdom. David was God's prototype of the Messiah, his Son.

Whatever my circumstances right now, I can rest in the fact that God fulfills his promises. His covenant is solid and sure. His program is moving along right on schedule. Just as he blessed David, he is about to touch my life in a unique way.

Personal Prayer
May I rest in the surety and certainty of your promises today, O Lord.

THE BEAUTY OF UNITY

ᕫᔢ Psalm 133 ᕫᔢ

How good and pleasant it is when brothers can live together! It is like fine oil on the head, running down on the beard, running down Aaron's beard, onto his robes. It is like the dew of Hermon falling on the mountains of Zion. For there the LORD has appointed the blessing—life forevermore (vv 1–3).

When Israel celebrated her great religious festivals, families came together to worship the Lord. These homecomings were accompanied by colorful pageantry and moving music.

Periodically, we have a Wyrtzen family reunion. How I love my own immediate family, but this gave me a chance to see members of my extended family too! My sister Mary-Ann and her husband, Dave Cox, are the founders and directors of the Word of Life Seminary in Brazil. My sister, Betsy, teaches at Mountainside Christian Academy in Schroon Lake, New York. My brother, David, with his wife Mary, pastors the Midlothian Bible Church in Texas. My brother, Ron, is a Christian businessman. His wife, Christine, is a prominent musician and author. My mom went to be with the Lord a few years ago, but he provided a wonderful new wife for Dad. Each one unique, yet with a common bond of love and unity.

In this passage David agrees that it is "good and pleasant" when believers live in unity and uses two striking word pictures to illustrate this idea—the "oil" that anointed Aaron and the "dew" from Mount Hermon. The oil of anointing ran down Aaron's beard and onto his breastplate containing the names of the twelve tribes of Israel. So also, the unity of worshipers in Jerusalem will consecrate the nation. Heavy mountain dew from the north fell on Zion, invigorating and nourishing the vegetation. So also, meaningful worship blesses the nation.

I need this reminder of the importance of family and community. In the press of publishing deadlines and concert commitments, I have a tendency to lose touch with family members and even with the local church support group of believers. Strong, creative leaders need to feel part of a caring fellowship and not live and work solo, independently of others.

Personal Prayer

O Lord, someday we will all come together for a great family reunion. Teach me that I belong to the greater family of God and make me accountable for keeping up family ties!

BENEDICTION TO THE PILGRIM PSALMS

∽ Psalm 134 ∽

*Now praise the LORD, all you servants of the LORD who stand in the LORD's house
at night! Lift up your hands in the holy place, and praise the LORD! May the LORD,
Maker of heaven and earth, bless you from Zion (vv. 1–3).*

I'm intrigued by the relationship between the act of leading people in worship
and the boon of personal blessing spelled out in this psalm. This unusual
benediction, given by the congregation to their leaders, exhorts the priests and
Levites to keep up the good work!

These ministers are encouraged to continue their personal times of devotion in order to undergird their public ministry. Leaders who have to bear heavy
burdens for others day and night (v. 1) are especially vulnerable to attacks from
the enemy. When they are physically and emotionally exhausted, their spiritual
guard is down. It is imperative, then, that they be lifted up in prayer by members
of their congregation, just as Aaron and Hur lifted up Moses' hands during the
long hours of the battle with the Amalekites (Exod. 17:8–16).

The final words of this psalm flow like a soothing balm across troubled
and tired spirits: "May the LORD, Maker of heaven and earth, bless you from
Zion" (v. 3). Our Lord—not the lifeless pagan gods of the ancient world, such
as the Canaanite god, Baal—created the universe and can certainly strengthen
his faithful representatives.

I am deeply touched by the significance of this psalm for my own life
and work. First, I'm reminded that the effectiveness of my public ministry is
dependent, to a great degree, upon keeping a vital and dynamic personal relationship with the Lord. I also have a number of close friends who regularly
and faithfully pray for me, and a corps of choir members and church musicians who remember to pray for me when they see my name on a piece of
music. I have no way of knowing what my life would be without this consistent, loving care and support!

The Language of Music

Benediction
The invocation of a blessing to
conclude public worship.

Personal Prayer

*O Lord, thank you for the intercessory
prayer of Christian friends. I am blessed
both by serving you and by the encouragement and concern of those who act as a
link for refueling my tired spirit.*

A Musical Mosaic
A LITANY OF PRAISE

❧ Psalm 135 ❧

Hallelujah! Praise the name of the Lord. Give praise, you servants of the Lord who stand in the house of the Lord, in the courts of the house of our God. Praise the Lord, for the Lord is good; sing praise to His name, for it is delightful. . . . House of Israel, praise the Lord! House of Aaron, praise the Lord! House of Levi, praise the Lord! You who revere the Lord, praise the Lord! May the Lord be praised from Zion; He dwells in Jerusalem. Hallelujah! (vv. 1–3, 19–21).

Because this psalm is a compilation of quotations from other Old Testament sources, the form is a musical mosaic of praise based on the Law, the Prophets, and the Psalms.

The theme, praise, should be the theme of my life. I am not always physically present in the "house of the Lord," but somewhere in transit, torn between the roles I'm called to play in the world in which I live. But I can make praise a priority—then spend those precious moments or hours meditating on God's goodness, greatness, and faithfulness—wherever I am.

Having a daily quiet time with the Lord is vital. I've used many different approaches over the years—reading the Bible through in one year, incorporating five psalms a day plus one chapter from Proverbs, studying a book of the Bible in depth with the aid of an excellent commentary, reading the Word aloud. A special blessing comes when I read the Bible and pray with Karen. How easy it is to neglect that precious time! What a missed opportunity!

No one is exempt from the roll call of the faithful. The houses of Israel, Aaron, and Levi (vv. 19–20) include all who fear and reverence the Lord. We are called to praise him in the house where he dwells—Jerusalem (Zion), for the ancient worshipper, our individual local churches, for the contemporary saint. The psalm ends as it begins, with a mighty "Hallelujah!" ("Praise the Lord!")

Praise is easy for a musician, you say, but what about the person who's tone-deaf or can't carry a tune? I would suggest that you try singing along with one of our major Christian artists on CD.

A faithful heart, an earnest desire to please the Lord, a life dedicated to his glory—*these* are the most eloquent songs of praise!

Personal Prayer
I join with my ancient Levite brothers, Lord, in praising your name for your goodness and faithfulness.

A MUSICAL MOSAIC

LONGING TO PRAISE

❧ Psalm 135 ❧

For the LORD has chosen Jacob for Himself, Israel as His treasured possession. For I know that the LORD is great; our Lord is greater than all gods. The LORD does whatever He pleases in heaven and on earth, in the seas and all the depths. He causes the clouds to rise from the ends of the earth. He makes lightning for the rain and brings the wind from His storehouses. . . . LORD, Your name [endures] forever, Your reputation, LORD, through all generations. For the LORD will judge His people and have compassion on His servants (vv. 4–7, 13–14).

My dad, Jack Wyrtzen, has had an aura of authority about him for as long as I can remember. A man of unusual strength and energy, he founded Word of Life International from scratch. He spent his life ministering in camps, Bible institutes, clubs, concerts, rallies, and through media all over the world.

As you might imagine, his presence had been strongly felt in our home. I always wanted to please him—to be the best I could be, to perform well in recital, to speak and teach effectively, to achieve so that he would be proud of me. His image, in my concept of reality, has profoundly affected my view of God, the transcendent Sovereign of the universe!

The motive behind the praise in this psalm is the sovereignty of God, who chose Israel as his "treasured possession" (v. 4), "does whatever He pleases" (v. 5), and still orchestrates all the events of Israel's history—past, present, and future (vv. 8–13).

Knowing that God never changes and that he is as concerned with the daily agenda of Don Wyrtzen as with the affairs of mankind, I am moved to write a song of praise.

Personal Prayer

Lord, I acknowledge you as Sovereign, my complete and ultimate Authority. I long to please you in everything I think and do.

The Language of Music

Mosaic

A decorative piece of art in which small pieces of multicolored material (i.e. tiles) are inlayed to form a picture or pattern.

Litany

A prayer consisting of invocations and supplications by the worship leaders with alternate responses by the congregation.

A Musical Mosaic
LEGACY OF PRAISE

∾ Psalm 135 ∾

He struck down the firstborn of Egypt, both people and animals. He sent signs and wonders against you, Egypt, against Pharaoh and all his officials. He struck down many nations and slaughtered mighty kings: Sihon king of the Amorites, Og king of Bashan, and all the kings of Canaan. He gave their land as an inheritance, an inheritance to His people Israel (vv. 8–12).

Two Hebrew words are linked to the concept of inheritance—*yaras*, which means "to become an heir" or "to take possession," and *nahal*, which indicates "giving or receiving property." The Lord promised an unbelievable inheritance to Israel, and modern Israel's expansion is motivated by a strong belief in this ancient right.

A forty-acre farm or $100,000 in bonds could never be compared to the inheritance of Israel. God's people inherited "many nations" (v. 10)! And the legacy lives on, to be fulfilled only when the Lord returns to reign in the new Jerusalem!

Again the historical events surrounding Israel's inheritance are catalogued—the "signs and wonders" God sent against the Egyptians, culminating in the killing of their firstborn (v. 8); God's leadership in the occupation of Canaan, including his divine intervention in the overthrow of heathen kings (vv. 11–12).

I share in this legacy of love and praise. I've been delivered from sin and have received God's gift of grace. I've felt his work in my life as he overthrows bastions of fear, insecurity, and depression. I've known the joy of walking in green pastures with my Lord. I've sensed his breath on my soul and have been inspired to compose songs and musicals to his glory. And someday I'll enter into the promised rest of Israel to enjoy his forever!

Personal Prayer
Lord, as you performed signs and wonders in Israel, please work supernaturally in my life and bless me with your inheritance of peace.

ANTIPHONAL PSALM OF LOVE

INTROIT: CALLING THE CONGREGATION TO PRAISE

✐ Psalm 136 ✐

Give thanks to the LORD, for He is good. His love is eternal. Give thanks to the God of gods. His love is eternal. Give thanks to the Lord of lords. His love is eternal. . . . Give thanks to the God of heaven! His love is eternal (vv. 1–3, 26).

In this marvelous antiphonal psalm, which was used liturgically in worship by ancient Israelis, one part of the congregation sang the theme, and the other responded with the refrain. Twenty-six times the refrain, "His love endures forever," is repeated. Today we would call this a "hook," the big idea, the major thesis, the central concept.

Because this was a favorite festival song and because its theme was predominant in the Old Testament, this psalm is often called "The Great Hallel." In the first few verses the psalmist commands his listeners to praise the Lord by giving thanks. Basic to this thanksgiving is the awareness and conviction of the Lord's goodness. Because he is good, his loyal love continues forever. He is eternally bound to his people by virtue of his solemn covenant (contract) with them. And who is behind this covenant, the nature of which is loyal love? "The God of gods" (v. 2). "The Lord of lords" (v. 3).

The original summons is restated in verse 26. "Give thanks to the God of heaven. His love is eternal." This is the only time in the Psalms where God is referred to as the "God of heaven," though Ezra and Nehemiah pick up the phrase in later writings (see Ezra 1:2 and Neh. 1:4).

When I'm tempted to revel in self-revulsion, self-pity, feelings of worthlessness and despair, I need to remember that God loves me with a loyal love that will endure forever! This is the only strong, adequate basis for any positive feelings about oneself.

The Language of Music
Introit
A short musical composition played or sung at the beginning of a worship service.

Personal Prayer

O Lord, I give thanks for your goodness and for your loyal love that stands forever firm, no matter how weak and indecisive I may be.

ANTIPHONAL
PSALM OF LOVE
SERVICE OF PRAISE:
PRAISING THE LORD FOR CREATION

✍ Psalm 136 ✍

He alone does great wonders. His love is eternal. He made the heavens skillfully. His love is eternal. He spread the land on the waters. His love is eternal. He made the great lights: His love is eternal. the sun to rule by day, His love is eternal. the moon and stars to rule by night. His love is eternal (vv. 4–9).

Preoccupied with business as usual, I have the tendency to sleepwalk through life, ignoring the beauties of creation around me. Television and films can dim our sight to a real visual experience, just as Muzak can jade our hearing so we don't really hear good music. Or I concentrate on biblical truth, while failing to observe God's testimony in nature. I believe it's possible to be too serious, too scholarly, too cognitive. Perhaps that's why so few people produce great art!

The psalmist is strongly motivated to give thanks because of his keen observation of God's magnificent creation. He alone "does great wonders" (v. 4). Mere man cannot even begin to fathom the genius and power necessary to fashion the heavens.

In poetic form the psalmist enumerates the splendors of nature—the land, the waters, the dazzling stars and planets—spread out like a diamond necklace against a black velvet curtain. All of these represent gifts of grace that contribute to our equanimity and well-being. Each one gives unique testimony to the eternally enduring love of God. We live in an ultimately benign cosmos, not a hostile universe, and behind it all is the unfathomable love of God.

Surprised by the full circle of a rainbow or the breathtaking sight of the aurora borealis, the great Northern Lights, I am moved to praise. "His love endures forever!"

Personal Prayer
Lord, I thank you for the astonishing beauty of your creation. Make me more aware of my surroundings as I brush against your brilliant designs and help me to hear this silent song of your love!

ANTIPHONAL
PSALM OF LOVE

SERVICE OF PRAISE:
THANKING THE LORD FOR HIS ACTS IN HISTORY

∽ Psalm 136 ∽

He struck the firstborn of the Egyptians His love is eternal. and brought Israel out from among them His love is eternal. with a strong hand and outstretched arm. His love is eternal. He divided the Red Sea His love is eternal. and led Israel through, His love is eternal. but hurled Pharaoh and his army into the Red Sea. His love is eternal. He led His people in the wilderness. His love is eternal. He struck down great kings His love is eternal. and slaughtered famous kings—His love is eternal. . . . and gave their land as an inheritance, His love is eternal. an inheritance to Israel His servant. His love is eternal. He remembered us in our humiliation His love is eternal. and rescued us from our foes. His love is eternal. He gives food to every creature. His love is eternal. Give thanks to the God of heaven! His love is eternal (vv. 10–18, 21–26).

God's loyal, enduring love extends to this century and to you and me on this special day. What greater cause for giving thanks?

Personal Prayer
O Lord, thank you for the thread of your love in the tapestry of human history. Along with my ancient Hebrew brother, I praise you today!

The Language of Music

Antiphonal
Relating to a response between two groups of singers (i.e., like two choirs echoing each other).

Andrea and Giovanni Gabrieli are known for brilliant antiphonal brass writing.

Songs of Zion in a Strange Land

WEEPING OVER JERUSALEM

∾ Psalm 137 ∾

By the rivers of Babylon—there we sat down and wept when we remembered Zion. There we hung up our lyres on the poplar trees, for our captors there asked us for songs, and our tormentors, for rejoicing: "Sing us one of the songs of Zion." How can we sing the LORD's song on foreign soil? If I forget you, Jerusalem, may my right hand forget [its skill]. May my tongue stick to the roof of my mouth if I do not remember you, if I do not exalt Jerusalem as my greatest joy! (vv. 1–6).

Sometimes crying is more appropriate than singing! I find myself at times feeling homesick for the past. I've looked back with longing to the days when I was growing up on Word of Life Island, Schroon Lake, New York, where we spent wonderful summers. Or the days when I was in public school in Maplewood, New Jersey. Or the beautiful high school campus of Hampden DuBose Academy in Zellwood, Florida. But we can never go back except in our memories. I can identify with the homesick Israelites.

The people of God are homesick for their beloved homeland. Captive in Babylon, hundreds of miles from Jerusalem, they lament the loss of their freedom. Even the tough Hebrew spirit, known for its fervor and fire, is quenched, and all they can do is weep. They have been deeply hurt by slavery and oppression.

When their captors demand entertainment, "one of the songs of Zion," they refuse and hang their harps on the poplar trees "by the rivers of Babylon" (vv. 1–3). The motivation for music making had been hammered out of their lives.

Instead, the psalmist reminisces about Jerusalem, where tribes and families once gathered to praise the Lord. He will remember those days at all costs and vows to consider Jerusalem his "greatest joy" (v. 6). Remembering will keep his zeal fresh.

This psalmist, like other musicians who despair over lost opportunities, is open to a deep work of God in his life. When the Lord restores his glory to Zion, there will be singing and dancing! But that will come later. Because God is good, the future will be good if we walk with him!

Personal Prayer

O Lord, do an exciting and colorful work in my life also, and may I burst out in creative worship of your mighty name and awesome power!

Songs of Zion
in a Strange Land

JUDGING ISRAEL'S CAPTORS

∽ Psalm 137 ∽

Remember, LORD, [what] the Edomites said that day at Jerusalem: "Destroy it!
Destroy it down to its foundations!" Daughter Babylon, doomed to destruction,
happy is the one who pays you back what you have done to us. Happy is he who
takes your little ones and dashes them against the rocks (vv. 7–9).

The Jews have never been reticent about expressing anger. These verses reflect their deep mourning while in exile as they cry out to the God of justice to repay their enemies for cruel and barbaric treatment.

The Edomites are singled out first. These pagan people celebrated while Jerusalem was destroyed (see Ezek. 25:12–14 and Joel 3). The Babylonians, guilty of a brutality that almost defies description, are next. Deep sadness and bitterness are poured out against these heathen oppressors who had smashed the Israelite children "against the rocks" (v. 9)! The victimized Israelites are demanding that God do the same to their enemies' children!

What do we have here? Certainly not the "turn the other cheek" ethic of the New Testament.

There is an honest facing up to the cold reality of violence and raw evil in the world. Apart from God's grace and his redemptive power in the human heart, people are capable of exacting terrible atrocities against their neighbors! Yet this psalm is, no doubt, a poetic catharsis. Pouring out bitterness and hurt can be the beginning of healing; pretending the hurt doesn't exist leads only to mental and physical illness.

I'm grateful for the honesty and candor of this ancient psalmist, but I'm even more grateful for the New Testament revelation that there is forgiveness for me as well as for those who have wronged me!

Personal Prayer
Lord, help me to acknowledge the deep, inner pain in my life.
I claim your forgiveness and grace for my life today.

DAVID'S VOW OF PRAISE
PRAISE FOR BOLDNESS

✑ Psalm 138 ✑

I will give You thanks with all my heart; I will sing Your praise before the heavenly beings. I will bow down toward Your holy temple and give thanks to Your name for Your constant love and faithfulness. You have exalted Your name and Your promise above everything else. On the day I called, You answered me; You increased strength within me. All the kings on earth will give You thanks, LORD, when they hear what You have promised. They will sing of the LORD's ways, for the LORD's glory is great (vv. 1–5).

King David has a full-hearted faith that he expresses uniquely and creatively. In these deeply satisfying verses, David praises the Lord before the gods of the pagans!

Dr. Elton Trueblood, in his book *Alternative to Futility*, said some time ago— The basic defect of the Protestant churches lies not in their divided condition but in their insipidity. They show so little imagination. The same kind of dull and lifeless service is repeated endlessly, whatever the occasion. We are in a time of crisis when we need a dynamic fellowship to turn the world upside down. What we are offered is a stereotype. A man, having become convinced that we are in a race with catastrophe, may seek the very bread of life, but in practice he is forced to sing sentimental songs with words he does not mean, listen to some comforting platitudes, and finally shake the minister's hand at the door, because there is no other way to escape! In short, this kind of church illustrates Professor Whitehead's dictum perfectly. "It is in full decay because it lacks the element of adventure."

We need adventurous fellowship. Like David, we need to take our stand boldly "before the gods," declaring our faith and singing praise to the Lord!

Personal Prayer

I long to praise you, Lord, wholeheartedly, courageously, and creatively. As I bow before you, inspire me with songs of praise and worship.

The Language of Music

Vow
A solemn promise or assertion by which a person binds himself to an act, service, or condition.

DAVID'S VOW OF PRAISE

PRAYER FOR FULFILLMENT

∾ Psalm 138 ∾

Though the LORD is exalted, He takes note of the humble; but He knows the haughty from afar. If I walk in the thick of danger, You will preserve my life from the anger of my enemies. You will extend Your hand; Your right hand will save me. The LORD will fulfill [His purpose] for me. LORD, Your love is eternal; do not abandon the work of Your hands (vv. 6–8).

I have long been intrigued with the idea of knowing God's will and have opened myself to his loving guidance and direction. He has led me specifically by his Word and his Spirit, and it is comforting to know that he cares more about my character than about my performance. He is gradually teaching me about reality and values as well. Because I believe he desires intimacy with me, I pray about every detail of my life. Sometimes he uses friends, circumstances, even books to point me in the right direction. Dr. James I. Packer's writings on guidance have been extremely helpful. And because I have a passion for music and communication, he allows me to be involved in creative projects for his glory and honor.

I understand David's plea for fulfillment in this psalm. Though I am not comparing myself with Israel's greatest king, I know something about the course of his career as a musician. From the description of his boyhood, it is obvious that David had talent and quickly became proficient. He was a skillful harpist. (The Hebrew roots for *skill* and *wisdom* are the same!) He was a passionate lyricist, responsible for at least half of the Psalter, a collection of poetry embodying intricate form. He was a man favored by God who preserved his life and gave it purpose.

As one who is prone to melancholy, the last part of this passage comforts and encourages me: "The LORD will fulfill [His purpose] for me" (v. 8). He designed me. He brought me into being. He is with me. He hasn't forgotten me. He hasn't overlooked me in the grand scheme of things. My life has a divine purpose and goal. I can stand with the apostle Paul and say, "I am sure of this, that He who started a good work in you will carry it on to completion until the day of Christ Jesus" (Phil. 1:6). What a promise!

Personal Prayer

Thank you, Lord, for promising to fulfill your purpose for my life! I believe it and claim it!

SYMPHONY OF
GOD'S ATTRIBUTES
FIRST MOVEMENT:
HE KNOWS EVERYTHING (OMNISCIENCE)

∽ Psalm 139 ∽

LORD, You have searched me and known me. You know when I sit down and when I stand up; You understand my thoughts from far away. You observe my travels and my rest; You are aware of all my ways. Before a word is on my tongue, You know all about it, LORD. You have encircled me; You have placed Your hand on me. [This] extraordinary knowledge is beyond me. It is lofty; I am unable to [reach] it (vv. 1–6).

This magnificent psalm opens with a frightening assertion of God's omniscience. Omniscience is a lofty theological term that means God knows everything—everything actual and everything possible. In fact, his knowledge covers both the realms of reality and the imagination.

God knew David inside out (v. 1). He knew what time he got up in the morning and what time he went to bed at night (vv. 2–3). He even knew David's thoughts before he framed them into words (v. 4).

The New Testament confirms this attribute of God. "He [Jesus] did not need anyone to testify about man; for He Himself knew what was in man" (John 2:25). This is terrifying news to the one whose mind is riddled with sinful thoughts and who acts on those impulses.

But to the person who understands God's unconditional love and acceptance, his omniscience is good news! Gloria Gaither's profound phrase sums it up so well: "For the one who knows me best, loves me most." This maximum exposure of my personality, combined with my Lord's total acceptance of me, boggles my mind. It is also what makes the gospel so unbelievably thrilling!

Personal Prayer

Lord, you know everything about me, yet you love me anyway!

The Language of Music

Symphony
A Greek term for "sounding together."

For all intents and purposes it is a sonata for orchestra. The most important form of orchestral music, it developed in the mid 18th century in a rather pure form and reached its highest development in Beethoven (who pulled, stretched, and expanded the form). Prime examples would be Beethoven's nine symphonies or Brahm's four symphonies.

Symphony of God's Attributes

SECOND MOVEMENT:
HE IS EVERYWHERE (OMNIPRESENCE)

∽ Psalm 139 ∽

Where can I go to escape Your Spirit? Where can I flee from Your presence? If I go up to heaven, You are there; if I make my bed in Sheol, You are there. If I live at the eastern horizon [or] settle at the western limits, even there Your hand will lead me; Your right hand will hold on to me. If I say, "Surely the darkness will hide me, and the light around me will become night"—even the darkness is not too dark for You. The night shines like the day; darkness and light are alike to You (vv. 7–12).

Upon learning that God knows the worst about him, David's first impulse is to run! Fallen, sinful humanity always attempts to flee from the presence of the absolute holiness of God. But there is no place to hide, for God is everywhere! He's omnipresent!

God is everywhere, but he is not *in* everything. That's pantheism. He is infinite and personal, but he is self-contained and separate from his creation. Nothing escapes his notice.

The comforting thought is that, if he is everywhere, he is also immediately accessible! I can make contact with him instantly. He is right here! Distance between God and me is created, not on his initiative, but by my sin and guilt. Where God is, there can be no evil. Light and darkness do not coexist at the same place at the same time.

Martin Luther once said, "Music is one of the greatest gifts that God has given us: it is divine and, therefore, Satan is its enemy. For with its aid many dire temptations are overcome; the devil does not say where music is."

I am newly encouraged to make music. For where God is, there can be no evil. Where God is, there is music!

Personal Prayer

O Lord, I'm happy that I can't flee from your presence.
I'm comforted by the fact that you are everywhere
and that music is praise to your name!

SYMPHONY OF
GOD'S ATTRIBUTES
THIRD MOVEMENT:
HE IS ALL-POWERFUL (OMNIPOTENCE)

∽ Psalm 139 ∽

For it was You who created my inward parts; You knit me together in my mother's womb. I will praise You because I am unique in remarkable ways.... My bones were not hidden from You when I was made in secret, when I was formed in the depths of the earth. Your eyes saw me when I was formless; all [my] days were written in Your book and planned before a single one of them began. God, how difficult Your thoughts are for me [to comprehend]; how vast their sum is! If I counted them, they would outnumber the grains of sand; when I wake up, I am still with You (vv. 13–18).

God is all knowing, ever present, and all-powerful!

These verses describing reproduction are among the most touching and tender in all the Bible. Realizing that he has been "fearfully and wonderfully made," David considers God's orchestration of his own conception and development: "You knit me together in my mother's womb.... My bones were not hidden from You when I was made in secret ... Your eyes saw me when I was formless" (vv. 13, 15–16).

God is fully cognizant of the union of sperm and egg, the attachment of the embryo to the uterine lining, and the development of that tiny life according to his timetable.

This passage gives every human being a remarkable basis for self-worth. From the moment of conception, God is present, and through every phase of development thereafter. How can people decide to abort what God deems so precious and valuable? The human embryo is not the result of a biological accident, no matter what the circumstances. Rather, it embraces the image of God and is not to be equated with junk or trash to be discarded! God presides over the mysteries of human reproduction. All life has meaning and eternal significance.

Personal Prayer

O Lord, I praise you for creating my inmost being. I praise you because I am fearfully and wonderfully made.

A Contemporary Song

Fearfully and Wonderfully Made

Fearfully and wonderfully made,
I'm unique, one of a kind,
Fearfully and wonderfully made,
My beginning was God's design.
He was with me before my birth
And formed my being with care,
I'm a person of infinite worth—
A masterpiece beyond compare!

Words and music by Don Wyrtzen © 1984 Singspiration Music.

Symphony of God's Attributes

Finale: David's Response

∽ Psalm 139 ∽

*God, if only You would kill the wicked (stay away from me, you bloodthirsty men)
who invoke You deceitfully. Your enemies swear [by You] falsely. Lord, don't I hate
those who hate You, and detest those who rebel against You? I hate them
with extreme hatred; I consider them my enemies. Search me, God, and
know my heart; test me and know my concerns. See if there is any
offensive way in me; lead me in the everlasting way (vv. 19–24).*

P iano tuning is a fine art. A piano has three strings for each tone. If the instrument is flat, the strings must be tightened; if it is sharp, the strings must be loosened. The piano tuner always has a point of reference—"A-440"—using either a tuning fork or an electronic device called a strobe tuner. But he also depends on his ear—perfect pitch or good relative pitch—and a thorough acquaintance with harmonic intervals.

After cataloging the sins of God's enemies, who are consequently his as well, David focuses on himself. Unlike those who "misuse" the name of the Lord, David prays, voluntarily submitting himself to God's tuning fork: "Search me"; "Test me"; "See if there is any offensive way in me" (vv. 23–24). In effect, he is saying: "Lord, let me know if my life is out of tune!"

As is true so many times in Psalms, David meets trouble with an expression of faith in the nature of God. He is both infinite and personal, transcendent and immanent—far above to watch over us yet within to guide us. He knows how it feels to be human because he came in the flesh and walked where we walk (John 1:1, 14).

David finds a deep wellspring of comfort and serenity in these harmonious attributes.

As the tuning fork is applied to my life, I can "hear" the flat keys. The Master Tuner may have to tighten the strings, thus producing temporary pain and stress. But the final result will be a beautifully voiced instrument of praise, fit for a heavenly concerto!

Personal Prayer

*O Lord, let me know if my life is out of tune! Search me, test me, and check me out.
I long to sing and play in perfect harmony with your plan!*

IMPRECATORY IMPROMPTU
DAVID PRAYS FOR JUSTICE

✍ Psalm 140 ✍

Rescue me, Lord, from evil men. Keep me safe from violent men who plan evil in their hearts. They stir up wars all day long. They make their tongues as sharp as a snake's bite; viper's venom is under their lips. Protect me, Lord, from the clutches of the wicked. Keep me safe from violent men who plan to make me stumble. The proud hide a trap with ropes for me; they spread a net along the path and set snares for me. I say to the Lord, "You are my God." Listen, Lord, to my cry for help. Lord God, my strong Savior, You shield my head on the day of battle. Lord, do not grant the desires of the wicked; do not let them achieve their goals. [Otherwise,] they will become proud. (vv. 1–8).

Again David vents his emotions, hence the title for this psalm. An *imprecation* is a curse on the wicked. An *impromptu* is a musical piece played extemporaneously. David is spontaneously engaging in an emotional outburst in song. The tone is harsh, strident, and dissonant.

In his opening prayer, David prays for justice and protection from the wicked. He then proceeds to curse them for their vicious character. Their tongues are poisonous; their hands do evil things; their minds devise all kinds of cunning plots to trap David and take him off the scene.

In verses 6–8, he praises God's sovereignty, using military imagery to affirm his protective power. David then concludes this section by praying for the divine restraint of the wicked.

David's prayer life is marked by honesty and openness. He never denies the reality of internal pressure. He is obviously fearful, and his emotions are churning, but he feels perfectly free to dump all of this junk on God. God is certainly big enough to take it!

The great psalmist was objective about his suffering, but because he acknowledged it and worked through it, he was able to cope with God's help. I can do the same!

Personal Prayer

O Strong Deliverer, I pray that you will protect me from the cunning schemes of ungodly persons. I pray also that you will protect me from myself and deliver me from unnecessary guilt and fear.

IMPRECATORY IMPROMPTU

DAVID'S RESPONSE TO HIS ENEMIES

∽ Psalm 140 ∽

As for the heads of those who surround me, let the trouble their lips cause overwhelm [them]. Let hot coals fall on them. Let them be thrown into the fire, into the abyss, never again to rise. Do not let a slanderer stay in the land. Let evil relentlessly hunt down a violent man. I know that the Lord upholds the just cause of the poor, justice for the needy. Surely the righteous will praise Your name; the upright will live in Your presence (vv. 9–13).

This psalm is best grasped against the backdrop of the Judeo-Christian ethic. God is holy, righteous, and pure. Man is evil, unfair, and deceitful. The morality is clear-cut and unrelenting. Because I desperately want to give people the benefit of the doubt, I sometimes tend to be "marshmallowy" about ethics.

David's intimate walk with God produced an objectivity that enabled him to see things monochromatically (in black and white). Artistic thinking in grays doesn't work in the areas of personal morality. This kind of reasoning results in a naïve and shallow view of sin. We need to learn how to hate evil as much as God does, but we are more addicted to happiness than committed to holiness.

While David's prayer may seem a little shocking to those of us living in a society tainted by secular humanism, we must bear in mind that his enemies were malicious men. They were as annoying as insects, as repulsive as reptiles, and as lethal as sharks. They were cunning and predatory—out to kill!

He responds with equal passion. He prays that the poisonous words of the wicked will boomerang. He prays that "hot coals" will fall on their heads like volcanic residue from Sodom and Gomorrah (Gen. 19). He prays that their slander will be self-defeating and that disaster will pursue them and bring them down.

Like the clash of cymbals, a stunning thought strikes my consciousness: *David's righteous wrath was not directed against his enemies but poured out to God in a prayer song!*

Personal Prayer

O Lord, I'm glad David was a passionate person too! And I've learned today that I don't have to act on my negative impulses but can pour them out before you in healing, restorative prayer and praise!

The Language of Music

Impromptu

An improvisation or composition suggestive of improvisation.

A piece that has a somewhat casual, spur-of-the-moment, feeling. The "pneumatic odes" of Ephesians 5:19 were somewhat like impromptus.

EVENSONG

SONG OF PROTECTION

∞ Psalm 141 ∞

Lord, I call on You; hurry to [help] me. Listen to my voice when I call on You. May my
prayer be set before You as incense, the raising of my hands as the evening offering....
But my eyes [look] to You, Lord God. I seek refuge in You; do not let me die. Protect me
from the trap they have set for me, and from the snares of evildoers. Let the wicked fall
into their own nets, while I pass [safely] by (vv. 1–2, 8–10).

For many people prayer is a one-liner beginning with "Gimme." For others it's a hasty thank-you mumbled over meals or a bedtime blessing left over from childhood. For David, prayer was a way of life.

Here David bows before the Lord during the evening sacrifices. We're allowed to peer over his shoulder as he observes this meaningful ritual. First, he calls on the name of the Lord—a name that, in its very use, promises power. His words rise like sweet perfume because they flow from a sincere heart. He lifts his hands in a posture of praise and commitment and prays, with open eyes fixed on his Lord.

The prayer itself is spelled out in specific terms—for the presence of the Lord (v. 1), for preservation of life (v. 8), for supernatural discernment of snares set by the wicked (v. 9), for vindication (v. 10).

I am reminded of the life of Queen Esther (Esther 1–10). Haman, the highest noble under King Xerxes, had a vendetta against the Jews, especially Mordecai, Esther's guardian. He even erected a gallows, seventy-five feet high, on which to hang Mordecai. Instead, Esther acted responsibly, God acted sovereignly, and the tables were turned!

What comfort there is in knowledge that God has a plan for us that will not be thwarted by the worst the wicked can do!

Personal Prayer

O Lord, I know you hear my prayers just as you heard King David's. Don't
let me fall into the traps set by the world, but let this humanistic society
hang itself by its own rope while "I pass by safely."

EVENSONG

SONG OF SANCTIFICATION

✑ Psalm 141 ✑

Lord, set up a guard for my mouth; keep watch at the door of my lips. Do not let my heart turn to any evil thing or wickedly perform reckless acts with men who commit sin. Do not let me feast on their delicacies. Let the righteous one strike me—it is [an act of] faithful love; let him rebuke me—it is oil for my head; let me not refuse it. Even now my prayer is against the evil acts of the wicked. When their rulers will be thrown off the sides of a cliff, the people will listen to my words, for they are pleasing (vv. 3–6).

David had the right idea. His aspirations were lofty; he was just too human to attain them! Still, he longed to be pure, blameless, and sanctified (set apart).

In this passage he submits three parts of his body to the Lord for cleansing—his lips and mouth, lest he speak evil (v. 3); his heart, lest he become involved in sensual pleasures (v. 4); his head, lest his mind toy with the evil schemes of the wicked (v. 4). In fact, he asks for corrective support from godly friends.

God never intended for us to face life alone. If we isolate ourselves from real, down-to-earth relationships, the enemy will subtly distract us, seduce us, and then devour us. My close friends regularly pray for me, communicate with me, and generally hold me accountable. Karen and I also attend small group Bible studies where we experience rich Christian fellowship in a private setting. Without this support, we would be depriving ourselves of one of the greatest blessings the Lord gives us—intercessory prayer.

In unity there is strength to endure temptation, to make a frontal attack on societal sins, and to stand firm against the enemy. God has set me apart for his ministry, but he has also blessed me with godly friends who pray for me and point out possible dangers I am too blind to see.

Personal Prayer

O Lord, I thank you again for prayer warriors who faithfully hold me up in prayer. I know you have brought these people into my life to help me fight the battle . . . and win!

LONGING AND LAMENT

I CRY ALOUD TO THE LORD!

✑ Psalm 142 ✑

I cry aloud to the Lord; I plead aloud to the Lord for mercy. I pour out my complaint before Him; I reveal my trouble to Him. Although my spirit is weak within me, You know my way. Along this path I travel they have hidden a trap for me. Look to the right and see: no one stands up for me; there is no refuge for me; no one cares about me (vv. 1–4).

David's circumstances couldn't be worse! He is hiding out in a cave with the murderous King Saul in hot pursuit. David is utterly helpless and alone.

His prayer is more of a demand than a polite request. He is crying "aloud," literally shouting at God!

Every trail and road is mined and booby-trapped, and David is spooked. He's afraid to make a single move! Isolated, he feels that "no one cares" (v. 4).

I understand this feeling. As long as I can remember, I've been quiet, introverted, high-strung, and overly sensitive. You probably wouldn't be able to tell from observing me, but deep inside is a fragile persona. There are times when I feel that I might as well drop out because no one cares. It's the price one pays for having the volume turned up too high on life!

David has "no refuge" (v. 4), no place and no one but God. Actually, that's exactly where the Lord wants us. The best place to be is in a position of absolute dependence on God. Most of us still believe we can make it on our own strength, that we make life work on our own. The real truth is that *he* gives us the power to do everything we do. "You may say to yourself, 'My power and the strength of my hands have produced this wealth for me.' But remember the LORD your God, for it is he who gives you the ability to produce wealth, and so confirms his covenant" (Deut. 8:17–18). Some people aren't blessed because they're depending too much on their own talent.

Personal Prayer

O Lord, I'm only too conscious of my weakness and vulnerability. Please show me your strength at the point of my deepest need!

An Appropriate Gospel Song

No One Ever Cared for Me Like Jesus

No one ever cared for me like Jesus
There's no other friend so kind as He;
No one else could take the sin and
    darkness from me,
O how much he cared for me!

Words and music by C. F. Weigle.
© 1932. Renewal 1959 by John T. Benson Jr.
Assigned to and © 1983 by Singspiration.

LONGING AND LAMENT

THEY ARE TOO STRONG FOR ME

∞ Psalm 142 ∞

I cry to You, Lord; I say, "You are my shelter, my portion in the land of the living."
Listen to my cry, for I am very weak. Rescue me from those who pursue me, for they
are too strong for me. Free me from prison so that I can praise Your name. The righ-
teous will gather around me because You deal generously with me (vv. 5–7).

Contemporary Christians are suffering from spiritual anorexia. Ignoring the Lord's bountiful feast spread out in his Word, we're literally starving ourselves to death! And instead of being strong and robust in the faith, we're weaklings, cowering in the face of real conflict and adversity. Like David, we look at the opposition and say, "They are too strong for me!" (v. 6).

How is it that a beautiful and gifted young woman like Karen Carpenter could literally starve herself to death? How could this skinny person look at herself in the mirror and think, *I'm too fat?* Why did she try to control her life through diet and exercise instead of turning to the Lord for answers to her problems? Psychology may provide some insights regarding the dynamics of this disease, but God's Word penetrates the mysteries of human existence and provides final resolution in Jesus Christ.

David did have the good sense to turn to the Lord. His consuming desire was to be able to praise the Lord and thus present a strong witness to other believers.

We don't have to fear the strength of our "enemies"—pride, out-of-control ambition, destructive use of sexuality, craving for status and things. The Lord has given us every resource needed to grow healthy, to build up our sin-immune system. We need to move from milk to meat! Everyone who lives on milk is inexperienced with the message about righteousness, because he is an infant. But solid food is for the mature—for those whose senses have been trained to distinguish between good and evil" (Heb. 5:13–14).

As we continue to eat heartily from God's Word, we'll be filled with his goodness and Spirit. Seeing the change, the righteous will "gather about" in open-mouthed wonder and praise to God!

Personal Prayer

O Lord, when there is so much rich food available for our spirits, why do we starve
ourselves? Lead me to the banquet table and let me feast on your Word so my brothers
and sisters in Christ may be fed and encouraged.

PATHETIQUE SONATA
FIRST MOVEMENT
MY SPIRIT GROWS FAINT WITHIN ME

∽ Psalm 143 ∽

Lord, hear my prayer. In Your faithfulness listen to my plea, and in Your righteousness answer me. Do not bring Your servant into judgment, for no one alive is righteous in Your sight. For the enemy has pursued me, crushing me to the ground, making me live in darkness like those long dead. My spirit is weak within me; my heart is overcome with dismay (vv. 1–4).

In this age of focus on physical fitness, I wonder if we give nearly as much thought to the condition of our spirits. The body can look pretty good on the outside while spiritual rigor mortis is in the process of setting in! Too many of us are "weak." We're spiritual wimps!

I'm impressed all over again with David's brutal honesty about himself. He doesn't attempt to project positive images or to numb himself into relief through positive mental attitudes. He's forthright and objective. His lament is real and rich in intensity. Emotionally, he has pulled the blanket of dark despair over his head. Because he's spiritually impoverished, he's ready for a mighty work of God in his life.

And he desperately needs one. In verses 3–4, he tells us that his enemies are still pursuing him relentlessly and that he is being forced to live in darkness like those that are dead.

In this psalm, I don't hear the mighty warrior king of Israel. Instead, I hear the pathetic plea of one who recognizes that power comes not from physical strength or military strategy but in trusting the faithfulness and righteousness of God.

Personal Prayer

O God, hear my prayer today. The macho image is not for me. I confess my inability to work out the details of my life or even to protect myself! Be merciful to me.

The Language of Music

Pathétique

A French word meaning "emotional" and "full of pathos" (not necessarily sad).

Beethoven's Sonata op. 13 in C minor is called "Sonate Pathétique." The Bible is full of emotional sensitivity, personal sympathy, and compassion. (See John 11 or Matt. 26:36–39.)

PATHETIQUE SONATA
SECOND MOVEMENT
MY SPIRIT FAINTS WITH LONGING

∽ Psalm 143 ∽

I remember the days of old; I meditate on all You have done; I reflect on the work of Your hands. I spread out my hands to You; I am like parched land before You. Answer me quickly, Lord; my spirit fails. Don't hide Your face from me, or I will be like those going down to the Pit (vv. 5–7).

David was no stranger to suffering. It became the foundation upon which the Lord erected a rich, intimate relationship with him.

The psalmist is now rescued through reminiscence. He considers God's mighty acts in history. He meditates on his supernatural works. These thoughts begin to restore and renew him.

Before, David's personality resembled a dry, parched land. Now he recognizes his inner thirst and longing for God and reaches out to his Heavenly Father. His request is of the utmost urgency. He feels as if he is about to die, "going down to the Pit" (v. 7). Perhaps his most horrifying thought is that the Lord will overlook him!

Spiritual pain is often the catalyst for change and growth. As I reach the end of my own limited resources, I grope toward God in desperation. He closes that great gap with his own presence and lets me know that he has not overlooked my need!

Personal Prayer

O Lord, please look beyond my fault to see my need. My soul thirsts for you like a parched land. Refresh me with the rains of your love.

He Looked Beyond My Fault

Amazing grace shall always be my song of praise—
For it was grace that bought my liberty—
I do not know just why He came to love me so—
He looked beyond my fault and saw my need.

I shall forever lift mine eyes to Calvary
To view the cross where Jesus died for me—
How marvelous—the grace that caught my falling soul
He looked beyond my fault and saw my need.

Words by Dottie Rambo. Music adapted from Londonderry Aire. © 1967 by Heart-Warming Music.

PATHETIQUE SONATA
THIRD MOVEMENT
MAY YOUR GOOD SPIRIT LEAD ME ON LEVEL GROUND

∽ Psalm 143 ∽

Let me experience Your faithful love in the morning, for I trust in You. Reveal to me the way I should go, because I long for You. Rescue me from my enemies, Lord; I come to You for protection. Teach me to do Your will, for You are my God. May Your gracious Spirit lead me on level ground. For Your name's sake, Lord, let me live. In Your righteousness deliver me from trouble, and in Your faithful love destroy my enemies. Wipe out all those who attack me, for I am Your servant (vv. 8–12).

A t the moment of rebirth, when the human spirit is "yielded and still," the Holy Spirit moves in to make his home and provide assistance for our pilgrimage with God.

Even David anticipated something of this divine exchange, I think. His despairing prayer, filled with strong, virile verbs, is the night sky against which the dazzling stars of God's grace through his Spirit are displayed.

Guide—David prays, "Review to me the way" (v. 8), sensing that God's guiding Spirit will not leave him stranded, not remove him from the unfailing love that is everlasting.

Enabler—"Rescue me from my enemies" (v. 9), he continues. It is the Spirit of God who enables and empowers. David's many military coups were a result of divine intervention by the Enabler.

Teacher—"Teach me to do Your will. . . . May your gracious Spirit lead me on level ground" (v. 10). The Holy Spirit is our Teacher/Interpreter. It is he who explains spiritual mysteries and levels the ground of our understanding.

Comforter—"For Your name's sake, LORD, let me live. . . . deliver me from trouble" (v. 11). God's Spirit whispers words of encouragement and calls to our minds his mighty works in our behalf. He banishes discouragement and puts a song in our hearts!

Personal Prayer
O Lord, fill me with your Spirit today. Guide me, enable me, teach me, comfort me. I need help as I continue my pilgrimage.

IMPERIAL MARCH

DAVID IN COMBAT: CELEBRATING THE PAST

∾ Psalm 144 ∾

May the Lord my rock be praised, who trains my hands for battle and my fingers for warfare. He is my faithful love and my fortress, my stronghold and my deliverer. He is my shield, and I take refuge in Him; He subdues my people under me. Lord, what is man, that You care for him, the son of man, that You think of him? Man is like a breath; his days are like a passing shadow (vv. 1–4).

David was the General MacArthur of his day—a conquering hero. He begins this stirring psalm by remembering past victories and enemies who have been subdued under him. But who forged David's career? Who gave him genius for military strategy? Who trained his hands for war and his fingers for battle? The Lord!

David had a personal relationship with God, who is strong, solid, and immovable, yet warm, loving, and intimate. He was David's Fortress, Stronghold, Deliverer, and Shield (v. 2). David went forth in God's strength to crush his enemies in battle. We are to do the same (see Eph. 6). God's character—his nature and attributes—sustained David and made him bold and courageous—a winner!

What is almost incomprehensible to me is that this mighty God of war invites me—weak and wandering though I be—into his presence to receive the same kind of strength that he gave David. He promises to be my Shield and Deliverer in the spiritual battles I must fight. Like David, I can be a conquering hero ... in him!

The Language of Music

March

Music for soldiers, usually involving strongly accented beats in groups of four.

Marches are usually dignified, ceremonial, and military. A good example is Arthur Sullivan's stirring hymn. "Onward Christian Soldiers."

Personal Prayer

O Lord, be my Rock, my Fortress, My Deliverer, and my Shield today. My battles are not as obvious as David's, but they are just as deadly!

IMPERIAL MARCH

DAVID IN COMBAT: PLEADING FOR HELP
IN THE PRESENT

✺ Psalm 144 ✺

Lord, part Your heavens and come down. Touch the mountains, and they will smoke.
Flash [Your] lightning and scatter the foe; shoot Your arrows and rout them. Reach down
from on high; rescue me from deep water, and set me free from the grasp of foreigners
whose mouths speak lies, whose right hands are deceptive. God, I will sing a new song to
You; I will play on a ten-stringed harp for You—the One who gives victory to kings, who
frees His servant David from the deadly sword. Set me free and rescue me from the grasp
of foreigners whose mouths speak lies, whose right hands are deceptive (vv. 5–11).

D avid set his faith firmly in divine intervention rather than in human strategy. He longed for a dazzling supernatural display of God's power! He wanted to see the heavens illuminated by holy fireworks, to see God's own Fourth of July celebration (v. 5)! He knew that when God sent forth lightning, enemies were scattered (v. 6), and when God sprung his bow and shot his arrows, villains were put to rout (v. 6).

David was praying for deliverance *now!* His enemies were foreigners with lying tongues, impure motives, and corrupt actions. He desperately needed a divine rescue action.

What inspiration for music! In ancient Israel the creative process worked like this:

Genuine need—God's people were backed against the wall.

Imminent danger—They faced the possibility of being wiped out.

Honest lament—They groaned and cried out to the Lord for salvation and deliverance. Whole families clothed themselves in sackcloth and ashes, fasted, and prayed.

Divine intervention—The Lord heard their cry and supernaturally delivered them.

Genuine praise—They worshipped God for his mighty works!

We often do it all backward today—cranking up a praise experience while nothing is happening in our lives! Yet David was so confident of success that he wrote this psalm of victory *before the fact!* Considering the unchanging nature of God and his faithfulness, I can begin *now* to compose music in gratitude *for who he is and what he is going to do for me!*

Personal Prayer

O Lord, even before you do your next exciting work in my life, may I burst
forth in creative worship of your mighty name and power!

Imperial March

DAVID IN COMBAT: ANTICIPATING PEACE AND PROSPERITY

∾ Psalm 144 ∾

Set me free and rescue me from the grasp of foreigners whose mouths speak lies, whose right hands are deceptive. Then our sons will be like plants nurtured in their youth, our daughters, like corner pillars that are carved in the palace style. Our storehouses will be full, supplying all kinds of produce; our flocks will increase by thousands and tens of thousands in our open fields. Our cattle will be well fed. There will be no breach [in the walls], no going [into captivity], and no cry of lament in our public squares. Happy are the people with such [blessings]. Happy are the people whose God is the Lord (vv. 11–15).

Only a survivor or a veteran of war in some strife-ridden part of the world can really appreciate the absence of conflict. Harry Bollback, Dad's colleague, is an ex-Marine who fought in World War II. But some of the guys—including Ike Eickleberger and Pete Monfore, who saw duty in the Korean conflict—never made it back. They died on Heartbreak Ridge. Whenever I return to the USA after being out of the country, I'm overwhelmed by our freedom. We owe it to men like these!

In this psalm David is projecting into a future when worldwide peace will reign once more. In order to understand his point of view, I have to do just the opposite.

I have to think about the hot spots of the world—especially the Middle East. Insulated from most physical violence as we are in America, I don't have to be overly concerned that my family will be harmed by a flying bullet or will step on a land mine (v. 12). I don't have to fear that bombs will destroy the farms of our country so that there will be no food in the supermarket (v. 13). I don't spend too much time wondering if I'll be captured and exiled by foreign invaders (v. 14). For his own reasons, God has blessed America . . . for now!

But David reminds us of the divine condition for peace and prosperity: "Happy are the people whose God is the Lord" (v. 15). There are definite signs of disintegration in our society: Families are in crisis, our economy is shaky, and our military strength is questionable. Could it be that we've forsaken the Lord?

Personal Prayer

O Lord, I long for your blessing of world peace. Take control of our economy, our national security, and international affairs, so that all nations will know that you are our God!

PRAISE TO THE KING
HIS ATTRIBUTES AND ACTS

❧ Psalm 145 ❧

I exalt You, my God the King, and praise Your name forever and ever. I will praise You every day; I will honor Your name forever and ever. The Lord is great and is highly praised; His greatness is unsearchable. One generation will declare Your works to the next and will proclaim Your mighty acts. I will speak of Your glorious splendor and Your wonderful works. They will proclaim the power of Your awesome works, and I will declare Your greatness. They will give a testimony of Your great goodness and will joyfully sing of Your righteousness (vv. 1–7).

This noble praise psalm begins the grand doxology (Psalms 145–150) of the entire Psalter, bringing this anthology of ancient worship songs to a mighty crescendo. Excitement builds, erupting in a fulfilling climax of praise in Psalm 150, the Old Testament Hallelujah Chorus!

David begins extolling God the King. He covenants with the Lord to praise his name on a daily basis. He vows to keep the relationship fresh, not taking anything for granted.

The psalmist praises the Lord for both his attributes and his acts. Only God is worthy of praise because of his divine personality and unprecedented acts in history. God is not an absentee landlord of his universe! Future generations will tell the stories revealing his glorious splendor and majesty.

What a model for my own praise experience! I need to celebrate daily the Lord's attributes and actions in my life. How does his character affect me personally? Can he ever act toward me in an unloving way? Is he capable of upholding and sustaining me?

These are the concepts I must meditate on. These are the things I must pray about. These are the images and pictures of God I must write down to preserve for future generations of believers. What poems, songs, and holy literature should spring forth from these exalted thoughts!

Personal Prayer
My God and King, you alone are worthy of daily and forever praise! I exalt and declare your goodness to all generations.

Praise to the King

HIS LOVE

∽ Psalm 145 ∽

The Lord is gracious and compassionate, slow to anger and great in faithful love. The Lord is good to everyone; His compassion [rests] on all He has made. . . . Your kingdom is an everlasting kingdom; Your rule is for all generations. The Lord helps all who fall; He raises up all who are oppressed. All eyes look to You, and You give them their food in due time. You open Your hand and satisfy the desire of every living thing (vv. 8–9, 13b–16).

When I think of God's Father love, I see his grace and compassion (v. 8), his goodness and compassion (v. 9), his faithful promises (v. 13), and his open hand (v. 16).

Our God is not stingy but lavish in his gift-giving. He is a God of extravagance. He delights in caring for his children. Over and over again in his Word, we are reminded of his gracious provision, both physically and spiritually: "They are filled from abundance of Your house; You let them drink from Your refreshing stream" (Ps. 36:8). "You crown the year with Your goodness; Your ways overflow with plenty" (Ps. 65:11). "The LORD is my shepherd; there is nothing I lack" (Ps. 23:1). The refrain is echoed in the New Testament: "I have come that they may have life and have it in abundance" (John 10:10).

That greatest Gift was God himself in human flesh!

Personal Prayer

My Father God, I thank you for your open hands which have satisfied the deepest desires of my heart through Jesus Christ . . . and keep on giving every day of my life!

PRAISE TO THE KING

HIS GLORY

✑ Psalm 145 ✑

All You have made will praise You, Lord; the godly will bless You. They will speak
of the glory of Your kingdom and will declare Your might, informing [all] people of
Your mighty acts and of the glorious splendor of Your kingdom. Your kingdom is an
everlasting kingdom; Your rule is for all generations (vv. 10–13).

I read the words of this passage and try to envision the kingdom described
here—its glory, its splendor, its everlastingness!

God's kingdom—not made with hands—is filled with his glory and
reflects his power and might. At the center—radiant and brighter than the
sun—is the King himself. His dominion is not transitory; it is an everlasting
kingdom, enduring through all generations (v. 13).

So moved am I that I break forth into a song of praise:

Personal Prayer

King of kings, I praise you for your mighty deeds in my life and look
forward to joining that "angelic rain" in glory!

Praise to the King

You are my God and King,
Of Your greatness I will sing;
I will thank You all my days
And thru eternity give Your praise.
I sing of Your wondrous fame
And bow before your name;
For You rule in sovereignty
And reign in glorious majesty.

I give thanks for Your goodness
And celebrate Your kindness.
I bow in humility
Before all You've done for me.
Then someday when You come for me
I'll be caught up to glory,
And I'll join the angelic train
To sing of Your sovereign reign.

Words and music by Don Wyrtzen © 1980 Singspiration.

Praise to the King

HIS LISTENING EAR

◇ Psalm 145 ◇

The Lord is righteous in all His ways and gracious in all His acts. The Lord is near all who call out to Him, all who call out to Him with integrity. He fulfills the desires of those who fear Him; He hears their cry for help and saves them. The Lord guards all those who love Him, but He destroys all the wicked. My mouth will declare the Lord's praise; let every living thing praise His holy name forever and ever (vv. 17–21).

Picture the Lord. What image do you see? He's a perfect King, infinitely powerful and totally just. But he is also a loving Father—intimately near, warm, and personal. He is just exactly what each of us needs. How sad that many of us try to keep him at arm's length most of the time!

King and Father. It may be easier to accept the image of God as King than as Father. Some, whose childhood memories are scarred by thoughts of unloving, insensitive parents, need to learn the definition of *father* by studying this psalm. This Father is never inattentive, neglectful, or too busy.

Even to those of us who were blessed with godly fathers, this concept may seem foreign to us. We're so busy declaring our independence, toughing it out alone, and proving ourselves that we lose sight of the truth that self-sufficiency never results in lasting satisfaction. We need to learn that we are most satisfied and safest in the arms of our Heavenly Father. He is "near all who call out to Him" (v. 18). How amazing!

Personal Prayer

My God and King, I'm so glad you showed me something of your heart through my dad and that I have only to turn to your Word to be further reminded of your active love and care.

The Ultimate Priority

PRAISING HIS GREATNESS IN CREATION

↬ Psalm 146 ↬

Hallelujah! My soul, praise the Lord. I will praise the Lord all my life; I will sing to the Lord as long as I live. Do not trust in nobles, in man, who cannot save. When his breath leaves him, he returns to the ground; on that day his plans die. Happy is the one whose help is the God of Jacob, whose hope is in the Lord his God, the Maker of heaven and earth, the sea and everything in them. He remains faithful forever (vv. 1–6).

Music has always been as necessary to me as breathing. Melodies tend to stick to me like glue, playing over and over in my "inner ear." A moving praise song such as "His Name Is Wonderful" evokes a whole emotional gestalt of feelings, memories, and associations. Certain songs, such as "In the Sweet By and By," "O That Will Be Glory for Me," and "When We All Get to Heaven" remind me of friends and loved ones who are waiting for us there. For me, music is a big part of the rhythm and meaning in life, and like David, I want praise to be the top priority of my life.

It's easy to praise the Lord when I see him at every turn—at the seaside, in the mountains, in the snow frosting the trees.

But God's unshakability is appreciated even more when seen against the backdrop of human weakness and transience. As David pointed out, "Man . . . cannot save" (v. 3). Their final destiny is the grave; on the day of death their well-strategized plans come to nothing.

As the year draws to a close, I need to reevaluate my commitment to the Lord. Have I kept my priorities in order? Have I praised the Lord every day through meditating on his Word, through prayer, through music? Have I let the plastic things made by humans blind me to authentic masterpieces created by God? Have I cultivated a sense of his presence, so that I can know him whom I've never seen? Am I worshipping him with my whole person or with my head? Objective knowledge is a poor substitute for subjective intimacy and involvement!

Personal Prayer

Dear Lord, I want to praise you as long as I live. Make me sensitive to your beauty in creation, and may I move from an awareness of your power and might to a warm, personal relationship with you.

THE ULTIMATE PRIORITY

PRAISING HIS GRACE IN PROVISION

∽ Psalm 146 ∽

Executing justice for the exploited and giving food to the hungry. The LORD frees prisoners. The LORD opens [the eyes of] the blind. The LORD raises up those who are oppressed. The LORD loves the righteous. The LORD protects foreigners and helps the fatherless and the widow, but He frustrates the ways of the wicked. The LORD reigns forever; your God, O Zion, [reigns] for all generations. Hallelujah! (vv. 7–10).

The Lord is to be praised not only for his greatness in creation but also for his provision on behalf of his people. He shows his loving favor in many ways.

There are many prophetic allusions to the marvelous gifts of God's grace (see Isa. 42:6–8). The New Testament records the fulfillment of this prophecy: "The Spirit of the Lord is upon me, because he hath anointed me to preach the gospel to the poor; he hath sent me to preach the gospel to the poor; he hath sent me to heal the broken-hearted, to preach deliverance to the captives, and recovering the sight to the blind, to set at liberty them that are bruised" (Luke 4:18 KJV). Indeed, the whole purpose of God's redemptive plan in history was "to the praise of His glorious grace" (Eph. 1:6).

God's grace was personified through his Son, the Lord Jesus Christ. It is through him and him alone that we can be saved (Eph. 2:8–9). He is the only true hope for fallen man.

The psalmist concludes by reminding us that the Lord reigns forever. He ends as he began—with a paroxysm of praise, "Hallelujah!"

Personal Prayer

Dear Lord, I thank you for your "glorious grace" and what it has done in my life. I thank you for the Lord Jesus Christ who personifies your grace—your undeserved favor.

A Contemporary Praise Song

To the Praise of His Glorious Grace

Let us praise the One who chose us;
Let us thank the One who knows us;
Set apart, blameless in His sight;
Through the Son we have faith, we
  have life—
To the praise of His glorious grace.

May the God of our Lord, the
  Almighty Father,
Give you wisdom and peace, His
  comforting Spirit;
That you may know His love,
And you may know His riches, and
  you may know His mighty
  strength—
To the praise of His glorious grace.
Words and music by Michael W. Smith and Deborah D. Smith.
© 1983 Meadowgreen Music Co.

A Very
Personal Doxology

HE HEALS ME

℘ Psalm 147 ℘

Hallelujah! How good it is to sing to our God, for praise is pleasant and lovely. The Lord rebuilds Jerusalem; He gathers Israel's exiled people. He heals the broken-hearted and binds up their wounds. He counts the number of the stars; He gives names to all of them. Our Lord is great, vast in power; His understanding is infinite. The Lord helps the afflicted but brings the wicked to the ground (vv. 1–6).

I've both experienced and observed brokenheartedness, and it's a devastating blow either way. The holidays, when families come together to make memories, are especially poignant and difficult for some of us who are still grieving. It's so hard to accept the fact that I will never again see my parents on this earth.

That's why this passage from Psalm 147 is so timely. David is referring, of course, to the exiled captives of Israel when he says, "He [the Lord] heals the brokenhearted and binds up their wounds" (v. 3), but he might be speaking of any broken heart anywhere.

Sometimes the "wounds" are caused by some significant "other" in one's life; sometimes they are self-inflicted through sin. But God loves to restore and rebuild. Just as he rebuilt Jerusalem after the Babylonian exile, he accepts any penitent sinner for remodeling. The only prerequisites are honesty, humility, and homage. The believer (or unbeliever) who truly repents and returns from sin is fully forgiven, restored, and radically rebuilt!

When we honestly face our grief or our sin and submit it to the Lord, He responds in grace by forgiving and healing. This profound, personal work then becomes the basis for authentic praise. I face an extravagant future with the Lord in glory, when I will see my parents again. We'll have a lot of catching up to do!

Personal Prayer

Praise the Lord! I join in praising your holy, precious name. I praise you for healing the brokenhearted and for setting us free to sing praise!

A Very Personal Doxology

HE DELIGHTS IN ME

∞ Psalm 147 ∞

Sing to the LORD with thanksgiving; play the lyre to our God, who covers the sky with clouds, prepares rain for the earth, and causes grass to grow on the hills. He provides the animals with their food, and the young ravens, what they cry for. He is not impressed by the strength of a horse; He does not value the power of a man. The LORD values those who fear Him, those who hope in His faithful love (vv. 7–11).

There are some things a father never forgets—his child's first steps, the first words, the first Christmas. I'll always remember the rush of pride I felt when our son, D. J., got the music award as a senior at Brentwood Academy. I felt the same deep emotion when his sister, Kathy, became the spelling champion of her class in Grand Rapids. My kids have delighted me on many occasions. I was especially proud of D. J. one time when he visited the Heaston family every day to see their daughter, Heather, who was recovering from the auto accident that took the life of her sister, Leesha.

Though it blows my mind, I know how the Lord must feel when his children do well! He "values in those who fear Him" (v. 11). God is unimpressed by brute strength, but he takes great pleasure and enjoyment in the reverence of his children. We are created to praise, and when we learn to do that well, we know we're pleasing him.

As we become aware of God's delight, we'll experience the gift of his glorious grace. We, in turn, will delight in him—a wondrous, intimate interplay between God, the Father, and his children.

Personal Prayer

Praise the Lord! I thank you and praise you for delighting in me. I place my confidence in your glorious grace and unfailing love today.

A VERY PERSONAL DOXOLOGY
HE GIVES ME PEACE

∽ Psalm 147 ∽

Exalt the Lord, Jerusalem; praise your God, Zion! For He strengthens the bars of your gates and blesses your children within you. He endows your territory with prosperity; He satisfies you with the finest wheat. He sends His command throughout the earth; His word runs swiftly (vv. 12–15).

David and the other psalmists had long been buried with their fathers when the angels sang the first Christmas carol: "Glory to God in the highest, and on earth peace to men on whom his favor rests" (Luke 2:14). How those ancient songwriters would have rejoiced at the coming of the Messiah—the "Prince of Peace" whom Isaiah foretold (Isa. 9:6)!

Here the psalmist exhorts the inhabitants of the holy city to praise the Lord. I can hear the harmony of soprano, alto, tenor, and bass as the "voices" blend in a choral anthem of peace.

Soprano—The high notes soar: "He strengthens the bars of your gates" (v. 13). These people need not fear invasion or attack.

Alto—Providing mellow, rich support is another voice: "And blesses your children within you" (v. 13). Blessing comes from his presence within. "Be born in me tonight," I echo.

Tenor—A strong male voice takes the lead and the song continues on a rising note of joy: "He endows your territory with prosperity" (v. 14). Peace! Peace! Where is peace in this chaotic world?

Bass—Deep and vibrant comes the reassuring word: "[He] satisfies you with the finest wheat. He sends His command throughout the earth; His word runs swiftly" (vv. 14–15). The Lord provides.

The Language of Music

Doxology
An expression of praise to God.
This term is based on the Greek word <u>Doxa</u>, which means "glory."

Personal Prayer

Praise the Lord! I thank you for the gift of your Word which sustains me. But I thank you even more for the gift of your Son, Immanuel—God with us!

A Very Personal Doxology

HE SUSTAINS HIS WORD

∽ Psalm 147 ∽

He spreads snow like wool; He scatters frost like ashes; He throws His hailstones like crumbs. Who can withstand His cold? He sends His word and melts them; He unleashes His winds, and the waters flow. He declares His word to Jacob, His statutes and judgments to Israel. He has not done this for any nation; they do not know [His] judgments. Hallelujah! (vv. 16–20).

What a wondrous wintertime scene is painted in this passage! The greatness of the Lord is perceived by the effect of his Word. He speaks, and the elements of nature obey. When he commands winter, blizzards occur. "He spreads snow like wool" and "scatters frost" (v. 16). "He throws His hailstones like crumbs" (v. 17). The icy blast is almost felt as well as seen in this graphic word picture.

Similarly, at his command the spring thaw sets in and rivers run, like the melting of an icy heart in the warmth of his love. His Word is inviolable, authoritative, and sure.

The most powerful display of his grace was the gift of his written Word. The magnificence of the Mosaic Law and the earth-shattering ethical insights of his decrees were his special gifts to Israel. No other nation then possessed the glory of his commandments.

Through Israel his Word comes down thorough the generations. It was the Word of God that sustained King David throughout his turbulent life. It is his Word that sustains us. Through his precious Word we receive his gifts of grace. Praise the Lord!

Personal Prayer

O Lord, I praise you for the gift of your written Word, which sustains and quickens my spirit.

CANTICLE OF PRAISE

ALL CREATION SINGS PRAISE

∽ Psalm 148 ∽

Hallelujah! Praise the LORD from the heavens; praise Him in the heights. Praise Him, all His angels; praise Him, all His hosts. Praise Him, sun and moon; praise Him, all you shining stars. Praise Him, highest heavens, and you waters above the heavens. Let them praise the name of the LORD, for He commanded, and they were created. He set them in position forever and ever; He gave an order that will never pass away (vv. 1–6).

On this night of nights, all creation erupts in a cosmic explosion of joy: "Hallelujah!" The psalmist's poetic expression is intensified by the use of personification. The luminaries in the heavens praise the Lord (v. 1). The angels—heavenly hosts—praise the Lord (v. 2). All the elements of nature praise the Lord (vv. 3–4).

What motivates all of creation to praise the Lord? The fact that its existence is based on the Word and decree of the Lord. On this night hundreds of years after this psalm was written, the Word became flesh and dwelt among us—like a candle igniting a forest fire that would banish the darkness forever (Luke 2).

But what if Jesus had not come?

Personal Prayer

Jesus, I'm so glad you came! I join with all creation in singing your praises!

The Language of Music

Canticle

In liturgy a Scripture text similar to a psalm but occurring outside of the Psalter.

Examples would be: "My soul doth magnify the Lord" (Luke 1:46), and "Lord, now lettest thou thy servant depart in peace" (Luke 2:29).

CANTICLE OF PRAISE

EARTHLY HOSTS SING PRAISE

∽ Psalm 148 ∽

Praise the LORD from the earth, all sea monsters and ocean depths, lightning and hail, snow and cloud, powerful wind that executes His command, mountains and all hills, fruit trees and all cedars, wild animals and all cattle, creatures that crawl and flying birds, kings of the earth and all peoples, princes and all judges of the earth, young men as well as young women, old and young together. Let them praise the name of the LORD, for His name alone is exalted. His majesty covers heaven and earth. He has raised up a horn for His people, praise from all His godly ones, from the Israelites, the people close to Him. Hallelujah! (vv. 7–14).

All nature sings to the Lord! The list of members in the great universal choir is a kaleidoscope of animate and inanimate creatures—sea creatures, lightning and hail, snow and clouds, small creatures and flying birds, kings and princes, rulers and nations, young men and maidens, old men and children—all crying out with joy, all praising the Lord together!

Why do they praise him? First, they are responding to the glory of his name (v. 13). Second, they realize that his glory transcends his creation (v. 13). Third, they are praising him in gratitude for the king he has given Israel (v. 14)—a prelude to the coming of Christ!

Why do I, who now know the Messiah, often neglect praise? Why is my heart sometimes unresponsive? Could I be guilty of worshiping the creation rather than the Creator (Rom. 1:25)? How do I alter this condition? By bowing again before his cradle throne, by cherishing this Gift from the Father, by adoring him!

Personal Prayer

O Lord, I adore you! I cherish the gift of your salvation and commit myself again to you with full fervor and joy!

A Christmas Carol

O Come, All Ye Faithful

O come, all ye faithful, joyful and triumphant;
Come ye, O come ye to Bethlehem;
Come and behold Him, born the King of angels:
O come, let us adore Him, O come, let us adore Him, Christ the Lord!

Yea, Lord, we greet Thee, born this happy morning;
Jesus, to Thee be all glory giv'n;
Word of the Father, now in flesh appearing:
O come, let us adore Him,
O come, let us adore Him, Christ the Lord!

Words—Latin hymn, 18th C. Trans. by Frederick Oakeley.
Music—Wade's *Cantus Diversi.*

MOTET FOR THE MEEK
MOTIVATION FOR PRAISE

↬ Psalm 149 ↫

Hallelujah! Sing to the Lord a new song, His praise in the assembly of the godly. Let Israel celebrate its Maker; let the children of Zion rejoice in their King. Let them praise His name with dancing and make music to Him with tambourine and lyre. For the Lord takes pleasure in His people; He adorns the humble with salvation. Let the godly celebrate in triumphal glory; let them shout for joy on their beds (vv. 1–5).

How quickly we forget! Once the gift is unwrapped and we exclaim over it, we lay it aside for a bigger and shinier one! What have I done with the gift of God's son and the salvation that cost him so dearly?

The psalmist prods my conscience when he calls on the people of Israel to sing a new song even while they are resting (v. 5)! I shouldn't have to be reminded. My joy in the Lord should be so full that it spills over in spontaneous praise!

Then I read on and am convicted all over again. Israel is commanded to express her joy with dancing and instrumental performance (v. 3). Not only are we to use our voices and musical instruments but also our bodies in complete, free, and uninhibited rejoicing. Yet dancing is an art form virtually unheard of in today's worship services! It is foreign to our culture, by and large, yet when we are too proper, too controlled, we may miss some of the blessings God has in store for us.

Consistent and creative praise keeps faith alive and growing. I must envision God as loving, caring, and delighting in me. Then I will be inspired to use all the gifts he has given me in exuberant praise!

Personal Prayer
Teach me a new song, Lord, and may I learn to express my joy with unrestrained enthusiasm!

The Language of Music

Motet
A polyphonic (many voices) choral composition on a sacred text usually without instrumental accompaniment.

MOTET FOR THE MEEK
SUMMATION OF PRAISE

∽ Psalm 149 ∽

Let the exaltation of God be in their mouths and a two-edged sword in their hands, inflicting vengeance on the nations and punishment on the peoples, binding their kings with chains and their dignitaries with iron shackles, carrying out the judgment decreed against them. This honor is for all His godly people. Hallelujah! (vv. 6–9).

God calls on Israel not only to praise his name but also to execute vengeance on the nations. The Israelites were to worship him, yes, but they were also to stand up for God's justice and to put down evil in the world. They would be praising with their mouths while brandishing a double-edged sword in their hands!

The psalmist gives us no romanticized view of God. He calls for the annihilation of heathen nations, for wicked kings to be fettered, and for his absolutely just sentence to be carried out. As his saints obey the Lord, they experience his glory.

What a study in contrasts—worship and vengeance, praise and power! If this seems strange, it may be because we are comfortable with double-mindedness. We want to be intimate with God while "cozying up" to evil on the side. The Lord wants us to be "wise about what is good, yet innocent about what is evil" (Rom. 16:19). We're open to praising God, but we're not as interested in balancing our worship with a holy hatred of sin. He calls us to praise and to prophesy. He needs some young Vance Havners who have the conviction to write and speak out against hypocrisy and evil. He needs worship leaders—praise spokesmen—but he also summons contemporary prophets—praise motivators—who will cry out against injustice and sin in our world.

Personal Prayer
May I have the inner strength not only to praise you, Lord, but to take a stand for righteousness in the circles where I live and work.

THE HALLELUJAH CHORUS

THE "WHERE" OF PRAISE

❧ Psalm 150 ❧

Hallelujah! Praise God in His sanctuary. Praise Him in His mighty heavens (v. 1).

This psalm is an orchestra of praise—every instrument imaginable poised and lifted up in worship, celebrating God's incomparable excellence.

Wherever his creatures live, God should be praised, the psalmist says. First, he encourages believers to praise the Lord in the sanctuary. Second, he urges the angels to praise the Lord in the sky, the vault of heaven. Since God's glory fills the universe, his praise must do no less!

Many of us organize our lives into neat, convenient categories—business, domestic, spiritual. We find it hard to think about praising the Lord at work, or while swimming or playing tennis, or at home with the family. Worship is slotted in on Sunday mornings. Many of us have fallen into the sacred versus secular dichotomy, which robs us of spontaneity and vitality in our relationship with the Lord. Such a narrow concept of praise leads to a life of truth without beauty, which, in turn, can result in legalism, disillusionment, or even rebellion.

We need to learn to praise the Lord wherever we are. We ought to try standing around the dinner table, holding hands with our loved ones, and singing the "Doxology" together. We ought to dare humming the tune to a hymn at break in the office. We ought to join some major community choir in the Easter or Christmas season, sing the "Hallelujah Chorus," and allow ourselves to lose control of our emotions, letting tears flow down our cheeks and the chills run up our spines. That will be a preview of heaven when we join the angelic choir of millions upon millions! Hallelujah!

Personal Prayer

*Dear Lord, may I be bold enough to praise you wherever I am today
You inhabit praise, so my joyful heart is your "sanctuary."*

Hallelujah Chorus

Hallelujah! Hallelujah! Hallelujah!
Hallelujah!
For the Lord God omnipotent
reigneth.
Hallelujah! Hallelujah! Hallelujah!
Hallelujah!
The kingdom of this world is become
the kingdom

The kingdom of our Lord, and of His
Christ;
And He shall reign forever and ever,
King of kings! and Lord of lords!
Hallelujah! Hallelujah! Hallelujah!
Hallelujah!

Words based on Rev. 19:6. Music by George Frederick Handel.

The Hallelujah Chorus

THE "WHY" OF PRAISE

∽ Psalm 150 ∽

Praise Him for His powerful acts; praise Him for His abundant greatness (v. 2).

Why should believers praise the Lord? The answer is simple: Because he deserves it!

He spoke the world into being, established the first couple in their garden home, then provided redemption for all mankind when they sinned. The Redeemer paid for your sins and mine on a Roman cross thousands of years later. We honor and extol him for these mighty deeds and saving acts. That's reason enough to praise him.

But there is more. If he did nothing at all, there would still be necessity for praise. We are created for communion with God. We are his admiring audience, his fans, who applaud him for the glory of his attributes and the beauty of his character.

We must move on from knowing the facts about him to knowing *him*. We must move from distance to intimacy. Then we can truly join the heavenly band in singing:

Gloria in excelsis Deo!
Angels we have heard on high,
Sweetly singing o'er the plains,
And the mountains in reply,
Echoing their joyous strains.
Gloria in excelsis Deo!

Old French Carol.

Personal Prayer

*Gloria in excelsis Deo! I'm eager to praise you
in celestial language, Lord. Teach me to sing like the angels!*

The Language of Music

Hallelujah Chorus

Perhaps the most famous of choral compositions.

Composed by George F. Handel for his oratorio, "Messiah," and Halleluhah Chorus is a definitive exclamation of praise to God. "Hallelujah" comes from Hebrew ("Hallelujah"—"Praise the Lord"). "Alleluia" is the Latinized spelling.

THE HALLELUJAH CHORUS
THE "WHO" OF PRAISE

∽ Psalm 150 ∽
Let everything that breathes praise the Lord. Hallelujah! (v. 6).

Who should praise the Lord? The psalmist answers in verse 6. "Everything that breathes" should praise the Lord. All of creation should be involved (Ps. 148:7–12). Infants and children are included (8:2). Even animals are included (Job 38–41). Worship is not the exclusive province of pastors, Christian celebrities, or worship leaders. All believers should join the creation in exalting and honoring the Lord. It's a privilege and joy!

In fact, when we sing, our Lord sings with us! When we worship, he worships with us (Ps. 22:22; Heb. 2:12). The believer has no higher calling!

Personal Prayer
Dear Lord, may I praise you with every breath I take!
And may I so inspire others with the music you give
me that all creation will join in the chorus!

A Praise Hymn

Our Sacrifice of Praise
We bow and worship Him, our Lord and King—
Forever and ever His praise we'll sing;
To Him all honor, love, and thanks we bring—
And to His attributes we cling.
We'll tell the world the glory of His name—
And tell how for sinners the Savior came;
We'll spread thru all the earth His wondrous fame—

Unchanging, always He's the same!
Jesus our Saviour lives forevermore—
He rose from the grave to die no more;
His mercy, grace and glory we explore—
And, winged by faith, our spirits soar.
He is deserving of all thanks and praise—
With joy overflowing our hearts we raise;
We'll sing and sing of Him for endless days—
This is our sacrifice of praise!

Words and music by Don Wyrtzen © 1973 Singspiration.
(Based on Hebrews 13:15.)

THE HALLELUJAH CHORUS

THE "HOW" OF PRAISE

✑ Psalm 150 ✑

Praise Him with trumpet blast; praise Him with harp and lyre. Praise Him with tambourine and dance; praise Him with flute and strings. Praise Him with resounding cymbals; praise Him with clashing cymbals (vv. 3–5).

We are to praise Yahweh with every kind of musical form and instrument available!

In ancient times great national feasts and sacred occasions were ushered in by the fanfare of the trumpet (2 Chron. 5:1–14). These trumpets were most likely rams' horns, primitive versions of modern valve trumpets and flugelhorns (Ps. 150:3). David's harp was also a simple instrument, which he played sensitively and gloriously, but was not a modern-day pedal harp.

Timbrels (tambourines), strings, and flutes are mentioned as vehicles of praise in verse 4. Joyous celebrations of victory were marked by the use of these instruments accompanied with dancing (149:3). Dancing was an integral part of Hebrew worship. Miriam danced to the tambourine (Exod. 15:20–21). So also did the women who greeted Saul and David in their moments of victorious celebration (1 Sam. 18:6–7). King David was so elated by the return of the ark of the covenant to Jerusalem that he broke into dancing (2 Sam. 6:14–16). Because of the influence of asceticism, many today feel that any movement of the body to music is evil. However, liturgical dance is certainly biblical, and the body is to be a reflector of his grace.

In verse 5, clashing cymbals are mentioned. In fact, Asaph, one of the premiere musicians in ancient Israel, was a cymbal player (1 Chron. 15:19). So we see that every kind of instrument, form, and sound is called upon to praise God—solemn and festive, percussive and melodic, gentle and strident, dissonant and consonant, fast and slow, stirring and meditative.

The church is just beginning to take advantage of the technological revolution—synthesizers, digital recording techniques, etc. Our challenge is to praise the Lord with our whole being and with every instrument at our disposal. We are to take the old-fashioned message of the gospel and translate it into the language of today. Luther did it in the sixteenth century. Sankey did it in the nineteenth century. Rodeheaver did it in the early twentieth century. Let us follow in their footsteps and in the steps of David, that greatest musician of the ancient world!

Personal Prayer

Dear Lord, help me to praise you with my whole being—heart, soul, mind, and body—and with all the instrumental forms, sounds, and inventions available to me.

POSTLUDE

WHAT I'VE LEARNED FROM THE PSALMS

⌘

A *Musician Looks at the Psalms* revels in three-part form. Each day of the journal has been divided into an exposition of the theme, a development of the theme, and a prayer (or recapitulation). The book itself also follows a three-part structure: prelude, body of work, and postlude.

A postlude is a closing piece of music, often an organ voluntary at the end of a worship service. I would like to use this postlude to share with you what I have learned from the Psalms. I can synthesize it into one big idea:

Only the Lord give us a clear, accurate picture of reality. Without his divine revelation we don't have an adequate basis for our identity, our values, or our morality.

To elaborate I will state seven basic principles I have learned from my study of the Psalter, the ancient hymnbook of Israel. They give beautiful, sensitive answers to the meaning of life and form the architecture of a Judeo-Christian philosophy of life.

First, my being and existence have eternal value because I am made in God's image. I have learned that God "created my inward parts" and that "I am unique in remarkable ways" (Ps. 139:13–14). I am a person of infinite worth and dignity, "a little less than God" and "crowned with glory and honor" (Ps. 8:5). In Genesis 1:27 the Word explicitly says that God created me "in his own image." I am never to believe the enemy's incessant message that I am valueless and worthless. Rather, I am crowned with meaning and majesty!

Second, my deepest longings to be loved and to be special are met in the Lord. I've learned that his loyal love endures forever (Ps. 136). Nothing I could ever imagine or experience can keep me from God's love (Rom. 8:38–39). Based on this love, I am safe and secure in him (Ps. 16). But not only do I possess inner security in the Lord; I am also adequate and special because of him. I am to rule over God's glorious creation (Ps. 8:6). Only the Lord defines the universe and brings meaning to the particulars of life. Only he has it all together. Therefore, when I experience deep longings—hunger and thirst—they are met in the Lord. "As a deer longs for streams of water, so I long for You, God" (Ps. 42:1; see Isa. 55:1–2). Therefore, I don't need to distort reality or distract

myself from pain because my Lord ultimately gives me all I need. My inner
core is only satisfied in him!

> Psalm to Jesus
> As a stream to the desert sand,
>   As a rain to the vine;
> As a shade to the barren land,
>   So Your heart is to mine.
> As a beam to the darkest night,
>   As a calm to the sea;
> As a kiss to the frightened child,
>   So Your love is to me.
> Yet, my heart longs for more,
>   Lord, my soul thirsts for more—
> My spirit hungers for more of You.
> As a rose in the summer sun,
> Thirsting for morning dew
>   So my heart longs for more of You!
> Words by Nan Allen. Music by Don Wyrtzen © 1988 by Singspiration.

Third, my mind can be renewed and refreshed by meditating on the Word. My
study of the Psalms has taught me that the real battles of life are fought in the
mind. One's perception of reality determines his response to life. The Jewish
nation was distinctive among the heathen people of the ancient world because
their minds were filled with the magnificence of the law. I have the capability of
running DVD's in my brain that either tear me down or lift me up. I can think
negatively or positively. You see, our lives can only be "transformed by the renewing of our minds" (see Rom. 12:2).

Joy comes from a refreshed and renewed mind. This is a major theme in the
Psalter. "The instruction of the LORD is perfect, reviving the soul; The testimony
of the LORD is trustworthy, making the inexperienced wise. The percepts of the
LORD are right, making the heart glad; the commandments of the LORD is radiant, making the eyes light up" (Ps. 19:7–8). Our thoughts, our cognitions govern
our lives. They affect our choices, and our choices predetermine our feelings. We
all bear scars from the fall of man. One of our major wounds is to think inaccu-
rately about moral truth. This is why we desperately need daily exposure to and
immersion in God's Word.

Fourth, my life can have direction and purpose through obedience to God's truth.
The whole subject of the will of man and how it relates to the sovereignty of
God is complex. But we can all grasp the fact that our choices are based on our

thoughts. We will not choose to go God's way until we begin to think his thoughts. Our minds function on a cybernetic principle: we are goal oriented. We will passionately pursue goals that we believe will give our lives meaning. The psalms teach us that the only ultimate meaning and deep personal fulfillment come from obedience to God's Word. The old hymn says it so simply, yet profoundly: "Trust and obey, for there's no other way to be happy in Jesus but to trust and obey" (John Sammis). David, the chief musician says, "But from eternity to eternity the LORD's faithful love is toward those who fear Him, and His righteousness toward the grandchildren of those who keep His covenant, who remember to observe His instructions" (103:17–18). We can choose to praise, adore, and worship the Lord, whatever our circumstances.

Fifth, my feelings can be experienced and expressed without fear or guilt. The Psalter really expresses two major motifs that are repeated again and again: Life is tough, but God is good. These psalmists, ancient songwriters, lived in a period of severe adversity and upheaval. They knew what it was like to suffer, to groan, and to cry out, but they worshipped a God who was big enough to handle their problems. Therefore, they poured out their souls to him. Their prayers were moments of catharsis: "Out of the depths I call to You, LORD! Lord, listen to my voice; let Your ears be attentive to my cry for help" (130:1–2). They knew that "weeping may spend the night, but there is joy in the morning" (30:5). We are called to be holy, not happy. But many of us are addicted to happiness rather than committed to holiness. We gladly trade ultimate joy for short-term relief. The psalmists teach us to face life squarely—to look life right in the eye! In the nature of reality, we will experience suffering and joy, pain and peace, adversity and felicity. Right now we're pilgrims—"just a passin' through." This world is not our home. It's abrasive. We're not comfortable here. We're not totally at home yet, not fully satisfied. We're restless until we find God because we were made for eternity! We can allow ourselves to lament individually and nationally.

Sixth, reality can only be grasped when I intimately embrace Jesus Christ as my Lord and Savior. Because the apostle Paul had further revelation from God, he knew more about the gospel than did King David. Yet, even in the Psalms, we see the gospel taking shape in seedling form. Here are the key ideas. I would encourage you to think about them, apply them to your own life, and then make some concrete decisions about them.

- *I'm a precious person made in God's image.* God "created my inward parts." "I am unique in remarkable ways" (Ps. 139:13–14; see Gen. 1:27).
- *I will live forever.* David said that he would "dwell in the house of the LORD as long as I live" (Ps. 23:6).

+ *I have sinned.* But David himself was flawed and sinful. He says, "Be gracious to me, God, according to Your faithful love; according to Your abundant compassion, blot out my rebellion. Wash away my guilt, and cleanse me from my sin" (Ps. 51:1–2).
+ *I need a Savior.* I believe Jesus Christ is the Messiah of the Psalms. Listen to the mournful music of these moving words: "My God, my God, why have You forsaken me?" That's a direct quote from Psalm 22:1. Those exact words were spoken by Christ as he bore the sins of the world on a Roman cross (Matt. 27:46)!
+ *I must choose to accept him or reject him.* Why must I choose? Why must I personally decide? Because "the LORD watches over the way of the righteous, but the way of the wicked leads to ruin" (Ps. 1:6). I must accept Christ as my Savior and must simply ask him to come into my life. "Yet to all who did received Him, He gave them the right to be children of God" (John 1:12). What gave him the authority? He rose from the dead (see Ps. 16:9–10; Acts 2:31). Why don't you choose to accept him right now as your Lord and Savior? He is the supreme Answer to the questions of life.

Seventh, my being and personality will live forever, either with the Lord or apart from him. David talks about being led "in the everlasting way" (Ps. 139:24). He says that he will be pursued by goodness and love all the days of his life. And he concludes the most sublime lyric ever written by saying, "I will dwell in the house of the LORD as long as I live" (Ps. 23:6).

J. S. Bach signed his works in a unique way. It is an apt closing, a perfect signature, to this journal.

Soli Deo Gloria!
"To God be the glory!"
Don Wyrtzen

SUBJECT INDEX

abortion 213
aging 176, 200
ambition 11, 223, 324, 348, 373
angels 44, 86, 96, 248, 271, 292–93, 388, 390, 394–95
anger 46, 89, 112, 116, 171, 194, 219, 221, 245, 270, 279, 314, 344, 361
anxiety 38, 42, 46, 73, 79, 101, 121, 130, 139, 254
arrogance 42, 214, 278, 348
authenticity 51, 78
blessings 185, 190, 342–43, 445
brokenhearted (the) 103, 386
comfort 61, 64, 85, 104–05, 163
commitment 233, 315, 386
compassion 196, 239, 270, 323
confession 79, 90, 92, 153–54, 189
contrasts 205–07, 247, 307, 393
counseling 282–83
creation 55, 68, 97, 252, 272–73, 294, 328, 347, 384, 390
creativity 68, 227, 267, 272–73
criticism 156
death 64–65, 67, 79, 121, 210, 327
deliverance 54, 93, 95, 105, 115, 164, 169, 171, 198–200, 213, 218, 280–81, 294, 297, 301, 333–35
dependence (on God) 56, 90, 199–201
depression 40, 49, 92, 130–31, 174, 314
discipline 116, 122, 173
disobedience 219
disorientation 172, 212
envy 207
eternal life 76
failure 101
faith 82, 99, 112, 118, 156–57, 163, 304, 367, 378
faithfulness (of God) 110, 165, 244, 275, 282, 299, 374
fear 38, 58, 120–21, 101, 162, 249
forgiveness 71, 73, 91, 93, 153–55, 185, 245, 279, 356
friends 33, 65, 117, 160, 172, 241
fulfillment 33, 61, 363
glory 43, 64, 70, 86, 274, 299
gossip 48, 326
grief 64, 107
guidance 71–72
guilt 73, 93, 116, 119, 155, 189

healing 127–28, 386
holiness 43, 69–70, 86, 99, 252, 263
Holy Spirit 316, 376
hope 71, 74, 122, 130, 186, 194–96, 200, 246
humility 78, 247
idolatry 50, 260, 295
illness 128
integrity 51, 69, 71, 75, 221, 266, 337
intimacy (with God) 63, 72, 117, 267
jealousy 65
joy 60, 87, 89, 91, 95, 124, 186–88, 191, 258, 265, 338, 392
justice 45, 47, 53 98, 166–68, 170, 202, 214, 368, 393
lament 42, 46, 54, 57, 104–05, 123, 129–32, 163, 211–13, 222–23, 231–32, 372
law (of God) 33, 55, 113, 124
leadership 211, 290, 353
life (brevity) 121–22, 246
loneliness 40, 117, 157, 191
love (of God) 49, 57, 66, 76, 95, 98, 110–11, 126, 133–38, 145, 153, 165, 181, 244, 261, 281–82, 299–300, 357–59, 387
lying 103, 152, 326
materialism 33, 50, 67, 147–49, 156, 208–09
mercy 127–28, 132, 195, 230, 372, 374
Messiah 85, 136–38, 202, 316
mid-life crisis 106
motives 98
neurosis 102
obedience 72, 294
omnipotence (of God) 68, 141
pain 58
patience 59, 82, 112, 118, 177, 347
peace 39, 42, 80, 89, 103, 170, 236, 327, 331, 343, 379, 388
perfectionism 39, 315
power (of God) 87–88, 97, 139, 186–87, 216, 218
praise 43, 45–46, 57, 60, 70, 77, 80, 84, 96–97, 99–100, 105, 107–08, 110, 125, 127–29, 131–32, 141–46, 165, 171–72, 180–82, 185, 191, 193, 198, 201, 214, 223, 227, 245, 250–51, 255–58, 270–71, 292–93, 296, 298, 302, 304–05, 324–25, 354–59, 362–63, 380–86, 390, 397
prayer 39, 41, 47, 53–54, 59–60, 71, 78, 83–84, 111, 119–20, 123, 126, 130, 135,

145, 154–55, 166–67, 176, 182–83, 189, 191, 198, 200, 219, 229–31, 241, 243–48, 251, 271, 294, 392–95, 404–05
pride 89, 253, 348
prosperity 67, 205–10
protection 70, 126, 140, 153
purity 68, 145, 266
rejection 81, 92, 160
refuge 47, 115, 140, 175, 178, 184, 199
repentance 119, 189
restoration 89, 154, 158, 194–96, 385
reverence 71, 102, 318, 342
righteousness 39, 41, 47, 53–54, 58–60, 71, 78, 83–84, 111, 119–20, 123, 126, 130, 135, 145, 154–55, 166–67, 176, 182–83, 189, 191, 198, 200, 219, 229–30, 241, 243–48, 251, 271, 294, 392–95, 404–05
sacrifice 123–25, 151
salvation 49, 79, 84–85, 88, 152, 158, 178, 185, 206, 261
security 42, 52–54, 57, 61, 74, 80, 94, 112, 127, 144, 157, 177, 248–49, 253–54, 336
self-esteem 34–35, 67, 70
servanthood 319
sin 73, 93, 109–10, 117, 126–28, 153, 278, 346
stress 40, 62–63, 162, 177
suffering 58–60, 223, 241–42, 247, 282, 292, 303, 366
temptation 89
thanksgiving 60, 84, 91, 126, 196, 265, 297–99, 325, 357–60, 373
vindication 108, 158, 168, 182
will (of God) 59, 63, 125, 363
witness 309
Word (of God) 34, 48, 55, 303–05, 324–25, 389
workaholism 62
worship 37, 70, 80, 96, 100–05, 129, 142, 150–52, 155, 157, 190, 209, 227, 233, 262, 292, 330, 350, 362

MUSICAL TERMS INDEX

Antiphonal 359
Appassionata 166
Aria 120
Ballad 161
Benediction 353
Canticle 390
Celebration 191
Chaconne 277
Concerto 187
Descant 49, 281
Dirge 48
Discord 50
Dorian Mode 334
Doxology 54
Drone-Pipe 183
Elegy 38
Fantasia 156
Hallelujah Chorus 395
Harmony 113
Hymn 73
Impromptu 369
Introit 357
Invention 256
Invocation 56
Jubilate 338
Kyrie 41
Leitmotif 77
Litany 355
Lugue 154
Madrigal 127
March 57
Melody 83
Mosiac 355
Motet 392
Ode 35
Opus 345
Pathétique 374
Plainsong 180
Polyphony 163
Processional 68
Recitative 350
Refrain 224
Sonatina 124
Song 60
Stanza 177
Symphony 364
Tocatta 282
Variations 80
Vow 362

SONG CREDITS

PRELUDE: *Adoration* Words and music by Don Wyrtzen. © 1984 by Singspiration Music/ASCAP.* (31). **JANUARY:** *Appreciation for Music* from *Psalm of My Life.* © 1987. Used by permission of David C. Cook Publishing Co. (33). *Psalm of My Life* Words and music by Don Wyrtzen. © 1975 by Singspiration Music/ASCAP.* (34). *My Everything* Words and music by Don Wyrtzen. © 1981 by Singspiration Music/ASCAP.* (36). *The Refiner's Fire* Words by Don Wyrtzen. © 1988. (48). *Make Me Real, Lord* Words by Don Wyrtzen. © 1988. (48). *Eternity's Values in View* Words and music by Alfred B. Smith. © 1941 by Singspiration Music/ASCAP.* Renewed 1969.* (69). **FEBRUARY:** *Finally Home* Words by L. E. Singer and Don Wyrtzen. © 1971 by Singspiration Music/ASCAP.* Music © by Don Wyrtzen. (65). *He Satisfies My Life* Words and music by Don Wyrtzen. © 1985 by Singspiration Music/ASCAP.* (84). *Unbounded Grace* Words by John E. Walvord. Music by Don Wyrtzen. © 1971 by Singspiration Music/ASCAP.* (85). **MARCH:** *We Will Glorify* Words and music by Twila Paris. © 1982 by Singspiration Music/ASCAP.* (100). *Love Was When* Words by John E. Walvoord. Music by Don Wyrtzen. © 1970 by Singspiration Music/ASCAP.* (109). *The Love of God* © 1917. Renewal 1945 by Nazarene Publishing House. (110). **APRIL:** *This World Is Not My Home* Arranged by Albert E. Brumley. © 1974. Renewal. All rights reserved. Used by permission. (123). *Stubborn Love* Words and music by Amy Grant, Gary Chapman, Sloan Towner, Brown Bannister, Michael W. Smith. © 1982 Meadowgreen Music Company/Edward Grant, Inc. (Meadowgreen adm. by Tree Pub. Co., Inc., 8 Music Square W. Nashville, TN 37203.) International copyright secured. All rights reserved. Used by permission. (145). **MAY:** *Something Beautiful* Words by Gloria Gaither. Music by William J. Gaither. © by William J. Gaither. All rights reserved. Used by permission. (155). *Secret Ambition* Words by Amy Grant and Wayne Kirkpatrick. Music by Michael W. Smith. © 1988 by O'Ryan Music, Inc./Emily Booth, Inc./Riverstone Music, Inc. International copyright secured. All rights reserved. Used by permission. (179). *Longing for God* Words and music by Don Wyrtzen. ©1980 by Singspiration Music/ASCAP.* (180). *As Long As I Live* Words and music by Don Wyrtzen. © 1982 by Singspiration Music/ASCAP.* (181). **JUNE:** *When Thou Passest Thru the Waters* (Isa. 43:2) Music by Don Wyrtzen. © 1979 by Singspiration Music/ASCAP.* (188). *El Shaddai* Words by Michael Card. Music by John W. Thompson. © 1981 and arr. © 1983 by Whole Armor Publishing Company. All rights reserved. Used by permission. (193). **JULY:** *Celebrate* Words by John E. Walvoord. Music by Don Wyrtzen. © 1971 by Singspiration Music/ASCAP.* (214). *Lord of Everything* Words and music by Don Wyrtzen. © 1988 by Singspiration Music/ASCAP.* (215). *Then I Remembered* Words and music by Don Wyrtzen. © 1988 by Singspiration Music/ASCAP.* (217). *Great Is Thy Faithfulness* Words by Thomas O. Chisholm. Music by William M. Runyan. © 1923. Renewal 1951 by Hope Publishing Company. All rights reserved. Used by permission. (244). **AUGUST:** Great Is the Lord Words by Deborah D. Smith. Music by Michael W. Smith. © 1982 Meadowgreen Music. (250). *Sing to the Lord* Words and music by Don Wyrtzen. © 1974 by Singspiration Music/ASCAP.* (262). *Sing Joyfully Before the Lord* Words and music by Don Wyrtzen. © 1971 by Singspiration Music/ASCAP.* (265). *How Great Thou Art* Words by Carl Boberg. Trans. and arr. by Stuart K. Hine. © 1953 by Stuart K. Hine, assigned to Manna Music, Inc. © 1955 by Manna Music, Inc. All rights reserved. Used by permission. (274). **SEPTEMBER:** *Because of Who You Are* Words and music by Bob Farrell and Billy Smiley. © 1982 by Paragon Music Corp./ASCAP. Used by permission of the Benson Company, Inc., Nashville, TN. (288). *Endless Praise* Words and music by Phil and Lynne Brower. © 1985 by Singspiration Music/ASCAP.* (296). *Teach Me to Sing Again* Words and music by Don Wyrtzen © 1985 by Singspiration Music/ASCAP.* (301). *Jesus Is My Music* Words and music by Don Wyrtzen. © 1978 by Singspiration Music/ASCAP.* (302). **OCTOBER:** *The Day That I Met Jesus* Words and music by Don Wyrtzen. © 1964 by Singspiration Music/ASCAP.* (307). *No Easier Way* Words by Clair Cloninger and Don Wyrtzen. Music by Don Wyrtzen. © 1984 by Singspiration Music/ASCAP.* (312). *I'll Walk and Talk with Him Today* Words and music by Don Wyrtzen. © 1975 by Singspiration Music/ASCAP.* (327). *There Is No Problem* Words and music by Don Wyrtzen. © 1981 by Singspiration Music/ASCAP.* (332). **NOVEMBER:** *To Be What You Want Me To Be* Words and music by Don Wyrtzen. © 1972 by Singspiration Music/ASCAP.* (337). *Fearfully and Wonderfully Made* Words and music by Don Wyrtzen. © 1984 by Singspiration Music/ASCAP.* (364). **DECEMBER:** *He Looked Beyond My Fault* Words by Dottie Rambo. © 1968 by John T. Benson Pub. Co./ASCAP.* (375). *Our Sacrifice of Praise* (Heb. 13:15) Words and music by Don Wyrtzen. © 1973 by Singspiration Music/ASCAP.* (396).

*Singspiration Music/ASCAP. All rights reserved. Used by permission of the Benson Company, Inc., Nashville, TN.